Buddhist Roles in Peacemaking:
How Buddhism Can Contribute to Sustainable Peace

Edited by Chanju Mun and Ronald S. Green

Blue Pine
Honolulu, Hawaii

Library of Congress Control Number: 2008943155
ISBN: 0977755347
ISBN: 9780977755349

CONTENTS

NOTES

1. The Pinyin system is used for Chinese terms, the Korean Government Romanization System revised in 2000 for Korean ones, and the Hepburn system for Japanese ones.
2. Diacritics are used on most of Sanskrit and Pāli terms.
3. Foreign terms, those not included in the *Webster English Dictionary*, appear in italics.
4. If authors have Romanized their names in ways contrary to East Asian Standard Romanization Systems, I have adapted their spellings.
5. If names have not previously been Romanized, I have done so using East Asian Standard Romanization Systems.
6. Standard PTS abbreviations are used for Pāli texts.
7. This book is edited based on the 15th edition of *The Chicago Manual of Style* (Chicago: University of Chicago Press, 2003).

Yun Goam (1899-1988), the First Spiritual Leader of Dae Won Sa Buddhist Temple: A Biography of His Peacemaking Activities

Chanju Mun

Yun Goam is the master of Daewon Ki, also known as Gi Daewon, who initiated the International Seminars on Buddhism and Leadership for Peace, biannually held seven times from 1983 to 1995. He religiously ordained, nurtured and educated his disciple Daewon Ki. Daewon Ki came to and established Dae Won Sa Buddhist Temple in Honolulu, Hawaii in 1975. He eventually made the temple the largest Korean Buddhist temple in North America. I wrote about him and his peace activities in detail in a paper entitled "Venerable Daewon Ki and Peacemaking" in my edited *Mediators and Meditators: Buddhism and Peacemaking* (Honolulu: Blue Pine, 2007), pp. v-xxv.

Daewon Ki concentrated his peace activities in two areas. First, he focused on making peace in the world by holding seven international seminars and disseminating Buddhist teachings on peace and justice. Second, as a Korean Buddhist monk, he dedicated his peace activities to bringing peace between North and South Korea. He visited North Korea eight times between July 1988 and December 1996. Between these visits, he hosted numerous meetings with many of the high-ranking administrators and politicians of the North Korean government and had thirteen official meetings with the Federation of North Korean Buddhists.

In 1978, Yun Goam visited the Dae Won Sa Buddhist Temple and earnestly encouraged his disciple Daewon Ki, founder of the temple, to propagate Buddhism in the West. In 1980, Yun Goam visited and became a resident monk at the Dae Won Sa Buddhist Temple in Honolulu and spiritually and religiously guided his disciple Daewon Ki. In 1982, Daewon Ki along with his followers instated his master Yun Goam as the temple's spiritual leader. Yun Goam served as the spiritual leader for Dae Won Sa Buddhist Temple from 1982 until he passes away in 1988.

In 2005, Daewon Ki assigned to me the task of revitalizing the discussions on Buddhism and peace. Accordingly, I edited and published four serial books on Buddhism and peace since then and along with my close colleague Ronald S. Green, am editing and publishing this current and fifth serial volume on the subject. I selected papers from the fifth seminar, held in Seoul, South Korea during November 18-21, 1991 on the theme of "Exploration of Ways to Put Buddhist Thought into Social Practice for Peace and Justice" and published them in my co-edited *Buddhist Exploration of Peace and Justice* (Honolulu: Blue Pine, 2006). The seminar was held under the joint sponsorship of Dae Won Sa Buddhist Temple and the Korean Buddhist Research Institute of Dongguk University. More than 60 participants came from Canada, China, Germany, India, Japan, Korea, Mongolia, Sri Lanka, Sweden, Thailand, Vietnam, and the United States.

I selected articles from the seventh seminar, held in Honolulu during June 3-8, 1995 on the theme of "Buddhism and Peace: Theory and Practice" and edited and published them in my edited *Buddhism and Peace: Theory and Practice* (Honolulu: Blue Pine, 2006). The seminar was held under the joint auspices of the Dae Won Sa Buddhist Temple and the Department of Philosophy at the University of Hawaii – Manoa. More than 40 scholars and religious leaders from Asia, Europe and the United States participated in the seminar.

I chose articles from the first and second seminars held in Honolulu during October 22-28, 1983 and in Tokyo Japan during

December 2-7, 1985 and published them in my edited *The World is One Flower: Buddhist Leadership for Peace* (Honolulu: Blue Pine, 2006). The first seminar proceeded under the auspices of the Dae Won Sa Buddhist Temple and the Department of Political Science, University of Hawaii – Manoa on the theme of "Buddhism and Leadership for Peace." The theme of "Buddhism in the Context of Various Countries" was examined in the second seminar under the joint sponsorship of the Dae Won Sa Buddhist Temple and the Peace Research Institute of Sōka University. Participants came from China, South Korea, Sri Lanka, Soviet Union, Thailand, and the United States in the first seminar. Individuals from these six nations well as from Bali, India and Mongolia participated in the second seminar.

I selected papers from the third seminar, held in Honolulu during May 23-28, 1987 on the theme of "Peacemaking in Buddhist Contexts" and edited and included them in my edited *Mediators and Meditators: Buddhism and Peacemaking* (Honolulu: Blue Pine, 2007). The seminar was cosponsored by the Dae Won Sa Buddhist Temple and the Peace Institute of the University of Hawaii – Manoa. Participants included those from China, Japan, South Korea, Mongolia, the Soviet Union, Thailand, and the United States. I also selected excellent papers among the numerous submitted to the editorial board of Blue Pine Books in 2006-7, editing and publishing them.

I was fortunate to have received so many excellent papers in 2007-8 and along with co-editor Ronald S. Green chose among them to fit the current volume, the fifth serial book on Buddhism and peace by Blue Pine Books. Because of their lasting importance, I also included in this volume two articles presented at the sixth seminar held in Honolulu November 24-28, 1993 on the theme of "A Buddhist Worldview and Concept of Peace," those by Y. Karunadasa and David Putney. The seminar was held under the joint auspices of the Dae Won Sa Buddhist Temple and the Department of Philosophy, University of Hawaii – Manoa. Participants included individuals from Korea, Sri Lanka, and the United States.

Because of the tremendous debt owed to his master Yun Goam by Daewon Ki and his peacemaking activities, the following biography is important. Even though both masters dedicated themselves to peace building, there are some basic differences in approach. For example, while Yun Goam tried to create peace at the individual and spiritual levels, his disciple Daewon Ki dedicated himself to making peace at the social and international levels. While Yun Goam prioritized individual and spiritual peace to social and structural peace, Daewon Ki prioritized social and structural peace to individual and spiritual peace.

Both shared Korean Buddhism's ecumenical view, that is, they inherited the tradition of promoting unity among religious groups.[1] They did not exclude other Buddhist doctrines and practices and did not place any specific philosophy or practice over others. They harmonized various Buddhist practices such as the meditation of Seon (Chn., Chan: Jpn., Zen), the chanting of Tantric spells, the recitations of the names of Buddhas and bodhisattvas, the recollection of Buddhist images, and other forms of practice, and did not arrange them hierarchically. They did not treat doctrines and practices as opposing each other, but as mutually complementing each other.

Peacemaking Activities: A Biographical Explanation

Yun Goam was born on October 5, 1899 at 425 Sikhyeon Village, Jeokseong Town, Paju County, Gyeonggi Province. He was the third son to his father Yun Mun and his mother Jeong Wonhaeng. His name was Jiho; his ordination name Sangeon; his honorific Dharma name Goam; and he gave himself the nickname Hwansan.

Before becoming a monk, he studied Confucian texts at a village schoolhouse from the age of nine in 1907 to the age of

---

[1] See Chanju Mun, "Wonhyo (617-686): A Critic of Sectarian Doctrinal Classifications," in *Hsi Lai Journal of Humanistic Buddhism* 6 (2005): 290-306.

twelve in 1910. He also attended Jeokseong Public Elementary School.[2]

His short autobiography entitled "Unsu saengae" (A Wandering Monastic Life) explains his activities from the age of 17 in 1915 until the age of 28 in 1926.[3] As the title suggests, he moved around the nation and from temple to temple. He did not want to become attached to any place and did not settle down in a temple. He continuously wandered to learn Buddhism from various masters and to propagate these teachings constantly to people who needed to hear them.[4]

In late summer 1915, he met a wandering monk and followed him to Mt. Dobong. He stayed at Hoeryong-sa Temple for one night. He separated from the monk and passed through Hwagye-sa Temple on Mt. Bukhan in Seoul where he saw several senior monks chanting Buddhist sūtras while striking a wooden floor with iron hammers at the temple's Hwagak Bojeon Pavilion. He was happy to listen the chanting.

An elderly monk, Jeon Wolhae, then the abbot of Hwagye-sa Temple and around 70 years old, welcomed him along with the other resident monks. At their request, he stayed at the temple for several months. While there, the temple reconstructed the affiliated hermitage called Samseong-am. He helped them with this project while studying Buddhism.

When the construction was completed, master Chunsan was supposed to stay at Samseong-am Hermitage. At the master's behest, Goam lived with him for a while at the hermitage.

---

[2] Yun Seonhyo, ed., "Goam seunim haengjang" (Biography of Master Yun Goam), in his edited *Goam keunseunim pyeongjeon: Nege han mulgeon i itteuni* (A Critical Biography of Great Master Yun Goam) (Seoul: Bulgyo yeongsang, 1994), 18.

[3] Yun Goam, "Unsu saengae" (A Wandering Monastic Life), in Yun Seonhyo, ed., *Goam daejongsa beobeo-jip: Jabi bosal ui gil* (Grand Master Yun Goam's Analects: The Ways of a Compassionate Bodhisattva) (Seoul: Bulgyo yeongsang hoebo-sa, 1990), 370-377. I heavily rely on the autobiography to introduce this period of his life.

[4] Im Hyebong, *Geu nuga keun kkum eul kkueotna* (Who Awakened from a Dream?), *Jongjeong yeoljeon* 1 (The 1st Series of the Biographies of Korean Buddhism's Supreme Patriarchs) (Seoul: Garam gihoek, 1999), 209-210.

However, because he felt heaviness in his chest, he left the hermitage and wandered without destination. He also visited several temples in Seoul.

In the fall of 1916, at his age of 18, he happened upon Imje Seon Propagation Center in Insa-dong, Seoul and occasionally attended lectures by Baek Yongseong (1864-1940).[5] He thought that he was a very wonderful master. In the summer of 1917, at the age of 19, Yun Goam took part in a series of preaching on the *Diamond Sūtra* with Baek Yongseong at the center.

One day, Goam asked the master, "According to the *Diamond Sūtra*, everything is empty and all forms are like a dream. How can you explain this sentence?"

After keeping silent for a while, Baek Yongseong responded to his question, "It exactly explains the Diamond Wisdom."

He was greatly impressed by the master's short answer and decided to consider Baek Yongseong his Dharma master.[6] He followed him to Mangwol-sa Temple on Mt. Dobong near Seoul and after a while, he moved down to Haein-sa Monastery where he met Gim Jesan (1862-1930).[7] Gim Jesan practiced Seon at Toeseol Hall in Haein-sa Monastery and was famous as a vinaya preceptor and a Seon master.[8]

Gim Jesan became Yun Goam's tonsure master and suggested he become a monk under Baek Yongseong. Yun Goam responded that he would become a monk under Gim Jesan, keeping in mind that he would serve Baek Yongseong as his Dharma master. He studied basic Buddhism at Haein-sa Monastery.

---

[5] I Jeong, ed., *Hanguk bulgyo inmyeong sajeon* (Dictionary of Korean Buddhist Names) (Seoul: Bulgyo sidae-sa, 1991), 288-289.

[6] Im Hyebong, 371.

[7] See the August 8th, 1967 issue of *Donga ilbo*, HBGJ 1.1.418-419. See Seonu Doryang, *Simmun euro bon Hanguk bulgyo geunhyeondae-sa* (The History of Modern Korean Buddhism through the Newspaper Articles), 4 volumes (Seoul: Seonu Doryang Press, 1995 & 1999). It published the first set of two volumes in 1995 and the second set of other two volumes in 1999. Hereafter, I will abbreviate the book title as HBGJ. Here, the first 1 in HBGJ 1.1.418-419 means the first set, the second 1 the first volume, and 418-419 the page numbers.

[8] Yun Seonhyo, ed., *Goam keunseunim pyeongjeon*, 21-22.

In 1918, when Gim Jesan moved back to his home temple, Jikji-sa, in the County of Gimcheon, North Gyeongsang Province, he wandered here and there. In the winter of 1918, he went to Hwajang-sa Temple in Gaeseong, Hwanghae Province, and took a winter intensive retreat at the temple from the 15th day of the tenth lunar month, 1918 and continued to the 15th day of the first lunar month, 1919.

When we review his monastic career, we see that he wandered here and there without stopping until his death.[9] For the most part, he did not stay at any one temple for more than six months. He thoroughly followed the model of a wandering monk and did not attach himself to any temple. Whenever people needed him, he served their needs. He delivered sermons and presided over the precept offering ceremonies at various temples all over the nation. Whenever he needed to see teachers in Seon and doctrinal Buddhism, he did so, visiting the temples and receiving teachings from them.

In 1919, the nationwide March 1st Movement for independence from Japan occurred. He also attended the movement for independence for more than one month along with the temple members. Because the Japanese police searched for monks who participated in the movement, he wore patched clothes, put on straw sandals, took a monastic knapsack on his back, and escaped to the mountains of Gangwon Province.

He visited and worshipped in the Hall of One Thousand Buddha Images and the Hall of a Stone Kṣitigarbha Bodhisattva Image at Simwon-sa Temple on Mt. Bogae in Cheolwon County, Gangwon Province. The temple was considered the holy site of the Kṣitigarbha Bodhisattva cult.

He visited and drank mineral waters at the Sambang Mineral Spring in Sambang Village, Sepo County, Gangwon Province. He went to Seogwang-sa Temple in the County of Anbyeon, South Hamgyeong Province. Someone guided him to various halls where he venerated the images enshrined there. The person also led him to the Hall of Five Arahans and explained its origin. He visited

---

[9] Im Hyebong, 209-210.

mountain hermitages affiliated with Seogwang-sa Temple for several months and left the temple for the beautiful beach called Myeongsa simni in Wonsan City, South Hamgyeong Province.

He walked down to the south along the coastal line of the East Sea. He finally arrived at the famous Mt. Geumgang (Skt., *Vajra*; Diamond). He visited Chongseok Pavilion in Tongcheon County, Gangwon Province, and arrived and bathed at Onjeong Village Mineral Hot Springs in Goseong County, Gangwon Province, located in the outer Geumgang Mountain area. He saw the "Ten Thousand Spectacular Scenes" on the mountain and entered Singye-sa Temple.

He visited and greeted the great master Im Seokdu (1882-1954) at Boun-am Hermitage affiliated with the temple. Im Seokdu[10] was the tonsure master of I Hyobong (1888-1966)[11] who had served two times as the highest patriarch of the Jogye Order of Korean Buddhism, from April 1958 until August 13th, 1959 and from April 11th, 1962 until October 24th, 1966. Yun Goam also visited Bogwang-am Hermitage, affiliated with Singye-sa Temple at which he observed the lay sculptor Choe Ginam carving stone Buddha images. We can see at Hwagye-sa Temple in Seoul the one thousand images that Choe Ginam carved. He then proceeded to Guryongyeon Falls.

He descended from Mt. Geumgang, passed through Goseong Town, and arrived at Geonbong-sa Temple. Baljing (d.u.)[12] established the "Society for Chanting Amitābha Buddha for Ten Thousand Days" at the temple in 758. When they finished the ten thousand day chanting in 785, 31 monks were said to have been born in pure lands without changing their physical bodies and 961 lay Buddhist members were said to have been born in Western Paradise. Here he learned the importance of Pure Land practice. He ascended to Bori-am Hermitage, affiliated with the temple, where he stayed for more than one month.

---

[10] I Jeong, ed., 116.

[11] *Ibid*, 204-205

[12] *Ibid*, 99.

He again left for Yujeom-sa Temple on Mt. Geumgang. At the time, the great scholar master Gim Dongseon (1856-1936),[13] who became a monk under Byeogam Seoho (1837-1911)[14] at Jeongam-sa Temple on Mt. Taebaek at the age of 18 in 1873, led the "Society for Reading the *Lotus Sūtra*." Several dozens of monks, whose ages ranged in their 30's and 40's, read and chanted the sūtra. He taught the sūtra to several dozens of student monks at the monastic seminary affiliated with the temple. More than 10 monks also practiced Seon meditation at the Seon Center, affiliated with the temple's Banya-am (Skt., *prajñā*; Wisdom) Hermitage. He also visited and worshipped the fifty-three Buddha images in the temple territory.

He went to Mahayeon (Skt., Mahāyāna) Temple in the inner Diamond Mountain. He observed that 50 to 60 Seon practitioners attended a series of lectures on the *Wisdom Sūtra* in 600 sets there. Two scholar monks Heo Mongcho (d.u.) of Tongdo-sa Monastery and Gim Gwanheo (d.u.) of Pyohun-sa Temple, one of four major temples on Mt. Geumgang, taught the sūtra two times a day before noon and after noon. Each scholar monk was charged with teaching once each day. While attending the lecture series, the monks practiced Seon meditation in the morning and in the evening. He went to Bodeok-gul, a cave near the temple and recollected the title(s) of Buddha(s) or Bodhisattva(s) for a little more than one month.

Yun Goam visited Pyohun-sa Temple and studied the four collections. These are the *Shuzhuang* (Letters) by Dahui Zonggao (1088-1163), the *Chan Preface* by Guifeng Zongmi (780-841), the *Chanyao* (Essentials of Chan Buddhism) by Gaofeng Yuanmiao (1238-1295), and the *Beopjip byeolhaengnok jeoryo byeongip sagi* (Excerpts from the *Dharma Collection and Special Practice Record* by Guifeng Zongmi with Personal Notes) by Bojo Jinul (1158-1210).

Generally, Korean Buddhist monastics learn the four collections in the intermediate class of a traditional monastic

---

[13] *Ibid*, 265.
[14] *Ibid*, 133-134.

seminary. They study them at an institutional monastic seminary affiliated with a big temple or monastery under a scholar monk's directorship, not under various scholars here and there. However, Yun Goam finished the coursework of the four collections under the personal tutorship of many scholar monks at many temples. [15] He studied them at Pyohun-sa Temple, Sinheung-sa Temple, Goun-sa Temple, Tongdo-sa Monastery, and the Haein-sa Monastery's Seoul mission center under various eminent monks. He studied four texts while meditating at Seon centers. He thus did not just concentrate on learning the texts.

He left Pyohun-sa Temple on Mt. Geumgang heading south and arrived in Mt. Seorak. He looked around Mt. Seorak and entered the Seon Center at Naewon-am Hermitage affiliated with Sinheung-sa Temple. While staying at the center, he studied the four collections and practiced Seon meditation for several months.

He departed from Mt. Seorak, moved to the south, and arrived at Bulyeong-sa Temple in Uljin County, North Gyeongsang Province. He again moved further to the south and visited Goun-sa Temple on Mt. Deungun in Uiseong County, North Gyeongsang Province. He entered the Geumdang Seon Center affiliated with Goun-sa Temple where he studied the four collections and practiced Seon meditation for several months, staying through the winter.

In the spring of 1920 at the age 22, he left Goun-sa Temple and arrived at Pagye-sa Temple on Mt. Palgong in Daegu. He met at the temple Jeong Geumo (1896-1968) [16] who led the Purification Buddhist Movement along with Ha Dongsan (1890-1965), [17] I Hyobong, and I Cheongdam (1902-1971). [18] When the great master Seolsan and the monk Danam came to Pagye-sa Temple, he visited their rooms and asked for Buddhist teachings from them.

He went to Donghwa-sa Temple on Mt. Palgong in Daegu near Pagye-sa Temple. He visited Geumdang Seon Center affiliated with Donghwa-sa Temple and asked for Buddhist teachings from

---

[15] Im Hyebong, 212.

[16] I Jeong, ed., 318.

[17] *Ibid*, 348-349.

[18] *Ibid*, 204-205.

the great master Seoram Uiseong. He left Donghwa-sa Temple for Eunhae-sa Temple on Mt. Palgong in Yeongcheon County, North Gyeongsang Province. He went to Gyeongju and visited Bulguk-sa Temple and its affiliate Seokgul-am Grotto.

He visited Tongdo-sa Monastery on Mt. Yeongchuk in Yangsan County, South Gyeongsang Province. Korean Buddhists consider Tongdo-sa Monastery as one of the three jewel temples in Korean Buddhism along with Songgwang-sa and Haein-sa Monasteries. Tongdo-sa Monastery represents the Buddha jewel temple, Haein-sa Monastery is the Dharma jewel and Songgwang-sa is the Saṅgha jewel. Because Jajang (? 590-? 658) took a head crown relic of the Buddha from China and enshrined it at Tongdo-sa Monastery, Korean Buddhists regard it as the temple representing the Buddha jewel in Korea.

He worshipped the stūpa of the Buddha's relic at Tongdo-sa Monastery and then moved up to Geurak-am Hermitage affiliated with the monastery and saw Sin Hyewol (1861-1937),[19] the most famous Chan master in the southern part of the Korean peninsula. Sin Hyewol was one of the four eminent disciples of Song Gyeongheo (1849-1912),[20] the revitalizer of Korean Seon Buddhism in modern times after the persecution of Korean Buddhism during the Joseon Dynasty (1392-1910). Along with Sin Hyewol (1861-1937), the other three disciples were Jeon Suwol (1855-1928),[21] Song Mangong (1871-1946),[22] and Bang Hanam (1876-1951).[23] While living at Geurak-am Hermitage in the summer, he practiced Seon meditation. He also went to the Seon center in Bogwang Hall located in the monastery.

He studied the four collections from Haemun, the spiritual leader of Bogwang Hall Seon Center at Tongdo-sa Monastery. I Hoegwang (1862-1933),[24] then the abbot of Haein-sa Monastery, established a propagation center in Seoul including a Seon center.

---

[19] I Jeong, ed., 342-343.
[20] *Ibid*, 144-145.
[21] *Ibid*, 221.
[22] *Ibid*, 210-211.
[23] *Ibid*, 275-276.
[24] *Ibid*, 123-124.

He invited Chan Master Haemun to be the spiritual leader of the
Seon center. When Haemun went to Seoul, Yun Goam also
followed him as an attendant. He studied the four collections from
him and learned meditation from him as well at the Haein-sa
Monastery's Seoul propagation center.

In 1921, at the age of 23, he entered Mt. Bogae in Gangwon
Province and spent the summer there. He took the monastic
curriculum [25] of the four teachings from the scholar monk
Yongseong (d.u.) on the mountain. The four texts were the
Śūraṅgama Sūtra, the *Awakening of Faith in Mahāyāna*, the
Diamond Sūtra, and the *Complete Enlightenment Sūtra*. Just as he
privately studied the four collections from many teachers at many
different temples, he learned the four teachings from various
instructors at various locations without having a fixed monastic
seminary or teacher.

He heard that Baek Yongseong assembled 50 – 60 Seon
practitioners at Mangwol-sa Temple, located in the vicinity of
Seoul and educated them in Seon Buddhism. He also attended the
teachings on Seon Buddhism. During his free time, he went to
Daegak-sa Temple in downtown Seoul and studied the four
teachings.

In the spring of 1922, at the age of 24, he attended the national
conference for monastics at Gakhwang-sa Temple, then the head
temple of Korean Buddhism, on January 7th of that year. The
participants in the national conference for monastics decided to
abolish the articles and bylaws of the association of 30 abbots of
the parish head temples, which guaranteed the thirty abbots a
monopoly on power in Buddhist society. They agreed to establish
the Central Secretariat Office of the Korean Buddhist Order of
Seon and Doctrine and unite all of the Korean Buddhist
organizations.

The progressive ten parish head temples such as Tongdo-sa,
Beomeo-sa, Haein-sa, Seogwang-sa, Baegyang-sa, Wibong-sa,

---

[25] I Jigwan comprehensively discusses the textbooks used in Korean
Buddhist monastic seminaries in his *Hanguk bulgyo soui gyeongjeon yeongu*
(Studies in Korean Buddhist Monastic Seminary Textbooks), 2nd edition (1969,
Seoul: Dongguk daehakgyo seongnim-hoe, 1983).

Bongseon-sa, Songgwang-sa, Girim-sa and Geonbong-sa Temples withdrew from the association of 30 parish head temples and established the Central Secretariat Office of Korean Buddhism at Gakhwang-sa Temple in Seoul. They elected Gwak Beopgyeong as its acting secretary general. The other pro-Japanese parish head temples organized the Central Administration of Korean Buddhism and also located its head office at Gwakhwang-sa Temple. Both organizations fought against each other to obtain hegemony in the order.

In 1920, just one year after the March 1st, 1919 Independence Movement, Gim Namjeon (1868-1936)[26], Gang Dobong (d.u.), Gim Seokdu (d.u.)[27] and others resolved to establish a representative Seon center in Seoul and revive traditional Korean Seon Buddhism.[28] Baek Yongseong, Song Mangong, O Seongwol (d.u.)[29] and others followed through on the project and began construction on August 10th, 1921 at Anguk-dong in downtown Seoul. Construction was completed on November 30th.

On two days, March 30th and April 1st, 1922, 82 monastics, including O Seongwol, Baek Hakmyeong (1867-1929),[30] Hwang Yonggeum (d.u.), and Song Mangong, established the Seon Practitioner's Association as an affiliate organization of the Center for Seon Studies at the center. They transmitted traditional Korean Seon and maintained the celibate monastic tradition during the colonial period. The association accepted only unmarried monastics as its members.

---

[26] I Jeong, ed., 30-31.

[27] *Ibid,* 134.

[28] See '2. Recent Korean Son Masters' (241-57) in Mok Jeong-bae, "Buddhism in Modern Korea," in The Korean Buddhist Research Institute, ed., *The History and Culture of Buddhism in Korea* (Seoul: Dongguk University Press, 1993), 219-261 and also Mok Jeongbae, "Yeoksa pyeon, Geun-hyeondae" (Korean Buddhist History – Modern and Contemporary Times), in Hanguk bulgyo chongnam pyeonjip wiwon-hoe, ed., *Hanguk bulgyo chongnam* (The Comprehensive Collection of Source Materials of Contemporary Korean Buddhism) (Seoul: Daehan bulgyo jinheung-won, 1993), 102-106.

[29] I Jeong, ed., 145-146.

[30] *Ibid,* 24-25.

The Seon Practitioner's Association had its headquarters at the Center for Seon Studies in Seoul. It also had local branches at nineteen temples such as Mangwol-sa Temple, Jeonghye-sa Temple, Jikji-sa Temple, Baegyang-sa Temple, Beomeo-sa Temple, Bulyeong-sa Temple, Geonbong-sa Temple, Mahayeon-sa Temple, Jangan-sa Temple, Woljeong-sa Temple, Gaesim-sa Temple, Tongdo-sa Temple, Singye-sa Temple, Namjang-sa Temple, Seogwang-sa Temple, Seonam-sa Temple, Cheoneun-sa Temple, Yonghwa-sa Temple and Haein-sa Temple.

The association assigned Yun Goam to establish a branch at Sangwon-sa Temple on Mt. Odae in Pyeongchang County, Gangwon Province. Because Ha Dongsan, a more senior monk than him, practiced Seon meditation at Sangwon-sa Temple at the time, he carried out Ha Dongsan's wishes and established a branch of the association. While practicing Seon meditation at the Seon center, he used to pray to the Buddha at the Hall of the Buddha's Relic, affiliated with Sangwon-sa Temple and continued his studies of the four teachings.

Around August or September of 1922, he descended from Mt. Odae. He visited and worshipped the Stūpa of the Buddha's Relic at Jeongam-sa Temple on Mt. Taebaek in Jeongseon County, Gangwon Province. He then headed for Daeseung-sa Temple on Mt. Sabul in Mungyeong County, North Gyeongsang Province. The temple hosted a seven-day service. He attended the service and worshipped the Buddha's relic, which was revealed to the participants in the closing ceremony. Next, he visited Gimryong-sa Temple on Mt. Undal in Mungyeong County, North Gyeongsang Province, Yongmun-sa Temple on Mt. Sobaek in Yecheon County, North Gyeongsang Province, and Bongmyeong-sa Temple. He finally arrived at Jikji-sa Temple on Mt. Hwangak in Gimcheon County, North Gyeongsang Province. There he served his ordination master Gim Jesan. He then returned to the Haein-sa Monastery where he was ordained and continued his studied of the four teachings there.

He visited Jeonghye-sa Temple, also known as Sudeok-sa Temple on Mt. Deoksung in Yesan County, South Chungcheong Province where he served the great Seon master Song Manggong and practiced Seon meditation under his guidance at its affiliate, the Neungin Seon Center. According to the record of the Seon Center, he attended the summer 1923 intensive retreat with 16 Seon practitioners[31] and he was in charge of the big bell while practicing Seon meditation at the center. It was also mentioned in the record that he was a monk of Mangwol-sa Temple on Mt. Dobong in Yangju County, Gyeonggi Province.

He went back to Daegak-sa Temple in Seoul and read the four teachings. Hwang Ilgu introduced Unmun-am Hermitage affiliated with Baegyang-sa Temple to Baek Yongseong and agreed to establish a Seon center with him at the hermitage. He went to the hermitage first and prepared to open the Seon center. Around 40 – 50 Seon practitioners participated in the 1923 winter intensive retreat and practiced Seon meditation under the guidance of Baek Yongseong. Ha Dongsan also attended the intensive retreat.

In 1924, at the age of 26, he also kept silent and practiced Seon meditation in the summer intensive retreat at Unmun-am Hermitage. He then went to Jikji-sa Temple where his vocation master Gim Jesan resided. He also visited the Toeseol Seon Center at Haein-sa Monastery and meditated there. Next, he went to Sudo-am Hermitage on Mt. Sudo in Gimcheon County, North Gyeongsang Province and practiced Seon meditation along with more than 20 Seon practitioners at its affiliate Seon center for the winter intensive retreat. He also met Jeong Jeongang (1898-1975)[32] and Wolsong, and discussed Seon Buddhism with them. Then, he spent the winter at the intensive retreat at the center.

In spring 1925, at the age of 27, he went to Jikji-sa Temple and practiced Seon meditation. He went to the Seon center of Sudo-am Hermitage where he practiced Seon meditation with the practitioners Haesan and Wolsong. During that time of practice, he remained in silence.

Baek Yongseong organized the "Society for Practicing Seon during the Ten Thousand Days" at Chilbul-am Hermitage on Mt.

---

[31] Buddhology Institute, ed., *Geundae seonwon bangham-nok* (Records of the Seon Practitioners at Modern Seon Centers in Korean Buddhism) (Seoul: Education Board of Korean Buddhist Jogye Order, 2006), 166-167.
[32] I Jeong, ed., 186-187.

Jiri in 1924. When Yun Goam heard that Baek Yongseong would continue the society at Mangwol-sa Temple, he went to Seoul to attend the society's intensive retreat. Around 50-60 Seon practitioners assembled and practiced Seon meditation. Seol Seogu (1875-1958), [33] the former highest patriarch of the Jogye Order, and Jeong Unbong (d.u.) led the society under the direction of its spiritual leader Baek Yongseong. All members of the society remained in total silence and did not eat any meals after noon. Their breakfast consisted of one bowl of rice soup and one other dish. They then held the chanting service in the main hall from 9:00 am to 11:00 am and later ate lunch with three side dishes, generally kimchi, miso soup, and a soy sauce.

In 1926, Baek Yongseong moved the society because its members could not live at Mangwol-sa Temple. He took them to Naewon-am Hermitage on Mt. Cheonseong, affiliated with Tongdo-sa Monastery, the County of Yangsan, South Gyeongsang Province. The government reclassified the forest of Mt. Dobong as a nature reserve, so the members could not use the forest to make firewood, without which they could not live through Korea's long winters. Yun Goam followed Baek Yongseong and remained in silent meditation along with 40 to 50 Seon practitioners at Naewon-am Hermitage.

In 1927, he participated in the summer intensive retreat at the Toeseol Seon Center of Haein-sa Monastery along with 16 Seon practitioners. [34] He served as the large bell manager. He also received an honorific Dharma name, "Hyangdang" as recorded in the list of Seon practitioners who attended the 1927 summer retreat at the Seon center. However, there is no record of who presented him with this name.

In January of 1936, at the age of 38, he presided over a seven-day special service for Avalokiteśvara Bodhisattva. He gave a sermon at the closing ceremony and requested all the participants to purify the world. [35] In the same year, he graduated from the

---

[33] *Ibid*, 116-117.

[34] Buddhology Institute, ed., 78-79.

[35] Yun Seonhyo, ed., *Goam daejongsa beobeo jip*, 53-56.

highest level of Great Learning at the monastic seminary affiliated with Woljeong-sa Temple.[36]

In 1938, at the age of 40, Baek Yongseong recognized Yun Goam's enlightenment and gave him an honorific Dharma name "Goam" with the words: "Who knows the eternal beauty of nature? When I privately interviewed Goam, the beauty of nature is eternal."[37] Since then, he was called Goam rather than Sangeon. He provided Yun Goam the following Dharma-transmission poem.[38]

A Buddha and a patriarch do not know each other,
Shaking a head, I do not know.
Yunmen Wenyan's[39] Chinese stuffed pancake[40] is round,
A radish of the County of Zhenzhou[41] is long.

Except for the second line, the above Dharma-transmission poem that Yun Goam received from his master Baek Yongseong in

---

[36] See the August 3rd, 1967 issue of *Joseon ilbo*, HBGJ 1.1.416-417. However, according to "Great Master Yun Goam's Chronological Record," in Yun Seonhyo, ed., *Goam daejongsa beobeo jip*, Yun Goam finished the highest level in the monastic seminary affiliated with Haein-sa Monastery on March 10th, 1923.

[37] Jo Ohyeon, "Jabi bosal ui musoyu silcheon, Goam" (Yun Goam: A Compassionate Bodhisattva's Non-attachment Practice), in (Gim) Ilta Seunim, *et al.*, *Hyeondae goseung inmul pyeongjeon* (Biographies of Modern Korean Buddhist Eminent Monks) (Seoul: Bulgyo yeongsang, 1994), vol. 2, 116.

[38] Yun Seonhyo, ed., *Goam keunseunim pyeongjeon*, 95, 130, 183, 204 & 208.

[39] Yunmen Wenyan, 864-949.

[40] Yunmen Wenyan used to instruct Chan practitioners with a Chinese stuffed pancake.

[41] See Yuanwu Keqin (1063-1135), comp., *Biyan-lu* (The Blue Cliff Record), T.48.2003.169c4-6. The *Blue Cliff Record* is the very famous collection of one hundred Chan Kōans. Thomas Cleary and J. C. Cleary translated and published *The Blue Cliff Record* (Boulder, Colorado: Shambhala, 1978). Its 30th Kōan originated from the following case: "A monk asked Zhaozhou Congshen (778-897), "I heard that you met Nanchuan Puyuan (748-835). Is it true?" Zhaozhou replied, "There is a big radish in the County of Zhenzhou."

1938 is identical to the following Dharma transmission poem that
Ha Dongsan obtained from the same master in 1935.[42]

> A Buddha and a patriarch do not know each other,
> They provisionally say that they transmitted (Dharma)
> from mind to mind.
> Yunmen Wenyan's Chinese stuffed pancake is round,
> A radish of the County of Zhenzhou is long.

In 1935 and in 1938, Baek Yongseong, who received
transmission from Hwanseong Jian (1664-1729), officially
transmitted the Dharma lineage to his two dharma-successors Ha
Dongsan and Yun Goam. Both of them later served as the highest
patriarch in the Jogye Order of Korean Buddhism.

Beginning in 1939, one year after his Dharma transmission
from Baek Yongseong, Goam served as a spiritual leader at
various Seon centers across the nation in temples such as Haein-sa,
Baengnyeon-sa, Pyohun-sa, Jikji-sa, Beomeo-sa Temples, where
he trained Seon practitioners.[43]

On October 10th, 1945, at the age of 47, he became the director
of the Seon Center at Dabo-sa Temple in Naju County, South
Jeolla Province. Lay Buddhists financially supported the Seon
practitioners and let them concentrate on Seon meditation at the
temple.[44] Dabo-sa Temple became one of the famous Seon centers
in the Jeolla Provinces at the time. Later, Seon master Uhwa (d.u.)
succeeded his directorship of the Seon center. When Dabo-sa
Temple became famous, he asked master Uhwa to take over as
abbot for a while to elude the distractions to one's practice inherent
in running a famous temple.[45]

Between 1945 and 1954, for ten years, Yun Goam propagated
Buddhism and presided over the precept-offering ceremonies in
various temples and propagation centers across the nation. He
transmitted the Bodhisattva precepts to monastics and lay

---

[42] Im Hyebong, 102.

[43] Yun Seonhyo, ed., *Goam keunseunim pyeongjeon*, 42-43.

[44] *Ibid*, 43.

[45] *Ibid*, 21.

Buddhists and helped them preserve the precepts. He inherited the vinaya lineage from three vinaya masters, Gim Jesan, Baek Yongseong, and Bang Hanam.

In his later years, he transmitted to Go Gwangdeok (1927-1999)[46] the vinaya lineage he inherited from Baek Yongseong; to Gim Tanheo (1913-1983)[47] the vinaya lineage he took from Bang Hanam; and to Jeon Gwaneung (1910-2004)[48] the vinaya lineage transmitted from Gim Jesan. Because Go Gwangdeok was a disciple of Ha Dongsan, a disciple of Baek Yongseong, he transmitted the vinaya lineage to him. Because Gim Tanheo was the most eminent disciple of Bang Hanam, he passed it along to him. Because Jeon Gwaneung was the disciple of Gim Jesan, he also gave it to him.[49]

The Korean War broke out on June 25, 1950 and it ended on July 29, 1953. During the war period, he would visit the Jaun Seon Center in Gwangju from Dabo-sa Temple in Naju. He allowed young Seon practitioners to escape the violence by travelling to other, secular places and lived at Dabo-sa Temple. He conversed with Jeong Jeongang (1898-1975)[50] who resided at Jaun Seon Center.

On August 25, 1955, at the age of 57, he was appointed abbot of Seongju-sa Temple in Masan, South Gyeongsang Province and he purified the temple of married monastics. Celibate Korean Buddhist monks officially initiated the Purification Buddhist Movement with President I Seungman's first presidential message issued on May 20, 1954 to cleanse the Japanized elements in Korean Buddhism and to recover traditional Korean Buddhism's celibate monasticism. Even though he was not a central figure in the movement like Ha Dongsan, I Hyobong, I Cheongdam, Jeong Geumo, and Son Gyeongsan (1917-1979),[51] he also participated in it.

---

[46] Hanguk bulgyo chongnam pyeonjip wiwon-hoe, ed., 527.
[47] I Jeong, ed., 319.
[48] Hanguk bulgyo chongnam pyeonjip wiwon-hoe, ed., 589.
[49] Yun Seonhyo, ed., *op. cit.*, 43.
[50] I Jeong, ed., 186-187.
[51] *Ibid*, 368.

On September 30, 1958, at the age of 60, he became the abbot of Jikji-sa Temple in Gimcheon County, North Gyeongsang Province. Later, when he normalized the temple's management, he handed over the abbotship to another monk. Jikji-sa Temple was his vocation master Gim Jesan's home temple. Between 1960 and 1968, he was the spiritual leader of Yongtap Seon Center at Haein-sa Temple at which his Dharma master Baek Yongseong's memorial stūpa was elected in July of 1941. The center was closely connected to his Dharma master Baek Yongseong. His relics and portrait were enshrined in the center. Baek Yongseong was ordained at Haein-sa Monastery in 1879. He bought the neighboring land and expanded the temple territory.

While serving as the spiritual leader at the center, he helped the director Bogwang, founded the Buddha's Relic Stūpa and enshrined three major stone images of Amitābha Buddha, Avalokiteśvara Bodhisattva and Kṣitigarbha Bodhisattva in a Stone Grotto. He organized the "Society for Amitābha Buddha and Seon for Ten Thousand Days." He had a special ceremony on 15th day of the ninth lunar month each year and raised fund with which he protected his master's memorial gravestone. [52] If other monks asked him to teach Buddhism and preside over the ceremony of offering Bodhisattva precepts at the temples, he never declined their requests. Even though he was the leader at the center, he did not always stay there. As he had done, if needed, he went out to help other temples for a while without fixing his residence in a specific place. He stayed at the center and wanted to preserve it from decline and protect his Dharma master's memorial gravestone. [53]

When President I Seungman (1875-1965), who strongly supported the celibate monastic group by issuing six presidential messages, resigned his presidential position due to a massive national demonstration on April 19, 1960, the married monastic group counterattacked the celibate monastic group and tried to regain hegemony in the temples and the order from celibate monks.

---

[52] *Ibid*, 20.
[53] *Ibid*, 50-51.

Celibate monks organized an emergency committee and reacted against the attacks from the married monks. Yun Goam was assigned to take charge of the temples on Jeju Island.[54]

In 1967, he was installed as the vinaya precept master of the prestigious Diamond Precept Platform at Beomeo-sa Temple and until this death on October 25th, 1988, he served as the precept master. During his term, he transmitted Korean vinaya precepts to a number of lay Buddhists and monastics and educated them in the importance of precepts in various temples. He held a myriad of the precept-offering ceremonies at temples throughout South Korea.

On April 24th, 1965, Ha Dongsan passed away at Beomeo-sa Temple. In 1943, Ha Dongsan became the vinaya master at Beomeo-sa Temple and until his death in 1965, he served as the vinaya leader of the temple. He ordained many monks and also transmitted Bodhisattva precepts to monastics and lay Buddhists on the ordination platform. He also presided over many ceremonies of offering Bodhisattva precepts to lay Buddhists and monastics at numerous temples across the nation.

After Ha Dongsan's death, resident monks at the temple wanted to install a precept master and could not find and establish an appropriate vinaya master for some time because many Korean vinaya masters received precepts from a Thai vinaya master of the Theravāda lineage when he visited Korea. They argued that they could not install as the ordination master of the prestigious Beomeo-sa Temple anyone who obtained the Thai vinaya precepts instead of the traditional Korean vinaya precepts passed from generation to generation for the long history of Korean Buddhism.

Even though most people knew that Yun Goam did not receive the Thai precepts, he did not announce that only he did not receive them in order to be considered by his colleagues as a vinaya master. When some representative monks from Beomeo-sa Temple went to Thailand and investigated the list of monks who received the Thai precepts, they discovered that Yun Goam did not receive the Theravāda precepts. As a result, they, along with the resident

---

[54] Im Hyebong, 219.

monks at Beomeo-sa Temple, recommended Yun Goam for the position of vinaya master.[55]

On July 25, 1967, the central assembly hosted its 16th session at Haein-sa Temple and on July 26th, it accepted the resignations of the order's 2nd highest patriarch I Cheongdam and secretary general Son Gyeongsan. The assembly elected Yun Goam as the order's third highest patriarch and Bak Gijong (1907-1987)[56] as its secretary general. Yun Goam was the director of Yongtap Seon Center, affiliated with Haein-sa Monastery and Bak Gijong was the abbot of the same monastery.[57] It recommended I Cheongdam to the chair of the Council of Senior Monks and Son Gyeongsan to the chair of the Committee of Legal Principles. I Cheongdam had retired to Doseon-sa Temple in the vicinity of Seoul and Son Gyeongsan to Jeokjo-am Hermitage in Donam-dong, Seoul.

These two highest figures in the order fought one another to obtain hegemony over the order and disagreed with each other on the order's major issues. While I Cheongdam was a radical in the Purification Buddhist Movement, Son Gyeongsan was a moderate. They also disagreed with each other on how to revitalize Korean Buddhism from its degenerate state. Because I Cheongdam advocated a speedy revitalization of Korean Buddhism, he wanted to secure funds by selling unused temple properties. However, Son Gyeongsan opposed his proposal. If they sold the temple properties, he felt this would set a bad precedent. He suggested the order invest some money and manage businesses for profit. He invested the order's money and lost more than 40 million Korean won. I Cheongdam asked Son Gyeongsan to resign his position as secretary general and take responsibility for this failure. Because Son Gyeongsan refused to do so, both sides fought continuously.

Yun Goam was well known as a very docile, gentle, compassionate, and forbearing monk among eminent monks. The public considered him the best choice for the symbolic patriarchate. Even though he was installed as the order's highest patriarch on

---

[55] Yun Seonhyo, ed., op. cit., 52-53.

[56] I Jeong, ed., 251-252.

[57] See the July 27, 1967 issue of Donga ilbo and the July 27th, 1967 issue of Gyeonghyang sinmun, HBGJ 1.1.415.

July 27th, 1967, he did not give an inauguration speech. As the highest patriarch, he gave his first, short speech on the closing day of the summer intensive retreat at the Toeseol Seon Center of Haein-sa Monastery on the 15th day of the seventh lunar month (August 20th), 1967.[58]

When he became the order's highest patriarch, the mass media began to spotlight the Yongtap Seon Center of Haein-sa Monastery. A reporter of the order's official newspaper *Daehan bulgyo* visited the center and reported on it in the September 10th, 1967 issue in which he mentioned that 18 senior laywomen had been practicing Seon meditation at the center.[59]

On September 20th, 1967, the highest patriarch Yun Goam announced that the order would establish a practice complex at Haein-sa Monastery where it would educate monks to enhance the quality of monastic education at the monastery.[60] In the tedious and long disputes between married and celibate monastic groups, many unqualified monks were admitted to the order and furthermore, the order did not educate them well. The public generally considered monks unqualified and incapable. According to his proposal, the monks would attend two regular intensive retreats per year, namely, the summer and winter intensive retreats with each retreat lasting for three months. In addition to the two regular retreats, they could attend irregular retreats in various Seon centers throughout the country. However, because the order did not systematically manage the practitioners, it did not know where, when and how long they should practice Seon under what master. Yun Goam suggested that the order reform the monastic education system. He argued that the order should strictly execute compulsory education for newly ordained monks for at least three years after the establishment of the practice complex. He asserted that Haein-sa Monastery should be the order's center even though its Secretariat Office should of course process the basic

---

[58] See the August 27th, 1967 issue of *Daehan bulgyo*, in Im Hyebong, 220-221.

[59] Im Hyebong, 221.

[60] See the October 4th, 1967 issue of *Gyeonghyang sinmun*, HBGJ 1.1.419.

administrative affairs. He strongly hoped that after constructing a building, the order would initiate his plan for the practice complex.

On November 26, 1967, the grand master Baisheng (1904-1989), the president of the national Association of Chinese Buddhism in Taiwan and the highest patriarch of Linji Chan Sect visited South Korea. And on December 2nd, he also visited Haein-sa Monastery and took a photo with Yun Goam, then the highest patriarch of the Jogye Order of Korean Buddhism.[61]

On January 1, 1968, Yun Goam, as the order's highest patriarch, issued to Korean Buddhists a speech commemorating the New Year entitled "If Our Minds are Purified, Our Lands are Purified." He often preached this same theme to Buddhists. A speech with the same title by him was included in the January 1, 1986 issue of the order's official newspaper *Bulgyo sinmun*:[62]

> The Buddha says, "If the mind is purified, the Buddha lands are purified."[63] It means that if our minds are purified, our nations are purified. When the Buddha was a crown prince, he observed a world in which people fought against each other ideologically and ethnically in each nation, were not in peace, anxiously competed with each other, and were stuck in a sea suffering birth, living, aging and dying. Even though I have reconsidered the observation of the Buddha's, these problems originate from sentient beings themselves. However, if we look back to the origin of human beings, this origin was brighter than the sun and there was a mysterious creature. This light surrounded the universe and nurtured all beings. Because the origin is an originally pure and bright light, we can call it "the awakened mind." The mind cannot raise an unwholesome mind at any time. If so, we can live well in an extensively pure and always bright nation. Therefore, the Buddha said that if the mind is purified, the nation is purified. This mind is always a new

---

[61] Yun Seonhyo, ed., *Goam daejongsa beobeo-jip*, 309.

[62] *Ibid*, 35-37.

[63] See the *Vimalakīrti-nirdeśa Sūtra*, T.14.475.538c7.

day, a new year and a new mind. Because it does not have the suffering of birth, aging, sickness, dying, anxiety, sadness, pain, and evil passions and it does not like, dislike, and envy others, people can live with joy. While propagating the teaching, the Buddha educated sentient beings with four methods adopted to attract people to Buddhism, (1) generosity, (2) lovely speech, (3) benefitting actions, and (4) a generous mind to allow sentient beings to see the benefit of practicing the Dharma. Sentient beings called him the Buddha and paid homage to him.

We should not make only ourselves liked. We should not make others disliked. Like the crown prince Gautama Siddhārtha, we should distinguish good from evil and recover the original light from which we come. We should transform dark worlds into light ones, suffering into happiness, and wicked friends into good ones with a new mind in the New Year. As the Buddha suggested, we should give rise to a new and always good mind, implement the four methods and live well in this troubled society.

Between March 31 and April 4, 1968, for five days, he presided over a ceremony at Jogye-sa Temple and offered the Bodhisattva precepts to 1,300 Buddhists. [64] It was the largest precept offering ceremony since the beginning of the Purification Buddhist Movement. He also outlined the Bodhisattva precepts in the ceremony over the course of one hour.

On 8th day of the fourth lunar month (May 5), 1968, as the order's supreme patriarch, he issued a message commemorating the Buddha's birthday, entitled "Born on the Street and Living on the Street." The message was included in the May 5, 1968 issue of the order's official weekly newspaper *Daehan bulgyo*. Yun Seonhyo, a disciple of Yun Goam, edited and published it in *Goam daejongsa beobeo-jip: Jabi bosal ui gil* (Great Master Yun Goam's

---

[64] Im Hyebong, 222.

Analects: The Ways of a Compassionate Bodhisattva) (Seoul: Bulgyo yeongsang hoebo-sa, 1990), 148-150.

On May 11, the lay leader I Hansang organized at Jangchungdan Park in Seoul the opening ceremony for the bronze statue of Master Samyeong Yujeong (1544-1610),[65] a leader of Korean Buddhist monastic soldiers during the Japanese invasion period (1592-1598). He was the CEO of Pungjeon Industry Corporation and financially supported Buddhist organizations. He also became the president of the order's official weekly newspaper *Daehan bulgyo*. Korean Buddhists have regarded Samyeong Yujeong as an idol of state protectionism. Yun Goam attended the ceremony and delivered an address.

On January 1, 1969, he issued, as the order's supreme patriarch, the New Year message to Buddhists, entitled "Let Us Purify the World with a Spirit of Harmony."[66] He listed six harmonies in this address:[67]

> First, the Buddha taught us to treat own bodies equally with other people's bodies. We should not feed only our own bodies but also other people's bodies. We should eat meals and wear clothes equally in our daily lives without discriminating against others. Second, the Buddha taught us to harmonize our speech with others and to avoid arguing with each other. If we see people fighting, we should step in and help them to resolve the disagreement. We should not side with one person but should treat both sides equally. We should use soft and lovely speech towards other people. Third, the Buddha requested us to think in harmony with others. We should not adhere to only our opinion but also listen to others. We should make friends with others. Fourth, the Buddha asked us to keep the precepts with others. We should not be proud of ourselves by saying that we preserve them, but we should equally praise others in

---

[65] I Jeong, ed., 215-216.

[66] Yun Seonhyo, ed., *op. cit.*, 119-121.

[67] *Ibid.*

maintaining moral standards. We should practice Buddhist ethics with others. Fifth, the Buddha taught us to view things in harmony with others. We should purify our view and see the positive qualities of others, not the negative qualities of others. Sixth, the Buddha taught us to maintain possessions in harmony with others. We should not benefit only ourselves but we should also benefit others quietly without letting them know what we have done. If we remove our own desires and help others, our world would be naturally harmonious.

On the 8th day of the fourth lunar month (May 23), he gave an address to celebrate the Buddha's birthday as the order's highest patriarch. He suggested Buddhists to confess their faults, celebrate the Buddha's birthday and endeavor to cultivate themselves.

In 1969, he was installed as the spiritual leader of Beomeo-sa Temple and until his death in 1988, he served that temple as its spiritual leader, guiding the monks in residence.[68] From the time of the former spiritual leader Ha Dongsan's death in 1965, the position was vacant until 1969. I Seongcheol (1912-1993), Ha Dongsan's monastic disciple, had served as the spiritual leader of Haein-sa Monastery since 1967. While his disciple served as the spiritual leader of presumably the biggest temple in Korea in 1969, his younger Dharma brother and the order's supreme patriarch Yun Goam was installed as Beomeo-sa Temple's spiritual leader at the time.

On September 11, 1969, Yun Goam became a director of the Board of Directors of the Daegak (Great Enlightenment) Foundation when the disciples and grand disciples of Baek Yongseong established the foundation at Daegak-sa Temple in order to inherit and propagate the spirit of Baek Yongseong. Daegak-sa Temple was the temple that Baek Yongseong himself established on April 8, 1911. At the time, his Dharma brother I Dongheon (1896-1983) was elected as the board's first president.

---

[68] Yun Seonhyo, ed., *Goam keunseunim pyeongjeon*, 51-52.

Baek Yongseong propagated Buddhism and developed the independence movement at the temple. He also officially established and systematized a new religion named Daegak-gyo (Great Enlightenment Religion) in 1927 and tried to modernize Korean Buddhism. He also endeavored to preserve Korean Buddhism's celibate monasticism from the onslaught of the married priesthood imported from Japan. Yun Goam inherited his master Baek Yongseong's emphasis on monastic precepts and the recovery of Korean Buddhism's tradition of celibacy from the Japanized system of a married priesthood infecting Korean Buddhism at the time. He presided over innumerable ceremonies of offering precepts to monastics and lay Buddhists at many temples all throughout the country.

On January 1, 1970, he gave a speech entitled "Geumgang bojwa" (Diamond Treasure Seat) as the order's supreme patriarch and asked Buddhists to practice the Dharma diligently.[69] On the 8th day of the fourth lunar month (May 12), 1970, the Buddha's Birthday, he gave a speech entitled "Let Us Purify the World with Peace and Mercy."[70]

In 1970, he was installed as the second spiritual leader of Haein-sa Monastery after the first and founding spiritual leader I Seongcheol. After married monks along with some celibate monastics established the Taego Order of Korean Buddhism on May 8th and completely separated themselves from the Jogye Order, the order hosted a special service for 49 days between August 23rd and October 10th at Jogye-sa Temple, the order's head temple in Seoul. During that time, Yun Goam presided over the ceremony for offering Bodhisattva precepts to Buddhist practitioners. In early September, he announced the 3rd session of the order's central assembly and on September 23rd, he gave a speech at the central assembly's opening ceremony.

On July 22, 1970, I Cheongdam, who had served as the order's Supreme Patriarch from November 30th, 1966 to July 26th, 1967, was appointed the order's lower-ranked Secretary General. He

---

[69] Yun Seonhyo, ed., *Goam daejongsa beobeo-jip*, 222-224.
[70] Im Hyebong, 224.

served in this position until his death on November 15th, 1971. I
Cheongdam contributed a great deal to the effort to regain the
hegemony of the celibate monks in Korean Buddhism from the
married monks. During his term as the order's Secretary General,
he actually had handled the order's administration and Yun Goam
just symbolically served as the order's patriarch.[71]

On January 1st, 1971, Yun Goam issued a message to all
members of the Jogye Order. On January 25th, the order revived its
Committee for Planning at a cabinet meeting with the intention that
the committee would advise the supreme patriarch. However, Yun
Goam did not utilize this committee. In March, the order's
Secretariat Head Office determined that the order would strongly
implement the order's three major missions of the education for
monks, the propagation of Buddhism to the masses, and the
translation of Buddhist texts in the vernacular Korean language
and convened the Committee for Planning to that end. On May 9th,
the 15th day of the fourth lunar month, the first day of the three-
month summer intensive retreat, he delivered a speech for the Seon
practitioners and strongly advised them to concentrate on their
Seon practice for the next three months.[72]

On June 26th, the executives of the order's Secretariat Head
Office determined that they would all resign from their posts if the
order's central assembly would not pass the revised constitution at
an extraordinary session to be held on July 5th. Because the
Secretariat Head Office wanted to strengthen its role and to
centralize the administration of the order as much as possible, it
submitted the revised constitution. The members of the order's
central assembly hoped to decentralize the order's administration
and to give greater autonomy to the parish head temples. Both
sides clashed with each other.

Around that time, Gim Gyeongu, the order's secretary of
general affairs, arbitrarily sold 60,000 *pyeong*[73] of land belonging
to Yeonju-am Hermitage on Mt. Gwangak near Seoul without

---

[71] *Ibid,* 224-225.

[72] Yun Seonhyo, ed., *op. cit.*, 328-330.

[73] A *pyeong*, a unit of area, corresponds to 3.954 square yards.

approval from the cabinet or the Secretary General. The order's Committee for Inspection investigated the case. The order's Inspector General, Secretary General and all cabinet members submitted their resignations to the order's central assembly. On July 27th, the central assembly accepted their resignations except I Cheongdam, the Secretary General and Song Wolju, the Secretary of Education at its 26th extraordinary session.

On August 16th, Yun Goam came to Seoul from Haein-sa Temple to solve the order's crisis. He discussed how to settle the current case with I Cheongdam and his secretaries. He also met some leading monks in Seoul. Over two days, from August 18th to 19th, Yun Goam hosted a meeting of the Council of Elder Monks at Jogye-sa Temple in which 13 elder monks participated. In the meeting, they decided to establish an Advisory Committee for the Order's Administration under the direct control of the supreme patriarch. The committee consisted of 22 members. When the speaker of the central assembly, the secretary general of the Secretariat Head Office, and the Inspector General recommend some candidates, the supreme patriarch appoints the members from among the candidates. The crisis originating from the illegal sale of the Yeonju-am Hermitage property by Gim Gyeongu allowed Yun Goam, the order's supreme patriarch, to officially step into the order's administration. He hosted committee meetings three times in 1971 in order to improve the order's administration.

On November 15th, 1971, I Cheongdam, the order's secretary general, suddenly passed away. When the order hosted a big memorial service for him at Dongdaemun Stadium on November 19th, Yun Goam attended the service and delivered an address of condolence. Go Gwangdeok, secretary of general affairs, served as the acting secretary general. The order's central assembly elected Gang Seokju, an independent and neutral monk, as the order's 7th secretary general at the order's 27th regular session. Gang Seokju did not belong to any particular faction.

On December 2nd, 1971, the 15th day of the tenth lunar month, the opening day of the winter intensive retreat, he issued an address as the order's highest patriarch in which he asserted that ignorance and suchness (enlightenment) are non-dual. [74]

On January 1st, 1972, Yun Goam gave a New Year's address. [75] He asked Buddhists throughout the country to think positively, open up a new era, and develop the order's three major missions in the January 2nd, 1972 issue of the order's official newspaper *Daehan bulgyo*. [76] He also announced the principal directions for purifying the order's monastics in six points. [77] We can understand his basic ideas on the purification of Buddhism through this article. The six topics he discussed in the article are (1) the order's organizational framework, [78] (2) the participation of religious practitioners in society, [79] (3) propagation originating from cultivation, [80] (4) the education of monastics, [81] (5) the propagation of Buddhism, [82] and (6) the harmony between traditional education and modern education for monastics. [83]

On January 2, 1972, he attended the 49th day memorial service for the late I Cheongdam, former Secretary General, at Jogye-sa Temple and delivered a memorial speech at the service. Monks also concurrently hosted a service at Songgwang-sa Monastery in Suncheon and Bohyeon-sa Temple in Daegu. [84]

On May 20th, the Buddha's Birthday, the 8th day of the fourth lunar month, the order's Secretary General Gang Seokju read a message on behalf of Yun Goam. He requested Buddhists to accumulate all wholesome merit. [85] On May 27th, the 15th day of the fourth lunar month he gave an address celebrating the beginning of

---

[74] *Ibid*, 293-295.

[75] *Ibid*, 231-232.

[76] *Ibid*, 229-230.

[77] *Ibid*, 102-112.

[78] *Ibid*, 102-103.

[79] *Ibid*, 103-106.

[80] *Ibid*, 106-107.

[81] *Ibid*, 107-108.

[82] *Ibid*, 108-110.

[83] *Ibid*, 110-112.

[84] See the January 16th, 1972 issue of *Daehan bulgyo*, cited in Im Hyebong, 226.

[85] Yun Seonhyo, ed., *op. cit.*, 153-154.

summer intensive retreat at Seon centers across the nation as the
spiritual leader of Haein-sa Monastery and as the supreme
patriarch of the Jogye Order of Korean Buddhism.[86] His speech
was included in Yun Seonhyo, ed., *Great Master Yun Goam's
Analects.*[87] He emphasized the unity between praxis and theory in
Seon Buddhism in this speech.

The order's third supreme patriarch Yun Goam's five-year
term was subject to finish on August 7th, 1972. The order's central
assembly hosted the 30th extraordinary session for two days from
July 20th to the 21st and unanimously recommended Yun Goam
once more as the order's 4th supreme patriarch. At the 30th session,
Yun Goam issued an address and urged the central assembly's
representatives to enrich the order's and their own inner wisdom
and not to merely strengthen the order's and their own appearance
with the following words.[88]

.... Modern society requests Buddhism to effectively
manage its organizations by strengthening its organizations,
enlarge its businesses, and socialize its structure. I well
know that our order accepts and implements these requests
of modern society. In the process, (however), we should
remember to make the internalization of the Buddha's
teachings a priority. We should understand that if we
superficially extend the order's external businesses,
strengthen its organizations and propagate Buddhist
teachings without enriching those inner understanding, it
will destroy the order's future. In order to extend the
order's influence externally into society, we should enrich
internally and educate ourselves in advance....

On August 23rd, the 15th day of the seventh lunar month, the
closing day of the three-month summer intensive meditation retreat,
Yun Goam delivered a sermon at Beomeo-sa Temple in Busan. He

---

[86] Im Hyebong, 226-227.

[87] See the June 4th, 1972 issue of *Daehan bulgyo*, in Yun Seonhyo, ed.,
Goam daejongsa beobeo-jip, 308-310.

[88] Yun Seonhyo, ed., *op. cit.*, 117.

taught the Seon practitioners that mind is the center of all things. He asked them to keep in mind the following four items: (1) Give rise to the great awakening mind and let it not backslide; (2) make good friends and let them not to be far away; (3) endure and let yourselves not indulge in anger; and (4) stay in a proper place and cultivate yourselves without being distracted until you achieve enlightenment.[89]

On August 27th, the order held an inauguration ceremony for Yun Goam's second term as the 4th supreme patriarch at Jogye-sa Temple to which numberless celebrities and 1,500 lay Buddhists attended to congratulate him. He said in the ceremony that if we purify our minds, our nations will become purified as well.[90]

From October 21st through the 22nd, for two days, he hosted a precept-offering ceremony at Jikji-sa Temple on Mt. Hwangak in Gimcheon, North Gyeongsang Province and offered the monastic and Bodhisattva precepts to the monks.[91] On November 20th, the 15th day of the tenth lunar month, the first day of the winter intensive retreat, he also delivered a speech at Jikji-sa Temple.[92]

On October 17th, 1972, he dictator Bak Jeonghui issued a special declaration, dissolving the National Assembly, and declared a nationwide emergency military vigilance.[93] Ten days later, on October 27th, the government's emergency cabinet notified the revised version of constitution called the Reformation Constitution by the military dictatorial government. The constitution allowed the president to control all three branches of administration, legislation, and judicature, changed the president's shorter term in office to a longer eight-year term, allowed the president to run for the presidency without any term limit, established the national convention for delegates, and let its members elect the president. On November 21st, the government passed the revised constitution through a national referendum. On

---

[89] *Ibid,* 290-291.

[90] *Ibid,* 96-101.

[91] Im Hyebong, 228.

[92] Yun Seonhyo, ed., *op. cit.,* 296-297.

[93] I Manyeol, ed., *Hanguk-sa nyeonpyo* (A Chronological Table of Korean History) (Seoul: Yeongmin-sa, 1985), 342.

December 27th, Bak Jeonghui was inaugurated as the South Korean Government's 8th president and promulgated the constitution. He campaigned to reform society in order to justify his unusual and improper actions.

During this period, Korean Buddhism was influenced by the socio-political atmosphere.[94] On December 7th, because the order, as a long-time pro-government institution, felt that it should support the government's measures, it convened a conference for the leading monks, giving them the opportunity to discuss how to reform Buddhism. Yun Goam assigned them to submit a list of twenty reforms for the order. They submitted the list to the order's central assembly and requested the assembly to enact all twenty points. They particularly discussed the order's ordination system and the reform of monastic robes. The assembly arranged a budget for implementing this proposal. On the same day, he issued a message asking them to discuss the order's issues, actualize the purification of Korean Buddhism from all Japanese influence and reveal the holy principles of the Buddha in this modern society.[95] On December 9th, he issued a message to the opening of the central assembly's regular session in which he suggested them to revise the order's constitution and discuss the order's urgent issues.[96]

On December 21st, the order initiated the secretariat office for the highest patriarch and Yun Goam appointed Im Wongwang as his chief secretary. He was ordained under Yun Goam at Dabo-sa Temple in Naju, South Jeolla Province in 1942.

On January 1, 1973, Yun Goam published the supreme patriarch's message in that day's issue of the order's official weekly newspaper *Daehan bulgyo*.[97] From January 23rd to the 25th, the order's central assembly held the 32nd extraordinary session and reshuffled the major position-holders in the order. Because Secretary General Gang Seokju resigned in December 1972, the position was vacant. The assembly passed a resolution that the order would protect its sovereignty from the government's

---

[94] Im Hyebong, 228-229.
[95] Yun Seonhyo, ed., *op. cit.*, 131-132.
[96] *Ibid*, 133-135.
[97] *Ibid*, 226-227.

intervention, an unusual action for a pro-government institution. It elected Son Gyeongsan as the order's 9th secretary general, Chae Byeogam as the speaker of the central assembly, and Gim Jihyo (1909-1989)[98] as its inspector general. On January 27th, Yun Goam conferred appointment letters to newly elected persons. Son Gyeongsan returned to the secretary general position after five years and six months. [99] Due to the power struggle with the supreme patriarch I Cheongdam, he resigned this position on July 26, 1967 along with I Cheongdam.

On February 17th, the 15th day of the first lunar month, Yun Goam attended the closing ceremony for the winter intensive retreat and delivered a speech at Jikji-sa Temple on Mt. Hwangak in Gimcheon, North Gyeongsang Province in which he suggested Seon practitioners to practice diligently. On May 17th, the 15th day of the fourth lunar month, he presided over the opening ceremony for the summer intensive retreat at Jogye-sa Temple in which more than 1,000 lay Buddhists and monastics participated. He asked them to cultivate their minds with endurance and to endeavor to remove ignorance. [100]

On May 29, 1973, the secretary general Son Gyeongsan requested the supreme patriarch Yun Goam to approve his dismissal of the director of the bureau of social affairs. [101] However, Yun Goam rejected Son Gyeongsan's request. Even though six major executives of the Secretariat Head Office, including the secretary of general affairs, ritualistically submitted their resignation letters to the patriarch Yun Goam, they did not expect the patriarch to accept the letters. However, Yun Goam accepted all six resignations.

Some people questioned whether or not the patriarch had the authority to do this under the order's bylaws. The problem in fact originated from the constitution's ambiguous rules on the

---

[98] I Jeong, ed., 286.

[99] Im Hyebong, 229.

[100] *Ibid.*

[101] Monastic Alumni Association of Dongguk University, ed., *Hanguk bulgyo hyeondae-sa* (The History of Modern Korean Buddhism) (Seoul: Sigong-sa, 1997), 46-47.

relationship between the patriarch and the secretary general. While the patriarch Yun Goam wanted to extend his authority, the then secretary general Son Gyeongsan understood that Yun Goam was just the order's symbolic spiritual leader and the secretary general should have full responsibility for administering the order. Since this case in the 1970's, because of structural and legal problems regarding the roles and responsibilities of the patriarch and the secretary general, the order's two highest administrators have competed with one another for control of the order's administration.

On April 22nd, 1970, the dictator Bak Jeonghui announced in a national meeting for provincial ministers the initiation of a new village-making movement. Since then, the movement patronized by the government became a nationwide movement. The government regularly intervened in and guided the movement in the 1970's. From 1970 to 1971, the government began to modernize farming villages through this movement. In 1972, the government implemented the movement on a national scale and in 1973, it systemized the movement. However, after his close aide Gim Jaegyu, then the director of the Korean CIA, assassinated President Bak Jeonghui on October 26th, 1979, the movement lost momentum and began to decline.

However, the Jogye Order had positively responded to the government and this government-sponsored movement.[102] On June 23rd, 1973, the order held a national conference for Buddhists for reforming the people's eating habits at the gigantic Jangchung Gymnasium in which more than 10,000 people participated. The supreme patriarch Yun Goam attended the massive conference and strongly recommended Buddhists to participate in the New Village-making Movement and to reform dietary habits.

On July 3rd, the order hosted a ceremony to celebrate Bulguk-sa Temple's one thousand year anniversary, having restored its original form after construction over the four years and two months.[103] Because President Bak Jeonghui also was interested in

---

[102] Im Hyebong, 229.
[103] *Ibid,* 230.

the restoration project and provided government funds for the project, he also attended the ceremony. Because the temple is located in Gyeongju, the capital for the former kingdom of Silla, it had been famous for tourism. The government's high-ranking officials and the order's high executives as well as more than five thousand Gyeongju citizens and Buddhists attended the ceremony.

From August 26th to the 31st, the 2nd international conference for World Buddhist Youth Leaders was hosted at various locations including Seoul and other major cities in Korea. [104] With 62 representatives from 12 nations such as South Korea, Thailand, the United States, Taiwan, Hong Kong, Indonesia, Malaysia, Laos, Khmer, Vietnam, Sri Lanka and Nepal attending, Yun Goam delivered his speech as the Jogye Order's supreme patriarch at the opening ceremony. [105] He requested them to purify the world with the Buddha's teachings.

In 1973, Sinheung-sa Temple, in which his disciple Mun Seongjun served as abbot, installed Yun Goam as its spiritual leader. Yun Goam then served as its spiritual leader between 1973 and 1976. On October 17th, he attended a ceremony in commemoration of the temple's successful remodeling of Sinheung-sa Temple on Mt. Seorak in Sokcho, Gangwon Province. He complimented the then abbot Mun Seongjun who had successfully reconstructed the temple buildings destroyed during the Korean War from 1950 to 1953 and recovered the original temple's atmosphere for his lay and monastic supporters. [106]

On December 5th and 15th, 1973, the supreme patriarch Yun Goam issued special messages stating that he would temporarily suspend the order's central assembly. [107] Since 1954, the minority of celibate monks kicked out the majority of married monks from the order and temples by relying on non-Buddhist methods, that is, physical violence and the support of the external government. Thus, they accomplished the Purification Buddhist Movement through the government's backing. During the movement, many

---

[104] *Ibid.*

[105] Yun Seonhyo, ed., *op. cit.*, 247-248.

[106] *Ibid*, 244-246.

[107] Im Hyebong, 230-231.

unqualified monks flooded the order and began to push for their interests. Because the order could not have educated the newly ordained monks properly during the movement period, 1954 – 1962, Yun Goam felt that it was time to purify and discipline the monks.

Secretary General Son Gyeongsan and his cabinet members as well as some members of the central assembly also supported the supreme patriarch Yun Goam's message.[108] On December 19th, the representatives of the order affiliated organizations and the leading monks held a meeting and passed a resolution that they would understand and follow the highest patriarch Yun Goam and his special address.

On the other hand, on December 20th, 1973, some monks opposed the patriarch Yun Goam's special address and met at Silleuk-sa Temple in Yeoju County, Gyeonggi Province. On December 28th, some leading monks, some abbots of parish head temples, and some central assembly members held a preparatory conference for organizing the Society for the Protection of the Order's Ecclesiastical Authority at Jogye-sa Temple. On January 3rd, 1974, they convened a meeting at Gwaneum-sa Temple in Daegu and, arguing the supreme patriarch's special address was unconstitutional, they passed five resolutions in the conference, including a resolution that they would request the central assembly's speaker to convene a session by January 15th. They also organized the Society for the Protection of the Order's Ecclesiastical Authority and elected O Nogwon, abbot of Jikji-sa Temple, one of the 25 parish head temples, as its president. On January 5th, they submitted the five resolutions to the order's Secretariat Head Office. Eight parish head temples formed the order's opposition group. The ruling side represented by the order's Secretariat Head Office and the opposition side by the Society fought against each other to obtain control of the order. On January 17th, 1974, the parish head temples met at Cheongnyong-am Hermitage in Seoul, organized the National Association of Parish Head Temples, and decided to manage their own

---

[108] *Ibid,* 213.

administration independently of the order's Secretariat Head Office.

On January 27th, the highest patriarch Yun Goam again issued a special message and asked Buddhists to work in harmony with one another and to accomplish the purification of Buddhism. From February 1st to the 6th, the supreme patriarch, the secretary general and the speaker of the ruling faction conceded to the opposition's request and held the central assembly's 32nd session. The two sides fought against each other at the session. The opposition party also informed the ruling group that it had decided not to host a national conference for monastics. On February 1, 1974, Goam issued a message at the opening ceremony and recommended the members of the central assembly to purify monasticism.[109] Even though the opposition side's representatives asked even the order's highest administrator Secretary General Son Gyeongsan to step down from his position, they did not succeed in removing him from his position. However, they did succeed in having three cabinet members of Son Gyeongsan's administration fired.

In mid April 1974, the highest patriarch Yun Goam presented eight principles for the order's monastic purification with the cosigners Secretary General Son Gyeongsan, Speaker Chae Byaegam, Inspector General Gim Jihyo and five major secretaries of the Secretariat Head Office.[110] The eight principles for the monastic order were (1) cultivation, (2) propagation, (3) translation, (4) discipline, (5) diligent work, (6) compassion, (7) state-protectionism, and (8) trust. He argued that the purification of the monastics could not be possible without increasing the qualifications of the monastics in the order. He recommended reflection on the order's previous steps and the accomplishment of monastic purification.

On May 24, 1974, the order's Secretariat Head Office (Secretary General Son Gyeongsan) appointed Hwang Jingyeong as the abbot of Bulguk-sa Temple. On June 3rd, the then abbot I Beomhaeng took the case to court and applied for provisional

---

[109] Yun Seonhyo, ed., *op. cit.*, 129-130.
[110] Im Hyebong, 232.

disposition to settle the matter. Due to an uncompromising struggle between Chae Byeogam and Bak Byeogan on the presidency of the Dongguk University Foundation, the government's Department of Education temporarily appointed 13 directors of the foundation on June 11th and instructed them to manage the foundation for three months. During that time, Seo Dongak resigned as the university's president and the foundation elected I Seongeun to replace him in that position.

The order convened a meeting for the Advisory Committee for the Order's Administration. [111] The committee members determined in the meeting that the order should settle the case of Bulguk-sa Temple by July 1st and appoint monks as directors within three months to solve the issues at Dongguk University. The committee reported these resolutions to the order's supreme Patriarch Yun Goam and requested him and the order's Secretariat Head Office to implement them.

Upon the committee's request, the order's Secretariat Head Office accepted Hwang Jingyeong's resignation and appointed Choe Wolsan as the temple's abbot with I Beomhaeng's cooperation. He was the elder Dharma brother of I Beomhaeng and was the director of the Seon Center affiliated with Bulguk-sa Temple.

On July 16th, a national conference for monks (Convener Yun Wolha) was convened by Yun Wolha to resolve the chaos occurring in the order. [112] Fully realizing his responsibility for finding a solution to the order's serious disorder, Yun Goam announced his resignation at the national conference and suggested the executives of the order's Secretariat Head Office and Inspector General Office resign from their positions. From July 18th to the 23rd, the order's central assembly hosted the 35th extraordinary session, accepted the resignations of the highest patriarch Yun Goam and those occupying the four major posts of the order's Secretariat Head Office except the Secretary General Son

---

[111] Im Hyebong, 233.

[112] Monastic Alumni Association of Dongguk University, ed., 47.

Gyeongsan and elected the 5th supreme patriarch I Seoong. His inauguration took place on August 3rd.

After removing himself from the order's politics in 1974, Yun Goam endeavored to propagate Korean Buddhism internationally and domestically even though he was by then a man of many years. Internationally speaking, in 1976, at the age of 78, Yun Goam visited Japan and Guam and hosted ceremonies of offering Bodhisattva precepts to lay Buddhists at several Korean temples. In 1978, he became the advisor to the Society for Memorizing the War Dead Overseas and then, he presided over memorial services in many places in the Pacific region. [113] On January 7, 1978, he visited Daewon-sa Temple (currently Muryang-sa Temple) in Honolulu and Gwaneum-sa Temple in Los Angeles where he presided over ceremonies of offering Bodhisattva precepts to lay Buddhists. On the way back to Korea, he visited four holy Buddhist sites in India. [114]

Domestically speaking, between 1977 and 1988, the year in which he passed away, he served as the director of the Daegak Foundation that Baek Yongseong originally founded. On November 5, 1977, he presided over the ceremony enshrining the Avalokiteśvara Bodhisattva image at Naksan-sa Temple in Yangyang County, Gangwon Province, belonging to the parish headquarter temple Sinheung-sa in Sokcho City, Gangwon Province, abbots of which were his disciples. More than seven thousand people attended. He delivered a speech at the ceremony. [115]

On May 6th, 1978, the order's central assembly held a meeting and again elected Yun Goam as the new supreme patriarch, Yun Wolha as the new secretary general and Gim Seoun as the new speaker. [116] It also revised the constitution and changed the head of the order's administration from the supreme patriarch to the secretary general, defining the supreme patriarch as the order's symbolic and spiritual figure. However, on May 10th, the then

---

[113] Yun Seonhyo, ed., *Goam keunseunim pyeongjeon*, 56.

[114] *Ibid,* 56-57.

[115] Im Hyebong, 234.

[116] Monastic Alumni Association of Dongguk University, ed., 53.

supreme patriarch I Seoong announced that he would continue his patriarchate.

At the time, the order was divided in two. The ruling group had its headquarters at Jogye-sa Temple, led by supreme patriarch I Seoong. This group advocated the then constitution that prescribed the supreme patriarch as the order's highest administrator. The opposition group had its headquarters at Gaeun-sa Temple. On March 10, 1978, the opposition group elected Chae Byeogam as their own group's supreme patriarch Chae Byeogam and Yun Wolha as secretary general. The group advocated revision of the constitution to change the head of the order's administration from the supreme patriarch to the secretary general.

Upon Chae Byeogam's resignation from the position of Supreme Patriarch for the opposition due to illness, the opposition group recommended Yun Goam as its own acting supreme patriarch. [117] On July 18th, the Seoul High Court also appointed Yun Goam to this position. On July 31st, the leader of the ruling group, Supreme Patriarch I Seoong, handed over power to Yun Goam. On August 2nd, Yun Goam appointed I Seongsu as the order's secretary general as well as other monks to other major cabinet posts. On August 3rd, he issued a special message in which he would normalize the order's management and recover its authority. [118] On August 11th, he agreed with the opposition group that he would concede his power as the order's acting patriarch to the central assembly. On August 12th, the abbots of 25 parish head temples convened a meeting and determined that they would support Yun Goam and his administration. With this support, Yun Goam announced that he would terminate the 4th central assembly's term and notified the opposition group that he would not continue with their agreement anymore.

On September 6th, he issued his 1st emergency order and organized an emergency central assembly, [119] appointing 65 representatives to this emergency central assembly. As the acting

---

[117] *Ibid.*

[118] Yun Seonhyo, ed., *Goam daejongsa beobeo-jip*, 136-138.

[119] Monastic Alumni Association of Dongguk University, ed., 53.

supreme patriarch, he completely disconnected his relations with the opposition group and wholeheartedly backed up the ruling group led by former supreme patriarch I Seoong. He who had supported the supreme patriarch-centered administrative system could not get along with the opposition group that advocated the secretary general-centered administrative system. Even though he had been the acting supreme patriarch with the support of the opposition group, he disconnected his relationship with the opposition and sided with the ruling group.

On September 9th, the emergency central assembly convened the 1st session and elected Choe Wolsan as the speaker and Gim Hyejeong and Im Wongwang as co-vice speakers. [120] At the 2nd session held from September 25th to the 26th, the central assembly again revised the constitution and changed the highest administer from the secretary general to the supreme patriarch. On September 26th, the assembly extended the supreme patriarch's power. For example, if needed, the supreme patriarch could issue emergency orders. At the time, the supreme patriarch could appoint the order's secretary general, inspector general, and even the abbots of the 25 parish head temples. [121] On September 30th, Yun Goam appointed the major cabinet members and executives in the order's Secretariat Head Office.

He led 15 delegates of Korean Buddhism and attended the 12th WFB (World Fellowship of Buddhists) General Conference held in Tokyo on October 1st through the 11th. He delivered an address at the conference and urged world Buddhist leaders to cooperate with one another and to create peace and prosperity through the Buddha's teachings in this struggling society. [122]

On October 18th, during the 3rd session, the central assembly elected Yun Goam as the order's Supreme Patriarch, Choe Wolsan as the Secretary General and Gim Jihyo as the Inspector General and nullified the opposition group's central assembly. He

---

[120] *Ibid*, 53-54.
[121] Im Hyebong, 237-238.
[122] Yun Seonhyo, ed., *op. cit.*, 281-285.

successfully returned the secretary general-centered administrative system to the supreme patriarch-centered administrative system.

On November 12th, the ruling group hosted the inauguration ceremony for the 6th Supreme Patriarch Yun Goam at Jogye-sa Temple. More than 3,000 people attended and celebrated his installment in the inauguration ceremony. He delivered a speech in which he enlisted three principles for the order's new direction. [123] The first principle was harmony. He requested Buddhists to act in harmony and to revive Buddhism from its state of decay. The second principle was religious cultivation and diligence. He proposed that lay Buddhists practice for themselves and propagate Buddhism for the masses. To disseminate Buddhism smoothly, he mentioned that the order should revise the constitution and centralized the distribution of power to the supreme patriarch. The third principle was to engage in creative activities. He recommended the Buddhists plan and implement long-term projects as he felt that the order should modernize and popularize Buddhism among the masses.

However, it is difficult to see his inauguration as being legitimate. Only one faction of the order elected and installed him as the order's supreme patriarch. The Jogye Order today also does not recognize him as the 6th highest patriarch, but considers I Seongcheol as the 6th supreme patriarch who began his term in January 10th, 1981. [124]

On the other hand, on October 23rd, the opposition group convened the 49th extraordinary session and opened the 5th central assembly. [125] After all, two central assemblies in one order were held. The ruling side and the opposition side organized their own 5th central assemblies. At the session, the opposition side's central assembly elected Son Gyeongsan as its speaker, did not agree the authenticity of the emergency central assembly and nullified the election of the supreme patriarch Yun Goam at the emergency central assembly's session.

---

[123] *Ibid,* 139-143.
[124] Monastic Alumni Association of Dongguk University, ed., 80.
[125] *Ibid,* 53-54.

On May 6th, 1978, Yun Goam became the president of the Association of Korean Buddhist Sects. On January 20th, 1979, he delivered a speech at the New Year's ceremony. He recommended all Korean Buddhist sects to cooperate to develop Korean Buddhism and help the nation.[126]

From the second half of 1979 to March 20th, 1980, both sides took several cases to court. The court ruled sometimes for and sometimes against the ruling side.[127] Based on the court's rulings, both sides went back and forth between their hopes and fears during that time. On March 30th, 1980, when monks of both sides attended the 100th day memorial service for the late Son Gyeongsan at Jeokjo-am Hermitage in Seoul, both sides agreed to dissolve the two separate central assemblies and hold a general election for the representatives of the 6th central assembly in 20 days.

On April 1st, both groups ratified the agreement and decided to hold a general election for the 6th central assembly's 69 representatives on August 17th and open the central assembly on April 26th.[128] On April 26th and 27th, 1980, the central assembly elected Song Wolju as the order's Secretary General, Hwang Dogyeon as the speaker and Yu Woltan and Jeong Chou as the vice-speakers. They could not make a recommendation for the order's supreme patriarch because of serious conflicts between the two factions.

Each side recommended its own supreme patriarch candidate as a candidate, I Seongcheol (1912-1993) and Choe Wolsan (1912-1997) respectively.[129] I Seongcheol was a disciple of Ha Dongsan (1890-1965) who was a disciple of Baek Yongseong (1864-1944). A resident monk of Haein-sa Monastery, I Seongcheol was a successor to Baek Yongseong's Dharma lineage. Korean Buddhists call this lineage the Beomeo-sa Temple Dharma lineage because of the connection of Baek Yongseong and that temple in Busan. He

---

[126] Yun Seonhyo, ed., *op. cit.*, 251-253.

[127] Monastic Alumni Association of Dongguk University, ed., 54-55.

[128] Im Hyebong, 240-241.

[129] Gim Gwangsik, *Uriga salaon hanguk bulgyo baengnyeon* (Korean Buddhism during Recent 100 Years) (Seoul: Minjok-sa, 2000), 164.

was also a Dharma nephew of Yun Goam, another disciple of Baek
Yongseong. Choe Wolsan, a resident monk of Bulguk-sa Temple,
was a successor to Song Mangong's Dharma lineage. He was a
disciple of Jeong Geumo (1896-1968), [130] a Dharma successor of
Bowol (1884-1924). Bowol was a disciple of Song Mangong
(1871-1946), a representative of Song Mangong's Dharma lineage.
Korean Buddhists call the lineage the Sudeok-sa Temple Dharma
lineage because of the connection between Song Mangong and the
temple in Yesan County, South Chungcheong Province. The newly
elected secretary general, Song Wolju and the vice speaker, Yu
Woltan were the younger Dharma brothers of Choe Wolsan. All
three monks were disciples of Jeong Geumo. These Dharma
lineages at times both competed and cooperated with one another
and were the two major Dharma lineages of modern Korean
Buddhism. The majority of monks in the Jogye Order belong to
one or the other of the two, although there are some minor Dharma
lineages. Even though each lineage supported the candidate
affiliated with its own lineage, neither of them received a majority
vote. [131]

On May 13th, Yun Goam handed over power to the newly
elected Secretary General Song Wolju. [132] The ruling faction
became the opposition faction and vice versa with Song Wolju
representing the opposition. Because he became the order's highest
administrator at the time, his became the ruling faction. The order
officially united, although, at the time, the two groups had their
own administrative head offices. The ruling group had its head
office at Jogye-sa Temple and the opposition group was
headquartered at Gaeun-sa Temple. Each group had its own
supreme patriarch and secretary general as well. They ultimately
united these two head offices into one that was moved to Jogye-sa
Temple.

During his time as acting supreme patriarchate, July 18th, 1978
to May 13th, 1980, Song Wolju engaged in many contradictory

---

[130] I Jeong, ed., 318.
[131] Gim Gwangsik, 164.
[132] Im Hyebong, 241.

actions. Even though he had a famous reputation as a compassionate monk and as a politically neutral and detached leader, he had behaved as a typical corrupt politician addicted to power during that difficult period. Even though he definitely had difficulty bringing the two factions together, he should have taken responsibility for engaging in such ugly politics. He was structurally subject to behaving as a monk-politician while serving as the order's acting supreme patriarch.

Yun Goam became the order's third supreme patriarch on July 26, 1967 on which date the supreme patriarch I Cheongdam and the secretary general Son Gyeongsan came into conflict with one another. He also became the acting supreme patriarch on July 18th, 1978 and took over as acting supreme patriarchate on July 31st, 1978 from the 5th supreme patriarch I Seoong. The order requested Yun Goam to intervene in the emergencies that arose and solve them. When he was installed as the supreme patriarch and as the acting supreme patriarch, the order was in crisis.[133] In this crisis, they seemed to need a monk who always emphasized harmony.

During the disputes between the ruling group and the opposition group, Yun Goam became the advisor to the government's Department of Unification on February 9, 1980, and a member of the Advisory Committee for the Government's Administration on February 18th. In 1980, he also became the spiritual leader of the association of Baek Yongseong's Dharma descendants,[134] as he had inherited the Dharma lineage from Baek Yongseong.

Because the order could not install its highest patriarch due to serious conflicts between opposition and ruling factions, on May 21st, 8th day of the fourth lunar month, the Buddha's Birthday, the supreme patriarch could not deliver a message. Due to the unavailability of a message from the supreme patriarch, Bak Gijong, chair of the Council of Elder Monks, gave the speech for the Buddha's Birthday.[135] After that, the central assembly tried

---

[133] Im Hyebong, 241.

[134] Yun Seonhyo, ed., *Goam keunseunim pyeongjeon*, 57.

[135] Im Hyebong, 241.

twice to elect the order's supreme patriarch, but it was unsuccessful.[136]

On August 31st, the newly elected Secretary General, Song Wolju, internally began to discuss how to purify Buddhism from within the order.[137] On October 20th, the order confirmed detailed directives to purify Buddhism independently of the government's intervention. On August 14th, the order also externally organized the Propulsion Committee for Revising the Government's Buddhism-related Laws and commissioned the committee to devise the revised laws. On September 15th and 16th, the order hosted the conference for demanding the government to revise the Buddhism-related government laws at Jogye-sa Temple and confirmed the order's revised versions of the laws that the committee had drafted. Two days later, on September 17th, the order submitted a tentatively revised version of the laws to the government's Department of Education and Information. Thus, Song Wolju's administration tried to reform Buddhism internally and revise the government's laws discriminating Buddhism externally. The order's reform movement originated in some ways from the social atmosphere after the death of the longtime dictator Bak Jeonghui.

On October 26, 1979, Gim Jaegyu, then the director of the Korean CIA, assassinated his superior, President Bak Jeonghui. After that, by taking advantage of the political situation, the opposition group demonstrated for democratizing South Korea. The government and the military suppressed the demand for democracy. On May 18, 1980, citizens and students in Gwangju protested against the military's intervention in politics and asked the government to democratize South Korea. On May 24th, the order sent a relief squad and a fact-finding mission to Gwangju.[138]

On October 27, 1980, the Martial Law Command dispatched the military to the order's Secretariat Head Office and major

---

[136] *Ibid.*

[137] Buddhology Institute, ed., *Hanguk geun hyeondae bulgyo-sa yeonpyo* (A Chronological Table for Modern and Present Korean Buddhism) (Seoul: Education Board of Korean Buddhist Jogye Order, 2000), 112.

[138] *Ibid.*

temples at four o'clock in the early morning under the pretext of social purification and it arrested 153 monks and lay Buddhists including the Secretary General, Song Wolju, Yun Wolha, Gim Seoun, Yu Woltan, I Hyeseong, and others.[139] One day later, on October 28th, the Martial Law Command announced that they were investigating 46 corrupt monks and lay Buddhists for religious purification based upon the requests of conscientious Buddhists. On October 30th, the command dispatched the police and the military to more than 3,000 temples of 18 sects across the nation under the pretext of searching for Communist sympathizers and criminals hiding in temples. On November 13th, the command announced that it had confined 18 corrupt monks, defrocked 32 monks, and confiscated from dishonest monks 20,060,000,000 won that they obtained improperly and took the amount back to the order. Korean Buddhists have called the persecution the "October 27th Persecution."

Yun Seonhyo, a disciple of Yun Goam, recorded in his *Biography of Master Yun Goam* that when he came to Daewon-sa Temple in Honolulu as an international missionary in 1981 after the persecution of October 27th, 1980, Yun Goam had arrived earlier than he had in 1980.[140] His other disciple Gi Daewon, also known as Daewon Ki, came to Hawaii in 1975 and established Daewon-sa Buddhist Temple in a rented office in Honolulu.[141] He bought some empty land and moved the temple to the new property on a mountainside in Honolulu's Palolo Valley in 1979. He began building the first structure in 1980 and finished it in 1982. Daewon Ki planned a larger complex in 1983 and began construction in 1984. It is a traditionally structured Korean Buddhist temple and the largest cluster of Korean traditional architectural works outside the boundaries of Korea. It consisted of the Four Heavenly Kings Gate, the World Peace Pagoda, the Bell Tower, the Memorial Hall to the Departed, Donor's Tablets, the

---

[139] *Ibid,* 113.

[140] Yun Seonhyo, ed., *op. cit.,* 58-59.

[141] See Chanju Mun's "Venerable Daewon Ki and Peacemaking" in his edited *Mediators and Meditators: Buddhism and Peacemaking* (Honolulu: Blue Pine, 2007), v-xxv.

Main Hall, a Statue of Maitreya Bodhisattva, the Buddhist Cultural Center Building, several residential houses and other structures.

When Yun Goam began to live at the temple in 1980, the temple was not completed and many of the buildings were just temporary structures. He served as a chef for temple residents at the time. He preached at Sunday services and at special services at the temple. He served as the spiritual leader of the temple from 1982 and until his death in 1988. On October 24, 1982, when Daewon-sa Temple finished the construction for the main buildings including the Buddha's Main Hall and Seon Center and hosted an establishment ceremony, he delivered an address in which he celebrated the completion of several Korean traditional architectural buildings along with other monks and lay Buddhists.[142] He emphasized the symbiosis of Korean Buddhism with other religions and other Buddhist traditions in the multi-cultural society of Hawaii and argued that we should dedicate the temple's main hall to purify and create a peaceful society. He also contended that we should contribute to Buddhism by engaging in the Buddhist effort to recover the sublime humanity inherent in all of us from the materialism and alienation rampant in human society today.

In March of 1981, when Professor I Jongik, a specialist in Bojo Jinul and a theorist of the Purification Buddhist Movement, visited and stayed at Gwaneum-sa Temple in Los Angeles, he met Yun Goam at the temple[143] as Yun Goam was visiting the temple. Gim Doan, abbot of the temple, was his Dharma nephew because he was a disciple of Bak Dongam, a disciple of Baek Yongseong. Over the course of two weeks, he traveled to various tourist sites in Los Angeles as well as in South California, Arizona and Nevada with I Jongik. He travelled to Las Vegas, the Grand Canyon, Zion Canyon, Bryce Canyon, Disneyland, the Huntington Library, Art Collections, and Botanical Gardens, among other places. A prominent lay Buddhist scholar, I Jongik also accompanied him. They discussed Seon Buddhism during their travels.

---

[142] Yun Seonhyo, ed., *Goam daejongsa beobeo-jip*, 286-288.

[143] Yun Seonhyo, ed., *Goam keunseunim pyeongjeon*, 111.

On the Buddha's Birthday, 8th day of the fourth lunar month, May 11th, 1981, he gave a sermon and celebrated the Buddha's Birthday at Daewon-sa Buddhist Temple:[144] "Despite our scientific and technological advancement, we are currently living in a troubled world in which conflicts, hunger and poverty cause humans to suffer. The suffering mainly originates from the self-centeredness of humans. The Buddha's birthday, (however), gives us a significant alternative. The Buddha's teachings provide us (with the means) to uplift our values and relieve human suffering. The Buddha and his teachings have brought a light onto this troubled society. The light of wisdom has the power to transform the world of suffering to a world of happiness and enlightenment. The Buddha provides the means to spiritual awakening to all sentient beings all over the world. We should take the responsibility of propagating the Buddha's teachings and instilling the hope that we can transform this struggling world into a Pure Land."

In March of 1985, at the age of 87, he visited several nations in South and Southeast Asia with India, Burma, Thailand, and Sri Lanka among them. In July of 1985, he visited Australia in which he presided over a ceremony offering the Bodhisattva precepts at several temples. He did not stop propagating Buddhism to people who needed him even though he was old.

When Daewon Ki, abbot of the Daewon-sa Buddhist Temple of Hawaii, hosted a fundraising party for establishing the Buddhist Cultural Institute in his temple on November 30th, 1986, he attended the party as the temple's spiritual leader and delivered a speech. He encouraged attendees to support this invaluable project and spread Korean culture and Buddhism in the local community as well as within the Korean-American community.[145] He asserted that if Daewon-sa Temple could establish a cultural center in Hawaii, a cultural bridge between the East and the West, it could propagate Korean Buddhism and Korean culture among Korean-

---

[144] Yun Seonhyo, ed., *Goam daejongsa beobeo-jip*, 274-279.
[145] *Ibid*, 280-281.

Americans and other Americans, relieve their mental stress and ease their social problems.[146]

In September of 1987, at the age of 89, he was installed as the president of the Daegak Foundation that the Dharma descendants of Baek Yongseong established on September 11th, 1969. He was appointed founding director of the Foundation in 1969, serving as a director from that time, and finally becoming its president in 1987.

In 1988, at the age of 90, he had a car accident in the United States. Due to the aftereffects, he went back to Korea and returned to his home hermitage, Yongtap Seon Center of Haein-sa Monastery on Mt. Gaya. On October 25, 15th day of the ninth lunar month, he passed away at the hermitage. Before his death, he called his disciples and gave his farewell poem:[147]

The red leaves become more reddish on Mt. Gaya,
We know from this that the season is autumn.
When it frosts, leaves fall down and return to the root.
The full moon of September shines in the sky.

On October 29th, the order hosted the funeral service for him at Haein-sa Monastery.[148] After cremating his remains in the Haein-sa Monastery crematorium, his disciples collected 16 serene relics. One year later, they established a gravestone on the western side of Haein-sa Monastery and memorialized their master Yun Goam.

I Seongcheol, the order's supreme patriarch, expressed his condolences. Because he was a disciple of Ha Dongsan, a Dharma brother of Yun Goam, he was his Dharma nephew and a grand disciple of Baek Yongseong. Yun Seonhyo introduced a condolence poem by I Seongcheol as follows:[149]

The moon brightly shines on Mt. Gaya,

---

[146] *Ibid,* 278-280.

[147] Yun Seonhyo, ed., *Goam keunseunim pyeongjeon,* 190.

[148] Im Hyebong, 244.

[149] Yun Seonhyo, ed., *Goam daejongsa beobeo-jip,* 29-30; and Yun Seonhyo, ed., *Goam keunseunim pyeongjeon,* 220-221.

The water violently runs through Hongnyu Valley.
The valuable birds loudly chirp,
The strange animals walk.
His compassion was limitless,
His edification covered nine continents.
He kept the precepts well.
He was the most respected preceptor on the Korean Peninsula.
He has repeatedly served as the order's highest patriarch,
All Buddhists respected him.
Because he transmitted precepts his whole life,
All the people took them.
Stars fly and twinkle in the sky,
The light of the stars swallows the whole universe,
Who can follow him in the past or present?
He suddenly came,
He suddenly went,
Mt. Sumeru is high and higher still.
He once frowned,
He once smiled,
The blue ocean is spacious and broad.
He lifted up his two hands,
He moved his two legs,
The sky is high,
The earth is deep.
When he opened his mouth and spoke,
The sound of thunder crashed,
It flashed.
Oh!
Who was he, Yun Goam?
He stood on one foot
on the top of Mt. Kunlun.
An auspicious wind fills the sky
With five-colored clouds.

INTRODUCTION

Chanju Mun
Ronald S. Green

Does Buddhism offer useful ideas and role models for peacemaking worldwide? If it does, which of its ideas are specifically applicable to the process and where are the examples of the individual or groups that have ever applied them? These are the major questions addressed in this volume.

While these articles offer evidence of the great potential for peacemaking through Buddhism, a number of recent news articles may have implied to opposite. Over the past several years, many of us from the outside have read reports of politically active monks of Southeast Asia with growing interest. We have seen newspaper images of protesters in Myanmar, in orchid robes with raised fists, yelling into megaphones. Monks in Sri Lanka have been shown in the press firing artillery cannons. These news stories typically point out that such images contrast greatly with our conceptions of monks. The general expectation in non-Asian countries is likely to be that either Buddhists would abstain from political conflicts entirely due to monastic vows and worldview, meet conflict with pacifism if forced, or at most use non-violent activist methods similar to those of Mohandas Gandhi, and then only in face of the utmost atrocious social injustices. Indeed, a number of articles in this collection find canonical support for such expectations.

Admittedly, in many respects, the faith and understanding maintained within the borders immediately affected by Buddhists

in political conflict is more important than the impressions
outsiders form based on partial information presented in the
foreign press. However, for our purpose, seeking to understand the
potential role of Buddhism in the larger process of peacemaking,
we are apt to look within those borders for outside applications as
well as examples of pitfalls to be avoided. This task is potentially
complicated when the media makes such statements about socially
engaged Buddhists as "Nirvāṇa is not the first thing their political
activism, past or present, brings to mind." [1] If we read this as
meaning activist Buddhists give up their religious goal in worldly
pursuit, non-Buddhists around the world may ask why bother
looking to Buddhism for ideas on peacemaking. In fact, Buddhism
may appear to be a throwback to an earlier age from an unrelated
part of the world, with a philosophy anachronistic for dealing with
modern crises.

Activist Buddhists have answered this concern similarly to
Venerable Yun Goam (1899-1999) of Korea: "Despite our
scientific and technological advancement, we are currently living
in a troubled world in which conflicts, hunger and poverty cause
humans to suffer. The suffering mainly originates from the self-
centeredness of humans.... The Buddha's teachings provide us
(with the means) to uplift our values and relieve human suffering.
The Buddha and his teachings have brought a light onto this
troubled society. The light of wisdom has the power to transform
the world of suffering to a world of happiness and enlightenment.
The Buddha provides the means to spiritual awakening to all
sentient beings all over the world. We should take the
responsibility of propagating the Buddha's teachings and instilling
the hope that we can transform this struggling world into a Pure
Land." [2]

---

[1] Somini Segupta, "Sri Lankan Government Finds Support from Buddhist
Monks," in *New York Times*, February 25, 2007.

[2] Yun Seonhyo, ed., *Goam daejongsa beobeo-jip: Jabi bosal ui gil* (Grand
Master Yun Goam's Analects: The Ways of a Compassionate Bodhisattva)
(Seoul: Bulgyo yeongsang hoebo-sa, 1990), 274-279. See Chanju Mun, "Preface"
entitled "Yun Goam, the First Spiritual Leader of Dae Won Sa Buddhist Temple:
A Biography for His Peacemaking Activities," page lv in this volume.

Most of the articles in this collection hold to this belief in one way or another, attempting to flesh out those values from various angles or provide examples of them. Particularly helpful in this regard is "Uprooting Sprouts of Violence, Cultivating Seeds of Peace: Buddhism and the Transformation of Personal Conflict" by Christiaan Zandt; "Re-imagining Socially Engaged Buddhism" by James Kenneth Powell II, "Peace through Moral Life: An Analysis Based on Early Buddhist Discourses" by Y. Karunadasa, and "A Buddhist Oriented Relational View of Transformation in Meditation" by Ran Kuttner.

In the preface "Yun Goam, the First Spiritual Leader of Dae Won Sa Buddhist Temple: A Biography for his Peacemaking Activities" by Chanju Mun, readers can see the detailed peacemaking activities of Venerable Yun Goam, religious master of Venerable Daewon Ki who founded Dae Won Sa Buddhist Temple, the largest Korean Buddhist Temple in North America. Based upon Master Yun Goam's spiritual influences, his disciple Daewon Ki held seven international conferences on Buddhism and peace and dedicated himself to forging peace between South and North Korea.

The publication of the current book as well can be traced to the original vision of Daewon Ki who assigned Chanju Mun to edit and publish articles submitted to the conferences in a series of books on Buddhism and peace. Two of the articles in this volume were originally presented at the sixth seminar held in Honolulu November 24-28, 1993, those by Y. Karunadasa and David Putney. The other articles were selected by the editors from many received though a general call for academic submissions on our topic.

In the opening article "Buddhism and Peace: An Overview" by Chanju Mun, readers will find a valuable outline of socially engaged Buddhism both in theory and practice. He investigates the Buddha and the Bodhisattva as ideal peacemakers and considers Huayan Buddhism and the ecumenical tradition as ideal philosophical and practical models for peacemaking. He also critically discusses modern Korean Buddhism and state protectionism in East Asian Buddhist contexts.

More examples of models for peacemaking are given in several articles about Japanese Buddhists. These include "How Faith Inspired the Save The Bell Movement," an article compiled by the Shōgyōji Archives Committee, "Reflections on the Ethical Meaning of Shinran's True Entrusting" by Victor Forte, and "Peace in Shin Buddhism and Process Theology" by Steve Odin. These writings are not only valuable in presenting information on exemplars of peacemaking. The authors have each uniquely contributed to our project by analysis and reflection.

Likewise, western philosophical concepts are applied as tools of reflection in "Paradigms of Buddhist Ethics: Judgment and Character in the Modern World" by David Putney, "A Dialectical Analysis of the Conception of "Self Interest Maximization" and Economic Freedom" by Mathew Varghese, and "Virtue, and Violence in Theravāda and Sri Lankan Buddhism" by Eric Sean Nelson. The latter article along with "Buddhist Protest in Myanmar: Basic Questions" by Ronald S. Green deals with some of the issues surrounding the abovementioned Buddhist involvement in crises in Southeast Asia. The volume is rounded out of by two articles that bring Christianity into our topic: "The Teachings of the Buddha and Jesus as Resources for a Doctrine of Peace" by J. Bruce Long and "Christianity and War by Kenneth A. Locke. The editors feel these articles may be especially informative for readers approaching our subject from a Christian background.

Bringing Selflessness into Peacemaking

Again, Venerable Yun Goam suggested, "We should contribute to Buddhism by engaging in an effort to recover the sublime humanity inherent in all of us from the material greed and alienation rampant in society." [3] In this sentence, we see a circularity that also applies to our task. It is a contribution to Buddhism to engage in the effort to recover our sublime humanity but it is through Buddhism that such is possible. In this book, we ask what appears to be an opposite question, not how we may

---

[3] See Chanju Mun, "Preface," page liv in this volume.

contribute to Buddhism but how Buddhism may contribute to the task of peacemaking. Yet, in some sense, we are also asking how our effort may contribution to Buddhism. According to a Mahāyāna idea, we all have the innate wisdom and compassion of the Buddha, known as "Buddha nature." It is impossible to contribute to this. At the same time, we do contribute to Buddhism by realizing our nature and putting it into practice. Styled in the seemingly enigmatic form so famous of Buddhists, because it is impossible to contribute to Buddhism, we are able to contribute to it.

As mentioned above, many of the contributions to this collection deal with specific Buddhist teachings that help us as individuals, groups and perhaps, as some suggest, universally to uplift our values and to relieve suffering. Perhaps the most prominently mentioned of these teachings here and elsewhere is the concept of no-self and the related idea of selflessness in giving and living. Not only is this understandably puzzling for those hearing it first time but it can continue to perplex longtime practitioners and even be denied by them. The first questions likely to arise include: To what conception of "self" do the Buddha's teachings refer? Did he mean there is (1) no "soul" or eternally abiding spirit; (2) no ego-self; (3) no physical, bodily self? How well does the English word "self" correspond to the sixth century BCE Indian notion of "*ātman*" (Pāli, *atta*) and, in fact, the other terms referred to by the Buddha for which we simultaneously use "self" as a translation? Is the Buddhist concept of "no-self" a statement about the nature of ultimate reality or about an ideal goal believed to be attainable by a few or all through meditation and other practices such as acts of charity and compassion? Where did the doctrine of no-self originate and has it developed over time in Buddhism? Perhaps most striking: how can Buddhists believe in both no-self and reincarnation? After all, if there is no self to survive death, what is left to be reincarnated? Drawing on the efforts of our contributors, the following is a simplified explanation, introducing some of the basic ideas as answers to these questions.

Existence, non-existence and "no soul" in Buddhism

Buddhist scriptures (Skt., *sūtra*; Pāli, *sutta*) surviving in the Pāli language are typically considered the earliest accounts of the Buddha's words. In these, scholars have searched in vain for a phrase equivalent to "the doctrine of no-self" often used to describe the Buddha's view. Although there may be no early mention of a specific "doctrine," a number of interrelated ideas are expounded by the Buddha in these texts. Early scriptures record the Buddha critically reevaluating two contrary religious or philosophical tendencies prevalent in India around the time he lived.[4] Buddhists believe these tendencies are common to people throughout history and across geographical borders but that their underlying assumptions are incorrect. The beliefs are in existence (*sassatavāda*) and non-existence (*ucchedavāda*). In the *Kaccayana Gotta Sutta*, the Buddha says the following to his learned disciple Kaccayana.[5] "This world, O Kaccayana, generally proceeds on a duality of the belief in existence and the belief in non-existence.... All exists, Kaccayana, that is one extreme. Naught exists, Kaccayana, that is the other extreme. Not approaching either extreme the Tathāgata[6] teaches you a doctrine by the middle way."[7]

Buddhism is called the Middle Way for a variety of reasons. It rejects extreme asceticism as well as extreme hedonism. It also refutes beliefs in existence and beliefs in non-existence. Many Buddhist writings address these issues. While some explicitly elaborate on the extreme positions, others proceed on the moderate assumption readers accept the Middle Way. But what exactly the

---

[4] The dating of the life of the Buddha is currently controversial among scholars. Conventionally his birth is dated around the mid-sixth century BCE.

[5] Kaccayana is traditionally considered one of the Ten Great Disciples of the Buddha.

[6] The Tathāgata is a name for the Buddha. While East Asian Buddhists translated it as "Thus-come," Tibetan Buddhists translated the same term as "Thus-gone." He is the one who has come from and gone to "thus-ness."

[7] Refer to *Saṃyutta Nikāya* 12.15, and based on the Pali Text Society version, *Saṃyutta Nikāya* II, 17.

Buddha meant by existence and non-existence is a matter of contention. Many Buddhists feel that by "existence" the Buddha was referring to the Indian equivalent of the western philosophical idea of substantialism, the doctrine that real matter constitutes phenomena. In this case, non-existence is interpreted as the equivalent of nihilism. Interestingly, Buddhism has often been variously charged with being either a substantialist or nihilist philosophy by critics, allegations Buddhists soundly deny.

Others find support in early Buddhist writings for saying the Buddha was referring to various Indian doctrines that attempt to explain humanity by positing the existence of a permanent soul that is distinct from the body.[8] An example of this we are likely most familiar with is found in the *Upaniṣads* of Hinduism. There and elsewhere, the true essence of an individual is said to be a permanent metaphysical self, independent of the physical body. This metaphysical self (*ātman*) is often called soul in English translation, or Self was a capital "s" to distinguish it from a physical self. It is envisioned as eternal and unchanging. Most if not all the Indian religions at the time of the Buddha seem to have incorporated this view, either as a development of Vedic thought or reaction against it. For this reason, it might be assumed that by "existence" the Buddha was referring generically to all the beliefs in an immortal soul. It is quite likely that the Buddha's rejection of the belief in existence precludes both substance and soul. In the first sermon, *Dhammacakkappavattana-sūtta* (The Sūtra Setting the Wheel of Dharma in Motion),[9] he explains that the individual is nothing beyond a composite of "five aggregates" or "five heaps": form, feelings, perceptions, mental fabrications, and consciousness.

---

[8] Evidence of this position may be found in *Dīgha Nikāya* I, 157, 188; *Saṃyutta Nikāya* IV, 392; *Majjhima Nikāya* I, 157; and elsewhere. For further analysis of this and some of the issue that follow, please see Y. Karunadasa, "Peace through Moral Life: An Analysis Based on Early Buddhist Discourses" in this volume.

[9] See *Saṃyutta Nikāya* 56.11. See T.W. Rhys Davids and Herman Oldenberg, trans., *Vinyaya Texts*, in F. Max Mueller, ed., *The Sacred Books of the East*, 50 vols. (Oxford: Clarendon, 1879-1910), Vol. 13, pp. 94-97, and 100-102.

So that none of the five aggregates would be seen as eternally substantial, the Buddha said, "Form is *anattā* (not soul/Self,) feelings are *anattā*, so too are perceptions, mental fabrications, and consciousness."[10] A famous phrase the Buddha uses in a number of scriptures to refute notions of existence is *"na me so atta,"* this is not my self/Soul.[11]

Can the refutation of the doctrine of Self be called a doctrine? Some would argue the Buddha did not create a doctrine of no-self but simply refuted what he saw as incorrect views of his time. Among those taking this perspective is perhaps the most famous of all Buddhist theorists, the Indian philosopher Nāgārjuna (150-250 CE). Claiming he was not an innovator but only a spokesperson for the Buddha's original messages, Nāgārjuna set about refuting all notions of reality, including those that had subsequently developed within Buddhism. In the end, Nāgārjuna claimed neither he nor Buddhism had a doctrine of any kind.

In fact, in the *Kaccayana Gotta Sutta*, and in other scriptures, the Buddha also opposes non-existence. But again, what does this mean? It may be, as some suggest, the Buddha is referring to another widespread belief of his time, one that held the physical body itself is a kind of soul.[12] According to this non-Buddhist view, the body is an individual's real essence and is annihilated at death. From the viewpoint of many modern Buddhists, any form of "materialism," past or present, which advocate a theory of the ultimate reality of a physical self that ends with death, are subject to the Buddha's rejection of theories of non-existence. Such a reading of the Buddha's message sees beliefs in non-existence and existence as instances of theories of the soul or Self (Pāli, *attavāda*; Skt., *ātmavāda*). One sees the soul as permanent and transcending. The other sees it as material, temporary and passing to nothingness. Concerning the latter the Buddha says, "Both formerly and now, I have never been a *vinayika* (believer in nothingness), never been

---

[10] See *Saṃyutta Nikāya* 3.196.

[11] For example, *Saṃyutta Nikāya* 3.46.

[12] See *Dīgha Nikāya* I, 34, 35; *Dīgha Nikāya* I, 157, 188; II, 333, 336; and *Saṃyutta Nikāya* IV, 392.

one who teaches the annihilation of a being, rather I taught only the source of suffering, and its ending."[13]

For today's readers, removed from the ancient Indian context, we are tempted to use modern descriptions for imagining what the Buddha meant by any of this. For example, if we interpret *anātman* as "no-soul" according to our conception of those words, we might mistakenly envision the following. Suppose that in the future, space travelers venture to another planet and find people just like us in every way except they have no souls. What would the difference be? Likewise, searching the internet for "people with no souls" turns up a bizarre variety of historical ideas about "black people," "white people," "redheaded people," and, of course, non-musical people.

For many Buddhists, the refutation of the view that there is an unchanging soul is a denial of any transcendental reality that would serve as ultimate grounds for existence. Others see it as less a specific denial of the possibility of such a reality than a part of the Buddha's broader ban on speculative philosophy. The Buddha discouraged talk about things we can never possibly know, whether about the existence of God or gods, the soul, or a universe just like ours underneath your fingernail. Spending time musing about unanswerable questions only distracts practitioners from the goal of overcoming suffering. This is one reason Buddhists often see Buddhism not as a religion but a way of practice, as focused on humanity rather than divinity. The Buddha says the following in *The Shorter Instructions to Māluṅkya.*

"So, Māluṅkyaputta, remember what is undeclared by me as undeclared, and what is declared by me as declared. And what is undeclared by me? 'The cosmos is eternal,' is undeclared by me. 'The cosmos is not eternal,' is undeclared by me. 'The cosmos is finite' is undeclared by me. 'The cosmos is infinite' is undeclared by me. 'The soul and the body are the same,' is undeclared by me 'The soul

---

[13] See *Saṃyutta Nikāya* IV, 400.

is one thing and the body another,' is undeclared by me.
'After death a Tathāgata exists,' is undeclared by me.
'After death a Tathāgata does not exist,' is undeclared by
me. 'After death a Tathāgata both exists and does not
exist,' is undeclared by me. 'After death a Tathāgata
neither exists nor does not exist,' is undeclared by me. And
why are they undeclared by me? Because they are not
connected with the goal...."[14]

In this way, the Buddha's idea of *anātman* is not a doctrine,
stating definitively that there is no soul but a tool to critique
ideologies. Accordingly, the Buddha addressed these issues out of
concern for the "psychological" wellbeing of meditative
practitioners on his path to liberation from suffering. In order to
overcome suffering, the Buddha taught we must eliminate our
desires and attachments. Among the most deep-seated may be the
desire to live forever. Hoping for this so strongly, various
individuals have posited the existence of an immortal soul.
However, cherishing this vision becomes a hindrance to liberation
from suffering because it is a strong attachment. On the other hand,
the belief in non-existence or non-being, if interpreted to mean
nothing survives death, may have arisen from the human desire to
be free from responsibility for living an immoral life or doing
anything that weighs heavily on the conscience. The belief that
nothing survives death or that nothing exists at all, frees an
individual from the fear of moral retribution whether that is
culturally envisioned as a day of reckoning in terms of karma or
otherwise.

In short, the Buddha does not say there is no soul. He says
those who believe there is a soul are mistaken and those who
believe there is nothing after death are equally wrong. The first
major problem with both views is that reality cannot be
conceptualized through such categories. You are justified in asking
now: Since the Buddha rejected views of existence *and* views of
non-existence, on what do Buddhists rely for dealing with life and

---

[14] See *Cula-Māluṅkya Sutta, Majjhima Nikāya* 63.

the world? The Buddhist idea of understanding phenomenal reality (or realities) is in fact different from the conceptions of many theorists. Buddhism rejects the very notion that it is possible to understand the phenomenal world by means of a theory. In the *Brahmajāla sutta* for example, the Buddha criticizes the promotion of any theoretical viewpoint and concludes that the world cannot be understood from the limitations set by any theory. Accordingly, theoretical understanding of the phenomenal world originates from our expectations and preferences rather than what actually happens. [15] If this seems like a theory, then it too should eventually be abandoned as a boat that helped you in the difficult crossing of barriers in the journey toward overcoming suffering.

Dependent Origination and "no self" in Buddhism

You have probably been asked or asked yourself the following question at some time in your life. If you could be anyone else in the world, who would you be? This is also a popular question online where the most common answers are movie stars and musicians. But what if we add a twist? You can be anyone else in the world but you will no longer be you. Would you still want to do it? In some conceptions of reincarnation (or even heaven), the situation imagined is somewhat analogous: you will be reborn but you will not remember this life. [16] While many Buddhist traditions vary in their interpretations of what reincarnates since it is not *ātman*, typically their answer is karma. That is, only the results of your actions continue and nothing you might call "you." [17] For those suffering from the fear of death who subconsciously hope to

---

[15] See the first of the long discourses of the Buddha. See Maurice Walshe's *The Long Discourses of the Buddha: A Translation of the Dīgha Nikāya* (Boston: Wisdom Publications, 1995).

[16] It should be noted that in Indian religions, Hinduism, Buddhism and Jaina, being reborn is not a good thing. Religious practices in these traditions are typically aimed at release from the cycles of rebirth.

[17] Some Buddhists suggest what we call "reincarnation" actually takes place in this life. For example, if your actions produce negative results you come to live in a kind of hell on earth. See Takashi Tsuji's article at http://www.buddhanet.net/e-learning/reincarnation.htm.

find consolation in a doctrine of eternal life, the idea that you will not be you is unlikely to be completely satisfying. Nor is it likely to match our view of soul connected with personality. Maybe even less satisfying are the Buddhist suggestions that you are not who you think you are now and ultimately there is no independent you at all.

We have seen above that the Buddha rejected ideas of permanence and annihilation as valid ways of understanding reality, and we questioned whether this applies to non-Indian conceptions of soul. In a like manner, we should ask to what extent the sixth century BCE Indian conception of self corresponds to the 21st century European, perhaps Judeo-Christian or even Freudian influenced idea of the self that we cherish today. Even though the Buddha did not live in our time, we can venture that, regardless of the differences, he rejected any possible conception that posits the existence of a real entity such as the independent self. This can be found specifically in his teachings about dependent origination.

Buddhism does more than simply reject the seemingly relentless conflict between existence and non-existence. It answers those concerned with such issues with the principle of dependent origination or dependent co-arising (*paticca-samuppāda*).[18] Most Buddhist traditions hold that this idea is the foundation of all other Buddhist ideas, that it is the Middle Path itself. The Buddha said, "Whoever sees dependent co-arising sees the Dhamma; whoever sees the Dhamma sees dependent co-arising."[19] This means, it is generally held in Buddhism, that the attainment of awakening is based on comprehension of the principle of dependent origination.

The principle of dependent origination proposes that individual existences are composed of interdependent physical and psychological elements that mutually condition one another. One element of this principle is the important Buddhist idea of non-substantiality. Since all "things" exist only as dependent on other

---

[18] For an account and critical analysis of this idea, see David J. Kalupahana, *Causality: The Central Philosophy of Buddhism* (Honolulu: University of Hawaii Press, 1975).

[19] See *Majjhima Nikāya* 28, http://www.accesstoinsight.org/tipitaka/mn/mn.028.than.html#t-4.

"things," nothing is independently substantial. Likewise, everything is changing and exists only in process, including what you have been calling your "self." References to "oneself," "I," "me," etc., are for Buddhists, made merely for the sake of conventional usages. Through meditative practice and acts of charity, we are to realize the hollowness of these concepts.

It might seem troubling that there is nothing we can point to as being an independent and unchanging entity that is the self. The Buddha well understood the anxiety you are likely to feel at the suggestion you give up this false notion. While today we tend to see meditation as a non-stressful activity, the Buddha continually encouraged followers to persevere in that practice with "fearlessness." If we look at it another way, the principle of dependent origination destroys our ego-centered worldview. When the Buddha advises us to observe all events from an interrelated perspective, this sets the guidelines for a symbiotic outlook on life. It rejects hostility toward an "other", antagonisms with neighbors, conflicts with "other" countries, attacks on animals and nature. In short, Buddhists believe that if otherness is rejected, ego-centeredness is destroyed. Modern Buddhists often say that as a result, peace and environmental responsibility can be realized.[20] According to scriptures, practitioners of meditation who are able to overcome their fear and finally renounce the belief in the ultimate reality of the five aggregates and the self, realize a release from suffering caused by clinging to those ideas. They experience an unattached bliss and abide in insightful wisdom (*prajñā*).

Because dependent origination advocates viewing with equal value what we conventionally call "ourselves" and "others," it encourages equal treatment of all. Not only should we live without being attached to self, we should not even give priority to what we call our self. When we hear on the news that a certain number of soldiers from the alleged "other side" were killed in battle, we should feel the same sympathy for them and their families that we

---

[20] As with adherents of most religious traditions, Buddhists have not always lived up to these ideas. See, for example, Brian Daizen Victoria, *Zen at War*, 2nd edition (Oxford: Rowman & Littlefield, 2006) and *Zen War Stories* (New York: Routledge Curzon, 2003).

feel for those killed from our country. In addition, the Buddhist notion of non-substantiality paves the road for another of its central themes: non-violence. By extension, according to the ideas of dependent origination and non-substantiality, to hurt others means to hurt ourselves. These ideas reject both the extreme egoist view focusing on maximizing one's own benefits and the extreme altruist view that only concentrates on the benefits of others. Neither oneself nor others can be prioritized. Seeing other human beings as the same, we should remove potential bases of discrimination such as age, gender, race, nationality, class, and so on. According to this outlook, we should consider all sentient beings, including the smallest of animals, equal in value.

Again, the Buddhist philosopher Nāgārjuna illustrates dependent origination by offering a series of examples and metaphors that bring into question common perceptions of reality and the self. Nāgārjuna asks about a burning log, where does the wood end and the flame begin?[21] If we consider the changes taking place on the surface of the log, beneath and above the surface, the exact range of the fire becomes uncertain at best and in a constant state of change. Likewise, all "things" including the "self" are impermanent and in a constant state of flux. Any entity that exists, only does so in dependence on other entities that condition its arising and are non-eternal. Therefore, whatever concept one might have of an abiding self is regarded as a delusion. Conceptualization of the self is just that and not ontological truth.

This appears to contrast with Judeo-Christian positions in several respects. First, in distinction from this Buddhist egalitarian outlook, Judeo-Christianity typically views the world as a creation with God the creator at the top of a hierarchy, followed by humans, and animals.[22] In addition, if the principle of dependent origination is accepted, we should not presuppose external forces or any *prima causa* to explain the origin of beings. Even God would have come from dependent co-arising. In this case, to conceive "I" as being in

---

[21] See chapter 10 in Kenneth K. Inada, *Nāgārjuna: A Translation of his Mūlamadhyamakakārikā* (Delhi: Sri Satguru, 1993).

[22] Other entities such as angels are seen as interspersed.

a process and not within fixed borders, removes boundaries between creator and created, subject and object, you and me, and other pairs often conceived of as polar opposites. Nor should we look for accidental forces to explain the origin of beings or events in history. When something happens, we should seek to understand it objectively and neutrally without looking for explanations in heavenly powers or accidental forces.

Perhaps one reason we hold on firmly to our love of a supposedly independent self is that we fear losing control of our lives. The Buddhist notion of "letting go" or "giving up" our egocentric selves likely seems like a loss of self-control to many. If that is your fear or objection, you should ask yourself how much control you have of your life now. Buddhists feel we are ordinarily led around by desires and hardly ever stop to think about it. What will I have for lunch, how can I meet a love interest, what car should I buy? We live with a constant barrage of such desire-driven questions or, more often, unacknowledged impulses. Maybe the desires are our own as human beings. But advertisers are betting high stakes that they can decide the direction of them. Did you really need the SUV you were persuaded to buy two years ago? Now you are being told to trade it in. Buddhists believe that it is not your life that you are giving up by letting go of your tendencies to grasp for things. Instead, those who are unconsciously led around by such desires are as if dead.[23] Only when we give up desires and false beliefs are we capable of living.

Later Buddhist writers illustrated the holistic worldview of dependent origination with a famous metaphor known as "The Jewel Net of Indra," Indra being a deity of ancient India. Imagine a large net spreading on and on across the heavenly abode of Indra. In each knot of the net there is a glittering jewel so that in all directions there appears to be an infinite number of them. When you look at one jewel, all of the many other jewels are reflected in its polished surface. Such is the case for each and every jewel. This symbolizes the universe as a potentially infinite number of

---

[23] See verse two of *The Dhammapada*, translated by Glenn Wallis (New York: The Modern Library, 2007).

connected relations among all beings with inter-identity and interdependence.[24] Buddhists see this as analogous to our situation. If we come to understand dependent origination, we awaken to the fact that each person, element of nature, planet and existent is not a separate "self" but an interactive and continually changing reflection of all those we erroneously supposed to be "others."

---

[24] See Thomas Cleary, trans., *The Flower Ornament Scripture: A Translation of the Avatamsaka Sutra* (Boston: Shambhala, 1993).

BUDDHISM AND PEACE: AN OVERVIEW

Chanju Mun

1. Prologue

Even though scholars in the Judeo-Christian tradition interpret the term history in different ways, that religious tradition generally understands it with some variations as follows: [1]

1. Through a teleological concept on the history of humanity and the universe, having a beginning and an end. Because history has a beginning, it is also supposed to be directed towards an end.
2. Considering history as the embodiment of a divine will or plan. Human beings cannot comprehend the ultimate plan, conducted by God, the Creator.
3. Centering only on the history of humans on earth, considered the center of the universe.

The above general characteristics of the Judeo-Christian tradition have decisively affected the history and the mentality of those from many non-Asian countries. The views on history could be analyzed as placing exclusive significance on human history in

---

[1] See the prologue in Garma C. C. Chang, *The Buddhist Teaching of Totality: The Philosophy of Hwa Yen Buddhism* (University Park & London: The Penn. State University Press, 1971).

relation to God, maintaining a human-centered and earth-centered orientation.

Unlike the Judeo-Christian tradition, the Buddhist tradition, especially Mahāyāna Buddhism, does not claim a unique significance for human history. The Buddhist view includes all beings, regardless of whether they are sentient or non-sentient, and everything in the universe, seeing Earth as one of the many planets. Buddhism generally characterizes history with some variations as follows: [2]

1. History has a beginning and an end only on a relative level, not an absolute one.
2. Human history has significance but this is not an exclusively human attribute. Buddhism presupposes numerous histories of other sentient beings on earth and in the universe and asserts that the histories of those beings have the same significance as the history of human beings.
3. Earth is only one tiny spot in the magnificent universe, i.e., the *dharmadhātu* (Infinite Dharma Realm). Buddhism does not postulate the earth as the only location Buddhists must consider.
4. History is not conducted and intervened into by God and it is the collective karma (activities) of sentient beings.

Buddhism views the assumed opposition implicit in the above-mentioned terms from a relative perspective, not an absolute one. It asks its followers to consider that those opposite conceptions are supplementary. Without the creator, the created cannot exist at all; without good, evil cannot exist; without the secular, the transcendental cannot exist; and so forth. In general, Buddhism advocates what we might call a symbiotic view. Symbiosis means the close association or mutually beneficial union of two dissimilar organisms.

---

[2] *Ibid.*

Buddhism does not divide the creator and the created. Buddhists should rely on themselves, not others, and on the teachings that the Buddha delivered. Generally stated, Buddhists do not look to God the creator transcendental deity to offer peace to humans as a gift through His Grace. God is not seen as the bringer of peace. Only humans can and should make peace. Peace is not a gift given by the outsider(s) or external force(s). Peace is not created by accident. Peace is the result of collective actions of peace activists.

Buddhism does also not dichotomize subject and object. We, as subject, have an impact on objects such as other humans, nature, societies and worlds. Objects also have an impact on us. Relations between subject and object are correlated and co-influential. If subject influences object, object influences subject. If we promote other objects, those objects promote us. One side does not bar the other side completely. Both sides are not exclusive, but complementary.

Based on its symbiotic view, [3] Buddhism advises its followers not to be antagonistic against, but to be cooperative and co-existent with other beings. Buddhism teaches how to cooperate with other religions, philosophies, ideologies, and so on. Unlike some individuals of other religions, generally Buddhists do not concentrate on proselytizing to win over others to their own religion. While not abandoning their religious teaching, they should develop cooperative relations with other religious persons. This ecumenical aspect of the Buddhist stance is strongly needed in problematic societies in which many religions are involved in the conflicts both worldwide and nationwide.

In his book *Buddhism: A Quest for Unity and Peace*, Johan Galtung, authority in peace studies, discusses Buddhism in terms of five areas where there are global problems, (1) nature, (2) human, (3) society, (4) the world, and (5) culture. Each of these areas is matched to a goal, (1) ecological balance, (2) (human) enlightenment, (3) (social) development, (4) (world) peace, and (5)

---

[3] Johan Galtung, *Buddhism: A Quest for Unity and Peace* (Honolulu, Hawaii: Dae Won Sa Buddhist Temple of Hawaii, 1988).

(cultural) *adequatio*. He states that the five areas and their respective goals are not operating separately but are very closely related. For example, if peace is discussed, it should be explained among nations, within societies, within cultures, among and within human beings and even within nature, without excluding any of the aforementioned five dimensions. Buddhists should interrelate the five dimensions holistically and dynamically and should not segregate them into separate dimensions.

Each of the above-listed five items should share two common factors, diversity and symbiosis. [4] Diversity and symbiosis might lead to ecological balance at the level of nature, to rich and mature human beings at the level of human beings, to pluralistic and democratic societies at the social level and finally to active peaceful coexistence between several systems at the world level.

Galtung clearly explains in the prologue why Buddhism quests for unity and peace in the following six cases, (1) species, (2) gender, (3) race, (4) nation, (5) classes, and (6) persons: [5]

> There is *no chosen species*, human beings, chosen over and above animals and the rest of nature, giving rise to cruelty to animals, to meatism, (and) to destruction of nature. From the very beginning, the unity with all life was proclaimed. There is *no chosen gender*, man, giving rise to cruelty and repression of all kinds of women, including discrimination. The Buddha saw women as equally capable of obtaining enlightenment. There is *no chosen race*, for instance, whites, or yellow people, giving rise to racism, slavery and colonialism. In fact, such practices are explicitly forbidden. There is *no chosen people or nation,* for instance, a country where the Buddha was born or where he worked, giving rise to nationalism and imperialism. Buddhism is found in many nations, none of them more chosen than the others. There are *no chosen classes* such as kings and rulers, military or merchants with both power and privilege, giving

---

[4] *Ibid,* 11.
[5] *Ibid,* 7-8.

rise to repression, exploitation, and class discrimination. In fact, from the beginning, Buddhism cut across the steep Hindu caste system. There are *no chosen persons*, such as the true believers, giving rise to all kinds of cruelty against the non-believers, inquisition, etc. On the contrary, there is the potential for Buddhahood in all of us. Nobody is divine, above the rest, but some may serve as better examples than others.

As above, any species, gender, race, nationality, classes, and persons should not be excluded and discriminated and should be equally treated without having any pyramid-like hierarchical stratum. Buddhism is a good and maybe ideal model in theory and praxis for environmentalism (nature's ecological balance), human enlightenment, social development, world peace, and cultural adequacy. It horizontally discusses each of those six subjects, i.e., species, gender, race, nationality, classes and persons, without vertically arranging any of them over others. It does not accept the superior position of a species, a gender, a race, a nationality and a class over other classes. It horizontally and equally treats any species, gender, race, nationality, and class without exception.

By overcoming three types of violence, (1) direct violence, (2) structural violence, and (3) cultural violence,[6] Buddhists can make a non-violent (peaceful) society in the troubled mundane world. If the three types of violence were eliminated, peace would be realized. Because Buddhism does not accept any kind of violence, it is a good model for removing it and for building peace.

First, counteracting direct violence, Buddhism expounds the doctrine of non-violence (Skt., *ahiṃsā*). It commands Buddhists not to kill any beings as the most important precept. It does not authorize any kind of violence, individual and social, in its discipline codes. Whenever Buddhists have disputes, disagreements, wars and other conflicts in society, they should use dialogues, persuasion, consultation, diplomatic measures and other peaceful means, not relying on violent actions. The Buddha hoped

---

[6] *Ibid*, 136-141.

to create a peaceful community in the monastic society at least and in the larger Buddhist one at best.

Buddhism has not brought war, violence and conflicts across the world in its name, even though we can easily find many examples of serious wars, violence and conflicts in Buddhist nations. Due to its symbiotic view, I think Buddhism might hold the greatest potential for constructively contributing to the peacemaking process in the world, perhaps more than other religious traditions.

Second, Buddhism suggests we remove structural violence that kills slowly and indirectly, replacing it with structural justice. The social structure of dictatorships produces such structural violence causing people to suffer in terms of human rights, free speech, and otherwise. Development-oriented governments lead to the destruction of nature. Stressful societies make people uncomfortable, distressed and disappointed. Sexist, nationalistic, racist, undemocratic, non-pluralist and caste societies structurally create violence. In opposition to these, a democratic society is strongly required to foster structural justice and eliminate structural violence.

Third, cultural violence is pervasive especially in religion and/or ideology, which backs up direct and/or structural violence. Even though there are many Buddhists who commit direct violence and support structural violence, there is no textual evidence in Buddhism that supports the previous two types of violence. If we live in a culturally peaceful society, we naturally have peaceful actions. Conversely, if we live in a culturally violent society, we easily commit violent acts. The society that culturally advocates competition naturally increases direct and/or structural violence.

The views of the Judeo-Christian tradition and traditional Western philosophy often involve divided pairs of opposites. For example, there is the creator and the created, good and evil, the secular and the transcendental, the nature and the function, noumenon and phenomena, sentient beings and non-sentient beings, subject and object, the Buddha and unenlightened beings, nature and human beings, enemies and friends, and so forth. However, Buddhism harmonizes each pair of opposites without excluding either of each constituent. Once again, due to the symbiotic view, Buddhism can be a strong theoretical and practical basis for peace.

2. The Buddha: An Ideal Figure of Peace

The Buddha, whose name is Śākyamuni, discovered the doctrine of dependent origination, the most important and central teaching in Buddhism. The doctrine of dependent origination explains that individual existences, composed of physical and psychological elements, are interdependent and mutually condition each other. This led to another central teaching, non-substantiality. Accordingly, all existences are existent based on interdependent relations and are not independently substantial. It is generally held in Buddhism that the attainment of enlightenment is based on the comprehension of the doctrine of dependent origination.

An early form of the doctrine of dependent origination shows the causal relationship between ignorance and suffering with twelve links. Each link leads to the next one. The twelve links begin with (1) ignorance, which produces (2) karmic action. Action causes (3) consciousness. Consciousness causes (4) name and form. Name and form cause (5) the six sense organs. The six sense organs cause (6) contact. Contact causes (7) sensation. Sensation causes (8) desire. Desire causes (9) attachment. Attachment causes (10) existence. Existence causes (11) birth; and birth causes (12) aging and death.

The twelve-linked dependent origination is seen from two perspectives, i.e., the perspective of transmigration and the perspective of liberation. If the perspective of transmigration is employed, (1) ignorance is led via ten links finally to (12) aging and death in the cycle of delusion and suffering. However, when the perspective of liberation is adopted, if (1) ignorance is removed, (2) action is automatically wiped out. Likewise, the case is consecutively applied to the next step and finally leads to (12) aging and death. One will be liberated from the cycle of life and death.

The doctrine of dependent origination destroys the ego-centered worldview. The Buddha advised us to observe all events with an interrelated perspective. The doctrine sets the guidelines for Buddhism to be a symbiotic religion of peace, not a non-symbiotic one of antagonisms. If ego-centeredness is emphasized, peace can in no way be constructed between oneself and others.

If the doctrine of dependent origination is accepted, we should not presuppose external forces such as God or other creators, to explain the origin of things. According to the doctrine, because everything is interdependently originated, even God should be originated interdependently. The Buddha negates deductive reasoning that assumes a primal originator (cause). If the doctrine is accepted, we should also not assume that accidental forces explain the origin of things. According to the doctrine, everything is conditioned by other things and there are no existents without causes and conditions. If something good or bad happens, we should understand objectively and neutrally why it happens without looking for external and/or accidental forces.

The doctrine of dependent origination leads to the doctrine of impermanence that everything is changing and exists in process. The doctrine does not eternalize anything and suggests we comprehend all facts and events as being in process. Even though this society is full of disputes, wars, violence, struggles and so forth, those unwholesome situations are not permanent. We can remove them and bring peace to a troubled society.

The doctrine of dependent origination also naturally leads to the doctrine of non-substantiality that excludes the possibility of a permanent soul or self. Unlike a concept of soul or self that is permanent and substantial, it does not remove something impermanent and changing. It negates the independent self as something eternal, unique, permanent and so on. It encourages all beings to treat others equally without being attached to oneself or giving priority to yourself. It conceives "I" as being in a process, not within a fixed border. Thereby, it removes boundaries between creator and created, subject and object, you and me, and other pairs often conceived of as polar opposites. We do not need to attach to ourselves because we are not permanent and eternal but continuously changing.

The doctrine equalizes the value of others and ourselves. It strongly calls for us to see other human beings equally without fixing borders such as age, gender, race, nationality, class, and so on, to consider even other sentient beings, including animals, as equal in value. It extends the quest for unity to everything, including other humans, sentient beings, and even non-sentient beings. To the contrary, Christianity explicates that the quest for unity should be extended upwards from humans to God through Jesus Christ, a mediator between humans and the creator. It justifies the hierarchical or vertical structure from bottom to top. It sees a just the rule of God over the created and of humans over nature. Because of these factors, Buddhists tend to see their worldview as being more egalitarian and conducive to peacemaking than that of Christianity. At its root Christianity appears to promote disharmony, starting with the creator and the created and moving to humans and nature.

The Buddhist doctrine of non-substantiality paves the road for another of its central doctrines, the doctrine of non-violence. If we extend the non-substantiality doctrine, "to hurt others" means "to hurt ourselves." All beings are existent in the continual process because their own permanent substance(s) are not existent. It also presupposes neither the egoist view focusing on maximizing one's own benefits nor the altruist view that only concentrates on the benefits of others, because neither of the two, oneself and others, can be prioritized in value. We should treat others as equal to ourselves. If we accept as an ethical norm that we should consider others equal to ourselves, there is no way we can justify violence against others.

The Buddha taught that the world is full of sufferings and contradictions. Buddhism can co-exist with other religions and ideologies. It is not a linear, one-sided religion and philosophy, but a cyclical, multi-sided religion and philosophy. It comprehends any facts and truth in the interactive process between action and reaction. Without excluding other faiths and ideologies, Buddhism can harmonize them. It naturally accepts diverse ideologies and religions without fighting and conflicts in a society.

Buddhists consider Nirvāṇa to be the final goal. It is not an extinguished negative mental status, but a vivid positive realization of the doctrine of dependent origination. It is peaceful mind at the individual level, conflict-free peace at the social, national and international level and ecological balance at the level of nature. It advocates not having a conflict-oriented mind but a harmony-oriented mind at the individual level, not being violence-oriented but peace-oriented at the social level, not being exploitation-oriented but environment-oriented at the level of nature.

The non-violence or non-killing precept is the first precept in five cardinal precepts, i.e., (1) don't kill; (2) don't steal; (3) don't engage in sexual misconduct; (4) don't use false speech; and (5) don't use intoxicants. All Buddhists, monastic and laypersons, should keep the precepts. While the five precepts are composed of negative sentences, the five activities comprise positive sentences. The five activities are as follows: (1) Increase compassion towards all sentient beings; (2) donate belongings and wealth to others; (3) positively control sexual conduct; (4) tell the truth; and (5) think wisely and reasonably.

If we combine the first non-killing (non-violence) precept of five precepts with the first deed of the five activities, we should not only remove violence but also increase compassion towards all sentient beings. We should not engage ourselves and others in violence, wars, conflicts, disputes, and so forth in the negative context and we should make peace, harmony, and so on in the positive context as well. Johan Galtung also says, "In the very center of Buddhism, there is a basis not only for negative peace, but also for positive peace, not only for absence of war, but also for positive relations."[7]

We should equate social well-being, natural environment, national security and economic development of other nations with those of our nation. If we destroy other humans at the individual or collective level, we also destroy ourselves because we are inter-connected with others. We should not see ourselves and others as being permanent, separate and independent, but as changing,

---

[7] *Ibid*, 16.

mutually dependent and interconnected. Buddhism strongly suggests we investigate our social well-being, natural environment, natural security and economic development in conjunction with others, not excluding but including opposite sides. We should not sacrifice social well-being, the natural environment, national security and economic development of others to build up those of things on our own side. In those areas of others, there should be cooperation with the same areas of our own and vice versa.

The Buddha also rejected caste-centeredness, a part of the hierarchical structure of society in India. For thousands of years, the caste system justified the social hierarchy in India, with the priest caste as the highest position, the warrior as the second position, the commoner the third and the slave the lowest or fourth caste. The Buddha declared the equality of all people, regardless of what social circumstance or family background one is born into, and negated the social discrimination of his day. Brahmanism, the Indian hierarchical religion of priests that the Buddha opposed, authorized racial discrimination and argued that Aryans are superior to native Indians.

The Buddha emphasized the middle path that avoided extreme standpoints as follow. [8] Epistemologically, he avoided both absolute substantialism and absolute skepticism. Ontologically, he negated both eternalism and annihilationism. He also ethically renounced both self-indulgence and self-mortification. He did not accept any extreme view as absolute. To take any particular view to the extreme naturally leads to conflicts because it refuses other views. This doctrine of the middle path is strongly needed to bring peace in this troubled society. It makes people see their own extreme views from the broader context and the more objective perspective, freeing them of their own dogmatic views.

The Buddha suggested that we not be extreme. For example, we should make a balance between prosperity and poverty, development and preservation, the poor and the rich, materialism

---

[8] David J. Kalupahana, "Ch. 16 Language and Peace: The Early Buddhist Perspective," in Chanju Mun & Ronald S. Green, eds., *Buddhist Exploration of Peace and Justice* (Honolulu, Hawaii: Blue Pine, 2006), 127.

and spiritualism, monism and dualism, theism and atheism, inequality and equality, diversity and unity, surplus and deficit, self-torture and self-indulgence, asceticism and hedonism, and so forth. The doctrine means Buddhists should not to be fanatics about religion and/or ideology. It means that Buddhists should not persecute believers in other religions but should take a pluralistic attitude towards them. It causes Buddhists to relinquish extreme attitudes that discriminate against other believers in their own religion and in other religions.

The doctrine of the middle path can be explicated as follows. If one eats too much, it is not good for one's health. If one eats too little, it is also not healthy. If one nation uses natural resources too much, it is not good for that nation. If one nation uses natural resources too little, it is also not good for its citizens. If one uses ones energy too much, it is not good for the body and mind. If one uses one's energy too little, it is also not good for one's body and mind. If one exercises too much, it hurts ones health. If one exercises too little, it is also detrimental to one's health.

Buddhists often refer to the Buddha with ten epithets as follows: (1) "Thus-Come," "the one who has Thus-come from enlightenment"; (2) "Worthy of Respect"; (3) "Correctly Enlightened"; (4) "Perfected in Wisdom and Action"; (5) "Thus-Gone," "the one who has Well-Gone to enlightenment"; (6) "Knower of the Secular World"; (7) "Unsurpassed"; (8) "The Tamer"; (9) "Teacher of Gods and Humans"; and (10) "World Honored One."

These names for the Buddha show him being seen as an ideal figure, perfect in theory and practice, capable of cultivating and educating all beings, those sentient and non-sentient, in order to bring about enlightenment and liberation without discrimination. That is, he is a person who actualized peace in himself and guided others to complete peace.

Buddhists believe the Buddha had the eighteen distinctive characteristics as follows: (1) Unmistaken action, (2) unmistaken words, (3) unmistaken intention, (4) meditative stable mind, (5) equanimous mind, (6) all-embracing mind, (7) determined aspiration, (8) determined endeavor, (9) determined mindfulness,

(10) determined wisdom, (11) determined liberation, (12) determined view to liberation, (13) all physical deeds that are practiced in accordance with wisdom, (14) all verbal deeds that are practiced in accordance with wisdom, (15) all mental deeds that are practiced in accordance with wisdom, (16) view of wisdom which is not blocked in the past, (17) view of wisdom which is not blocked in the present and (18) view of wisdom which is not blocked in the future.

We can see by these eighteen characteristics, the Buddha put equal emphasis on both sides, i.e., theory and practice, without neglecting either side to realize peace within him. He is an active peacemaker because he attained a peaceful state within his mind and continuously persuaded all beings to build peace.

Buddhists believe that when the Buddha attained enlightenment, he obtained ten auspicious powers or ten perfect knowledge(s). These are: (1) Knowledge of right and wrong; (2) knowledge of the karmas of all sentient beings of the past, present and future; (3) knowledge of various meditations; (4) knowledge of the capacities of sentient beings; (5) knowledge of the desires of all sentient beings; (6) knowledge of the different conditions of every individual; (7) knowledge of the results of various practices; (8) knowledge of the transmigratory states of all sentient beings and their accompanying thoughts; (9) knowledge of the past lives of all sentient beings and the Nirvāṇic state of non-defilement; and (10) knowledge of the destruction of all evil passions.

The 10 perfect knowledge(s) lead the Buddha to engage actively in saving all sentient beings in this mundane world. The Buddha's ten knowledge(s) are always accompanied by the Buddha's concrete practical actions with the following four confidences. Theory and practice are two wings of a bird in Buddhism.

The Buddha is endowed with four fearlessnesses or confidences as follows: (1) Confidence in complete supreme enlightenment, (2) confidence in complete destruction of defilement, (3) confidence in teaching defilement to hearers (*śrāvaka*s) and (4) confidence in leading *śrāvaka*s to the destruction of defilement.

The Buddha advised Buddhists to observe five precepts as follows: (1) abstaining from killing, (2) not taking what is not given, (3) refraining from sexual misconduct, (4) abstaining from unjust speech and (5) refraining from intoxicants. He prioritized non-killing (non-violence) as the most important precept in Buddhist ethics for Buddhists to observe. He also strongly urged his followers to maintain symbiotic relations with others and not to hurt them financially or mentally. He did not authorize any kind of violence in Buddhist ethics.

3. The Bodhisattva: An Ideal Activist for Peace

There are two main types of Buddhism practiced in the world today, Theravāda Buddhism and Mahāyāna Buddhism. In Mahāyāna Buddhism, which is the predominate variety practiced in East Asia, the model practitioner is called a Bodhisattva. The Bodhisattva is an ideal activist for peace in Mahāyāna Buddhism in particular and in Buddhism in general. From the Mahāyāna point of view, while other traditions may seek personal liberation, Mahāyāna Buddhism tries to attain enlightenment for the sake of all beings. The Mahāyāna attitude is embodied in the Bodhisattva, the ideal figure of Mahāyāna Buddhism, actively conducting altruistic practice. The Bodhisattva even postpones the complete entry into Nirvāṇa until all beings attain enlightenment.

The Bodhisattva practices ten perfect virtues: the following six major ones, (1) generosity, (2) discipline, (3) patience, (4) endeavor, (5) meditation and (6) wisdom, and the following four additional ones, (7) right means, (8) vow, (9) manifestation of the ten knowledge(s), and (10) knowledge of the all existences.

The six major perfect virtues can be explained a little more as follows. (1) Generosity includes the beneficent activities and the Bodhisattva dedicates it to saving all beings. (2) Discipline indicates proper activities conducive to eradicating all passion. (3) Patience and tolerance arise from insight. (4) Endeavor is resolute effort, which does not have any diversion and distraction. (5) Meditation is the way of wiping out illusion and (6) wisdom is the realization of supreme insight.

The rules of discipline, designed to ensure personal purity for monks and nuns and harmony in the religious order, saṅgha , are dominant in the monastic community.[9] A major alternative to the monastic model of ethics is the Bodhisattva precepts, which advocate social activism. Many different texts of Mahāyāna Buddhism provide various examples of practices and values for the bodhisattva life.

There are a number of different sets of bodhisattva precepts,[10] among which the Fangdeng list of twenty-four vows and the Fanwang set of fifty-eight vows are representative in East Asian Buddhism. The Fangdeng precepts are based on an Indian scripture, but the set of ten major and forty-eight minor vows in the *Fanwang jing* (Skt., *Brahmajāla-sūtra*) may have been compiled in China. The Fanwang vows became the most famous and the most used. Monks and nuns in Sino-Korean Buddhist tradition usually receive these precepts after receiving their monastic vows at their full ordination.

The ten major Bodhisattva precepts, included in the *Fanwang jing*, are as follows: (1) Don't kill; (2) don't steal; (3) don't engage in sexual misconduct; (4) don't use false speech; (5) don't use intoxicants; (6) don't gossip; (7) don't boast about selves and insult others; (8) don't be stingy and don't insult the needy; (9) accept repentance and avoid ill will; and (10) don't slander the Buddhist community.

While around twenty-nine minor precepts of 48 in the *Fanwang jing* are dedicated to maintaining the Buddhist teachings and the religious order, the remaining sixteen minor precepts deal with social actions beyond the Buddhist community as follows:[11]

---

[9] Refer to H. Saddhatissa, *Buddhist Ethics: Essence of Buddhism* (New York: George Braziller, 1970).

[10] The *Upasākaśīla-sūtra* has six major and twenty-eight minor precepts for the laity and the Yogācāra tradition has four major and forty-three minor bodhisattva precepts.

[11] David W. Chappell, "Chapter 10 Bodhisattva Social Ethics," in Chanju Mun & Ronald S. Green, eds., *Buddhist Exploration of Peace and Justice* (Honolulu, Hawaii: Blue Pine, 2006), 59-60. I adopted his translation for the sixteen minor Bodhisattva precepts.

2. Don't consume intoxicants or deal in intoxicants;
3. Don't eat meat;
4. Don't eat the five pungent plants;
9. Care for the sick as the foremost field of blessing;
10. Don't collect deadly weapons, nor seek revenge;
11. Don't act as a military envoy;
12. Don't conduct uncompassionate business dealings (for example, slavery, being an undertaker, keeping domestic animals);
13. Don't deliberately slander others;
14. Don't ignite destructive fires;
16. Help the needy, even if you have to give your own body, and then teach them the Dharma;
17. Don't curry favor with the powerful for the sake of selfish manipulation and to gain advantage over others;
20. Seek to liberate all beings (physically and spiritually) based on your kinship with all beings;
21. Don't seek revenge and kill others;
29. Don't conduct deviant livelihoods;
30. Don't conduct other deviant livelihoods but choose purer activities; and
32. Don't harm living beings.

While the Bodhisattva precepts are altruistically oriented, the monastic ones aim primarily at the attainment of personal merits. While monastic rules center on the formalistic or external aspects, the Bodhisattva precepts are more concerned with the intentional or internal ones. The violation of rules in monasticism has a strict punishment, including even expulsion from the monastic community. However, the violation of rules in Mahāyāna Buddhism can be excused if they violate the precepts for the sake of the welfare of other beings.

4. Huayan Buddhism: A Chinese Totalistic View

In China, Huayan Buddhism is the most representative philosophical Buddhist tradition along with Tiantai Buddhism. It teaches the equality of all beings, sentient and non-sentient, and the interdependence of all things. Its teaching is called the teaching of totality. The fundamental teaching of Huayan Buddhism is the interdependent origination of the *dharmadhātu* (universal Dharma realm), in which everything in the universe is inter-related without obstruction. The realm of principle, the static aspect and the realm of phenomena, the dynamic aspect, interpenetrate each other without obstruction.

The view of Huayan Buddhism is explained in the division of the universe to four realms as follows: (1) the realm of phenomena; (2) the realm of the principle; (3) the realm in which phenomena and principle interpenetrate; and (4) the realm in which all phenomena exist in perfect harmony and do not obstruct each other. The last realm must be an ideal world in which the status of complete peace and interpenetration is realized.

Fazang, systemizer of Huayan Buddhism, explains the interdependent origination of the *dharmadhātu* with the six characteristics as follows:[12]

First, if we list the names [of the interdependent origination of the six characteristics], they are the characteristics of (1) universality; (2) particularity; (3) identity; (4) difference; (5) integration; and (6) disintegration. (1) Universality means that one includes many virtues. (2) Particularity means that the many virtues are not identical because the universal is necessarily made up of many dissimilar particulars. (3) Identity means that many aspects [which make up the universal] are not different because they are identical in forming the one universal. (4) Difference means that each aspect is different from the standpoint of any other aspect. (5) Integration means that [the totality of] interdependent

---

[12] T.45.1866.507c5-19. I adopt the translation by Francis H. Cook with a few of revisions. Refer to his book *Hua-yen Buddhism: The Jewel Net of Indra* (University Park & London: The Pennsylvania Sate University Press, 1977), 76-77.

origination is formed as a result of [the collaboration of] these [elements]. (6) Disintegration means that each aspect remains what it is [as an individual with its own characteristics] and is not disturbed [in its own nature].

Second, this teaching [of the six characteristics] can be explained as follows: this teaching is to show such things as the interdependent origination of the *dharmadhātu*, which is the perfect doctrine of the one vehicle [i.e., Huayan], the infinite interpenetration [of all things], the unimpeded identity [of all things], all other matters including the infinite interrelationship of noumenon and phenomenon, and so on, shown in the symbol of the net of Indra.[13] These aspects reveal all of the obstacles. When one obstacle is overcome, all are overcome. One acquires the destruction of [moral and intellectual faults of] the nine times and ten times. In practicing the virtues, when one is perfected, all are perfected, and with regard to the essence, when one [part] is revealed, everything is revealed. All things are endowed with universality and particularity, beginning and end are the same, and when one first arouses the aspiration for enlightenment, one also becomes perfectly enlightened. Indeed, the interdependent origination of the *dharmadhātu* results from the interfusion of the six characteristics, the simultaneity of cause and result, perfectly free identity, and the fact that the goal is inherent in causal practice. The cause [of enlightenment] is the comprehension and practice, as well as enlightenment, of Samantabhadra Bodhisattva, and the result is the infinitude which is revealed in the realm of the ten Buddhas, all the details of which can be found in the *Huayan Sūtra*.

---

[13] The simile of the golden lion explains the Indra's net, which symbolizes the interdependent relation without obstruction. See the *Treatise of the Golden Lion*, attributed to Fazang, included in the Taishō canon, T. 45.1880.663a1-667a5.

The *dharmadhātu* does not have a teleological meaning at all. It has neither a beginning or end, nor a division between the creator and the created. It cannot be directed by a divine plan and it should be explained only in terms of its own inner dynamic functions. All things are interpenetrated and interdependent without obstruction in the universe. It does not exclude any elements, but harmonize them in the universe. It is a self-creating, self-maintaining, and self-developing universe.

While Judeo-Christian tradition adopts an exclusive approach, Huayan Buddhism adopts an inclusive one. While the theist religions adopt the exclusive importance of God to which all beings are subordinate, Buddhism does not have the concept of exclusiveness and equalize God with all beings. Based on the non-teleological view, Huayan Buddhism does not exclude other religions, philosophies, races, classes, genders, cultures and others.

The Huayan universe is essentially a universe of inter-identity and interpenetration. It has no hierarchy. There is no division between center and circumference and between the creator and the created. The doctrine of inter-identity is identical with interdependence. No being can exist independently of other beings. Existence is empty because it does not have substance or essence within it. Existence derives from the interdependence.

The inter-identity is the static relationship among things and the interpenetration the active relationship. Inter-identity and interpenetration are two sides of the same coin or two wings of the same bird. The two aspects cannot be separated at all. They are interrelated. Based on the doctrine of emptiness, Huayan has a totalistic view of beings. The rafter is a part of the whole building in its inter-identity and interdependence with the rest of the building. Without the rafter, the whole building cannot exist. Without the whole building, the rafter cannot exist.

The totalistic world is a living and organic body in which the part and the whole interpenetrate and inter-create. It firmly follows the doctrine of impermanence, delivered by Śākyamuni Buddha in early Buddhism. Śākyamuni Buddha emphasized the doctrine along with the doctrine of non-substance. The Huayan universe is continuously changing without intervention. All beings are living under a changing stream of activities.

Huayan scholars explain the totalistic world with a famous metaphor of the jewel net of the great god Indra. Imagine a wonderful net in the heavenly abode of Indra in which there is a glittering jewel in each knot and there are infinite jewels. When we select and look at one jewel, so many other jewels are reflected in its polished surface. Likewise, in each jewel's polished surface, the other jewels are reflected. There could be an infinite reflecting process without limit. This symbolizes a Huayan universe in which there are the non-obstructed relations among all beings in terms of inter-identity and interdependence.

Huayan Buddhism strongly negates ego-centeredness and human-centeredness. However, it is generally said Judeo-Christian tradition has a hierarchical view in which the creator occupies the highest position, human beings the middle one, while other animals, plants, rocks and things occupy a lower position. Huayan Buddhism idealizes the universal peace and harmony among humans and even between humans and their surrounding environment.

5. The Ecumenical Tradition in Sino-Korean Buddhism

As in many other religions, sectarian Buddhists accept the teachings to which they are affiliated and hold theirs to be superior to other Buddhist teachings in many ways. Likewise, sectarian antagonistic attitudes against other traditions in Buddhism created many sectarian conflicts throughout the history of Buddhism across nations. However, ecumenical Buddhists recommend co-existence and cooperation with other traditions without making trouble with them.

I think it is natural to extend the ecumenical attitude among Buddhist sects in Sino-Korean Buddhism in particular and in Buddhism in general to include the many religious traditions. Because there are so many religious traditions in the United States, brought here from the rich traditions of the world, the inter-religious ecumenical movement is strongly needed here for the construction of a peaceful society. If we exclude other religious traditions, it automatically leads to conflicts among them.

I published a research book of 498 pages on doctrinal classifications of Chinese Buddhism [14] in which I categorized doctrinal classification systems into two groups, i.e., the ecumenical systems and the sectarian systems and explained the ecumenical lineage. Sino-Korean Buddhist ecumenists define the Buddha's teachings from ecumenical perspectives. They consider that all of the Buddhist teachings are equal in values without discriminating among teachings and traditions. They adopt the expression "one voice teaching" for their own ecumenical scriptural evidence. Based on an individual's mental or spiritual capacity, he or she understands Buddhism in a certain way. Others understand Buddhism in different ways according to their own capacities. In contrast to this ecumenical view, sectarians create systems to show how their doctrines and practices are superior to those of other Buddhist traditions.

The connotation of the term "sect" in Sino-Korean Buddhism is entirely different from its usage in Christianity as well as in Tibetan and Japanese Buddhism. It is impossible to clearly delimit boundaries among the sects, which are not exclusive. Since the classification of sects is not based upon differences of doctrine and practice, the notion of a "sect" is essentially nominal. For instance, if a monk is living in a monastery founded by a master in the Huayan School, he is automatically classified to a monk of the Huayan School, regardless of his mastery or familiarity with some other doctrine or practice. In this context, sect has a genealogical meaning in Sino-Korean monasticism. [15]

In terms of monastic genealogy, eminent monks are generally supposed to have three lineages, i.e., the tonsure linage, the ordination linage and the dharma lineage. Thus, a monk might simultaneously belong to various lineages. Monks living in the same monastery might belong to different traditions based upon

---

[14] Chanju Mun, *The History of Doctrinal Classification in Chinese Buddhism: A Study of the* Panjiao *Systems* (Lanham, Maryland: University Press of America, 2006).
[15] *Ibid.*

three lineages. For example, if a monk was shaved under a master in the Tiantai sect, he belongs to the Tiantai sect. If the same monk was ordained under a Vinaya (discipline) master, he belongs to the lineage of the preceptor. And if the same monk was trained under a Linji Chan (Kor., Seon; Jpn., Zen) master, he belongs to the lineage of the Linji Chan sect. Each monk has multiple interactive relations among various sects. Thus, a monk might belong to one of the Chan sects by lineage, but study Huayan doctrines by his doctrinal preference and recite the name of the Amitāyus Buddha as his practical method.

In a typical monastery, there are different centers, e.g., a Chan center, a Vinaya center, a doctrinal seminary, a center for Pure Land practice and so on. In a Chan center, Chan practitioners focus on meditation. In a seminary, Buddhist scholars conduct research and educate monk students in Buddhist theory. In a Vinaya center, moralists center their practice on their strict observance of various precepts and teach Buddhist ethics to novice monks. And in a center for Pure Land practice, practitioners endlessly recite the name of Amitāyus Buddha as their own practical method. Without having any contradiction, the residents in the monastery can select any center or all of them based upon their own preference for their practice.

Sino-Korean Buddhists generally categorize the sects into three categories. First is the category of doctrinal sects, represented by the Tiantai Sect, Huayan Sect and Faxiang Sect. Second is the category of practical sects, represented by the Chan Sect and Pure Land Sect. Third is the Vinaya (discipline) Sect. Since all monks take precepts in the ordination ceremony, they should always keep them. Historically, we assume that Sino-Korean monks live without having strong rivalry and exclusiveness toward other sects. As a hypothesis, we might suggest that it is the third vinaya (rules) that creates a non-sectarian environment. They do not completely exclude other doctrinal and practical sects. Rather than kicking out other sects, they synthesize various sects or tenets in their own doctrinal and practical systems.

From the time of the introduction of Buddhism in China and Korea, there have been no institutionalized sects that resemble

Western religious sects or Japanese Buddhist sects. For example, the scholars of the Huayan sect do not have strong sectarianism, compared to Japanese Buddhist sectarianism and western Christian sectarianism. The "Huayan sect" refers simply to the group of scholars who are interested in Huayan Buddhism. Therefore, a scholar who is categorized under the rubric of the Huayan sect can also be included in another sectarian category. So, when the term "Huayan sect" is used, it means those who hold Huayan Buddhism as a central tenet. [16]

Sino-Korean Buddhist ecumenists, technically speaking, are the Mahāyāna ecumenists, arguing that the Mahāyāna teaching is higher than the Hīnayāna. However, because there is no sect representing Hīnayāna Buddhism in East Asia, their assertion is nominal. East Asian Buddhists generally use the term "Hīnayāna" didactically and ethically, to delineate what Buddhists should not do. It is secure for us to define them as ecumenists, just not Mahāyāna ecumenists.

They do not hierarchically evaluate various scriptures and they advocate that the scriptures are basically equal in value. From the ecumenical perspective, they suggest that various scriptures should not be understood as lesser than other scriptures because each has their own unique valuable tenets. To iterate, because they believe that all the scriptures have their own unique tenet, they do not evaluate all of the Mahāyāna scriptures.

6. Wonhyo (617-668): An Ecumenist Model of Korean Buddhism

Wonhyo formed the ecumenical tradition of Korean Buddhism. His ecumenical interpretation of various Buddhist teachings had a tremendous impact on the formation of Korean Buddhism. His ecumenical stance on previous doctrinal disputes was extended to include conflicts about practices and disputes among religious traditions. Whatever thoughts and religions Korean Buddhists have

---

[16] See Yoshizu Yoshihide, *Kegon-zen no shisōshi-teki kenkyū* (Research in the History of Huayan-Zen Buddhism) (Tokyo: Daitō shuppan-sha, 1985), 16-17.

met, they tried to harmonize new ways with Korean Buddhism.
They do not dichotomize their thinking into two camps of friends
and enemies.

Wonhyo is a very complex persona. [17] Early in his life, he was a
part of an elite youth corp. After this, he became a Buddhist monk.
Later, he abandoned his monastic robes and returned to secular life.
He also had a love affair with a princess. While he belonged to a
street gang, he continuously propagated the teaching of the Buddha
wherever he went, adopting an easy practical method for
commoners to chant the names of Buddhas and Bodhisattvas and
to seek rebirth in the Pure Land. Wonhyo removed a dichotomous
border between secularism and monasticism in his activities.

One of the most famous Chinese Buddhists in history,
Xuanzang (602-664), introduced and translated new a massive
amount of Buddhist texts into Chinese Buddhism. Loyally
following the ecumenical perspective on various Mahāyāna
scriptures from the preceding ecumenical systemizers, Wonhyo
opposed Xuanzang's sectarian doctrinal interpretation in which
Xuanzang championed the superiority of the Yogācāra Buddhism
over various Buddhist traditions and philosophies.

Wonhyo set the cornerstone for the syncretic and ecumenical
tradition of Korean Buddhism. His ecumenical position is by
called the Korean term "hwajaeng," which can be translated as
"Harmonization of All Disputes". Through the ecumenical position,
Wonhyo endeavored to reconcile all doctrinal debates to unify and
synthesize all sectarian perspectives into a comprehensive
Buddhist teaching.

Korean Buddhism is generally characterized as having a highly
syncretic and conciliatory nature. The Korean Buddhist syncretic
and ecumenical pattern of thinking is owed to Wonhyo and his
works, especially the *Shimmun hwajaeng-non* (Treatise on the
Harmonization of Ten Disputes). He dedicates the book to
harmonize various Buddhist opposing traditions with ten different

---

[17] Sung-bae Park, "Ch. 26 Wonhyo's Theory of Harmonization," in Chanju
Mun & Ronald S. Green, eds., *Buddhist Exploration of Peace and Justice*
(Honolulu, Hawaii: Blue Pine, 2006), 233.

topics. The text comprises two fascicles. However, some fragments of the text, consisting of eleven woodblock pages, were discovered in 1937 in Haein-sa Temple where the woodblock version of Korean Buddhist Tripiṭaka is preserved.[18]

Of ten disputes, there are three found in the fragments and several Korean scholars such as I Jongik, I Manyong, Gim Unhak and O Beopan reconstructed the remaining seven disputes from Wonhyo's texts and other references.[19] I will list the ten disputes based on O Beopan's reconstructions,[20] the first three of which are included in the extant fragments. Wonhyo harmonizes all disputes in ten aspects, i.e., (1) harmonization of the disputes between Being and Emptiness (Non-being); (2) harmonization of the disputes on whether or not Buddha nature exists; (3) harmonization of the disputes between subject and object; (4) harmonization of the disputes on Nirvāṇa; (5) harmonization of the disputes on Buddha Body;[21] (6) harmonization of the disputes on Buddha nature; (7) harmonization of the disputes on (Yogācāra's) Three Natures;[22] (8) harmonization of the disputes on (Yogācāra's) Two Hindrances;[23] (9) harmonization of the disputes on ultimate and conventional truths; and (10) harmonization of the disputes between three vehicles[24] and one vehicle.

Many later eminent Korean monastic scholars incorporated Wonhyo's ecumenical understanding on Mahāyāna Buddhist texts. Later Korean Buddhists try to harmonize Seon Buddhism and Pure

---

[18] See O Beopan's *Wonhyo ui hwajaeng sasang yeongu* (Wonhyo's Theory of Harmonization) (Seoul: Hongbeopwon, 1989), 10 & 195.

[19] *Ibid,* 83-108, 309-366.

[20] *Ibid.*

[21] The most famous theory on Buddha body is the *Trikāya* doctrine literally meaning the three bodies of the Buddha, (1) *Dharmakāya* (Body of Great Principle), (2) *Saṃbhogakāya* (Body of Delight), and (3) *Nirmāṇakāya* (Body of Transformation).

[22] Three Natures are (1) the nature of discrimination, (2) the nature of interdependence, and (3) the nature of ultimate reality.

[23] Two Hindrances are (1) the hindrance of the object of knowledge and (2) the hindrance of defilement.

[24] Three Vehicles are (1) the vehicle of hearers, (2) the vehicle of solitary realizers and (3) the vehicle of Bodhisattvas.

Land Buddhism, Seon Buddhism and doctrinal traditions, Seon
Buddhist groups, doctrinal traditions and furthermore among
different religious traditions, represented by Confucianism and
Daoism.

There are two major traditions of practice in East Asia. One is
Pure Land Buddhism and another is Seon Buddhism. Pure Land
Buddhism recites the title of Amitāyus Buddha through which its
practitioners concentrate their minds. The practitioners use external
object(s) to meditate and visualize. However, Seon practitioners
cultivate their minds without relying on any other external images
and objects.

With the introduction of Chan Buddhism to the Korean
peninsula, some Korean monks, represented by Jinul (1158-1210),
adopted an ecumenicist position to harmonize between doctrinal
traditions and Seon practical ones. Jinul is considered the actual
founder of the current Jogye Order of Korean Buddhism. His
ecumenical books were incorporated into the monastic educational
curriculum in the Korean Buddhist tradition. The Korean
monastics are naturally supposed to be trained under the
ecumenical education atmosphere.

Wonhyo himself tried to harmonize Pure Land Buddhism with
doctrinal traditions. His syncretic attitude between Pure Land
Buddhism and other doctrinal traditions directly and indirectly
influenced later ecumenists to harmonize between Pure Land
Buddhism and its opposing Seon Buddhism.

Based on the strong influence of two ecumenists, Wonhyo and
Jinul, Korean Buddhists are free to choose any kind of practices for
their cultivation. There are several practical methods available for
Korean Buddhists. These include Seon, the recitation of the title of
some Buddhas and Bodhisattvas, chanting mantras, reading texts,
copying texts, participation in ceremonies, social activities, and so
on. They do not accept only one practice exclusively for their
cultivation. If needed, they choose one and/or multiple practices
based on their inclination and/or their capacity.

7. State Protectionism: East Asian Buddhist Contexts[25]

Buddhism was first introduced to China during the reign of Emperor Ming (r. 58-75) of the Later Han Dynasty (25-220).[26] After the Later Han Dynasty fell in 220, a long period of chaotic disunity continued until to 589 when the Sui Dynasty united China. Non-Chinese rulers, mostly of Turkic and Tibetan origins, established their short-lived dynasties and ruled native Chinese in north China from 316 for less than three hundred years. Chinese literati, officials, and learned monks left north China to south China and transplanted their own civilization in uncivilized south China.

Exiled Chinese (re)established the Eastern Jin Dynasty (317-420) in south China, considering itself as the real successor of the (Western) Jin Dynasty (265-316) in north China. Because of (relatively) strong influences from Chinese Confucianism and Daoism, Buddhist monks "emphasized both Buddhist and Chinese learning, philosophical discussions, literary activities, a mixture of Taoist and Buddhist ideas, and congenial association between monks and the cultured elite of Chinese society. Since the imperial house was generally weak, the monastic community was able to assert its independence from secular authority."[27]

Indian Buddhism pretty well preserved the separation between religion and state. Monks governed the monastic community based the vinaya codes, not state rules. The state gave the monastic community autonomous governing authority. The rulers might respect a monk of even a lower-class family background. However, Chinese bureaucrats strongly opposed the Indian concept of the separation between religion and state based on their traditional

---

[25] Ronald S. Green also discussed state protectionism in East Asian Buddhism in his article entitled "Institutionalizing Buddhism for the Legitimation of State Power in East Asia," in Chanju Mun, ed., *Mediators and Meditators: Buddhism and Peacemaking* (Honolulu, Hawaii: Blue Pine, 2007), 219-213.

[26] Kenneth Ch'en, *Buddhism in China: A Historical Survey* (Princeton, NJ: Princeton University Press, 1964), 29-31.

[27] Ch'en, 57-58.

Confucian ideology. Confucianism ideologically authorized only
the ruler to rule the state in all areas, including law, politics,
diplomacy, religion, education, rituals, and so on. Confucians even
referred to the emperor even as the Son of Heaven. Confucians
subordinated religion to politics.

Confucian bureaucrats, Yu Ping and Huan Xuan, could not
accept extraterritorial positions for Buddhism and wanted to locate
Buddhist organizations under the government's direct control.
Buddhists, Ho Chung, a sincere layman and Huiyuan, a famous
monk, defended the separation status between the monastic
community and the state. Especially in his famous work entitled
Shamen fujing wangze lun (Treatise that Monks Do Not Need to
Pay Respect to the Rulers),[28] Huiyuan divided Buddhism into two
groups, i.e., the laity and the monks. He asserted in it that because
the laity follows the Buddhist teachings in society, lay Buddhists
should pay respect to the ruler and because the monks transcend
society and do not have worldly affairs, they do not need to pay
respect to the ruler based on the ordinary social norms.

Unlike in the south where the Buddhist monastic community
pretty much had autonomous and independent status, many non-
Chinese rulers used Buddhism for political purposes in the north.
Many eminent monks who were active in the north were political
and military counsels. Those such as Fo-tu-cheng and
Dharmakṣema exercised magical techniques for their rulers and
nations in order to propagate and popularize their religion. It
sometimes served as a state religion. Some non-Chinese rulers
gave strong favors and sympathy to Buddhism of non-Chinese
origin because they also were non-Chinese.[29] Non-Chinese were
not happy to follow conservative Confucianism of Chinese origin,

---

[28] Michihata Ryōshū comprehensively discusses the *Shamen fujing wangze
lun* (Treatise on the Separation of the Buddhist Monastics and the State) and the
topic between the state and the monastic community in the 10th chapter of his
Bukkyō to jukyō rinri: Chūkoku bukkyō no okeru kō no mondai (Buddhist and
Confucian Ethics: The Concept of Filial Piety in Chinese Buddhism) (Kyoto:
Heiraku-ji shoten, 1968), 163-218.

[29] Ch'en, 80 and 206.

which identified non-Chinese as barbarians. They embraced Buddhism in their strong antagonisms against Confucianism.[30]

Emperor Taizu (r. 386-409), the founder of the Northern Wei Dynasty (386-534), possibly of Turkic origin, appointed Faguo the national chief of monks and let him exercise administrative control over the monastic community. According to the Buddhist doctrines, he should be prohibited from participating in secular politics as a government official and from paying respect to the ruler as a monk. To the contrary, he even stated that because Emperor Taizu was the Buddha, not the ruler, when he respected him, he respected him as the Buddha, not the secular ruler.[31]

Emperor Wencheng (r. 452-465) of the same dynasty appointed Shixian, presumably died in 460, the national chief of monks and systematized the monastic bureaucratic system. The highest governmental office for controlling the monks was the *jianfucao* (Office to Observe Merits). His deputy was called *du-weina*. The government established provincial offices called as *sengcao* (Office of Monastic Community) in various provinces and the national head of monks appointed the provincial head of monks, called *zhou shamen-tong* and his assistant *weina*. The government bureaucratized the monastic community and temples to control Buddhism very smoothly. Following the bureaucratic model of Buddhism from Shixuan, Tanyao furthered bureaucratized Buddhist temples and activities under the centralized government.

The reasons why Buddhism rapidly grew during the period of disunion are as follows.[32] First, Buddhism became popular when a strongly centralized government that Confucians idealized as its ideology became dissolved. Many Chinese considered Buddhism for an alternative of Confucianism, their traditional social ethics, and political ideology.

---

[30] *Ibid,* 206.

[31] Ch'en, 145-146; and *Foguang dacidian* (Fo Guang Dictionary of Buddhism), supervised by Master Xingyun and edited by Ven. Ciyi, 5th edition (Kaohsiung, Taiwan: Foguang chupan-she, 1989), 3360. You can also use the digital version at URL http://sql.fgs.org.tw/webfbd/index.htm.

[32] Chen, 203-209.

Buddhism and Confucianism are contradictory in many ways such as the following. (1) The Buddhist monastic celibate system is opposed to Confucian familism. (2) While Buddhism backs up the separation between the state and religion, Confucianism thinks religion is subordinated to the state. (3) Buddhism that theoretically advocates an egalitarian society is contrasted with Confucianism that theorizes a hierarchically structured unequal society. (4) The Buddhist view that the world as full of suffering is opposed to the Confucian view that the world is filled with harmonious happiness.

Second, Buddhist monks with sophisticated rituals that included chanting spells and charms and predicting the future, helped popularized the tradition for the public and ruling group especially in north China. Using the aforementioned ability, they also supported the state and in return, they received strong support from the state.

Third, many persons who wanted to escape from the military and labor services during the continuous warring period became Buddhist monastics. When they joined the monkhood, they were also free from the secular regulations and taxations that their governments imposed.

Fourth, many literati and scholars who could not find opportunities to exercise their knowledge and talents in the state politics relied on Buddhism. They withdrew from the contemporary problematic society and found mental tranquility and happiness by means of theory (knowledge and study) and praxis (meditation) in Buddhism. The upper class, especially in south China, also enjoyed conversations with Buddhists on metaphysical and mysterious issues.

Fifth, Buddhism was very adaptable during the troubled period. (1) Confucianism did not satisfy the religious demands of the people in the uncertain and instable society. (2) The doctrine of karma helped the oppressed and the hopeless have hope, at least for the future. According to this idea, if people are involved in wholesome activities, they are guaranteed to be reborn in a better position. (3) The doctrine of Buddha nature also provided the possibility for all beings to obtain Buddhahood and salvation. (4)

Pure Land Buddhism that provided easy practical techniques and salvation to the commoners popularized Buddhism.

Emperor Wen (r. 581-604), the founder of the Sui Dynasty (581-618), a general of the Northern Zhou (556-581), superseded the nation in the north and by conquering the Chen Dynasty (557-589) in the south, finally united all of China after the long disunion of more than three hundred years. He issued edits for the promotion of Buddhism several times during his reign. He helped Buddhists construct the forty-five national temples in the prefectures. He also issued a decree for the establishment of Buddhist temples at the five holy mountains[33] and donated land to support and maintain the temples.

After uniting south and north China, he used Buddhism as a unifying ideology in his nation. He endeavored to locate himself as a universal emperor in the Buddhist tradition. "The emperor's motive was very clear. He hoped that all classes of society would share in the merits of worshiping the sacred relics. The stūpas were the symbols of the imperial support of Buddhism, and were erected in places where the scenery was especially excellent. By the ceremony of simultaneous enshrinement of the relics, with the official and clerical community participating, he sought to convey the idea that the entire empire was united in its support of Buddhism."[34]

Emperor Yang (r. 604-617) killed his father and ascended the throne. Like his father, he was also a sincere Buddhist and supported Buddhism in many ways. He carried out a gigantic construction project, linking by canal Chang'an and Loyang, the two capitals, one in the north, the other in the Yangzi Valley of the south. He imposed taxes on the citizens and their properties to support the two capitals and to construct palaces in each. He unsuccessfully exercised three military campaigns against Goguryeo (37 BCE – 668 CE). Because of the afore-mentioned

---

[33] Chinese considers that the five holy mountains are Taishan in Shandong, Huashan in Shanxi, Heshan in Anhui, Hengshan in Hebei, and Songshan in Henan.

[34] Ch'en, 200-201.

problems, the Sui Dynasty ended in 618. After that, Buddhism lost its position as the state's official ideology.

The Tang Dynasty (618-907) succeeded the united nation that the previous Sui Dynasty established. Its founder claimed that the royal family clan was the direct descent of Laozi, the legendary founder of Daoism. The dynasty naturally favored Daoism and also treated other religions pretty well, newly imported religions such as Nestorian Christianity, Islam, and Manichaeism, and established religions, Buddhism and Confucianism.

Buddhism was tremendously influential among all classes of people from the imperial family to the commoners. Chinese Buddhists incorporated into their traditions the massively translated texts that previous and current translators had introduced and they sinicized Buddhism on their own soil. They created their own Buddhist traditions, doctrinal and praxis, for instance, Chan, Tiantai, Huayan, Pure Land, and others. The government strongly supervised and controlled Buddhism in the Tang Dynasty. It arranged monastic officials under the control of state officials. "Under previous dynasties, monks accused of major crimes, such as murder, were tried by the state, but those guilty of minor infractions were judged by monastic law. Now, under the Tang, all crimes committed by monks were judged by civil laws."[35]

East Asian Buddhists exercised state-protection ideology under the name of their own religion, even creating an apocryphal text entitled the *Renwang huguo banruo jing* (Wisdom Sūtra on How Benevolent Rulers Can Protect Their Own Nations) (the *Renwang jing* for abbreviation).[36] They used to recite the scripture along with the *Lotus Sūtra* and the *Jinguang-ming jing* (Skt., *Suvarṇa-prabhāsa-sūtra*; Eng., Sūtra of Golden Light)[37] in special ceremonies in order to protect their own nations.[38] The three texts are considered the three major texts for protecting nations in East Asian Buddhism.

---

[35] Ch'en, 215.

[36] *Foguang dacidian*, 1217.

[37] *Ibid*, 3524.

[38] *Ibid*, 6868.

It is told that if rulers and commoners recite "the chapter for state protection" in the *Renwang jing* and "the chapter for state protection by four heavenly kings" in the *Jinguang-ming jing*, they can remove seven disasters[39] and are able to comfort and protect their own nations. Chinese Buddhists popularly recited and gave lectures on the two texts from early history of Chinese Buddhism during Southern and Northern Dynasties (386-589). The chaotic and endless warring between southern and northern dynasties made the two texts popularized and let Buddhists, the rulers and the ruled, rely on them to protect their own nations. Many eminent monks commented on the texts and implemented ritual manuals for protecting nations.

During the Sui and Tang Dynasties (581-907), the rulers established temples at the central government and provincial government levels where Buddhists particularly prayed for the nation's prosperity and comfort. For example, Emperor Taizong (r. 626-649)[40] issued decrees that monks should hold consolation services for the dead heroes, should pray for a rich harvest and by

---

[39] See the entry on seven disasters in the *Foguang dacidian, op. cit.,* 123. There are at least four different sets of seven disasters in the *Renwang jing,* the *Yaoshi liuliguang rulai benyuan gongde jing,* the *Lotus Sūtra* and the *Yi tuoluoni ji jing* respectively. First, the *Renwang jing* lists seven disasters as follows: (1) a disaster that sun and moon do not appear at a proper time; (2) a disaster that stars do not appear properly; (3) a conflagration; (4) a flood, (5) a wind disaster; (6) a poor harvest; and (7) wicked enemy armies. Second, the *Yaoshi liuliguang rulai benyuan gongde jing* lists seven disasters as follows: (1) a sickness disaster; (2) a disaster that neighboring nations invade; (3) a rebellion; (4) a disaster that the operation of stars became strange; (5) a disaster that the sun and the moon operated very improperly; (6) an untimely wind; and (7) an untimely rain. Third, the *Lotus Sūtra* introduces seven disasters as follows: (1) a fire disaster; (2) a flood disaster; (3) a disaster that unwholesome Rākṣasa ghosts create; (4) a sword-fighting disaster; (5) a disaster from unwholesome ghosts; (6) a disaster from criminals; and (7) a disaster from malicious enemies. Fourth, the *Yi tuoluoni ji jing* lists seven disasters as follows: (1) a disaster from rulers; (2) a disaster from enemies; (3) a flood disaster; (4) a big fire disaster; (5) a disaster from unwholesome Rākṣasa ghosts; (6) a disaster from unwholesome ghosts; and (7) a disaster from detrimental medicines.

[40] See Ch'en, 216-219 in which Ch'en discusses Emperor Taizong's attitude toward Buddhism.

reciting the *Renwang jing* and the *Dayun jing* (Skt., *Mahāmegha-sūtra*; Eng., Sūtra of the Great Cloud) [41], should pray for the prosperity and protection of the empire. He also patronized some important temples on holy mountains for the spiritual welfare of the empire.

Emperor Gaozong (r. 649-683) established state-sponsored temples called Guofen-si Temples in each prefecture in order for the monks residing in the temples to pray for the protection and prosperity of the empire and to spread and propagate the good aspects of the emperor to the masses. [42]

Empress Wu (r. 684-705) very strongly supported Buddhism and sponsored the carving of various images in the grottoes of Longmen even before taking over the government administration. She justified her control of the state not from Confucianism, which discriminates against women obtaining political power, but from Buddhism. She used the *Dayun jing* for her political purposes. There are two translation versions for the text, one by Zhu Fonian and another by Dharmakṣema, consisting of thirty-seven chapters. Some scholars claimed that a monk or monks concocted the sūtra by Empress Wu's edict to solidify her power ideologically. [43] In the text, the Buddha answers questions posed by the Bodhisattva Dayun and manifests his teachings.

Especially, in the 4th fascicle of the Dharmakṣema translation, the Buddha said "that as a result of her having heard the *Mahāparinirvāṇa sūtra* from a previous Buddha, she was now reborn as a female deity (named Ching-kuang), but that having encountering his super-mundane profound teaching, she would transform her female deity form to a universal monarch ruling over nation." [44] In the 6th fascicle of the same text, the Buddha told that seven hundred years after he entered the death (Nirvāṇa) by the skillful means, a princess named Zengzhang, of a small kingdom in South India succeeded the kingship after her father passed away

---

[41] *Foguang dacidian*, 757.
[42] *Ibid*, 219.
[43] *Foguang dacidian*, 757.
[44] Ch'en, 221; and T. 12.387. 1098a3-5.

and extended her rule over all of the world. While she ruled the nation, she propagated Buddhism in her nation and educated her citizens with it. The Buddha even predicted that she would become a Buddha named Zengzhang.[45] The female ruler used the *Dayun jing* to cultivate the mind of her citizens and with the merits of reading and copying the text for twenty years, she was able to be transformed to the female body.[46]

Empress Wu distributed the *Dayun jing* at the national level and established a Dayun-si Temple in each province across the nation to justify her unjust accession to the throne and her establishment of a new dynasty called Zhou as a female ruler. In order to get the support from people ideologically, Huaiyi and others used the popular Maitreya cult during the time and even claimed that Empress Wu was the reincarnation of the future Buddha Maitreya on this mundane world. She prioritized Buddhism over Daoism in her imperial edit of 691 and changed the basic policy on religion, implemented during the reigns of the previous rulers of the Tang Dynasty, which gave favor Daoism over Buddhism.

Emperor Zhongzong (r. 683-710) took back the throne from Empress Wu and restored the Tang Dynasty in 705. He tried to treat Buddhism and Daoism equally and by changing the titles of existing temples, established in every prefecture Zhongxing-si Temple in 705, renamed Longxing-si Temple in 707.

Emperor Ruizong (r. 710-712) issued a decree in 711 for the equal treatment of Buddhism and Daoism in all royal ceremonies. Emperor Xuanzong (r. 712-756) gave priority to Daoism over Buddhism and recommended the public read the Daoist texts. Even so, he did not discriminate against Buddhism and in addition to existing public temple Longxing-si Temples, he established Kaiyuan-si Temple in all prefectures across the nation. He let Buddhists pray for the nation's protection and defense at the two official temples. They performed various nation-protecting

---

[45] Ch'en, 221; and T. 12.387.1107a8-b10.
[46] T. 12.387.1107a24-26.

ceremonies and rituals. Even so, he attempted to control Buddhism under the governmental administration.

The very famous persecution against Buddhism by Emperor Wuzong (r. 840-846) in 845, called the Huichang Suppression,[47] can be explained by the following reasons. First, ideologically, Daoists developed their long-time antagonisms against Buddhists. Second, Confucian officials, one of two major political groups, sided with the emperor's persecution measure while the eunuchs the other of the two, allied with Buddhism to defend it. Third, economically, the emperor wanted to appropriate huge tax-free temple lands and wealth and to tax numerous tax-free monastics.

He ordered the government administration to investigate the number of monastics and temples in the fourth month of 845. According the census, the number of temples was around 4,600, the number of monastics more than 265,000. He issued an edict in the fifth month of the same year that except four temples in each of the two capitals and only one temple in each county and prefecture, all temples should be destroyed. Only 30 monks were able to live in each capital temple and of the county and prefecture temples, 20 monks were allowed to live in the large-sized temples, 10 monks in the middle-sized temples, and 5 monks in the small-sized temples. Except the above-allowed monks and nuns, all should be defrocked. He also ordered that the bronze images and bells be made into coins, iron images be changed into agricultural tools, golden, silver and jade images be turned over to the government. He issued an edict in the eighth month of 845 and revealed his determined intention for persecution against Buddhism.

Emperor Wuzong died of an illness in the third month of 846. Two months later, Emperor Xuanzong (r. 846-859) arrested and executed 12 Daoist priests, including three key figures, i.e., Zhao Gueizhen, Liu Xuanjing, and Deng Yuanchao, who cooperated to persecute Buddhism. He cancelled the suppressive measures against Buddhism that previous Emperor Wuzong implemented and issued favorable measures on Buddhism. In the third month of

---

[47] Ch'en, 226-233; and *Foguang dacidian*, 5473.

847, he issued an edict to revitalize Buddhism from the 845 persecution.

The persecution was tremendously influential in the history of Buddhism in China. It was the most extensive suppression of Buddhism in China. The previous suppressions by the Northern Wei Dynasty in 446 and by the Northern Zhou Dynasty between 574 and 577 were limited to the northern part of China. After the persecution, the connection between Buddhism and the state became weaker throughout the history in China. The intellectual and academic atmosphere of Buddhism drastically decreased and only two practical forms of Buddhism, Chan and Pure Land Buddhism, continued to be preserved and to be prosperous into modern times.

Buddhists, particularly in Korea, have also been proud of fighting against invading nations and of protecting their own nations from them. Even monks voluntarily became soldiers and bravely fought against the invading nations. Buddhists, including monastics and laypersons, in medieval Japan, had continuously used violence and wars for their sectarian and political purposes. Buddhists, especially in modern Japan, justified Japan's attacks on neighboring nations and participated in the invading wars. They described defensively the fact that Buddhism has served as a nation-protecting ideology and boasted of Buddhism as a religion of protecting the nation and the people.[48]

By violating the rule of separation between religion and state, many monks even joined government officialdom and carried out activities to rule the state. Regardless of whether or not their actions were just, the monks prayed for the well-being, prosperity and longevity of the rulers. They did not question their unjust activities. In East Asia, some rulers made bureaucratic systems for monastics at the government level, appointed national advisors, royal advisors and even the lower monastic bureaucratic posts and let them control Buddhism under their directions. Buddhists

---

[48] Bong-choon Lee, "Introduction: Buddhism from India to Korea," in *The History and Culture of Buddhism in Korea*, edited by The Korean Buddhist Research Institute (Seoul: Dongguk University Press, 1993), 31-32.

supported the government to gain and maintain positions and power without listening to voices from the oppressed masses. They cooperated to nullify the just voices of the people for democracy and for free speech.

In modern times, when Japan invaded neighboring nations, while a few of Buddhists voiced up to oppose the unjust war, the majority of Japanese Buddhists kept silent or supported it reluctantly or actively.[49] During Japan's occupation period, while a few Buddhists demonstrated against the unjust war, the majority of Korean Buddhists kept silent about the war or supported it reluctantly and strongly.[50]

We should question the unquestioned bureaucratism, nationalism, and patriotism that East Asian Buddhists have generally accepted. Can we justify the use of violence and wars for defensive fighting in Buddhism? Does Buddhism allow nationalism and patriotism? How should we judge many of the monks and laypersons who proudly employed violence and killing for protecting their own nations? Even East Asian Buddhists, at least in Korea and in Japan, respect them and consider them as national heroes.[51] Can we say that their arguments are proper and appropriate according to original and fundamental Buddhist teachings?

---

[49] Brian Victoria demonstrates how much Japanese Zen Buddhist masters strongly participated in unjust wars in his two books *Zen at War* (NY & Tokyo: Weatherhill, 1997) and *Zen War Stories* (London: RoutledgeCurzon, 2003).

[50] Im Hyebong explains the extent Korean Buddhist leaders actively supported wars during Japan's occupation period in his two books *Chinil seungnyeo 108 in* (One Hundred Eight Pro-Japanese Korean Buddhist Monks during Japan's Occupation Period) (Seoul: Cheongnyeon-sa, 2005) and *Chinil bulgyo-ron* (Essays in Pro-Japanese Korean Buddhism during Japan's Occupation Period), 2 volumes (Seoul: Minjok-sa, 1993).

[51] Korean Buddhists characterize their Buddhism as a religion of protecting their nation and Japanese Buddhists their Buddhism as a religion of comforting and protecting their nation.

8. Peacemaking: A Case of Modern Korean Buddhism

In 1910, Japan annexed Korea and in 1911, the Japanese Governor-General Office established regulations for Korean Buddhist Temples, effectively colonizing Korean Buddhism.[52] The regulations heavily influenced modern Korean Buddhism during the occupation period (1910-45) and continue to do so to the present. In complete acquiescence to these regulations, the Korean government passed the Law of the Management of Buddhist Properties in 1962 to control all Korean Buddhist Temples under the hands of the dictator, Bak Jeonghui. Because progressive Buddhist activists protested against the undemocratic law under the name of the Minjung (Liberation) Buddhist movement,[53] the government substituted it with the Law of the Preservation of Traditional Temples in 1987. Even though the scope of the government's control was reduced from all Buddhist temples to the traditional temples, the current Korean government is still imposing undemocratic laws to manipulate Korean Buddhism by continuously revising it to appease Korean Buddhist opposition.

Based on the regulations, the Japanese colonial government organized all Korean Buddhist temples under its bureaucratic hierarchy and established a system of thirty parish headquarter temples in which the vertical relations between the headquarter temple and its respective branch temples are strictly regulated. In

---

[52] For information on Korean Buddhism during the Japanese occupation period (1910-1945), see Chanju Mun, "Imperialism and Temple Properties: A Case Study of Korean Buddhism during Japan's Occupation Period (1910-45)," in *Hsi Lai Journal of Humanistic Buddhism* 7 (2006): 278-294.

[53] For information on Minjung Buddhism, see Chanju Mun's two articles, "Historical Introduction to Minjing Buddhism (Korean Liberation Buddhism) in 1980's," in *Kankoku Bukkyōgaku Semina-* (Journal of Korean Buddhist Seminar) 9 (2003): 239-270, and "Minjung bulgyo gyopan-reul seugi wihan siron" (Some Attempts to Establish the Doctrinal Classification of Minjung (Liberation) Buddhism), in *Dongguk sasang* (Annual Journal of the Buddhist College of Dongguk University) 24 (1991): 109-138.

order to easily rule Korean Buddhism, the Japanese Governor-General Office approved the abbots, in contrast to the Korean Buddhist tradition in which abbots are appointed in accordance with the unanimous recommendations of monastic members. The articles and bylaws of the thirty parish headquarter temples also had to be approved by the government. The regulations stipulated that all Korean temples must report their temple affairs in detail to the government.

While or after pursuing education in Buddhist Studies at universities in Japan, many Korean monastics got married, due to the influence of married monasticism of Japanese Buddhism. The Japanese colonial government encouraged the thirty parish headquarter temples to change their articles and bylaws so that married, pro-Japanese monastics could become abbots through whom Japan could smoothly control Korean Buddhism. Because their abbotships were approved by the government, it was economically and politically prudent to be loyal to its will. The married monastics also privatized temple properties to support their families. In short, the Japanese-derived system destroyed traditional Korean celibate monasticism and brought about the loss of monastic properties.

On one hand, Korean progressive activists reacted against Japanese control of Korean Buddhist temples and properties and began to demand that Japan's Governor-General Office abolish the regulations and the parish system in the early 1920s, that is, just since the massive March 1, 1919 movement for independence from Japan. However, they were unsuccessful in nullifying the regulations because pro-Japanese abbots and Japan's colonial government crushed the movement. On the other hand, Korean Seon practitioners initiated the Center for Seon Studies in 1920, just after the March 1 movement, and tried to recover Korean Buddhism's celibate tradition and other conventions of Korean Seon Buddhism.

There have been two major movements in the Buddhist history of South Korea since the liberation of that country from Japan on August 15, 1945. Chronologically, the first to appear was the "Purification Buddhist Movement" (Jeonghwa Bulgyo Undong), [54] the more recent being the Minjung Buddhist Movement.

The Purification Buddhist Movement began in 1954 and was largely concluded by 1962. This movement focused on the cleansing of the influence of Japanese Buddhism from Korea and the purification of the monastic order. The movement was initiated by the executive order of the first South Korean president, I Seungman, to expel married Buddhist priests from traditional monasteries. Essentially, the Korean monastic order had kept the precept of non-marriage until the Japanization of it by the Japanese government. This occurred during the colonial period from 1910 to 1945. During that time, the Japanese Governor-General in Korea forcibly caused Korean Buddhist monks to marry in order to facilitate control over the Korean Buddhist order.

The unmarried monks obtained the leadership in the order after the national monastic conference on August 12 – 13, 1955. The married monks, who lost the leadership, strongly reacted against the unmarried monks' leadership. The confrontations between two groups continued until to the establishment of the united order in April 1962. The married monastic group broke away from the united order because of the discriminating measures from the unmarried monastic group in September 1962.

The Supreme Court finished the long and tedious legal procedure between the married monastic group and the unmarried monastic group and authorized Purification Buddhism over married Japanized Buddhism in 1969. The married monks established the independent new order called the Taego Order and the government approved the registration of the new order based on the Law of the Management of Buddhist Properties in 1970.

---

[54] Refer to Chanju Mun's article, "Purification Buddhist Movement, 1954-62: The Recovery of Traditional Monasticism from Japanized Buddhism in South Korea," in *Hsi Lai Journal of Humanistic Buddhism* 8 (2007): 262-294.

Purification Buddhism had two major missions. First, it was to recover the celibate monastic tradition of Korean Buddhism from the married priesthood of Japanese Buddhism. The married monks privatized temple properties to support their families financially. To obtain and keep their higher positions in Buddhism, they were loyal to their appointers, Japanese officials.

The second mission of Purification Buddhism was to revitalize the Seon practice tradition of Korean Buddhism. Seon practitioners lost the temples in which to practice because married abbots and higher order administrators controlled almost all Korean temples at the time. The movement closely mirrored the spirit of the Center for Seon Studies. The Seon practitioners actively participated in the Purification Buddhist Movement in this context.

The characteristics of the Purification Buddhist Movement can be summarized as follows. First, the movement heavily resorted to the state for support. Two rulers supported the movement, President I Seungman and President Bak Jeonghui. President I Seungman issued six messages between May 21, 1954 and August 5, 1955 and President Bak Jeonghui issued official statements several times to support the Purification Buddhist Movement.

Second, the movement violated the separation policy between religion and state, which is described in the constitution. President I Seungman initiated the Purification Buddhist Movement by issuing his first presidential message on May 21, 1954. Prior to the message, Korean Buddhists tried to purify Korean Buddhism and obtained almost none of their goals. After the first message by President I Seungman, the government administrative units became actively involved in the religious affairs.

Third, both groups, married monks and celibate monks, defined the monastic order in different ways based on their interests. The celibate monks conservatively defined the monastic order based on the monastic codes which the traditional Buddhist orders had kept. The married monks suggested that the monastic order could be a combination of celibate monks who might concentrate on cultivation and enlightenment without being distracted by secular lives and married monks who could focus on propagating Buddhism through mundane lives.

Fourth, the process of the Purification Buddhist Movement was heavily dependent on the court and the state's intervention. The two groups took their cases to court and to the state to back up their own behaviors. The court and the state generally favored the celibate monastic side. Korean Buddhism wasted its properties and money in legal fees. In the process, Korean Buddhism became a pro-Government religion and automatically voiced government support. It ignored the social injustices of the undemocratic regimes. Meanwhile, the government manipulated the conflict between the two Buddhist groups for their purposes.

Fifth, the behaviors of both sides were non-Buddhist. Violence was used, some disemboweled themselves and intruded into the court, and the harmony of the Buddhist community was generally broken. Gangsters were even employed to attack the opposite side and to take temples. Even though the goals of Purification Buddhism could be justified, the methods they adopted could not be authorized under the name of Buddhism. Buddhism strictly prohibits Buddhists from using violence.

Because the aim of the Purification Buddhist Movement was to recover this aspect of the monastic order from the Japanese influence, the movement was basically for reformation of Korean Buddhism inside the religious area. In contrast, the Minjung Buddhist Movement is fundamentally an attempt to construct a type of Pure Land in the society by introducing such universal issues as human rights, justice, peace, labor, democracy, reunification, and so on.

Below, I discuss Minjung Buddhist Movement in terms of its history, development and meaning within the larger context of Korean Buddhism and society. I also indicate when and how the two movements came into conflict with each other. While Minjung Buddhism was a socially engaged movement, Purification Buddhism was a religious one. While Minjung Buddhism was active to work for social justice, Purification Buddhism was indifferent to the social issues. Purification Buddhism was successful based on the government's backing so that it was automatically institutionalized under the government's control.

The term "Minjung" means "masses," "people," "populace" and so on, strongly associated with the oppressed class. Minjung Buddhism became a movement in its collective and continuous activities aimed at the accomplishment of particular social, political and religious ends. As the representative movements in contemporary Korean Buddhism, the above-mentioned have greatly affected the formation of current Korean Buddhism. Minjung Buddhism continues to be a vital force in that respect.

Minjung Buddhism experienced its greatest period of influence as a progressive religious movement in the 1980's. There are two major reasons why the Minjung Movement has been declining since the early 1990's. One stems from international conditions, namely, the economical and political collapse of the Eastern European Communist bloc and the Soviet Union. Minjung Buddhism is indebted for its theories and practice to Marxism and socialism. As the Eastern European Communist bloc collapsed, Minjung Buddhism lost one of its most important models.

The second reason for its decline is related to domestic conditions. In 1992, a longtime opposition party leader, Gim Yeongsam, was elected president, even though this involved collaboration with the conservative ruling camp. Although many Korean intellectuals considered his victory in the presidential election incomplete in terms of overthrowing the dictatorship, it definitely decreased the need to push for democratization through extra-parliamentary means. After assuming power, Kim recruited radical and progressive opposition leaders to fill some important positions in his cabinet and ruling party. His measures brought democratization to many areas of administration and served to nullify the power base of the long time ruling conservative group, even though he was elected by the support of that group. His aim was to diminish the influence of conservative politicians and their supporters, including businessmen, bureaucrats, bankers, and so forth, in order to establish a strong democratic hegemony in the ruling circle.

The characteristics of Minjung Buddhism can be outlined as follows. First, it maintains an acutely critical stance towards traditional or established Buddhism. Their criticisms in this respect are aimed primarily at practice as opposed to theory or doctrine itself. If the oppressed masses are not liberated, Minjung Buddhists assert, the true ideal of Buddhism cannot be realized. They charge the traditional Buddhists with standing in opposition to this by maintaining the *status quo*.

Second, Minjung Buddhists believe that they can alleviate the real suffering of the masses by the transformation of contradictory structures in politics, economy, and society. In order to do so, they adopted the idea of class struggle as one of their major principles. For this reason, the Minjung Buddhist method of salvation is quite different from that of traditional Buddhism, which tries to destroy the suffering of sentient beings by purely "spiritual" means.

Third, Minjung Buddhist activists do not interpret doctrine with the traditional *panjiao* (doctrinal classification) system but by reference to the modern social sciences. For example, Minjung Buddhism does not see suffering as originating from human internal desire or ignorance but from the external social structure. For this reason, their solution to suffering focuses upon structural contradiction rather than individual ignorance.

Forth, Minjung Buddhist activists exercise a cliquish exclusionism, considering that they are endowed with an advanced consciousness. They believe they are justified, simply based on this assumption, in strongly criticizing those who do not follow their line.

Fifth, traditional Buddhists and other scholars disagree with Minjung Buddhism in terms of its doctrines as well as its practices. They ask whether Minjung Buddhism is Buddhism and consider it instead a new Buddhism or heretical Buddhism. They strongly ask Minjung Buddhism to not rely on the non-Buddhist method of violence to propagate its agendas.

9. Closing Remarks

Buddhism has two forms, the ideal and the actual. As discussed above, Buddhism strongly advocates peace in principle. It is the ideal form of Buddhism. Many Buddhists might represent a contradiction between real Buddhism and ideal Buddhism.

Buddhist scholars and leaders should inform the two different types of Buddhism to promote peace in this problematic world.

If we look at the actual history of Buddhism across the world, we can easily find so many cases that Buddhists have been very tolerant of undemocratic social structure, such as dictatorship, militarism, imperialism, and so on and have very seriously ignored social justice, human rights, unjust economic policies, inequality, racism, sexism, nationalism, and others problems. [55]

Buddhists easily accept unjust political leadership if the leaders give special favors to them. According to Johan Galtung, [56] we can easily find cases of nations where dictators give favor to Buddhism, possibly, in Thailand, Sri Lanka, Burma, Korea, and elsewhere. For instance, when the atrocious dictator Bak Jeonghui, a South Korean Buddhist, supported unmarried monks in favor of the Purification Buddhist Movement, the celibate monks did not protest against his undemocratic actions and further authorized his dictatorship. [57]

In many cases, we can easily see the negative sides, i.e., isolationism, escapism, retreatism and ritualism, in the history of Buddhism across the world. There are many instances of Buddhist monks having privatized their own ideal teachings on peace and social justice in their own monastic communities at the micro level and having not activated the teaching in terms of social, governmental and world affairs at the macro level. Buddhists made a very peaceful and egalitarian model in monastic communities. They did not endeavor to extend their monastic model to the broader contexts, such as village, government, world and even nature. They have kept silent in social issues, for instances, political equality, democracy, environmentalism, human rights, social justice, world peace and so on. [58]

---

[55] Johan Galtung, 28.

[56] *Ibid*, 30.

[57] This author explains the relationship between ex-President Bak Jeonghui and Purification Buddhist Movement in detail in his article, "Purification Buddhist Movement, 1954-62: The Recovery of Traditional Monasticism from Japanized Buddhism in South Korea."

[58] Johan Galtung, 28-30.

The Buddhist view of cyclical processes, not linear ones, easily results in a high possibility of fatalism in some way, not always, making Buddhists accept failure too easily. The cyclical view of history assumes failure. If we meet failure, we easily accommodate ourselves to it without strongly trying to overcome it. If we have failure, we also anticipate success. If we have success, we also expect failure. When peoples encounter failure, they might have two opposite responses. Some might respond to it very positively and anticipating success, others would try to overcome it. Some may react to it very pessimistically, others might accept it as a natural phenomenon. [59]

There is the doctrine of Buddha nature or *Tathāgatagarbha* in later Mahāyāna Buddhism. The doctrine explains that all sentient beings have Buddha nature or *Tathāgatagarbha* without exception. Some can interpret it substantially in terms of ontological context. [60] Others can interpret it as a provisionally needed logical apparatus for a soteriological purpose. [61] Some scholars argue that Buddha nature served as an ideological background for social discrimination, Japanism, nationalism, and ethno-centralism. [62] One can find many historical cases of rulers and the ruling class

---

[59] *Ibid*, 30.

[60] Two major Japanese Critical Buddhists, i.e., Hakamaya Noriaki and Matsumoto Shirō, argue that the doctrine is based on substantialism, an anti-Buddhist theory. See several articles on Critical Buddhism, introduced from original Japanese, in Jamie Hubbard & Paul L. Swanson, eds., *Pruning the Bodhi Tree: The Storm over Critical Buddhism* (Honolulu, Hawaii: University of Hawaii Press, 1997). You can see the list of Hakamaya Noriaki's articles on Critical Buddhism in Hubbard & Swanson, eds., 491-495. You can also refer to the list of Matsumoto Shirō's articles on Critical Buddhism in Hubbard & Swanson, eds., 496-497.

[61] To understand defensive arguments for the doctrine of Buddha nature, see especially Sallie B. King's "The Idea of Buddha Nature is Impeccably Buddhist," in Hubbard & Swanson, eds., 174-192.

[62] See Hakamaya Noriaki's "Thoughts on the Ideological Background of Social Discrimination" (339-355), Matsumoto Shirō's "Buddhism and the Kami: Against Japanism" (356-373), Ruben L. F. Habito's "Tendai Hongaku Doctrine and Japan's Ethnocentric Turn" (374-387), and Matsumoto Shirō's "The *Lotus Sūtra* and Japanese Culture" (388-403) in the *Pruning the Bodhi Tree: The Storm over Critical Buddhism* edited by Hubbard & Swanson.

utilizing the doctrine for a social discrimination. One also can see opposite historical cases that the oppressed masses appropriated it for their own political purpose such as egalitarian social well-being, rebellions and others, particularly in the Three Stages Sect.[63]

Buddhists should overcome the negative aspects of actual Buddhism prevalent in the history of Buddhism across the world and should actualize the positive aspects of ideal Buddhism in concrete historical and social contexts. Buddhists need to explore seriously how to remove direct, structural and cultural violence and as a result how to build peace in Buddhist institutions and societies in particular and throughout the world in general.

They can see some practical models from the peace activities of Buddhist leaders,[64] for example, U Thant, a Burmese and the late UN Secretary-General; Sulak Sivaraksa, a Thai and the leader for democracy; H. H. the 14th Dalai Lama, the political and religious leader of exiled Tibetan government in India; A. T. Ariyaratne, a Sri Lankan and the leader of Sarvodaya Shramadana Sangamaya; Thich Nhat Hanh, a Vietnamese and the leader of the Plum Village community in France; Aung San Suu Kyi, a Burmese and the leader for democracy; and others.

Buddhists can also get invaluable teachings on peace from non-Buddhist leaders, for instance, Mohandas K. Gandhi, an Indian Hindu and the leader for independence from Britain; Martin Luther King, Jr., an American Christian and the leader of civil rights movement; Petra Kelly, a German and the founder of Green Party; Ham Seokheon, a South Korean Quaker and the leader for democracy; Desmond Tutu, a South African Catholic and the leader for democracy; N. Radhakrishnan, an Indian Hindu and the founder of the Shanti Sena (Peace Corps) and the G.

---

[63] See Mark Edward Lewis, "The Suppression of the Three Stages Sect: Apocrypha as a Political Issue," in Robert E. Buswell, Jr., ed., *Chinese Buddhist Apocrypha* (Honolulu: University of Hawaii Press, 1990), 207-238. See, for a comprehensive understanding on Three Stages Sect, Yabuki Keiki's *Sangaikyō no kenkyū* (Research in Three Stages Sect) (Tokyo: Iwanami shoten, 1927).

[64] Chanju Mun introduces worldwide renowned Buddhist peacemakers in "Buddhist Peacemakers in Modern Times," in his edited *Mediators and Meditators: Buddhism and Peacemaking*, 1-47.

Ramachandran School of Non-violence; Leo Tolstoy, a Russian Christian and the world-renowned novelist and peace activist; and others.

We can find good examples of peacemaking from many religious institutions that promote peace across the world, e.g., the Jains of India, Quakers of England and America, the Universal Peace and Brotherhood Association of Japan, the Buddhist Plum Village community in France, the Simon Kimbangu Church in Africa, the Boukhobor (Spirit Wrestler) pacifists of Russia and Canada, the Jewish Peace Fellowship in the United States, and so on.[65]

Every day we see many articles in newspapers dealing with violence, both individual and institutional. Of course, all religions, including the three Abrahamic religions, i.e., Judaism, Christianity and Islam, might give their own answers and solutions. However, as this author argued continuously, while the Abrahamic religions and traditional Western philosophies polarize all things into opposites, for instance, the black and the white, the good and the bad, the truth and the false, the center and the circumference, the creator and the created, humans and nature, and so forth, Buddhist doctrine says we should harmonizes them. Buddhism has this to offer other religions and philosophies as an outlook with great potential for peacemaking.

Buddhist doctrines, such as non-substantialism, impermanence, the middle path, interdependent origination, and so forth, negate human-centeredness, ego-centeredness, class-centeredness, race-centeredness, religion-centeredness, and so on. I firmly believe the Buddhist symbiotic view is a strong theoretical means for bringing about peaceful coexistence in the world. Based on this view, we can make peace, unity, cooperation and harmonization between different groups in terms of race, religion, class, and so forth.

---

[65] Glenn D. Paige, *Nonkilling Global Political Science* (Philadelphia, Pennsylvania: Xlibris, 2006), 48.

UPROOTING SPROUTS OF VIOLENCE, CULTIVATING SEEDS OF PEACE: BUDDHISM AND THE TRANSFORMATION OF PERSONAL CONFLICT

Christiaan Zandt[1]

Introduction

There is suffering. The body hurts, a dear one dies, or a marriage breaks up. One type of distress that most, if not all, human beings experience on a daily basis, is personal conflict. When dealt with effectively, small-scale personal conflicts can bring a sense of progress and development that fills an immediate need for relief or happiness. There seems to be a promise in Buddhist sources from the Buddha's discourses (*sutta*s) to the writings of modern-day Buddhist authors, that Buddhism gives clear and practical aid in dealing with these conflicts. In the *Madhupiṇḍika Sutta*[2] for instance, the Buddha summed up his

---

1 This article is a summary of a dissertation written under the guidance of Professor Peter Harvey (University of Sunderland in UK). Many people contributed by sharing ideas, reviewing drafts or just by being present. I feel grateful for their feedback and support.

2 See *Majjhima Nikāya* (I.109-114), translated by Bhikkhu Ñāṇamoli and Bhikkhu Bodhi, *The Middle Length Discourses of the Buddha* (Boston: Wisdom Publications, 1995). Reference is to the volume and page number of the Pāli Text Society edition of the *Majjhima Nikāya*. 'I.109-114' refers to volume I, pages 109-114. These can be found as i.109-114 at the top of the pages

teaching as 'enabling a person to live without entering into conflict with anyone.' In the *Upāsaka-śīla-sūtra*, a Mahāyāna sūtra on the moral code for lay followers of Buddhism, there is a vow to bring people together in harmony when he or she sees them 'separate due to discord.'[3] Despite practical aid and insights, there are numerous and quite recent examples of Buddhists engaging in violence and even war. Richard Gombrich has even wondered how anyone ever came by the idea that Buddhism predisposes its believers and practitioners to being less violent in public affairs than other people.[4] It is not my intention to present or defend the worth of a spiritual philosophy. It is my intention to contribute to discussion and applications of Buddhist philosophy. I tend to agree with Mahinda Deegalle, who states that Buddhists, as practising religious people, have a need to express their condemnation of violence both in their reflections as well as in their behaviour.[5] For many people, a state of conflict provides the greatest challenge to refrain from harmful conduct. Therefore, the goal of this article is to present an introduction to Buddhist analysis of conflict and to point out some elements of Buddhist philosophy which can be useful in the transformation of conflict on a personal scale.[6]

Sprouts of violence: Buddhist analysis of conflict

1.1 Towards a definition

Anton Chekhov once wrote down in his notebook:

---

in Ñāṇamoli and Bodhi's translation.

[3] See Heng-ching Shih's translation, *Upāsaka-śīla Sūtra: The Sūtra on Upāsaka Precepts* (Berkeley: Numata Center for Buddhist Translation and Research, Bukkyō Dendō Kyōkai, 1994), 36. This is a translation from the Chinese of T.24.1488.1034a-1075b).

[4] Richard Gombrich, "Is the Sri Lankan War a Buddhist Fundamentalism?" in Mahinda Deegalle, ed., *Buddhism, Conflict and Violence in Modern Sri Lanka* (London and New York: Routledge, 2006), 22-38.

[5] Deegalle, ed., 4-5.

[6] I have chosen to generally refer to persons with 'he' or 'him.' This is done for the benefit of readability. The reader is cordially invited to read 'she' or 'hers' in its place.

If you cry "Forward," you must without fail explain in
which direction one must go. Do you not see that, if
without explaining the direction, you fire off this word
simultaneously at a monk and at a revolutionary, they will
proceed in precisely opposite directions?[7]

In a similar fashion, when one wants to resolve or transform
conflict, some clarity on how conflict is perceived is beneficial.
Organizers of a workshop on conflict management held by the
Sinhalese and Buddhist Sarvodaya Shramadana organization made
sure the first step taken was in the direction of a definition of
conflict. One team came up with over fifty responses, which were
then narrowed down by consensus to a list which included notions
ranging from competition, opposition and hatred, to fear, division,
injustice, and social discord.[8] What definition of conflict is being
used here? And can it be shared by Buddhists?

The Latin verb *confligere* means 'to hit against each other' or
to collide. 'Conflict' basically means that there is a perceived
collision. But if I accidentally bump into a street-lamp, we would
not call this conflict. So there seems to be more to conflict than
two (or more) things colliding. A satisfactory definition of conflict
has to take into account some sort of perceived incompatibility of
the impulses, needs, tendencies, people, or parties involved. I
propose to use the following working definition of conflict:

*Conflict is an antagonistic state or action of incompatible,
divergent phenomena. These internal or external phenomena
can be mental or physical needs, drives, ideas, wishes, interests
or demands.*

---

[7] A. P. Chekhov, *Note-Book of Anton Chekhov*, trans. S. S. Koteliansky and
Leonard Woolf, 2004, online at The Project Gutenberg eBook,
http://www.gutenberg.org/files/12494/12494-8.txt.

[8] Robert Burr, "Buddhist Conflict Management," in Chanju Mun, ed.,
Buddhism and Peace: Theory and Practice (Honolulu: Blue Pine, 2006), 179-
180.

When two things or persons do not accord, and seem irreconcilable, we use an intransitive verb to say that they conflict. I will refer to this first type of conflict as either **inner conflict,** for friction within oneself, or **implicit conflict,** for friction which involves others. When the disagreement leads to some overt action, things or people are 'in conflict,' they struggle, fight, battle or even wage war. This second type of conflict will be referred to as **overt or open conflict**. Of course, when handled too rigidly, this distinction between inner, implicit and overt conflict becomes inadequate: even when inner or implicit conflict does not lead to overt action, it might (and probably will) influence the people around the person who feels torn. And during overt conflict, one will be assessing whether it is worth continuing the struggle, weighing the immediacy of different needs.

1.2 A state of mind

Though most Buddhists would agree with the definition just presented, they would add that conflict starts in the mind (even when the triggers for conflicts seem to lie outside oneself). An 'antagonistic state' or an 'incompatibility of phenomena' clarifies first of all a certain state of mind. Because of this, it is not the existence of conflict itself which we need to focus on, but an understanding of its causes and the way it is dealt with, to prevent it from leading to open conflict. Ignorance, hatred and greed are seen as the roots of *all* unskilful behaviour of sentient beings. The Theravādin *Dhammapada*[9] holds that ignorance is 'the worst stain of all.' [10] When the 14th Dalai Lama, the temporal and spiritual leader of the Tibetans, attended a meeting of trainees at the Tibetan Center for Conflict Resolution in Dharamsala, he said: 'According to the Buddhist philosophy, the main source of conflict is hatred and attachment, and the root cause of these conflicting emotions is

---

[9] The *Dhammapada* is a part of the Pāli canon and can be found in the *Khuddaka-nikāya* section of the *Sutta Piṭaka*.

[10] *Dhammapada,* v. 243.

ignorance.'[11] It is safe to say that this is the general Buddhist position. As long as ignorance reigns, there will be conflict, collisions of delusions, a continuation of misunderstanding.

When Buddhists talk about ignorance (Pāli, *avijjā*; Skt., *avidyā*) or delusion as the root of conflict, they are not referring to stupidity in an ordinary sense. First and foremost is meant a lack of experiential knowledge of the four Noble Truths (*Nidāna-saṃyutta*, S.II.4). Secondly, there is ignorance or a lack of insight into the real nature of phenomena. Let us have a closer look of these interrelated appearances of ignorance and their bearing on conflict.

The four Noble Truths – In the first discourse the Buddha gave after his awakening, he spoke of four Noble Truths. These can be found in the canons of various Buddhist schools:

1. There is suffering.
2. There is a cause to suffering, namely craving.
3. There is an end to suffering, namely the complete fading away of craving.
4. There is a path leading to the end to suffering, consisting of eight parts.

What the Noble Truths imply is that dealing with the deep causes of suffering (and conflict) will lead to its extinction. The first Noble Truth acknowledges that there is hardly a reason to be surprised when conflict arises: Conflict is part and parcel of the world that we live in. Nor is there reason to become angry, at ourselves or others, because of the thought that there should not be conflict. Not understanding that suffering is an inherent part of the conditioned existence, sentient beings try to avoid or get rid of things perceived as the causes of particular pains. They tend to be content with temporary solutions which are subject to change. When this change happens, suffering and pain arise anew. While people are in pain and experience inner conflict, they tend to hurt

---

[11] T. Dhondup, "Buddhism and Conflict Resolution", *The Times of Tibet*, the Jan 20, 2005 online at http://www.buddhistchannel.tv/index.php?id=8,667,0,0,1,0 and *The Buddhist Channel*, May 31st, 2007, http://www.buddhistchannel.tv/ > Opinion > Conflict and Buddhism.

others through overt conflict.[12] Not knowing the way to appease inner conflict and to arrive at a state of peace, people thus keep creating the conditions which contribute to open conflict.

Another insight that the Noble Truths offer is that conflict, as a form of suffering, might have some sort of craving as its cause. Several discourses explain how craving and conflict are tied up. In a discourse on quarrels and disputes, the *Kalaha-vivāda Sutta*,[13] the cause of conflicts is traced back to the tendency of the mind to label, evaluate and then elaborate on every perception with lightning speed.[14] People, upon evaluating what they perceive, long for or grasp at something, so as to affect the nature of their mind and body. This situation is one of the elements that influence contact, which is the coming together of a sense-organ (including the mind-organ which is crucial for mental contact), a sense-consciousness and an object. As soon as this contact has appeared, there is 'appealing' and 'unappealing.' What is appealing, one desires to have close. This desire makes a thing become dear to a person. And from what is dear arise, says the *sutta*, 'quarrels, disputes, lamentation, sorrows, along with selfishness, conceit and pride, along with divisiveness.'[15] In the *Araṇavibhanga Sutta*[16], the Buddha explores conditions of a state of non-conflict. Not pursuing sensual desires which are 'low, vulgar, coarse, ignoble and connected with harm' is first in the list. Pursuing sensual pleasures or sense desire can cause all kinds of suffering, ranging from internal conflicts to fights or even wars. Similar analysis can be found in the *Mahādukkhakkhanda sutta*[17] and the *Mahānidāna Sutta*, where the Buddha provides us with an example of how conflict over possessions is directly caused by craving: Craving is

---

[12] Thich Nhat Hanh, *Creating True Peace: Ending Violence in Yourself, Your Family, Your Community and the World* (New York: Free Press, 2003), 14.

[13] *Sutta-nipāta*, translated by Thanissaro Bhikkhu, http://www.accesstoinsight.org/tipitaka/kn/snp. 4.11 (Reference is to verse number).

[14] Peter Harvey, *The Selfless Mind: Personality, Consciousness and Nirvāṇa in Early Buddhism* (London and New York: Courzon, 1995), 139.

[15] *Sutta-nipāta*, 4.11.

[16] *Majjhima Nikāya*, III.230-237.

[17] *Majjhima Nikāya*, I.86-88.

the cause of pursuit, and pursuit will lead to seeking gain. Gain leads to decisions, which lead to desire and passion. Out of desire and passion arises tenacity, which leads to possessiveness. When one possesses something, this will cause avarice. Avarice will lead one to guard property, which will have quarrelling and fighting as a result.[18]

The nature of reality – People have a mistaken view of the nature of reality. Firstly, people fail to see that phenomena in Saṃsāra, or the endless cycle of rebirth, are 'interconnected.' Actions (*karma*) and the intention behind them bring forth results, which will affect the actor. Thus, the cycle of rebirth is perpetuated because certain conditions bring about certain results. This is *paṭicca-samuppāda* (Skt., *pratītya-samutpāda*), which has been translated in various ways, from Conditioned Arising and Dependent Origination to Interdependence and Interbeing. Most people, Buddhist or not, have a gut-feeling that their own behaviour contributes to the way, a relationship, a family, or even society at large functions. When it comes to conflict, it is difficult to grasp or pinpoint the exact nature of this relationship between a lack of inner peace and outer turbulence. This fundamental lack of really seeing or understanding the principle of Conditioned Arising is an important aspect of ignorance.

Secondly, there is a lack of awareness of something that some Buddhists call 'Buddha nature' (*Tathāgatagarbha*). Although the idea of a Buddha nature has its precursors in the Pāli Canon,[19] it has been developed and discussed mainly in the Northern (i.e., Tibetan) and especially East Asian traditions of Buddhism. It might be described as an inner purity or the potential that all sentient beings have to attain enlightenment, to free ourselves from the endless cycle of rebirth. It is a fundamental quality that all sentient beings are said to share equally. To some it was the innate

---

[18] *Dīgha Nikāya* translated by Maurice Walshe, *The Long Discourses of the Buddha* (Boston: Wisdom Publications, 1995). Reference is to the volume and page number of the Pāli Text Society edition of the *Dīgha Nikāya*. 'II.58-60' refers to volume II, pages 58-60. These can be found as ii.58-60 at the top of the pages in Walshe's translation.

[19] e.g., AN.I.7-11.

bright purity of the mind, to others it was a corollary of the lack of acceptance of a fixed nature, and therefore the potential of every sentient being to awaken into a Buddha. Modern Buddhist authors talk mostly about a basic goodness, or a shared humanity. The famous Vietnamese Buddhist monk, scholar and poet Thich Nhat Hanh translates Buddha nature into an inherent goodness in every human being that may be covered up by ignorance.[20] Because we do not see this inherent goodness, we are tempted to think that some beings are fundamentally 'bad' or 'evil.' And because we are not aware of Conditioned Arising, we tend to hold onto fixed images, especially during conflict, of what a person 'is'. This brings us to a third aspect of a deluded perspective on reality.

Because of delusion, people conceive reality in a way that is full of conceit. One of the most convincing conceits is that there is something that one could an 'I' or 'me,' or 'you.' We experience a 'conventional' self, an identity based on the thoughts we have, the body we experience or the name we carry. We mistake these, Buddhism holds, for an Absolute Self. We even cherish this identity, this self, and want to protect it or satisfy its needs and greed. Especially, this notion of there being a Self, according to Buddhists, fuels inner, implicit and overt conflict.[21]

1.3 From the mind into the world

In 2006, members of the Buddhist Peace Fellowship (BPF) were offered a chance to join a retreat that was announced under the title: 'Peace in Our Hearts, Peace in the World: Wholehearted Practice in Difficult Times.' Earlier that year, a World Buddhism Forum convened in Zhejiang (China) to discuss the theme 'A harmonious world begins in the heart.' Awareness of how inner and overt conflict, or inner peace and outer peace, relate is a

---

[20] Thich Nhat Hanh, *Creating True Peace*, 182-183.

[21] Bhikkhu Bodhi, an American Buddhist monk and translator of many important texts, sees a view of self not as ignorance but as an aspect of clinging. He is supported by AN. V. 116 (16-21). Clinging is conditioned by craving, which in its turn is conditioned by ignorance (*The Connected Discourses of the Buddha*, p. 728, n. 8).

crucial feature of the Buddhist approach to conflict. How does Buddhism enhance the understanding that peace of mind conditions peace in the world?

First of all, many clarifications of the workings of Conditioned Arising can be found. Well known from the Pāli canon are the 12 links that tie up physical and mental processes to all sorts of discomfort we experience. To me, the following explanation indicates, among other things, that the better we understand the ways that our body and mind interact, the better we understand the prolonging of Saṃsāra:

> Spiritual ignorance → constructing activities → (discriminative) consciousness → mind-and-body → the six sense-bases → sensory stimulation → feeling → craving → grasping → existence → birth → 'ageing, death, sorrow, lamentation, pain, grief and distress.'[22]

We have seen above what is meant by spiritual ignorance. 'Constructing activities' are states of mind or tendencies that influence ones character and determine action. They can be intention or 'volition,' but also determination, joy or anger. These constructing activities direct ones consciousness. 'Mind-and-body' refers to the coming together of mental and physical processes, most commonly the sentient organism with its sense-bases. Only with the sense-bases and consciousness present can there be sensory stimulation and pleasant, unpleasant or neutral feelings. Feelings lead to craving, either to get rid of something or to get close to it. And this craving leads to a more active pursuit, called grasping, which in turn prolongs existence. This existence can be considered to be the effect of one's actions in this life, or in a next life, after a new birth.[23]

The sequence of 12 links shows how, because of ignorance,

---

[22] *Mahāpadāna Sutta, Dīgha Nikāya*, II.32-33. Because of its clarity, I have made use of Harvey's translation of this passage instead of Walshe's. Peter Harvey, *An Introduction to Buddhism: Teachings, History and Practices* (Cambridge: Cambridge University Press, 1990), 55.

[23] Harvey, 59.

tendencies arise which might fuel inner conflict. Since these states of mind condition consciousness, they influence how one perceives the world and the distinction between pleasant, unpleasant and neutral phenomena. By sustaining violence in ourselves, we cultivate the roots and conditions for violence to occur in our community and society. Conversely, by investigating what violence we hold in our bodies and minds, and by transforming these, a change in perception and perspective is possible. The extent of craving that arises based upon certain feelings *can* be modified,[24] which in turn might dampen down the transition from implicit conflict to overt conflict. This explanation provides insight and inspiration: insight how Conditioned Arising works, and trust that there are links in the chain which offer a chance for change.

Insight and inspiration can also be found with many contemporary Buddhist peace-makers: Daisaku Ikeda, a Nichiren Buddhist and leader of Soka Gakkai International[25] has written a book in which he outlines several paths that can lead to global harmony.[26] Throughout the book, Ikeda illuminates the connection between the mind and outer peace. His 'first path' is taken alone, consisting of self-restraint and introspection, leading to self-mastery.[27] Ikeda's 'second path' is one of dialogue; being an open, respectful connection that leads to the deinstitutionalization of war. The same perspective can be found with Sulak Sivaraksa, a Thai Buddhist and activist for democracy and human rights. He holds as follows:

A personal understanding of violence in ourselves and meditating, praying, contemplating – in order to lessen the violence inside us – obviously cannot by itself be a singular

---

[24] *Ibid*; my emphasis.

[25] Soka Gakkai International is a Buddhist school that is based on Japanese Nichiren Buddhism, which promotes international education exchange and the establishment of world peace (www.sgi.org).

[26] Daisaku Ikeda, *For the Sake of Peace, Seven Paths to Global Harmony, A Buddhist Perspective* (Santa Monica: Middleway Press, 2001).

[27] Ikeda, 12.

force for social change. What it can do is to give clear vision, not clouded by hatred. [28]

This is done by looking at our inner conflict, our own violence, by becoming knowledgeable and dissolving little parts of our delusion or ignorance about it. Sivaraksa continues:

It can help us link our head and heart and also to draw strength from Mother Earth, as did the Buddha. When we identify the seeds of violence, perhaps we may not uproot them, but we plant seeds of peace in their place. All of this is necessary in order to cultivate the inner strength to persist in non-violent struggle. [29]

Although the quality of our inner and overt conflict management is *conditioned* by the mind, it sometimes takes more than the mind to end conflict. There are several reasons to be cautious with the assumption that because conflict starts in the mind, it also ends in the mind. First of all, it seems sensible not to rely *solely* on the development of our minds to transform violence around us. It takes a highly developed mind to be able to apply enlightened insights in daily conduct. These highly developed minds are quite rare. Sometimes there are other means to resolve conflict, even though they might not last as long as peace of mind. Secondly, there are other conditions than our mind that determines outer conflict. One's individual inner peace (or lack of it) is only one part of the outer conflict at hand. [30] This insight might help one refrain from becoming frustrated or disillusioned when outer conflict persists, despite one's inner peace or effort to dissolve it. A third and final reason for caution is that individualistic spiritual practice, driven by determination to better the world, might reinforce the 'I am'-conceit, a sense of a separate Self. It was noted

---

[28] David Chappell, ed., *Buddhist Peacework: Creating Cultures of Peace* (Boston: Wisdom Publications, 1999), 44.

[29] *Ibid.*

[30] Nico Tydeman, a Dutch Zen teacher, pointed this out during a personal interview in January 2007.

in the *Mahāyāna Tathāgatagarbha Sūtra* (third century CE) that meditators should not spend too long sitting in the meditation hall, but that they should go out and apply the benefits of meditation.[31] We now turn to some qualities that support transforming conflict on a personal scale.

Seeds of peace: Ingredients for the transformation of conflict

Just like a cook uses several ingredients to make a meal, there are several factors that can contribute to dealing with suffering in the form of conflict. We will have a look at ingredients that support constructive transformation of inner, implicit and overt conflict. Since greed, hatred, and delusion are at the basis of the Buddhist analysis of conflict, their antidotes (wisdom/insight, loving-kindness/compassion and generosity) form a good place to start. Buddhists have worked for millennia to strengthen these antidotes by practicing insight or wisdom (Pāli, *paññā*; Skt., *prajñā*), practicing ethical conduct (Pāli, *sīla*; Skt., *śīla*), and practicing meditation or concentration (Pāli/Skt., *samādhi*). According to the fourth Noble Truth, this practice consists of eight aspects, which became known as the Noble eightfold path:

Wisdom	1.	Right view or understanding
	2.	Right intention or thought
Ethical conduct	3.	Right speech
	4.	Right action
	5.	Right livelihood
Concentration	6.	Right effort
	7.	Right mindfulness
	8.	Right concentration

---

[31] W. H. Grosnick, "The Tathāgatagarbha Sūtra," in Donald S. Lopez, ed., *Buddhism in Practice* (Princeton: Princeton University Press, 1995), 92-106.

The terms 'noble' and 'right' require some explanation. It is said that, during the process of awakening, one passes through several stages. During these stages, ones wisdom, conduct or concentration might be in accord with the Dharma. These are then called 'mundane' or ordinary right view, intention, speech, etc. The thoughts and actions of an enlightened one, whose mind is noble and taintless, are called 'Noble' or supramundane.[32] 'Right' or 'noble' in this context points to the spiritually ennobling effect of following this path, as well as to a supramundane way of understanding, intention, etc.

The richness of the Noble Eightfold path and its implications fill many books. Here, I introduce eight ingredients of conflict transformation, cast in the Buddhist mould and distilled both from the factors of the Noble Eightfold path, as well as from what has been presented so far:

1. The power of truth: Developing wisdom (cf. path factor 1)
2. Compassion and cherishing others (cf. path factors 2-5)
3. Deep listening, right speech (cf. path factor 3)
4. Mindfulness or awareness (cf. path factor 7)
5. Inner transformation through meditation (cf. path factors 6-8)
6. Equanimity (cf. path factor 8)
7. Non-violence (cf. path factor 4)
8. Skill in means (cf. path factors 1-2)

To me, these ingredients mutually enhance one another, as do the factors of the eightfold path. For instance, equanimity supports the awareness needed to listen deeply. And cherishing others provides skill in means with human warmth. Here, I shortly give

---

[32] The *Mahācattārīsaka Sutta* (*Majjhima Nikāya,* 117) offers a clear explanation of the differences between the 'mundane' and the 'supramundane' view, intention, speech, action, etc. There are many books which explain the many facets of the eightfold path. Concise introductions can be found in Piyadassi Thera's *The Buddha's Ancient Path* (Kandy: Buddhist Publication Society, 1974) and Rupert Gethin's *The Buddhist Path to Awakening* (Oxford: Oneworld, 2001), 190-226.

some background information from Buddhist sources as well as a few remarks on their possible application during personal conflict.

2   The power of truth: Developing wisdom

In early Buddhist *suttas*, outer conflict was traced back to the tendency of the mind to immediately evaluate (and thereby in a way 'complicate') perceptions. [33] When we do not see how our mind shapes our experiences world, we start to think that there exists such a thing as an 'enemy' outside of our own mind:

> The processes that compound the picture of the enemy occur within the mind of the perceiver. *Phassa* might give us accurate data, causing feelings to arise (*vedanā)*, the raw material of emotion, but the process of concocting a picture of the other person then takes place within us. The enemy is an extension of our own self-picture and is intimately related with it. [34]

This does not mean that there is no such thing as a world that can be known outside of the mind. Buddhists have been discussing this for a long time. The Theravādins for instance consider reality as consisting of *dhammas* that make up all phenomena (including people). Although the Theravādins they do not deny that a physical reality can lead up to mental ones, [35] the authors of the *Dhammapada* explicitly state that all that people are, is the result of, founded on and made up of what they have thought. [36] In the Mahāyāna Yogācāra tradition, the role of the mind in constructing

---

[33] *Sutta-nipāta,* 4.11.

[34] J. McConnell, *Mindful Mediation: A Handbook for Buddhist Peacemakers* (Bangkok: Buddhist Research Institute, 1995), Part 1 chapter 3.

[35] Peter Harvey, "The Mind-Body Relationship in Pāli Buddhism: A Philosophical Investigation," in *Asian Philosophy* 3.1 (1995): 39; T.A. Kochumutton, *A Buddhist Doctrine of Experience: A New Translation and Interpretation of the Works of Vasubandhu, the Yogācārin* (Delhi: Motilal Banarsidass, 1982), 1-3; and Griffiths, *On Being Mindless: Buddhist Meditation and the Mind-Body Problem* (Delhi: Sri Satguru Publications, 1986), 37.

[36] *Dhammapada,* vv. 1-2.

the world is emphasized up to the point that the perceived world is 'thought-only' (*citta-mātra*), or representation-only (*vijñapti-mātra*). The objectivity of things and subjectivity of oneself only exist in the mind. Whereas modern science tends to view the empiric side of experience as related to the physical senses, and the mind to be ungraspable, the Yogācārins took it the other way around. For them, the psychic complex which makes up an individual is empiric, while everything else simply cannot be known by ordinary human beings.[37] As ordinary human beings, they hold, we have no direct experience of this Absolute Truth, although we can (and do) experience a relative, everyday truth.

Developing wisdom can contribute to the transformation of conflict in two ways. On a 'deep' level (the Right Understanding which is the first step of the Eightfold Path), it is a knowing and understanding of the Dharma. By becoming more aware, one's understanding of reality deepens. This understanding helps dissolve the ignorance that lies at the root of our conflicts. A growing understanding of the way things are will strengthen inner peace and conduct that is in harmony with the way things are. It can help resolve inner conflict by penetrating the different thoughts and mindsets that make up the conflict, and see that there is a choice how to deal with these conflicting inner elements. Secondly, developing wisdom on a conventional level is about 'getting the facts right.' It is important to assess the situation and investigate what is true for the people involved in outer conflict. The power of truth can be applied in many ways. One way to practice with it during conflict is trying to distinguish between observation and evaluation or interpretation.

2.1 Compassion and cherishing others

Many people acknowledge that compassion, a concern for the problems of others who wish for peace and happiness and wish to overcome suffering, is crucial in any important relationship. 'Compassion,' says Daisaku Ikeda, 'signifies the sublime

---

[37] Kochumuttom, 219.

endeavour to share the suffering of another from the stance of our common humanity.'[38] This common humanity can be understood as a universal application of the concept of 'Buddha nature' that some Buddhist traditions share. At the same time, it is the Right Intention of the Noble Eightfold Path. If we are concerned for the welfare of other sentient beings, we change the attitude or illusion which holds our self (or even our alleged Self) as most important. It is an experiential way to increase an understanding of reality. The implicit conflict fuelled by the cherishing of a self is put on hold, but the *ability* to cherish is used to the benefit of others.[39]

Training oneself to be so filled with compassion, with concern, with love, has the practical benefit of being able to deal with all kinds of outer conflict. But for the untrained it might need tremendous effort to have compassion, for oneself or others, during conflict. When you find it difficult to have compassion during conflict, you might want to try and *be* compassionate – acknowledge and mourn that a gap remains between your ideal and the current situation. Smile and celebrate that you are aware of this!

2.2 Deep listening, right speech

Compassion, mindfulness and equanimity provide a motivation and an atmosphere that can strengthen our ability to listen and speak at the right time. According to Thich Nhat Hanh, deep listening and loving speech can stop new anger and fear from arising.[40] In the case of inner conflict, listening well to what is actually going on that causes inner turmoil, often helps to lighten the burden. Often this provides the space needed to create calm or even a solution. The same can hold true for overt conflict: deep listening and right speech can allow the parties to get things off

---

[38] David Chappell, ed., 130.

[39] K. Thrangu, *The Tibetan Vinaya: A Guide to Buddhist Conduct*, trans. Sonam Palden and Chojor Radha, Bibliotheca Indo-Buddhica Series # 188 (Delhi: Sri Satguru Publications, 1998), 38.

[40] Thich Nhat Hanh, *Creating True Peace, Ending Violence in Yourself, Your Family, Your Community and the World* (New York: Free Press, 2003), 93-94.

their chest and provide clarity in the turmoil of emotions. Deep listening helps us connect mindfully to what is alive in ourselves and others. It goes beyond the words that are being spoken. At the same time, these same words might be given back to the other party to establish a connection that aids conflict resolution. We have to develop the flexibility to understand words and definitions that are used by the other party and be able to use them freely.

In the *Araṇavibhaṅga Sutta,* a few hints are given as to what is this right way of speaking.[41] First of all, one should not utter covert speech which is untrue, incorrect and unbeneficial. 'Unbeneficial' in the case of conflict could mean: not aiding the transformation or resolution of conflict. If we think we know something about the other person, but we are not sure whether it is true, and we want to utter it just to confront or even hurt the other, this is best left unsaid. Covert speech which is true, correct and unbeneficial is also best avoided whenever that is possible. Even when we know something as a fact, it might still be better to leave it unsaid, in order to solve the conflict. When covert speech is true, correct and beneficial, one has to know the right time to utter it. Secondly, the same approach is advocated for the use of overt sharp speech. Speaking sharply is not avoided per se, if it is true, correct and beneficial, but one should know the right time. Hearing the truth might be hurtful. Yes, there is suffering (this is the first Noble Truth), but one has to allow time for healing as well. Thirdly, one should speak without haste. Speaking hurriedly costs a lot of energy and wears the body down. Moreover, it is quite hard to hear and understand what one is saying. Finally, we should not rely on specific local vocabularies and meaning alone, but be able to freely use language as an instrument. In addition to this, we find an explanation by the Buddha in the *Abhayarājakumāra Sutta*[42] where he explains that, based on his compassion for sentient beings, he only utters speech which he knows to be true, correct, and beneficial, whether or not others find it agreeable to hear.

---

[41] M.III.234.
[42] M.I.395.

When you are involved in a conflict, check our intention just before you open your mouth to speak. What need are you trying to meet? When you listen to others, try to be with them with all your being, like when you are reading an exhilarating book.

2.3 Mindfulness or Awareness

We saw earlier how ignorance, the root cause of conflict according to most Buddhists, can be interpreted in different ways. Insight as an antidote is supported by mindfulness or awareness (*sati*). *Sati* refers to a bare attention for what is (or was) happening, without egocentric judgement or other forms of attachment. It is a great aid in experiencing more clearly the real nature of phenomena (people included).

The act of being mindful as well as the right understanding that can be its result serve conflict transformation in at least two ways. First of all, being mindful is being aware of the changes that occur in body and mind, moment by moment. If one observes carefully, one sees that inner conflict changes. It is intense at one moment, and weakens the next. It is fuelled by different thoughts and mindsets that come into being and fade away. These lessons from mindfulness can be extended and applied to outer conflict, to social situations: things will and do change. There will be new sides to this story, to this outer conflict. Mindfulness thus helps in being attentive, rising to the occasion when the tide changes. Secondly, the right understanding that grows upon mindfulness helps see that there is always something like a 'different perspective,' as long as we are dealing with conventional everyday truth. When we understand that life is made up of physical and mental processes, and not of solid, permanent elements, we are opening up to the possibility of change. We tend to look less for conventional truths based on conventional facts, and look more at the processes and needs that arise in the moment because of certain conditions.

Bernie Glassman Roshi, cofounder of the Zen Peacemaker order, explains that for him an important ingredient of making peace is 'bearing witness' or 'unknowing.'[43] These terms are sometimes used, I believe, as Zen Buddhist synonyms for mindfulness. By 'unknowing,' I understand Glassman to mean letting go of conditioned responses and treasuring the creativity that arises from being open to the moment, instead of being stuck to what we think we know:

> When we penetrate the unknown we don't see the meal, we see the ingredients. (...) In the present moment, there are no thoughts, no concepts, just – THIS![44]

By staying open, the chance is that there is a greater awareness of the elements which make up the situation, instead of our usual (deluded) perception of it. So mindfulness becomes a very practical tool that supports outer conflict transformation aimed at present needs, not at alleged 'truths.' This openness or receptiveness, however, does not mean that one trims ones sail to every wind. It is being 'response-able': able to confidently deal with conflict's capriciousness. We can find a clear illustration of this position in the Pāli Canon: When prince Abhaya came to the Buddha questioning whether the Buddha would ever say unwelcome or disagreeable things to others, the Buddha gives him a detailed answer (see below, 'right speech'). Prince Abhaya then posed a second question: Does the Buddha think beforehand about how he is going to respond to a certain situation, or do the answers occur on the spot? The Buddha responded with an analogy: Somebody who is an expert on the different parts of a chariot can promptly and spontaneously answer any questions that arise about a chariot. Since the omniscient Buddha has fully penetrated the way things are, the answers to questions occur when they are posed.[45]

There are many ways to apply mindfulness in case of conflict. The breath is always with us as an instrument of awareness.

---

[43] B. Glassman, *Bearing Witness: A Zen Master's Lessons in Making Peace* (New York: Bell Tower, 1998), 71.

[44] *Ibid.*

[45] M.I.395.

Becoming aware of the in-breath and the out-breath can quickly
bring us back to the present moment. Like in walking meditation,
slowing down the conversation, either within oneself or between
people, can bring a new sense of awareness as well. Thich Nhat
Hanh urges us to practice mindful breathing, mindful walking and
gives a specific meditation that can help transform anger and
irritation into openness and the ability to listen with love and
compassion.[46]

2.4 Inner transformation through meditation

Mindfulness is a key ingredient of most forms of Buddhist
meditation. One of the most important expositions of Buddhist
meditation in the Pāli Canon and in the Theravāda school is the
Satipaṭṭhāna Sutta, [47] a discourse on the foundations (or
applications) of mindfulness. Meditation is a tool. It can help
develop insight, compassion, awareness and patience. By watching
the breath, for instance, or thoughts or any bodily sensations that
arise when one sits for an extended amount of time, we learn to see
our actions and habits for what they are: conditioned phenomena,
processes that arise and fade away. For Senauke meditation
practice is the essence of what he calls 'inner disarmament.'[48] It is
becoming intimate with the pain we experience as well as how we
react to it.

The ability to sit and watch comes in handy during outer
conflict: we become more skilful in observation, distinguishing
between egocentric evaluation of our observations and evaluation
based on wisdom or insight. One develops patience to see what
happens. We thus create the choice not to act out of habits that got
one in the mess in the first place. Meditation then becomes a tool

---

[46] Thich Nhat Hanh, *op. cit.,* 22.

[47] M.I.55-63.

[48] H. A. Senauke, "Cultivating Peace, Dismantling War: Inner and Outer
Disarmament," http://www.bpf.org/html/whats_now/2005/disarmament.html,
The *Buddhist Peace Fellowship,* May 31, 2007, www.bpf.org > Resource Center
> Essays & Reflections > February 2005: Cultivating Peace, Dismantling War:
Inner and Outer Disarmament.

to learn to abstain from unethical conduct with body, speech, and mind, and strengthen the ability to act ethically.

2.5 Equanimity

The *Kakacūpama sutta*[49] tells of the monk Phagunna, who is associated over much with the community of monks around him. Whenever somebody makes an unkind remark about the community, Phagunna becomes upset. The Buddha admonishes him to be mindful of 'urges and thoughts which are worldly' when he is reproached to his face or even hit by hand or some other means. He should train himself to the effect of being gentle and calm even under dire circumstances out of respect for the teachings. Even if bandits were to sever a monk limb by limb with a saw, the training of monks should be not to utter harsh words, but remain calm and try to encompass their own minds as well as the bandits and the whole world with a mind imbued with loving-kindness.[50] This is equanimity (Pāli, *upekkhā*; Skt., *upekṣā*). Equanimity clearly is not indifference or desperation. It is the experience of spaciousness based on a growing absence of hostility and ill will.

Even though *sutta*s like the *Kakacūpama sutta* were directed at monks with their high and exacting standards, it is sound advice for all involved in conflict not to build upon fickle reputations and to work on patience, loving-kindness and compassion. The danger of emotional involvement in outer conflict is first of all the effect that these emotions have on our minds. A reaction of anger is an act on the part of the doer 'and by it you co-operate with your assailant's wish to bring harm to you.'[51] Providing a stronghold for conflict through anger, the conditions for karmic traces or imprints are made. Furthermore, patience and equanimity help to keep a focus on deeds and processes, instead of what something or

---

[49] M.I. 118-129.

[50] M.I. 129.

[51] Peter Harvey, "The Buddhist Perspective on Respect for Persons," in *Buddhist Studies Review* 4.1 (1987): 36.

someone allegedly *is*.[52]

Equanimity helps in remaining impartial and even-minded, aiding the skilful transformation of inner and outer conflict. In fact, being able to remain impartial during inner conflict can help acknowledge emotions or thoughts that one would rather not have. We can use and strengthen this equanimity during outer conflict by investigating the different sides to a story, hearing all parties involved, and desiring to look for alternatives. In the *Vinaya*, texts on Buddhist discipline, at many instances where there is conflict among the monks, the first thing that is done is to hear the parties.[53] This helps get clear what are the different versions of the truth.

2.6 Non-violence

Although Indian philosophical and religious traditions have been a strong advocate of the non-violent way of solving conflict, there has also been awareness that in certain situations, the use of force or even violence was justified. In the *Bhagavad Gītā*, direct violence is justified when there is no way left open to restore righteousness.[54] Early Buddhism took a radical different position

---

[52] A focus on the process, on deeds, on acts, does not dismiss certain sensitivity to the reaction that this focus causes in others. Knowing how to express oneself and listening carefully (or 'deeply') are important instruments.

[53] The *Vinaya* also offers several practical rules on how to deal with litigations (*Vinaya Piṭaka* II.93-104). One source for these rules is the *sutta*s, for instance a passage of the *Sāmagāma sutta* (*Majjhima Nikāya* II.247-250). The seven ways of settling a dispute that are presented by the Buddha in this *sutta* are: reaching a consensus, majority voting, overlooking monastic offences which the person charged cannot remember committing, overlooking apparent offences committed when a person was out of his mind, setting aside an acknowledged offence with the promise not to repeat it, censure of a monk who at first denied an offence, 'covering up with grass.' Cf. Peter Harvey, *An Introduction to Buddhist Ethics: Foundations, Values and Issues* (Cambridge: Cambridge University Press, 2000), 248. This last way consists of the acknowledgement of any offences by a wise monk related to each of the disputing sides, and then letting the matter rest.

[54] K. N. Upadhyaya, "Early Buddhist Attitude to War and Peace," in Mun, *Buddhism and Peace: Theory and Practice*, 87.

from the contemporary dominant view and influential Indian works like the *Gītā*.[55] All forms of abuse, be it mental, verbal or physical, directed towards oneself or others, are defined in early Buddhist scriptures as possible examples of 'violence.'[56] Some regard the abstention of violence as a lofty ideal, as something for saints, an absolute standard impossible to adhere to and not a practical approach to conflict.[57] Deegalle reminds us that the original context for the often quoted *Dhammapada* verses on non-violence was very concrete indeed, being a dispute between monks over the construction and possession of material property.[58] But is it possible to always deal with conflict without causing harm? Isn't it impossible *not* to resort to the use of force in certain circumstances or positions which require 'peace-keeping'? There is an account of the Buddha thinking over the possibility of reigning without killing, conquering or grief.[59] Before he could come up with an answer, however, the 'tempter' Māra stopped by to persuade him into becoming a king himself. Because the Buddha was interrupted in his train of thought, it remains unclear whether he thought it was possible to rule without killing or grief. Some authors[60] indeed hold that early Buddhism considers a 'peace-loving defender' as moderately good. To these authors, the gap between early Buddhism and contemporary religious traditions was not that big on the stance of violence. Khantipalo Bhikkhu, a Theravādin monk, acknowledges that some people think that sometimes force or punishment is needed to have fools not do acts of violence.[61] In cases like these, forceful action is seen as an act of compassion. Khantipalo is sure that nowhere in 'the original collection of the Buddha's discourses' is such a doctrine included. According to

---

[55] *Ibid*, 85.

[56] Deegalle, ed., 3.

[57] See K. Kraft, ed., *Inner Peace, World Peace: Essays on Buddhism and Nonviolence* (New York: State University of New York Press, 1992), 5.

[58] Deegalle, ed., 5-6.

[59] *Mārasaṃyutta sutta, Saṃyutta Nikāya*, I.103-127.

[60] Upadhyaya, 94.

[61] Khantipalo, *Aggression, War, and Conflict: Three Essays* (Bodhi Leaves no. B 108 (Kandy: Buddhist Publication Society, 1986), 29-30.

Khantipalo, Dharma-practice does not recognize means that use violence from a compassionate motivation as *Dharma*-means: 'Means are important if ends are to be attained, but only *Dhamma*-means will lead to a *Dhamma*-end.' Perhaps Khantipalo is referring to the *sutta*s of the Tripiṭaka only, and does not take other Buddhist scriptures into account. Since, in the Mahāyāna traditions, the liberation of all sentient beings is the Dharma-end, intervening forcefully or even violently to protect beings from greater suffering or a prolonged stay in Saṃsāra, might well be called a dharma-means. A version of the Mahāyāna *Parinirvāṇa sūtra*, that was composed before the 5th century CE, even urges lay followers to protect 'true Buddhist teachings' with weapons if necessary.[62]

For early Buddhism, the motivation to avoid violence and to protect the lives of other beings derives from a fundamental conviction that all beings share a similar position with respect to their own lives.[63] All beings, to paraphrase the *Dhammapada*, tremble at violence and fear death.[64] Non-harmful conduct can be considered to be a necessary element on the way to liberation, both as three of the factors of the Noble Eightfold Path, as well as part of the (right) resolve to practise harmlessness.[65] Although space is lacking here to go into a definition of violence, I think that the ability to distinguish between conflict and violence supports a non-violent transformation of conflict. Unable to make that distinction, anyone striving for harmlessness is lured into thinking that conflict itself is harmful and violent. Thinking that it should be stopped immediately, we might lose any valuable information that aids the structural relief of conflict. Conflict is not violent per se. The way we deal with it might be. So, one application of non-violence during personal conflict is: try to slow down and let the conflict be. Ask others and yourself whether there is anything more that needs to be said or done. This way, you create the conditions for transformation, instead of solutions which support some apparent

---

[62] M. Zimmermann, "War," in Robert E. Buswell, Jr., ed., *Encyclopedia of Buddhism* (New York: Macmillian Reference, 2004), 894.

[63] Deegalle, ed., 5.

[64] *Dhammapada*, vv. 129-130.

[65] *Magga-vibhanga Sutta, Saṃyutta Nikāya*, V.9.

needs, but violate other, less obvious ones.

2.7 Skill in means

Bearing witness, acting compassionately, being mindful, listening or speaking rightly, aiming for non-violence all are suitable approaches that contribute to the recipe of peace. Without wisdom, applying (Buddhist) principles might lead to serious problems. Without wisdom, equanimity might lead one to condone domestic violence, or non-violence to destruction. So how do Buddhists determine when to use which tool? And what to do when circumstances require means that seem to oppose rules of conduct that Buddhists hold as important?

In the history of Buddhism, this discussion often centred around the topic of skilful means (Skt., *Upāya-kauśalya Sūtra*). 'Skilful means' or 'skill in means' came to the fore in exegesis and Buddhology. It was not a term or an issue that was prominent in early Buddhism,[66] although the logic behind the skill in means stories that we encounter in the Mahāyāna tradition, can be found in Theravāda-texts as well. In the first century CE, the idea that everybody could attain Buddhahood and the availability to all of the spiritual career of a bodhisattva started to evolve.[67] This greatly influenced the values that were considered central for Buddhists. Compassion (Pāli/Skt., *karuṇā*) became central from this time on. And so, with a compassionate motivation, a bodhisattva could choose means which in early Buddhism would certainly entail a breach of precepts. There was a shift in dominance from the principle of non-violence to that of compassion. Buddhists in the Mahāyāna traditions generally accept that certain beings can commit transgressions of certain modes of conduct that they consider ethical or skilful, because their intention is to benefit other sentient beings. Stewart MacFarlane sees the Buddha making promises which he has no intention of delivering, for the spiritual

---

[66] M. Tatz, trans., *Upāyakauśalya Sūtra: The Skill in Means Sūtra* (Delhi: Motilal Banarsidass, 1991), 10.

[67] Zimmermann, 894.

benefit of the persons involved.[68] He connects with the concerns at hand, and uses them as a spiritual springboard to a higher understanding and insight into the causes of suffering. An example of this is the case of a woman named Kisagotami, as narrated in a commentary to the Pāli *Therigāthā*.[69] She asks the Buddha for a medicine that will cure her son, who has recently died. The Buddha seems to agree to provide the medicine as he asks Kisagotami to bring him a handful of mustard-seed. When the girl is about to leave, the Buddha adds that the mustard-seed must be taken from a house where no one has lost a child, husband, parent, or friend. Kisagotami goes from house to house, only to find out that everywhere she goes, some beloved one had died. Tired and hopeless, Kisagotami sits down, watches the lights of the city which slowly extinguish during the night. It is likewise with the lives of all men, she discovers: they flicker up and are extinguished, death is common to all. Kisagotami eventually had the body of her dead son buried and took refuge in the Buddha and the Dharma. So here we see how the Buddha's approach is both practical (addressing the concerns of the person or parties who are engaged in conflict) and spiritual (opening up new insights).

The concept of 'skill in means' was also used to explain certain puzzling events in the Buddha's life, seeing them as means by which the Buddha taught. The *Upāya-kauśalya Sūtra*, of the early Mahāyāna school and probably dating from the first century BC, was composed to offer explanation for instances which were hard to understand.[70] How should one, for example, understand the fact that the one time Buddha had a thorn in his foot? People surrounding him wondered whether this was bad karma ripening, being some residue of unskilful past deeds? The Buddha then used the observation to make the point that there is no place where one can go to escape the effects of his deed. He tells his audience of a previous life, when he was captain of a ship.[71] This captain, who

---

[68] Stewart McFarlane, "Skilful Means, Moral Crises and Conflict Resolution," in Mun, *Buddhism and Peace*, 158-159.

[69] *Therigatha Atthakatha*, X.1.

[70] *Upāyakauśalya Sūtra*, 2.

[71] *Upāyakauśalya Sūtra*, 132-137.

some sources refer to as Captain Great Compassionate[72] and others as Captain Courage,[73] steers a ship manned by five hundred merchants. One of them, however, has planned to kill the merchants as soon as they have collected their possessions. The Captain is warned by the ocean's deities, who tell him in his dream of the plans of the man. The deities also paint the karmic consequences of such a deed for this person and they urge the captain to come up with skilful means to prevent the person from killing and thus perpetuating his own suffering from karmic consequences. The captain reflects upon this for seven days. Eventually he concludes that the only way to prevent a tremendous amount of suffering is by killing the man himself. He will bear the consequential pain from the hellish rebirths that killing a man may lead to. Twenty people in the city of Śrāvastī, upon hearing this story, abandoned plans of killing their enemies.[74] So the Buddha used skill in means to teach persons and inspired them *not* to kill.

Another important sūtra in the discussion on the use of violent means is the Sarvāstivāda *Mahāparinirvāṇa sūtra*.[75] The issue of skilful means is addressed at several points, to bridge the gap between early Buddhist principles and their seeming contradiction with ideas presented in this sūtra. In short, the Buddha uses skilful means to teach different people in different circumstances. The *sūtra* has been used repeatedly as a scriptural source for supporting the use of force in certain circumstances. The sūtra describes an episode in a previous life of the Buddha, where he killed several Brahmins who were about to slander Buddhism. By doing this, he saved them from the karmic consequences of such an act. The sūtra goes on to state that followers of the Mahāyāna should bear

---

[72] *Upāyakauśalya Sūtra*, 132.

[73] Thrangu, 85.

[74] *Upāyakauśalya Sūtra*, 138-145.

[75] It is a long text which exists in several versions of which it is not always clear how and when they originated. See Paul Williams, *Mahayana Buddhism: The Doctrinal Foundations* (London and New York: Routledge and Kegan Paul, 1989), 98. Together with the *Lotus Sūtra*, it has been tremendously important for many of the Eastern Buddhist traditions. This *sūtra* is not to be confused with a non-*Mahāyāna sutta* of the same name which can be found in the Pāli canon as the *Mahāparinibbāna Sutta* (*Dīgha Nikāya*, II 72-169, *sutta* XVI).

weapons and ignore their moral code if this is necessary to defend the Dharma.[76]

Skill in means enables Buddhas and bodhisattvas of a high stage (*mahāsattvas*) to act with compassionate motivation in a way that aids the permanent liberation of other sentient beings, even when it seems to go against the temporal relief of suffering. From stories like the one about Captain Courage, it seems evident that skill in means can even serve as a validation for violent actions to prevent wider violence. I want to point to two important caveats which greatly reduce the strength of an argument in favour of skilful use of violence. First of all, Mahāyāna texts which touch upon the subject of skilful means often describe cases and crises where drastic measures and extremely skilful means have to be employed. In these stories, there is almost always a real or potential conflict.[77] What becomes clear is that these are uncommon situations, and are ones which require measures which can only be judged correctly by one with great insight and a pure motivation. Stories about the Buddha in previous lifetimes often describe him as a bodhisattva. It is the bodhisattva's extensive knowledge which provides for the assurance that what is done is actually best in a certain situation.[78] One needs 'fundamental assumptions about the operation of karma, the acceptance of responsibility for actions, as well as the need for insight, understanding and compassion for those involved.'[79] Without sufficient wisdom and compassion, we try to provide help and later on regret that our 'help' turned out to be harmful.[80]

Besides a compassionate motivation, complete insight is a requisite for the skilful use of violence. Note, that in the story of captain Courage, it is not the captain who can read the intentions of the villain. The ocean's deities inform him. And even then, it is not immediately clear to the captain what he should do. He ponders over the issue for days. So penetrative insight, help and time are

---

[76] Williams, 161.
[77] McFarlane, 159-160.
[78] Tatz, trans., 6.
[79] McFarlane, 166.
[80] Thrangu, 90.

relevant factors in skilfully determining the appropriate means in a situation. Before one uses violence and inwardly or outwardly validates it by saying it is the skilful use of means, we have to look deeply inside and outside ourselves. We have to have penetrating insight in the causes and effects of those processes which surround us. Or we should have the ability to be guided by people with these qualities. Most people simply do not qualify. It is exactly for this reason that the Buddha cautions his audience in the end of the *Upāya-kauśalya Sūtra*, that the given explanation of skill in means is to be kept secret: Only a bodhisattva of a high level is 'a fit vessel' for this teaching. Common people have too little merit to be able to benefit from it.[81] For one who looks for ethics that are prescriptive and universal, not situational and dependent on the actor, this hierarchy in a moral or spiritual sense might be quite hard to deal with.

How is the discussion on the issue of skilful means related to attempts to resolve or transform conflict? First of all, skill in means can help understand, manage or even transform outer conflict constructively. Anyone who finds himself in a conflict, or is asked to help resolve it, benefits from investigating thoroughly. Only then can he try and translate his principles to this specific situation. Secondly, the ability to adapt to circumstances and to the character and capacity of the people involved, requires an absence of prejudice.[82] It takes great insight and the compassion of a bodhisattva to judge with certainty what means to happiness and salvation for those involved would fit a situation best. Thirdly, this implies that there is no ultimate or 'best' way to solve conflict. Skill in means enable one to adapt and creatively use the means at hand to benefit a constructive solution of conflict. And fourthly, forceful means to prevent or resolve outer conflict might be opted for, according to many Buddhists, in extreme situations. Until one is a bodhisattva of great capacities, however, it seems wise not to opt for it.

---

[81] *Upāyakauśalya Sūtra*, 174.
[82] Ikeda, 45.

3. Conclusion

From the Buddhist perspective, as long as ignorance reigns, it will cause greed and hatred, and these three will misguide people's intentions. Collisions of delusions and a continuation of misunderstanding will persist, leading to suffering on a daily basis. For Buddhists, inner conflict has its origin in a mind that is deluded. Some Buddhists would even state that outer conflict is nothing more than mind: the reality that we perceive as verbal disagreement or struggle between two persons, is not something that is 'out there.' The Noble Truths make clear that dealing with suffering in general, and conflict in particular, requires a multi-pronged approach. Buddhism, moreover, stresses the importance of transforming wisdom and experience into everyday conduct. A Buddhist approach to conflict therefore is both practical and spiritual. It addresses the needs involved, and also opens up new insights through self discipline, inner calm and cultivation of mindfulness and wisdom. I have suggested that these might be broken down into eight aspects: (1) a search for what is the truth that supports conflicting needs or parties; (2) the ability to have compassion, for (the needs of) oneself and others; (3) mindfulness of what is actually going on during conflict; (4) equanimity which supports even-mindedness and impartiality amidst the turbulence of conflicting needs and emotions; (5) the ability to communicate constructively by listening deeply and speaking constructively; (6) concentration and the ability to transform experiences into wisdom through meditation; (7) the intention not to harm others; and finally, (8) flexibility and creativity to adapt one's methods according to circumstances.

Spirituality can be a practical resource in handling problems. Most if not all of the skills just mentioned can be found in the methods of other religious and spiritual traditions, as well as in communication processes that have been developed recently. Someone who experiences conflict as a one-time event (even when it occurs repeatedly) might choose to focus on any of the presented tools. He might take the admonition to be flexible and creative in solving outer conflict, based upon his own abilities, without really caring for the happiness of others involved. Some Buddhists have facilitated this by translating the assumptions underlying these tools into concepts that seem to be universal and supported by modern science. For a Buddhist, this fits well into the bodhisattva-ideal of helping people become or remain free of suffering. 'Buddha nature,' a complex concept which most Mahāyāna Buddhists hold to be the potential of every being to become a Buddha, has been watered down to inherent goodness or a 'humanity' which we all share. Conditioned Arising is presented without its corollary that all phenomena lack inherent substance. There is a danger, however, that the coherence and motivation that underlie these tools are lost.

To me the power of ancient Asian thought, and in particular of the Buddhist traditions, lies in the fact that it points to our individual peace as the fundamental source for dealing skilfully with conflict. Neither this individual peace, nor the *elements* that make up the inner transformation that Buddhism professes as a requisite for peace, are 'Buddhist.' The Buddhist twist, I believe, is both in the way these skills are presented as a coherent whole, as well as in the assumptions or motivation underlying this coherence. Like a medicine that has a certain composition and a certain way of usage. The ingredients that make up a medicine to alleviate pain might be used in a different composition with a different effect. And the medicine itself, used with a different motivation, might even be an instrument to harm. Together, tools and motivation form a 'Buddhist' whole that can be truly called a way or a method: Without wisdom, a compassionate attitude might lead to condoning behaviour that is harmful. Equanimity without compassion might actually be indifference. The flexibility of a skill in choosing and using means without insight and compassion tends to trickery. For a Buddhist, understanding of and belief in the Buddhist teachings will likely help him see the coherence between the several tools of conflict transformation. It will help him gain a personal and experiential understanding of the Buddhist teachings, which goes beyond the ideas and insights that have been presented in this dissertation. A practice confined to meditation and retreat is bound to hamper the sense of connection needed to skilfully resolve conflict. Ending conflict is a road travelled with the body, our speech and our mind.

Bibliography

Bhikkhu Bodhi, trans. *The Connected Discourses of the Buddha.* 2 vols. Boston: Wisdom Publications, 2000.

Chappell, David, ed. *Buddhist Peacework: Creating Cultures of Peace.* Boston: Wisdom Publications, 1999.

Deegalle, Mahinda, ed. *Buddhism, Conflict and Violence in Modern Sri Lanka.* London and New York: Routledge, 2006.

Dhondup, T. "Buddhism and Conflict Resolution." In *The Times of Tibet.* January 20, 2005. Http://www.buddhistchannel.tv/index.php?id =8,667,0,0,1,0 *The Buddhist Channel,* May 31st 2007, http://www.buddhistchannel.tv/ > Opinion > Conflict and Buddhism.

Gethin, Rupert M. L. *The Buddhist Path to Awakening.* 2nd ed. 1992. Oxford: Oneworld, 2001.

Glassman, Bernie. *Bearing Witness: A Zen Master's Lessons in Making Peace.* New York: Bell Tower, 1988.

Griffiths, Paul J. *On Being Mindless: Buddhist Meditation and the Mind-Body Problem.* Delhi: Sri Satguru Publications, 1986.

Harvey, Peter. "The Buddhist Perspective on Respect for Persons." In *Buddhist Studies Review* 4.1 (1987): 31-46.

_____. *An Introduction to Buddhism: Teachings, History and Practices.* Cambridge: Cambridge University Press, 1990.

_____. "The Mind-Body Relationship in Pāli Buddhism: A Philosophical Investigation." In *Asian Philosophy,* 3.1 (1993): 29-41.

_____. *An Introduction to Buddhist Ethics: Foundations, Values and Issues.* Cambridge: Cambridge University Press, 2000.

Horner, I. B., trans. *The Book of the Discipline.* 6 vols. London: Luzac & Company, 1938-1966.

Ikeda, Daisaku. *For the Sake of Peace, Seven Paths to Global Harmony, A Buddhist Perspective.* Santa Monica: Middleway Press, 2001.

Khantipalo. *Aggression, War, and Conflict: Three Essays.* Bodhi Leaves no. B 108. Kandy, Sri Lanka: Buddhist Publication Society, 1986.

Kochumuttom, T. A. *A Buddhist Doctrine of Experience: A New Translation and Interpretation of the Works of Vasubandhu the Yogācārin.* Delhi: Motilal Banarsidas Publishers, 1982.

Kraft, K., ed. *Inner Peace, World Peace: Essays on Buddhism and Nonviolence.* New York: State University of New York Press, 1992.

McConnell, J. *Mindful Mediation: A Handbook for Buddhist Peacemakers.* Bangkok: Buddhist Research Institute, 1995. [I made use of the draft that was provided to me by Dr. McConnell: "Mediation and the

Dhamma – A Handbook for Buddhist Peace-Makers" (June 1994).
References are, as Mr. McConnell requested, made to this draft].

Mun, Chanju and Ronald S. Green, eds. *Buddhist Exploration of Peace and Justice*. Honolulu: Blue Pine, 2006.

Mun, Chanju, ed. *Buddhism and Peace: Theory and Practice*. Honolulu: Blue Pine, 2006.

Piyadassi Thera. *The Buddha's Ancient Path*. Kandy, Sri Lanka: Buddhist Publication Society, 1974.

Senauke, H. A. "Cultivating Peace, Dismantling War: Inner and Outer Disarmament."
http://www.bpf.org/html/whats_now/2005/disarmament.html, The *Buddhist Peace Fellowship*, May 31st 2007, www.bpf.org > Resource Center > Essays & Reflections > February 2005: Cultivating Peace, Dismantling War: Inner and Outer Disarmament.

Tatz, Mark, trans. *Upāyakauśalya Sūtra: The Skill in Means Sūtra*. Delhi: Motilal Banarsidass Publishers, 1991.

Thrangu, K. *The Tibetan Vinaya: A Guide to Buddhist Conduct*. Trans. Sonam Palden and Chojor Radha. Bibliotheca Indo-Buddhica Series # 188. Delhi: Sri Satguru Publications, 1998.

Walshe, Maurice, trans. *The Long Discourses of the Buddha: A translation of the Dīgha Nikāya*. Boston: Wisdom Publications, 1995.

Williams, Paul. *Mahayana Buddhism: The Doctrinal Foundations*. London and New York: Routledge and Kegan Paul, 1989.

Primary sources

Austin, Jack, trans. *The Dhammapada from the Khuddaka Nikāya of the Sutta Piṭaka*. 1945. 6th ed. London: The Buddhist Society, 1988. Reference is to verse number.

Bhikkhu Ñāṇamoli and Bhikkhu Bodhi, trans. *The Middle Length Discourses of the Buddha*. Boston: Wisdom Publications, 1995. Reference is to the volume and page number of the Pāli Text Society edition of the *Majjhima Nikāya*. "M.I.109-114" refers to volume I, pages 109-114. These can be found as i.109-114 at the top of the pages in Ñāṇamoli and Bodhi's translation.

Bhikkhu Bodhi, trans. *The Connected Discourses of the Buddha*. 2 vols. Boston: Wisdom Publications, 2000. Reference is to the book (*vagga*) or part of the volume of the *Saṃyutta Nikāya* and page number of the Pāli Text Society edition of the *Majjhima Nikāya*. "S.I.103-127" refers to book I, pages 103-127. The page number can found in square brackets in the texts of Bodhi's translation.

Walshe, Maurice, trans. *The Long Discourses of the Buddha*. Boston: Wisdom Publications, 1995. Reference is to the volume and page number of the Pāli Text Society edition of the *Dīgha Nikāya*. "D.II.58-60" refers to volume II, pages 58-60. These can be found as ii.58-60 at the top of the pages in Walshe's translation.

Thanissaro Bhikkhu, trans. *Sutta-nipāta*. Access to Insight Website. http://www.accesstoinsight.org/tipitaka/kn/snp. Reference is to verse number.

Olendzki, trans. *Therigatha Atthakatha*. 2005. Access to Insight Website. http://www.accestoinsight.org/index > Tipitaka > Therigatha (accessed May 31, 2007).

Tatz, Mark, trans. *The Skill in Means Sūtra*. Delhi: Motilal Banarsidass Publishers, 1991. Reference is to the page number in Tatz' translation.

Shih, Heng-ching, trans. *The Sūtra on Upāsaka Precepts*. Berkeley: Numata Center for Buddhist Translation and Research, Bukkyō Dendō Kyōkai, 1994. This is a translation from T.24.1488.1034a-1075b. References are to page number in Shih's translation.

Horner, I. B., trans. *The Book of the Discipline*. 6 vols. London: Luzac & Company, 1938-1966. Vols. I-III are translations of *Vin*. III and IV, vols. IV and V are translations of *Vin*. I and II. "*Vin*.II.93" refers to volume II and page 93 of the Pāli Text Society edition, to be found in part V of Horner's *The Book of the Discipline*.

HOW FAITH INSPIRED THE SAVE THE BELL MOVEMENT:

An historic chapter in the life of the Venerable Dharma master Daigyōin, demonstrating his philosophy of peace and his efforts to try to bring about peace in this world.

Compiled by the Shōgyōji Archives Committee[1]

Introduction

When a person stands on the verge of a spiritual breakthrough, there is no need for them to answer to anyone as to who one is or what one knows. All that matters is how to break free from this state of suffering in which one has long been imprisoned. It is only when one arrives at this critical impasse wherein one turns at last to take refuge in the Three Treasures that a true resolution comes about. In more familiar terms the

---

[1] The present text was originally compiled by Reverends Shinohara Kōjun and Senō Eshū, of the Shōgyōji Archives, Shōgyōji Temple, Fukuoka, Japan, under the editorial supervision of the Venerable Reverend Takehara Chimyō; English translation and annotation were carried out by W. S. Yokoyama, of Kyoto, in collaboration with Reverend Satō Kemmyō Taira, of the London Shōgyōji branch. The text has greatly benefited from the extensive critical editing by Mrs. Dilly Suzuma of London.

Three Treasures of Buddha, Dharma, and Saṅgha are, respectively, (1) the excellent person of ideal qualities who is awakened to the truth, (2) the teaching of the truth that veritably speaks to us, and (3) the community of seekers who have awakened to that truth. Thus, those who have turned to take refuge in the Three Treasures are the ones who have crossed the threshold of salvation and realized what it truly means to be saved. Today, as wars continue to rage, there is little sign that the forces of world conflict threatening to destroy such Treasures will ever abate.

During World War II, the Buddhist community in Japan was forced to stand helplessly by as many of their irreplaceable temple treasures, which should be regarded as items belonging to the Three Treasures estate, were put in jeopardy and in fact ran the risk of being lost forever. Although our own temple was ordered by the military government to hand over our historic temple bell to the drive to assemble scrap metal, one lone monk had the courage to step forward and engage in a long and bitter struggle to protect that precious bell through a faith-inspired campaign that claimed it as the heritage of our Saṅgha. Nor was the scope of his monk's campaign restricted to preserving this treasured bell for our postwar Saṅgha alone. His struggle, rather, was a continuation of his lifelong efforts to create a living Saṅgha community that was culturally rich in such items of Three Treasures estate. The name of that Dharma master was the Venerable Daigyōin, also known as Reverend Takehara Reion.

The Venerable Daigyōin was born at Shōgyōji in Fukuoka prefecture on December 24, 1876 and lived to the advanced age of seventy-five, his long career coming full circle with his death at the same temple on November 12, 1951. Daigyōin was a priest of the Jōdo Shinshū School, a form of lay Buddhism established some eight hundred years ago by Shinran Shōnin (1173–1262). Known as Jōdo shinshū, or Shin Buddhism, it is now the largest school of Japanese Buddhism, comprising some twenty-thousand traditional branch temples and a combined congregation estimated modestly to be upward of one million members. The Venerable Daigyōin Reion was the thirteenth head priest of

Shōgyōji, a temple established over four hundred years ago on the outskirts of Hakata, in northern Kyushu.

Our temple, Shōgyōji, built in the medieval period during a time of civil war, was founded by the sixteenth century Dharma master Ryōen, originally hailing from the *bushi*, or warrior class, attached to the powerful Asō clan that in those days ruled the Asō district of Kyushu.[2] Ryōen was forced to stand by and watch as the Shimazu clan, the rulers of southern Kyushu, attacked the Asō clan and brought them to ruin. As a liege of the defeated Asō clan, Ryōen fled northwards, at which time he must have acutely felt the impermanence of this world. By chance he met the twelfth Honganji leader, Kyōnyo Shōnin (1558–1614), who happened to be touring the area, delivering sermons. Ryōen pledged allegiance to the Honganji and was ordained into its priesthood.

With the support of a devoted follower, who was a lord of the Ōga family,[3] Ryōen built a hermitage, or small temple, in Chikushino on the site of modern day Shōgyōji. Ten years after he became a monk, Ryōen's hermitage came into its own as a full-fledged temple when the main Honganji temple bestowed upon it an official temple name and furnished it with the requisite Buddha statue carved of wood.[4] Just the previous year, in 1592, Hideyoshi Toyotomi dispatched his first wave of troops to Joseon Korea (the so-called Bunroku no eki, Imjin Waeran) and then five years later, in 1597, a second wave that invaded the whole peninsula (Keicho no eki, Jeong'yu Waeran). Thus, when we look at the background to our founding master Ryōen, it is

---

[2] Next to the Imperial lineage and the Izumo Sen family, the Asō family of Kyushu is one of the oldest traditional clans in Japan. Since the Sengoku period, they have served as the head of the Shinto shrines in Asō, the present day head being the ninety-first descendant of the line.

[3] The Ōga family continues to be supporters of Shōgyōji, with the oldest member currently serving as one of the most responsible trustees of the temple today.

[4] Shōgyōji was at one time affiliated with the Shinshū Ōtani-ha (Higashi Honganji) denomination. Nowadays it has independent status but still enjoys cordial relations with the Tokyo Honganji, successors to Shinran Shōnin's blood line.

evident that such continuous war-related affairs must have swayed his decision to enter the Buddhist order. Nor can we deny the impact that such events in the modern era must have had on the Venerable Daigyōin as he set out to formulate his own philosophy of peace.

In the modern age, along with the tremendous progress in scientific technology, we have witnessed a quantum leap in the massive killing power of weapons and an unrelenting rise in the overall scale of warfare. The First and Second World Wars resulted in the deaths of ten million and thirty million people, respectively. In imperial Japan, the only country to suffer atomic bombing, at Hiroshima and Nagasaki some one hundred and twenty thousand lives were incinerated in the blink of an eye.

After her defeat, Japan was obliged to declare in her Constitution a wish for everlasting peace with the words, "We desire to occupy an honored place in an international society, striving for the preservation of peace and the banishment of tyranny and slavery, oppression and intolerance for all time from the earth." Recognizing the equal rights of all peoples to live in peace, Article 9 of the Japanese Constitution further states that "We recognize that all peoples of the world have the right to live in peace, free from fear and want." These points are reiterated in further articles of the Japanese Constitution expressing the noble ideals that Japan shall forever abandon war, shall not maintain armed forces, and shall reject the right to wage war.

Awakening of Faith

The inspiration for the Buddhist path of peace that the Venerable Daigyōin walked during his long life of seventy-five years came from his own personal awakening of Faith that took place a full century ago in April 1907. As he relates in his *Record of My Awakening of Faith* (*Nyūshinroku*), once he noticed a young nobleman, who was a priest ordained to the traditional Higashi Honganji order, standing on the brink of moral ruin. During this period, he did his best to go to that young man's aid, and apart from that, even helped spur a religious revival amongst the general populace. Nevertheless, in the midst of striving to resolve these problems, he came to suddenly realize the futility of such altruist efforts on his part, or what Shin Buddhists call *jiriki*, literally, "self power." At length he found himself impelled to renounce forever the idea he could change anyone by applying any such external means.

Hard upon the heels of that realization, the Venerable Daigyōin had to confront what was for him the vexing problem of taking a wife. He reckoned that anyone who married him, given his role as Buddhist priest and spokesman, would have to go through hell and high water at his side, and so for his own purposes he wanted someone well able to endure whatever hardships they might encounter together. Yet how utterly false this line of reasoning was, was revealed to him by the light of the Tathāgata, which purged him of his self-centeredness and showed him how caught up he was with thinking only in terms of himself alone. The religious convictions he had held up to then were completely overturned and he found himself swept up and emptied of this false way of being. It was as if the voice of the Tathāgata spoke to him, saying, "Come what may, I will take upon myself all your burdens and shoulder them on your behalf." Interestingly, a similar episode is known to have occurred with Shinran Shōnin, the Shin Buddhist founder, who, when faced with the decision whether to marry or not, was overjoyed to hear a voice in a dream vision assure him that it was the right thing for him to do. Thus, in the same year as his religious awakening, the Venerable Daigyōin was also able to cross the threshold of married life.

In *Record of My Awakening of Faith* (*Nyūshinroku*), the Venerable Daigyōin expresses the deep joy he felt upon reading a passage from the Buddha's sermon in the *Larger Sūtra of Eternal Life* that goes, "There are sentient beings who, having encountered this Light, find that their three defilements have simply vanished and their bodies and minds have now become soft and supple. They dance for joy as they discover to their intense surprise that a warm heart has been awakened within them. When those caught up in the suffering of the three mires behold this radiant Light, they will all of them recover from their misery and never have to endure such anguish again. After their lives come to an end, all of them will don the cloak of liberation" (*Larger Sūtra of Eternal Life*, Scroll One). For the Venerable Daigyōin this passage perfectly expressed the brilliant expanse of living faith that now cradled him, body and soul, in her ocean-like embrace.

While still on the subject of peace, it should be noted that Buddhism, in order to spread its message, has never once resorted to arms. Let us now look at some of the several ways in which peace has been defined: "the state of no war," "the state of non-aggression towards neighboring countries," "the absence of civil war," "the state of no conflict between a State and its citizens." In each case, peace is defined negatively as "a state of no war." It is rare indeed to come across a positive definition of peace as comprising a specific kind of state. Such nostalgia for a war-free state or for the construction of a war-free world should remind us in what high esteem humanity holds these ideals and how universal they actually are. Ever since the beginning of recorded history, however, an errant mankind has demonstrated time and again it has learned nothing from its deplorable tendency to engage in war. Buddhist teachings point out that as long as we let our self-view, self-delusion, self-conceit, and self-love persist, our personal interests are bound to come into conflict with those of others, compelling us to engage in endless conflict.

Thus, it is not until each and every one of us achieves Inner Peace or tranquility of being, known in Buddhism as Nirvāṇa, that can we hope to be released from the vexing forms of karmic suffering that torment us at every turn. When every individual attains for themselves, a state of Inner Peace, it will be reflected in the peace of the State, the peace of the people, and ultimately, the peace of the world; other than that there can be no real way to achieve World Peace. This is why His Holiness the Dalai Lama has constantly been referring to Inner Peace as the wellspring of World Peace. Such a state of inner tranquility has been clearly exemplified by numerous Buddhist figures, as well as by countless leading individuals and their likeminded followers. What we ourselves should be thinking about today is finding the way for each of us to achieve that state of peace within, or Inner Peace, that leads to World Peace.

With this in mind, let us take a brief look at the way devised and tested by the Venerable Daigyōin, retracing the steps he took at various points in his career.

Petition to save the temple bell

The most potent symbol of how our Master, the Venerable Daigyōin, set about putting into practice his prayer for World Peace was the Save the Bell movement initiated by him in 1943, when the world was in the throes of World War II. By 1943, the situation of the Japanese Army on the battlefield was rapidly deteriorating and it was abundantly clear that Japan itself was on the road to defeat. On February 1st, the Japanese Army began its retreat from Guadalcanal; on April 18th, Admiral Yamamoto Isoroku, Commander in Chief of the Japanese fleet, was killed; and on May 30th, the Japanese garrison on Attu Island, in the Aleutians, was completely destroyed. It was against this somber background that the Venerable Daigyōin, in his mission to restore peace in our hearts, implemented the Save the Bell movement. In the following, we will attempt to give an outline of the key Buddhist activities undertaken by him in his campaign to bring about peace.

In May 1942, with the rapid depletion of strategic materials and arms, the country found itself so lacking in scrap metal that the Government was at last forced to turn to the public sector for further supplies, issuing what came to be known as the Metal Collection Directive. All over the country temples were forced to hand over any Buddhist items that were made out of metal such as statues and bells. The Administrative Headquarters of the Shinshū Ōtaniha (Higashi Honganji) denomination, to which Shōgyōji was at that time affiliated, sent word that July to all its temple branches that it would be conducting a special drive to collect all such metal, and in September again initiated a further campaign to step-up scrap metal donation. By September 1943, the Higashi Honganji Headquarters had managed to accumulate ten and a half tons of so-called scrap metal, including amongst these other treasures its own bells and the bronze base of the lotus fountain from in front of its very gates.

As one of the Honganji branch temples, our Shōgyōji, too, received a directive regarding scrap metal collection from the local administrative office of the main temple in June 1942. Given the situation, there appeared to be no alternative but to hand over the temple bell and other Buddhist artifacts, since turning one's back on a government edict would have been tantamount to refusing to obey the Emperor's orders, and, in religious circles at least, to be labeled unpatriotic traitors would have amounted to the temple faithful digging their own graves.

The Venerable Daigyōin, however, spurning the abuse of those around him, urged people instead to assume the standpoint of *monpō*, or Dharma listening, and "to nurture the Buddha-dharma in their hearts." In time he was able to gather together a loyal circle of likeminded followers, with whom he solemnly initiated a movement to petition the government to please not requisition their bell.

It should be particularly noted that the fundamental purpose of this movement was not to absolutely oppose the drive to collect scrap metal, but rather to submit with all deference a petition for our bell to be exempted. There was never any intention of opposing the militarists in control of the government; rather, as was firmly proclaimed to one and all, this was a religiously inspired movement on behalf of the Shōgyōji Saṅgha, that sought to obtain exemption from the round up of scrap metal for the temple's beloved bell and other Buddhist treasures, which were originally intended for the peaceful alleviation of suffering. Japan at that time was engaged in what had by now escalated into a war against other nations on a worldwide scale. At the very heart of that conflict, and with no signs of stopping or abating, was Japan's own voracious self-infatuation, that is her adoration of self as a centre of power. This is what Shin Buddhists term *jiriki*, or "self-power." The essential core of the

Venerable Daigyōin's Dharma movement was the desire to overcome our destructive attachment to such "self-power."

In the course of the eleven-year period between 1938 and 1948, the Venerable Daigyōin wrote out Dharma messages one by one on hundreds of sheets of plain Japanese paper, distributing them to all his loyal followers. These essays were later compiled into his *One-page Dharma Message* (*Ichimai hōgo*). In one of these, he writes: "For the past three hundred and fifty years, this bell has been tolling, filling the temple precincts with its resonance: you must listen to the voice of that bell! The Bell is saying: *From ancient times right down to the present day not one single person has ever really listened to me. I might as well go off with the army, let them drag me away!* These are the words I hear the bell saying and they are perfectly justified. Even if we are doomed to let the bell go, if we hand her over first without listening to her voice, no matter whether we are traditional temple members (benefactors) or the head priest (the petitioner) in person, no words of apology can ever suffice. I am left speechless to think there is nothing I can do to save that bell from the scrap heap; that is indeed a bitter cup to drain. Never did I dream it would come to this." (Shōgyōji Archives, ed., *Ichimai hōgo: Daigyōin goroku* (*One-page Dharma Message: A Record of the Words of the Venerable Daigyōin*), § 158; official edition; to be published).

From this Dharma message, we can see the basic stance taken on religious grounds by the Venerable Daigyōin towards the scrap metal drive: a Buddhist temple bell and other such treasures are precious tools for peace, meant to rid the nation's people of their blind passions and to treat the delusions enshrouding their hearts. Never should such tools of peace be allowed to be melted down and transformed into weapons of war and mass destruction.

Being forced to hand over the Shōgyōji temple bell on government orders was a situation that left him speechless. As head priest of Shōgyōji, his being asked to part with that bell was as painful to him as having to cut off his own arm. Nor was there anything he could say to his followers by way of apology,

especially not to the temple's chief benefactor, a descendant of
the Ōga clan that had helped to establish the original Shōgyōji.

In another essay (*One-page Dharma Message* (*Ichimai hōgo*),
§ 24; adapted), the Venerable Daigyōin writes, in effect, "If the
temple bell were the private property of the temple complex, then
handing her over to the authorities would be less of a problem.
But everything, from the temple precincts themselves with their
buildings and equipment right down to the Buddhist artifacts and
temple bell, belong to the Buddha. As devotees on the path of the
nembutsu, we must realize that nothing of what we are being
asked to hand over to the government is originally ours. Now at
long last we are getting down to the fundamental practice of the
Buddha-dharma. At this point let us hand over to the Buddha the
very possessions we treasure most: our body, our life, our
property." The fact that Daigyōin had dedicated his entire being
to Buddha, Dharma, and Saṅgha enabled him to become now a
spokesman for the great Dharma of the Tathāgata, summoning
one and all to action. Thus the senseless demand of the
government scrap metal collection directive was reinterpreted by
the Venerable Daigyōin as the great command of the Tathāgata
for him, Daigyōin Reion, to muster his courage and take a stand.

In the course of the three hundred and fifty years since
Shōgyōji was first established, there had been many a follower
who had heard the sound of the bell pealing out in every
direction, but there had been none who had listened to the bell's
voice speaking to them from her basic source: the soundless
sound from which her voice drew being. The source of the bell's
voice was the voice of Amida Tathāgata's Great Compassion,
calling to us from the Pure Land. But nobody up till then had
listened to her voice in quite that way, and so, until such time as
people should hear the bell and come forth to encounter the Great
Compassion, the Venerable Daigyōin could not resign himself to
letting her simply be tossed on the scrap heap.[5]

---

[5] Regarding the voice of the bell, in another entry the Venerable Daigyōin
writes, "The reason I had hoped to keep the bell around was because our
followers are sometimes like people without eyes or ears who can neither see
nor hear religious faith. All I was plotting to do was to get them to encounter

The result was that a core group of Shōgyōji members who supported the Venerable Daigyōin's spiritual convictions gathered round him. Though they were well aware of the risk they were running by taking what appeared to be a stand against government policy, they succeeded in initiating a petition to save the bell. One representative of the traditional temple members actually took the petition to his hometown of Futsukaichi where, by circulating it among the citizens, he was able to rally support and gain considerable sympathy for the Venerable Daigyōin's views. Had everyone who was involved, from the contributors, to the government authorities and collectors, all shared a consistent understanding of the Buddhist teachings, there would have been little need to oppose the scrap metal collection so vigorously, but unfortunately this was not the case. As it gained momentum, the petition movement had members scurrying in every direction in search of support. A record of what the petition movement entailed can be gleaned from the following items that appeared in the Shōgyōji in-house publication *All That Has Been Done For Us* (*Go-On*).

1. The work of producing the Save the Bell petition (*Bonsho kyoshutsu horyū tangan shō* [A request to exempt the temple bell from the scrap metal collection], dated December 21st, 1942) in the Shōgyōji magazine *All That Has Been Done For Us* (*Go-On*), No. 163 (1968)). In those days, famous antique bells of aesthetic or artistic value fell into the category of cultural assets worthy of preservation, hence it was standard government policy at the time to exclude such temple bells from being requisitioned as scrap metal. Knowing this, Daigyōin arranged to have an enlightened woman disciple of his, named Nonaka Ekaini (1899–1998), draw up the Save the Bell petition with the help of a number of other followers, subsequent to which the work of circulating the petition began in earnest.[6] Part of that petition

---

religious faith [through the voice of the Bell]" (*One-page Dharma Message* (*Ichimai hōgo*) 68).

[6] Ekaini, the first disciple of the Venerable Daigyōin, had her spiritual awakening in 1925. During the Venerable Daigyōin's lifetime, she was a

reads: "More than National Treasures sequestered for their meritorious value in days gone by, more than bells that have long fallen silent, set aside from ancient times on account of their craftsmanship, the Temple Bell of Shōgyōji plays a role in the veneration of the spirits of our ancestors and in continuously opening up the spiritual hearts of those of us who are their children. Along with our honored head priest (the Venerable Daigyōin), who has appeared to us in the present global confusion as a universal savior, that Bell is our Living National Treasure, one that we cannot live without at this desperate point in time" (*Bonsho kyoshutsu horyū tangan shō*, extract).

2. In October 1942, Ekaini called upon the Manager of Shrines & Temples and the Manager of the Conscription Section at Fukuoka Prefectural Government headquarters to plead against the compulsory handing over of the temple bell.

3. Around the same time, to ascertain whether it might be possible to refuse to surrender the temple bell, Ekaini took the petition to Hikata Ryūshō (1892–1991), professor of Kyushu University, who was one of the editors of the Taishō Buddhist Tripiṭaka as well as a member of the Fukuoka Prefecture Cultural Assets Survey Committee.

4. In April 1943, Ekaini went up to Kyoto to plead her case before the Minister of Agriculture and Forestry, Yamazaki Tatsunosuke, who also came from Kyushu.

Immediately after that, Ekaini all on her own went to visit the nationalist activist Tōyama Mitsuru (1855–1944), a man who wielded great power in the world of Japanese politics.

---

capable Dharma worker to whom he entrusted many of his projects. In the postwar era, after his death, it was to her that the task of editing his published works befell. She also played an important role as Dharma mother, nurturing new members of the Saṅgha. Further information on her life and work can be gleaned from *The Wheel of Light Knows No Limits* (*Kōrin kiwanaku*) that contains her writings as well as a chronology of her life, compiled by Shōgyōji, and published in 2007.

Journeying all the way to Nagano prefecture, she related to him
the spiritual understanding of the matter she had received from
the Venerable Daigyōin, taking several hours of his time to
explain their quest to preserve the temple bell. Tōyama was
moved by her single-minded devotion and there and then
approved a stay of execution that was sent to Fukuoka
Prefectural Government headquarters and Fukuoka City Hall.

In addition, Ekaini called upon the Administrative Chief of
the Shinshū Ōtani-ha (Higashi Honganji) Headquarters, a large
number of notable Shin Buddhist scholars, the manager in charge
of scrap metal collection at Fukuoka Prefectural Government
Headquarters, members of the Diet, the chief secretary of one of
the political parties, members of the prefectural assembly and the
mayor of Futsukaichi-chō, as well as various other individuals.
Nor did Ekaini merely plead her case. Instead she presented each
one of them with her vivid understanding of the Venerable
Daigyōin's religious convictions in such a way that every visit
became an occasion for serious discussion of the problem.

On the occasion of her meeting with the Administrative
Chief of the Higashi Honganji Headquarters, Ekaini leveled a
sharp criticism, declaring, "The Honzan Headquarters should be
the gathering place of our school's most prominent intellectuals.
For them to be among the first to contribute the metal items in
their Buddhist repository to the drive for scrap metal is not in
accord with the spiritual faith of our founder, Shinran Shōnin.
Especially at times like these, we need to strive to live up to our
ideals, to guide our community beyond the demands of State, and
to bring to fruition our religious teaching. Is this not the mission
sent down to us from the great citadel of Dharma?"[7]

---

[7] Ekaini was sharply critical in her remarks on more than one occasion
during the war years; see *All That Has Been Done For Us* (*Go-On*), no. 163
(1968): 9, and *The Wheel of Light Knows No Limits* (*Kōrin kiwanaku*) Vol. 3, §
46. On one occasion leading Shin Buddhist scholar Kaneko Daiei (1881-1976)
was present (see *The Wheel of Light Knows No Limits* (*Kōrin kiwanaku*) Vol. 2,
§ 41). Though he felt obliged to cooperate with the military government during
wartime, Professor Kaneko was also a man of deep faith and was no doubt

But on May 18, 1943, despite all the desperate efforts of the followers to promote the movement, an altogether unexpected event befell Shōgyōji, as related in *A Short Biography of the Venerable Daigyōin (Daigyōin shōden)*.

Stirred up by state-sponsored wartime fervor, a band of some thirty vigilantes from Futsukaichi, led by former servicemen, suddenly stormed into Shōgyōji and began to forcibly make off with the temple bell.[8] Even though the people inside the temple pleaded with them, saying, "We have filed a petition with the prefectural office to allow us to keep the bell, please give us more time," it was to no avail. The leaders of the young patriots argued, "After all, if one temple were allowed to keep its bell, then other temples might follow suit, and this could undermine the whole war effort. Shōgyōji would be branded a community of unpatriotic citizens who had refused to cooperate." There was no knowing what that hot-blooded group of vigilantes might have got up to next, rather like those terrible bands of armed monks from Mount Hiei in the olden days who violently attacked the temples of other sects.

The sounds of a scuffle filled the temple precincts, and as urgent word reached Daigyōin's disciple Ekaini, she rushed out without thought for her own safety and placed herself squarely in the path of the departing bell. Barefoot, having had no time to put on her shoes, there she stood, hands raised to block the group's progress, saying," You menfolk, have you never heard the teaching of the Buddhist prince Shōtoku Taishi? He says that a premium should be placed on harmony, and that it is absolutely crucial you revere the Three Treasures!"

Struck by Ekaini's compelling words, the vigilante band stopped in their tracks and set down the bell. The Venerable Daigyōin then calmly spoke with the leaders of the band,

---

moved when he heard her declare that cooperating with the government in this way was not in the spirit of Shinran Shōnin's teaching.

[8] The young patriots who came to remove the bell by force were members of the Auxiliary Youth Movement (*Yokusan sonen dan*), an organization initiated by former war veterans that formed part of a nationwide network and permeated every town and village throughout Japan.

explaining to them how inappropriate it was to fashion weapons of war out of Buddhist instruments of peace. At length, with the fight gone out of them, the men reluctantly withdrew from the scene, flustered and angry.

Seeing how selflessly Ekaini had acted, the Venerable Daigyōin shed tears of joy, praising her with the words, "To respond as you did, with all your heart, that is something that happens only when a person puts all other practices aside and turns solely to the *nembutsu* in which they entrust themselves absolutely to Amida (Skt., Amitāyus or Amitābha) Buddha. You are like our temple bell come alive!" By calling her the living embodiment of their temple bell, the Venerable Daigyōin was in effect saying that, as a person who truly lived Buddhism, Ekaini was just as important as the bell itself. Indeed in the postwar era she went on to become one of the great spiritual pillars of the Shōgyōji Saṅgha community.

Nevertheless, the whole event was a matter of great concern to Daigyōin, for he recalled how in the Kamakura period, during the Jōgen Dharma persecution of 1207, a number of Pure Land monks had been executed for no reason. It occurred to him that Ekaini, by her actions, might have crossed that same line and thus put her life in jeopardy. Knowing how in history things are all karmically linked, he now noticed how a single thread of karmic coincidence connected the government authorities, the metal collectors, and Shōgyōji itself, and realized that the time had now come to hand over the bell.

One day, about six months later, in the wake of a solemn ceremony of sūtra chanting that took place in front of the temple bell placed in the main hall, the Venerable Daigyōin delivered a sermon that touched even the hearts of that band of vigilantes. Then, as members of the community repeated the *nembutsu* with palms together in *gasshō*, it was time to bid a fond and tearful farewell to the Bell as she quietly disappeared through the temple gates forever.

The central committee could see how much losing the bell grieved the Venerable Daigyōin and so, rather than give up hope entirely, they set out some time later to try and track the bell down. They finally managed to catch up with her at the Japan Mining Industry Saganoseki Smelter and Refinery. Informing the manager of their deep concerns on religious grounds, they discovered that he too was a Shin Buddhist follower who hailed from Echigo (present day Niigata prefecture). Ekaini and the others found the manager extremely sympathetic to their cause and the night before the temple bell was to be melted down he secretly arranged for the dragon-head crown (where the life of the bell is said to reside) to be cut off and delivered back to Shōgyōji. To this day in the sūtra repository of Shōgyōji the dragon-head crown remains safely preserved, a temple treasure testifying to the peace movement first set in motion by the Venerable Daigyōin.

Reverence for the Buddhist prince Shōtoku Taishi

The Venerable Daigyōin sought to establish a source of peace for the entire world. In the midst of World War II, he deeply lamented the global situation and is reported as saying, "The last thing we should be doing is waging war against those very countries to whom we are most indebted, particularly China and Korea with whom we have a long history of cultural exchange, including the transmission of the kanji writing system and the whole Confucian tradition. It is the height of arrogance on our part." Pointing out Japan's responsibility for her actions, he also stated, "The Second World War is one that Japan started, and as such, it must be one that she has to settle by herself" (*One-page Dharma Message* (*Ichimai hōgo*), 920; paraphrase). In the same entry he writes, "The means to bring an end to this world war is to be found in the battle of the holy *inner* war"; that is, it lies in the struggle for the Buddha-dharma or, more precisely, the inner struggle to establish the Three Treasures. In the case of Shōgyōji Temple, this struggle can be traced back to the establishment of the temple some four hundred years ago, and in the case of the Japanese state, to the era of the Buddhist prince Shōtoku Taishi, who drew up the first Japanese Constitution, about one thousand four hundred years ago.

We shall recall how Prince Shōtoku, at a time when the Japanese state had yet to achieve stability, laid down his Seventeen Article Constitution as the bedrock of the Yamato Imperial Court. The first article of the Constitution reads, "We shall value harmony above all else," and the pathway to realizing that ideal is indicated by him in the second article, "We shall hold the Three Treasures in the highest respect." Nor was Prince Shōtoku content with merely making such a declaration to his people. In 596, he himself engaged as his own personal teachers the Buddhist high priests Hyeja and Hyechong, from Goguryeo and Baekje, who had come over to Japan and, while learning from them the finer points of Buddhist doctrine, he also wrote a work that was later celebrated even in China called the *Three Sūtra Commentary* (*Sangyō gisho*), a set of three studies in praise of the *Vimalakīrti* (*Yuimakyō*), *Lotus* (*Hokkekyō*), and *Śrīmālādevī* (*Shōmangyō*) Sūtras.

The Venerable Daigyōin's reverence for Prince Shōtoku was above all inspired by the way that, in the midst of a life-and-death struggle for imperial power, Prince Shōtoku had sat in meditation in the Yumedono, internalizing the conflict as his own problem and seeking a resolution through inner religious struggle. Realizing that there was a connection between experiencing this terrible world war and being born in the present age of the Last Dharma (*mappō*), the Venerable Daigyōin felt that it was up to him to bring this war to a close by taking up the spiritual legacy of Prince Shōtoku Taishi. He paid reverence to the statue of Prince Shōtoku Taishi morning and evening and, taking Prince Shōtoku Taishi's own thoughts as a starting point, came to the conclusion that to achieve peace in the outside world, one first needed to realize a state of Inner Peace.

Inner Peace can only be found in the world of Awakening, the Buddha world. Recognizing this, the Venerable Daigyōin tells us that the source of Inner Peace is "what we build within ourselves and what we build within ourselves is an eternal, unchanging, and everlasting temple where peace can at last prevail" (*One-page Dharma Message* (*Ichimai hōgo*), § 37; paraphrase). This state of inner calm is created by the interplay of our inner and outer religious striving for peace.

On August 15th, 1945, when the Venerable Daigyōin heard the Emperor's voice on the radio announcing Japan's unconditional surrender and the end of the war, he is reported to have said, "Thank goodness for that. It was a senseless war for Japan to have got herself into in the first place . . . what was she thinking of, fighting against those very countries (America, China, and Korea) to whom she owed so much?"[9]

To the Venerable Daigyōin's mind, the world of material goods offered no solution: the more you have, the more you want, and there is simply no way out. In the world of great spiritual awakening, by contrast, even though on first reflection we may see ourselves as inextricably bound for hell, the moment our hearts become oriented along the axis of religious awakening, that dark and doom-laden state suddenly transforms itself into the bright and welcoming world of true reality. Thus, for those living on the plane of great spiritual awakening, the Buddha-dharma emerges ever stronger through confrontation with adversity. Truth arises when we least expect it and, as the heart undergoes spiritual conversion, we realize we are no longer continuously drowning in the endless sea of suffering that is birth and death, but feel ourselves instead coming back to life.

The Venerable Daigyōin denounced the war, saying, "Now, as to the present great conflict, this is all the result of our jealous heart" (as cited from the uncompiled items to *One-page Dharma Message* (*Ichimai hōgo*)). All those terribly evil worlds brought about by the wars in which Japan was involved, such as the Sino-Japanese War that Japan herself instigated and the First and the Second World Wars, originally sprang from the Three Poisons

---

[9] See Ekaini's recollection of the Venerable Daigyōin's words in *The Wheel of Light Knows No Limits* (*Kōrin kiwanaku*), Volume 3, § 37, where she tells of hearing the Venerable Daigyōin utter these words after the Emperor's radio announcement of Japan's unconditional surrender on August 15, 1945. When an overwrought Ekaini cried out, "Why, if I didn't have religious faith I might go out and kill myself," she recalls that the Venerable Daigyōin strode up to her with a glowering expression and, standing over her, slapped her on both cheeks, left and right, military style.

and Five Desires of the blind passions that rule the heart of Ignorance. Regarding the hell unleashed by atomic bombs, he writes: "Alas, that holocaust is what has been caused by my own state of Ignorance" (cited from the uncompiled items to *One-page Dharma Message* (*Ichimai hōgo*)). In so saying, the Venerable Daigyōin takes upon himself full responsibility for the war in all its terrifying aspects as being the product of his own human karma. His confession is utterly uncompromising, reminding us that, even if our country has been seared by the blast of atomic bombs, unless we realize the terrifying nature of our own inborn karma that caused such a war and arrive at a penetrating insight into the frightful impact that human karma exercises on a global scale, then sad to say we can never arrive at a thoroughly penetrating religious self-realization conducive to Inner Peace.

Resisting the 1929 Religious Organizations Bill

The defining moment of Daigyōin's path to religious conviction came about as he sought to deal with several major problems that came his way. One problem was the Religious Organizations Bill. In January 1929, the Japanese Government of the time, having decided some kind of regulation of religious organizations was called for, formed a select committee in the House of Peers to draw up a bill especially for this purpose. The essence of the bill proposed by the government was that "Religious sects (*kyōha*) and denominations (*shūha*), as well as religious orders (*kyōdan*), would be placed under the jurisdiction of local government administrators (prefectural governors) and supervised by the Ministry of Education (Mombushō)." But subjecting religious organizations to state control in this way, of course, would seriously undermine the freedom of religion.

The religious world, the media and public opinion all demonstrated strong opposition to what would amount to ideological control by the State. The Venerable Daigyōin himself joined the Association Opposed to the Religious Organizations Bill, founded by his close friend Reverend Chikazumi Jōkan

(1870–1941),[10] and together the two men and their colleagues built the movement into a nationwide crusade. The Venerable Daigyōin portrayed the guiding principle of the movement as "one that is beyond the dichotomy of 'I agree' or 'I oppose'; what is called for is an opposition so absolute that it utterly annihilates such a bill, an opposition grounded in the absolute religious conviction of Other Power faith" (*The Solution to the Problems of Society (Shakai mondai no kaiketsu)*, 1929).

The crux of the problem of Religion versus State and the grounds for opposition to the bill are summed up by the Venerable Daigyōin in the following four statements: (1) The government errs when it seeks to establish its goal of public safety and state-appointed social order by using its jurisdiction over religion to its own advantage. (2) The government errs when it guarantees the impartial treatment of Buddhism, Shintōism and Christianity but seeks to use its own discretion to decide whether other religions are good or bad. (3) The government errs when, rather than leaving religious problems to the religious world to solve, it sees the political as superior to the religious sphere and seeks instead to discuss such problems as part of its own remit. (4) Unless politicians themselves attain peace of mind on a religious plane and transcend their dualistic views on right and wrong, good and bad, friend and foe to arrive at a state of unwavering respect for others, they can never truly be in a position to discuss the problems of the religious congregation.

---

[10] Reverend Chikazumi Jōkan was a leading Buddhist activist who, like the Venerable Daigyōin, came from the Shinshū Ōtani-ha denomination. Close in age, the two became close Dharma friends. In 1910 it was Reverend Chikazumi who confirmed the Venerable Daigyōin's awakening of faith, something that the Venerable Daigyōin had arrived at of his own accord without any actual teacher (see *Record of My Awakening of Faith (Nyūshinroku)*, compiled in *My Encounter with That Light (Gushikō)*, Vol. 1, p. 27). In the ensuing years, the Venerable Daigyōin often made the journey to Tokyo to see and work with Reverend Chikazumi. Reverend Chikazumi had numerous books and articles on Shin Buddhist themes, many of them based on talks he gave at his striking architectural landmark, the Kyūdō Kaikan, or Seekers Hall, established near the main gateway of Tokyo University.

In March 1929, just before the bill was to be enacted, the Venerable Daigyōin published a book entitled *The Solution to the Problems of Society* (*Shakai mondai no kaiketsu*), expressing his opposition to the Religious Organizations Bill on religious grounds, and sent out thirteen thousand copies to religious communities, the media and members of the intellectual classes. He also initiated a campaign amongst his compatriots to get people to sign a petition. In the end, on March 19th, the bill was thrown out. The movement Daigyōin initiated was thus never just another run-of-the-mill opposition movement, but evolved instead out of a sense of deep religious conviction. It represented what he himself confessed to being his "ferocious inner struggle against a host of demons in my mind". [11]

Establishing the Taya house system for the Shōgyōji Saṅgha

The Venerable Daigyōin made a lasting contribution to promoting the Three Treasures in the public consciousness by establishing the Taya house system. The actual concept of the Taya house made its first appearance in the history of the Shinshū community in the olden days when the Honzan, or Main Temple, as well as branch temples, began providing accommodations, called *kyūdō shukuhaku sho*, to visiting Dharma friends for their convenience.

The origins of the Taya house system can be traced back to the time when Rennyo Shōnin (1415–1499) sought to circumvent the persecution of the Shin Buddhist community by the powerful Enryakuji temple on Mount Hiei, and took shelter in the distant province of Echizen in the Hokuriku district (present day Fukui prefecture) where he constructed a *dōjō*, or temple, on a hillside known as Yoshizaki, facing the Sea of Japan. Once there, accommodations soon had to be provided for his followers on the order of several hundred such dwellings.

---

[11] In his Introduction to *Record of My Encounter with That Light* (*Gushikō roku*); in the compilation of this work in *My Encounter with That Light* (*Gushikō*), volume two, 1953, this statement regarding his "ferocious inner struggle with a host of demons in my mind," appears on p. 142.

With the establishment of the Yoshizawa religious center, fellow Dharma seekers came to listen to the teachings of Rennyo Shōnin from as far away as Tōhoku, or northeastern Honshu, as well as from the provinces of Ōshū, Dewa and Shinano and from all over Hokuriku, with priests and laymen, men and women, arriving in droves. It is recorded that within the main *dōjō* area there were permanent houses for Rennyo Shōnin's immediate disciples, who protected the temple, but, as more and more fellow visitors began to arrive to pay their respects to Rennyo Shōnin and receive his teaching, more and more accommodations had to be built and soon Taya houses began suddenly springing up as if out of nowhere.

The visiting Dharma friends who came from many provinces were able to commute from the Taya houses to the Main Hall on the hill, where they could hear the sermons of the Master, Rennyo Shōnin, and also listen to the Dharma talks of the priests who were his disciples. In addition, whilst living in a Taya house, any Dharma friend suffering from one or other of life's problems, as symbolized by "birth, ageing, disease, and death," could listen and benefit from the advice from those who were more advanced. This would lead them to an awakening of religious faith and thereby enable them to arrive at a solution to their problems.

The Venerable Daigyōin had a clear understanding of how the dynamics of the Taya house system had played a crucial role in the development of the Shin Buddhist community from the time of Rennyo Shōnin onwards and wanted to incorporate this feature into Shōgyōji on a permanent basis for the benefit of the Shōgyōji Saṅgha. With the Taya house system, as both priest and layperson alike engage in the Jōdo Shinshū practice of listening to the Buddha-dharma, the basic distinction between priest and layperson vanishes and the concept of the Mahāyāna as a great path leading to Universal Awakening takes on an even deeper meaning. As far as religious faith is concerned, the Taya house is an ideal setting where priest and layperson alike mutually seek religious awakening by listening and learning from one another.

In his *One-page Dharma Message* (*Ichimai hōgo*), the following three guidelines are given for the Taya house. (1) The

Taya house shall be a *dōjō*, or place of religious practice, where all attachment to self, career or possessions are set aside, and each person entrusts themselves to the Buddha-dharma in order to attain birth in the Pure Land. (2) The Taya house shall be a place where priest and layperson alike illumine one another so that each may come to experience the awakening of faith. (3) The Taya house shall be a place where those awakened to faith, as a result of their faith-experience, have decided to embark upon their spiritual journey unto the very end of their lives. Also it shall be the religious crucible wherein they communicate through faith with other family members living outside the temple.

In Buddhism, the Sanskrit word "Saṅgha" refers to the community of those that receive the teachings of the Buddha and of their good friends or spiritual guides, known as *kalyāṇamitra*. The particular process whereby members of the Saṅgha pass on to other members the teachings of the Buddha, represents the notion of precept-holding in Buddhism in general (*One-page Dharma Message (Ichimai hōgo)*, §§ 45, 81, 434). Even though Shin Buddhism is a form of lay Buddhism, the Taya house system can nevertheless be seen as incorporating the formal precept-holding aspect of regular Buddhist monastic life as the cornerstone of Saṅgha practice.

After the Shinshū restoration initiated by Rennyo Shōnin in the fifteenth century the Taya house system admittedly fell into virtual disuse. Although there were already a few Taya-style houses in Shōgyōji during the 1920s and 1930s, the first Taya house built in 1932 by Ekaini, based on Daigyōin's idea of providing Taya houses for the Shōgyōji Saṅgha, was called quite simply Taya house Number One. Taya house Number Two, erected at the request of Ekaini, was built by her sister-in-law. These two buildings, which they used as Taya houses, were known as the Enokidera Taya, and were also the living quarters of Ekaini and of Ekaini's sister-in-law and family. Nowadays, in the vicinity of Shōgyōji main temple, there are seven Taya houses and a number of other ordinary households, in which upward of one hundred and eighty people, young and old, male and female, live and practice. In addition, there are another fourteen Taya houses in Tokyo, Kyoto, Osaka, London and other places with a further seventy people in residence.

In recent years, Reverend Seongwon (Chanju Mun) of the University of Hawai'i - Manoa, on the introduction of his teacher, the Venerable Jeongwoo, head priest of Guryongsa[12] in Seoul, has visited Shōgyōji on several occasions, attending morning and evening service and taking part in the *Eza*, or Saṅgha assembly. Sensing the peace and harmony of the Taya house system at Shōgyōji, he wrote, "Shōgyōji is a place where equality is finely balanced between the sexes; it is an environment free of discrimination, where social plurality is duly recognized. What I witnessed was a melding together of priest and layperson in a process of mutual growth. Herein may lie the key to resolving the problems of religion in the future." These words encouraged us considerably, as the number of other Shin Buddhist temples in Japan that promote the Taya house system is virtually nil, and as a result, as far as the lay population goes, the power of Buddhism to infuse the lives of the ordinary people has been greatly curtailed. In our Taya house Saṅgha, on the other hand, we are constantly being forced to ask ourselves whether what we are doing is truly leading us to the realization of Inner Peace. To achieve this goal requires that we diligently explore the question together and view the problems of daily life as an invitation to engage personally in Buddhist practice.

Retreating into oneself to open up the flow of Buddha-dharma

---

[12] The Japanese Shin Buddhist priest, Reverend Kamada Kōmei (1914–1998) of Kyōganji temple, Toyama prefecture, at the end of his life, sought the help of Shōgyōji in carrying on his pioneering work of improving relations between Korea and Japan and introduced a Korean Buddhist Venerable Jeongwoo, abbot of Tongdo-sa Monastery, one of the biggest monasteries in Korea, to Shōgyōji. Venerable Jeongwoo in turn introduced his sincere disciple Reverend Seongwon (Chanju Mun), the chief editor of Blue Pine Books to Shōgyōji. cf. Reverend Kamada's book *A Bell Tolls in Baekje* (*Kudara ni kane wa naru*). It is through this karmic connection that the present essay came to be contributed to the book that Reverend Seongwon is currently editing and publishing.

During the war, while the Venerable Daigyōin was engaged in developing the Taya house system, a subtle development came about in his way of thinking. This had to do with the concept of *Shokai*, a word the Venerable Daigyōin coined to mean "to retreat into oneself to open up the floodwaters of spiritual awakening," and which he himself frequently made use of when instructing his followers (cf. *One-page Dharma Message (Ichimai hōgo)*, § 287). *Shokai* is, in fact, a subtle play on words on the very similar-sounding Japanese term for evacuation or dispersal, *sokai*, which came into everyday use towards the end of the Second World War. At that time, Japan was being regularly firebombed, and people were being told to get women and children of the cities out of harm's way by evacuating them to a safe place in the countryside. The Venerable Daigyōin took this word that was on everyone's lips and fashioned a new word with a Buddhist twist: *Shokai*, "to retreat into oneself." While the wartime word for evacuation simply meant to disperse from the busy city centers, the Venerable Daigyōin's own coinage had the deeper implication to "retreat into oneself away from the maddening *Sahā* world in order to practice in an environment conducive to the pursuit of religion." Indeed, *Shokai* retreats, inspired by the Venerable Daigyōin's idea, may one day become an important item on the Shōgyōji Saṅgha agenda.

In his philosophy, the Venerable Daigyōin felt it incumbent on the Saṅgha to demonstrate its own unique form of activity, inherent in its identity as a place of religious practice, and from his new vantage point, the Venerable Daigyōin strongly recommended that we flee the *Sahā* world, a world consumed by fighting and the flames of war, and escape to Buddhist territory, such as the Taya houses of Shōgyōji, where the power of the Buddha will most surely protect us. In the ideal environment of this newly discovered land perfectly suited to Mahāyāna Buddhism, the pursuit of religious practice will cause the floodgates of Awakening to burst asunder, allowing its free-flowing waters to irrigate the thirsty soil of our long-parched land, in both the real as well as in the spiritual sense. It is through the release of these waters that our world within and our world without will at last be brought into equilibrium.

This reminds us of an episode that took place during the Second World War, when American citizens of Japanese ancestry were rounded up and incarcerated in so-called relocation camps. Amongst those confined within the walls of these concentration camps were a number of devout Shin Buddhists who worked together to raise the level of religious awareness of their fellow inmates. By sublating the feelings of confusion that the war had stirred up in them, this small handful of brave individuals managed to encourage others to live lives brimming with the joy of religious awakening. As a result, once the war ended, many of the incarcerated were able to return to ordinary life in a more positive frame of mind. Like the Venerable Daigyōin, they strove to create a more perfect environment for the pursuit of religion in a less-than-ideal world.

Sermon to his disciple, Sudō Kaneomi, at his government office

In another wartime episode, the Venerable Daigyōin's admonitions to one of his disciples make patently clear his own religious convictions, convictions that can be seen as exactly resembling those of Amida Buddha, for whom a warm and healthy respect for other religions, other peoples, and other cultures is paramount for building a peaceful world.

In a career in which he served as governor of several prefectures, Sudō Kaneomi (1896–1994) was appointed by the Ministry of Home Affairs to become Chief of the Fukuoka Prefectural Police, and it was through his connection to this office that he first met the Venerable Daigyōin and had the opportunity to receive from him instruction in the Buddha-dharma. At that time, Mr. Sudō was under considerable pressure to try and keep the left-wing elements under control. Troubled by the ideological contradictions that lay in carrying out his official duties, he was finally able to resolve his dilemma through experiencing a deep personal understanding of Other Power faith.

Subsequently, on more than one occasion, he related the following account, that, "In 1942, just before I was assigned to the post of Military Governor of the Japanese-occupied territory of Celebes, my revered teacher (the Venerable Daigyōin) came to explain some Buddhist guidelines to me at my government headquarters. This sermon was such a magnificent gesture and one for which I was so immensely grateful that even now words still fail to express how I felt then." Below is a similar entry by Mr. Sudō from *The Wheel of Light Knows No Limits* (*Kōrin kiwanaku*), vol. 5.

"In 1942, just before I was appointed to the post of Military Governor (attached to the Japanese Navy) of the former Dutch colony of Celebes (present day Sulawesi, Indonesia), my teacher (the Venerable Daigyōin) made the long journey to the capital (Tokyo), to set out for me in straightforward terms, A, B, and C, just exactly how one should conduct oneself as governor of an occupied territory when one is a person who is committed heart and soul to the *nembutsu*. He told me in the most unequivocal terms that, in occupied territory, one should not build Japanese shrines or force people to worship there. One must respect the religions native to that territory. And one must never recklessly impose Japanese customs or Japanese ways on native people." The instructions he received from the Venerable Daigyōin, in short, ran diametrically counter to the ideology of the Japanese military regime presiding over Japan at that time. Mr. Sudō goes on to write, "Thanks to his instruction, I was able to conduct my military governorship of the Celebes in a relatively uneventful manner, working harmoniously with the native peoples, and did not end up accused of being a war criminal." In October 1951, in accordance with the last will and testament of the Venerable Daigyōin, Mr. Sudō entered the Shōgyōji Sangha, living in a Taya house and devoting the rest of his long life to the practice of the Buddha Way.

Taking delivery of our Gagaku instruments during wartime

During the closing years of the Second World War, the American armed forces stepped up their aerial bombardment, leaving the country strewn with rubble and ashes. In the long history of the Venerable Daigyōin's efforts to realize peace, there is yet one more episode occurring around that time that deserves special mention, and that is in connection with the set of traditional Gagaku musical instruments that he purchased and bequeathed to Shōgyōji which are still carefully preserved here to this day.

In June 1944, American bombers attacked northern Kyushu; in July, Saipan fell, followed by the loss of Guam and Tinian; and in October wave upon wave of American troops landed in Okinawa. As the American armed forces' saturation bombing threatened to reduce one region after another into so much scorched earth, the Venerable Daigyōin lamented the fact that he might be forced to die without leaving behind him any Gagaku music by means of which people could offer up praise from this world to the land of the Buddha. Earlier, when the Venerable Daigyōin was around age fifty, his keen appreciation of Buddhist chanting had led him to make the acquaintance of leading Buddhist musicologist Hatsuka Kenshi (1893–1975), later Chief of the Music Section of Higashi Honganji. It was through Hatsuka's introduction that in 1944 the Venerable Daigyōin was able to place an order for a full set of Gagaku musical instruments, dispatching Ekaini and others to Nagoya to take delivery of them. They transported these instruments via the wartime train service which was in a state of confusion such as the little party had never before experienced. Nevertheless the party and their shipment arrived safely at Shōgyōji on December 26, thanks in no small part to the timely intervention of an influential member of the temple. The Venerable Daigyōin's cherished wish for Gagaku music to be performed as a means of offering praise to the Buddha land continues to be honored to this day in the form of the Shōgyōji Gagaku music group.

Gagaku music boasts a fourteen-hundred-year history in

Japan and is the oldest form of music to be handed down continuously right until the present day. It was originally an ancient art form brought to Japan as part of the East Asian cultural interchange, and was transmitted via the countries along the Silk Road, from distant India, to China, along the Korean peninsula, to Japan. There it fused with an ancient form of music and dance, especially in vogue during the Heian period, to become the traditional Gagaku music we know today.

The Venerable Daigyōin's deep and undying respect for the Buddhist prince Shōtoku Taishi is intimately tied in to the fact that the prince is known to have issued an imperial edict to conduct a Pūja ceremony for the Three Treasures to be celebrated by a varied program of continental music. This event, dated Suiko 20, or 612, is reported in the *Short Biography of Prince Shōtoku* (*Shōtoku Taishi denryaku*). A similar event also took place during the Nara Period, in 752, at the Rakkyō-e, the inauguration of the Tōdaiji Great Buddha. On that occasion, over five hundred musicians took part in a grand Gagaku performance staged as part of the Buddhist Pūja ceremony.

While Gagaku is traditionally regarded as "the Pūja of Music offered up to the Three Treasures" and "the performance of music dedicated to the gods and buddhas," its essence is best captured in the observation that, "when it comes to transporting us beyond the realm of human emotions, that ranges from happiness and anger to sorrow and joy, it is Gagaku music that best conveys to the heart the song of Peace and Harmony of the Pure Land." Throughout its history, Gagaku has thus long been appreciated as a special form of religious music. Its sound has a unique resonance that conveys the highest aspiration of humankind to realize Peace and Harmony in this world. Thus, a Pūja of Music offered to the Buddha is an important form of religious music.

In the closing years of the Second World War, the Venerable Daigyōin's preoccupation with his extraordinary desire to promote and safeguard the performance of Gakaku music may have made him appear to many as somewhat obsessed. To the Venerable Daigyōin, however, Gagaku music had the potential to convey the absolute importance of Inner Peace. During the final phase of bitter fighting against British and American troops, when the barest necessities of life were in short supply and dreaming of the heavenly strains of Pure Land music was the last thing on people's minds, the Venerable Daigyōin set out to purchase a complete set of Gagaku musical instruments, declaring it absolutely vital that Gakaku music be performed at Buddhist services. The musical instruments obtained at that time are still carefully preserved by the Shōgyōji Gagaku group, now known as the Chikushi Gagaku Music Ensemble. Today the membership of the Chikushi Gagaku Music Ensemble has swelled to over seventy participants and their hall is still the only place in Japan devoted exclusively to Gagaku music where the music performed is offered up to the Buddha.

The Venerable Daigyōin is said to have remarked, "Even if our country loses this war, the one thing that she absolutely must not lose is this Gagaku music that transcends the power of words." The Pūja of Music offered up to the gods and Buddhas should thus remind us that music is not simply for one's own personal enjoyment. Before a symphony of sound can be performed, one must first tune in to the soundless sound of Peace beyond the din of conflict and listen to the Harmony that resounds therein. Borne along on the symphony of sound that such deep listening brings, there comes to us an Inner Peace that we can share with others, an Inner Peace that could yet make possible a state of peaceful coexistence in this world.

In the oppressive atmosphere of wartime, the Venerable Daigyōin alone let his thoughts dwell exclusively on the idea of preserving Gagaku music for the world, nor did he ever relinquish his efforts until his wish was finally realized. The Venerable Daigyōin's earnest desire to perform the Pūja of Music well expresses the spirit of peace and harmony that we should seek to realize in the world today. Though his prayer that peace and harmony should be brought about by Gagaku music may go far beyond our ordinary ways of thinking, the Venerable Daigyōin well understood that the performance of Gagaku music constitutes a concrete way for the inconceivable and mysterious workings of such a spirit to manifest itself right before our eyes in an actual, tangible event in the real world. The Venerable Daigyōin's wish for harmony has thus been perpetuated in the form of the Shōgyōji music tradition that continues to flourish down to this very day.

Gagaku music itself is part of a centuries-long transmission of Buddhist continental culture from China and Korea. Thus, when the Chikushi Gagaku Music Ensemble was invited to perform its Pūja of Music abroad, the members found themselves presented with a unique opportunity to express thanks for all the kindness these two countries have historically shown to our country, Japan. In July 2000, the Ensemble was invited to Yeoraesa temple in Korea to perform a ceremony of goodwill, and in May 2007, they were likewise invited to the International Festival of Modern Music in Beijing. These performances in the homeland of Gagaku music were given on behalf of all Japanese people as an expression of our deepest gratitude for everything Japan has received from these two countries over the centuries. After the Beijing performance, many music lovers from China came forward to offer their compliments to the Ensemble, saying how pleased they were to find the music of ancient China was still preserved intact to the present day. In addition, through the performance of its Pūja of Music before the statue of Confucius at the Institute of Confucian Studies at Renmin University of China, Beijing, the Ensemble was able to give sympathetic expression to the music of religious rites inspired by the teachings of Confucius that still flows deep within the hearts and minds of the Chinese people.

In September 1993, the Chikushi Gagaku Music Ensemble was invited by Sir Derek Roberts, Provost of University College London, and Professor John White, Pro-Provost of the same college, to perform at the unveiling ceremony of a stone monument dedicated to the memory of the first foreign students from Japan who came to study at the university at the end of the Tokugawa Period. This opportunity to perform their Pūja of Music in London also led indirectly to the creation of an annual ceremony to pray for world peace and reconciliation between

British and Japanese war veterans who fought in Burma, with memorial services held at Westminster Abbey, Coventry Cathedral, Canterbury Cathedral and the London branch of Shōgyōji Temple, known as the Shin Buddhist Centre of Three Wheels. Fifty-six years have passed since the death of the Venerable Daigyōin, and, thanks in part to the international performances of Gagaku music by the Chikushi Gagaku Music Ensemble, we can say that his deepest wish for the realization of peace and harmony in the world is now starting to be fulfilled.

Conclusion

Of the writings on Buddhism and peace compiled in Chanju Mun, ed., *The World is One Flower: Buddhist Leadership for World Peace* (Honolulu: Blue Pine, 2006), the Venerable Daewon Ki's essay, "Why I dedicate the temple to world peace," is a moving piece that should open the eyes of many people to what Buddhism intends. The Venerable Daewon Ki writes that "The Buddhist temple does not exist to glorify the Buddha, but comes into the world in order to be returned, with Buddha's light inside, to humankind and to the world…. Buddha did not ask that a temple be dedicated to him or anyone else. He simply asked that it be returned to all humanity" (*The World is One Flower*, p. xxxviii). This powerful assertion brings an important point to our attention. The Venerable Daewon Ki is telling us in frank terms that we, as Buddhists, have to rethink our basic attitude toward our own tradition, otherwise we will never be able to demonstrate the Inner Peace that is the essential quality of Buddhism. In the following, we will briefly introduce three elements of Shin Buddhist teaching: 1. Awareness of one's past karma as "good"; 2. Responding gratefully to the kindness shown us by the Buddha-dharma; and 3. Realizing the state of selflessness in real terms. These points well complement what the Venerable Daewon Ki teaches and in future may serve as guidelines to realizing Inner Peace as a cornerstone of World Peace.

1. *Awareness of one's past karma as "good."* In Buddhist literature, there is an episode where Śākyamuni Buddha, who has yet to become a Buddha, first aspires to Enlightenment. At that time, he is said to have met a primeval Tathāgata through whose encounter he somehow learned to affirm the totality of his past karma as "good"; it was only then that he was at last able to become a Tathāgata himself. In this episode, the Buddha, after long years of reflection on the many untold hardships he had undergone, is said to have remarked nostalgically, "All these years have passed but, though coat upon coat of dust and dirt have covered my body like moss, never once has it ever occurred to me to rub off the dust and grime." [13] This statement well illustrates the Buddha's awakening to the totality of his past karma as "good" (*shukuzen*), ushering in a deep and lasting sense of inner peace when we own up to and embrace everything about our lives up to now, whether good or bad, or clean or dirty;

---

[13] This passage is quoted from the writings of Nakamura Hajime (1912–1999), *Gotama Budda: Shakuson no shōgai* (Gotama Buddha: The Life of Śākyamuni) (Kyoto: Hōzōkan, 1958), a work that was well received, reprinted numerous times and even translated twice into English (Hajime Nakamura, *Gotama Buddha* (Los Angeles: Buddhist Books International, 1977); and Hajime Nakamura, *Gotama Buddha: A Biography Based on the Most Reliable Text*, trans. G. Sekimori (Tokyo: Kōsei Publishing, 2000). The title is compiled as volume 11 of the Nakamura's selected works, with this particular quote appearing on p. 335. The exact source of the quotation is not indicated by Nakamura, but Professor Shimoda Masahiro of Tokyo University has directed us to the *Mahasihanada Sutta* (The Greater Discourse on the Lion's Roar), the twelfth item of the *Majjhima Nikāya*, or *Middle Length Sayings*. The I. B. Horner translation (*The First Fifty Discourses* (*Mulapannasa*) (London: Pāli Text Society, 1954), 105) reads: "In that Sariputta, there was this for me through loathliness: on my body there accumulated dust and dirt of years, so that it fell of in shreds. Just as the stump of the *tinduka*-tree comes to accumulate the dust and dirt of years, so that it falls off in shreds, even so, Sariputta, on my body there accumulated the dust and dirt of years, so that it fell off in shreds. But it did not occur to me, Sariputta, to think: '*Indeed now, I could rub off this dust and dirt with my hand, or others could rub off this dust and dirt for me with their hands.*' It did not occur to me thus, Sariputta. This then was for me, Sariputta, through loathliness." While the latter interpretation may appear to vary from that of Nakamura, this is due possibly to historical accretions that we are loath to dismiss, its literary source would seem to be the same.

indeed, in this awareness we are loath to part with any bit of it, so dear have they become to us. Thanks to our past karma, the significance of which we once were not fully aware, we have now arrived at the solid bedrock of understanding our total life experience commensurate to its scale, for which development we are most grateful. This shows that, in the long and arduous process leading to the inner peace of Buddhahood, as one's spirituality deepens and matures, one at last comes to realize the "good" or fortuitousness of everything that comprises one's life, wherein everything is conserved and embraced in its totality, and not the least bit of it is ever wasted or abandoned as meaningless. In Shin Buddhism, the agency taking our often painful past karma and rendering into "good" is known as the light of Other Power, its working enfolding us just as we are, with all our joys and sufferings intact, bringing us to reach a new peak of self-understanding characterized by wholeness of being infused with spiritual insight.

The medieval Shin Buddhist leader Rennyo Shōnin, whom the Venerable Daigyōin deeply revered, also placed a premium on the notion of "past karma as good" (*shukuzen*) and understood it to mean not merely good karma carried forward from the past, but the affirmation, in the present, of our total life experience as "good." Such an affirmation takes place as a process of self-emptying, fulfilling a prime condition for spiritual rebirth known in Shin Buddhism as *shinjin*.[14] Once we awaken to such Other Power faith, in that state of selflessness we realize that everything in our life up to now is as it should be, that there is no

---

[14] The Shin Buddhist term *shinjin*, which can sometimes understood simply as "faith," refers specifically to Other Power faith. (1) In Shin Buddhism the essence of such faith lies in awakening: (a) an awakening to oneself or the reality of one's karmic existence, and (b) an awakening to the Buddha or the unconditional love of the Buddha's Original Vow; this is called *nishu jinshin*, or the "two kinds of deep faith." (2) The concept of faith in Shin Buddhism also connotes the seeker's "entrusting oneself to the Buddha," or *tanomu*, that is, giving up our altruistic self-power to at last receive Other Power faith. (3) The Shin Buddhist faith has the element of instantaneous leap, or *ōchō*, the so-called leap of faith. (4) As a result one arrives at the Shin faith of "purified heart" or the "purification of mind," known as *jōshin* (Skt., *prasāda*).

part of it that is meaningless, and that in fact there is nothing in our past that was not meant to be; our life up to now is thus seen as "good," a life worth living. Once the awareness of our past karma as "good" deepens and a change takes place in us via Other Power, the sense of gratitude we have for the Buddha-dharma serves to further refine and purify our Other Power faith. In other words, it is not that we must have good karma in our past nor is it necessary for us to reinforce our life with good karma in the present; rather, when at last we become aware of all of our karma as "good," we can affirmatively embrace our total past karma and are grateful to the role that all of our karmic conditions have played in making us what we are. Herein, our affirming the totality of our life experience and finding it to be "good" comes about through our involvement in the Buddha-dharma.

2. *Responding gratefully to the kindness shown us by the Buddha-dharma.* Our school of Buddhism places a premium on gratitude. This sense of gratitude may be said to derive from Rennyo Shōnin, who had a unique interpretation of gratitude to the Buddha-dharma. Rennyo Shōnin particularly explained that such gratitude meant our *responding gratefully* (*hō-on*) to the kindness shown us by the Buddha, and that the defining act takes place when the seeker says the Name of the Buddha, or *nembutsu,* in effortless response. In its very effortlessness, we can see that our saying of the Name of the Buddha is neither moral deed nor ethical act; that is, it is not what we strive to do out of our own purported good; it flows forth rather of itself from the depths of the heart in grateful response to the kindness the Buddha has shown us in our hour of need.

Indeed, the Buddha has made a deep prayer for humanity's sake out of compassion for the many people who are helplessly caught in the depths of suffering. This compassionate prayer, known as the working of the Original Vow, appears to us in the midst of ordinary life, when we are desperate and have nowhere to turn. When, in the depths of suffering, we at last hear the call and awaken to this prayer, we respond effortlessly to the Buddha with a grateful heart, the *nembutsu* flowing effortlessly from our lips in Other Power faith. In that moment when we awaken to the great compassion, we realize that this Vow of Amida Buddha is one that has constantly manifested itself throughout history through countless individual cases like our own. As the urge to say the Name of the Buddha emerges from within, we realize the truth that others too have discovered: that a deep prayer has been made on our behalf by the world of Awakening, though we have done nothing to deserve it. This most wonderful gift is being given us without our asking, and as it flows from our lips, it marks the beginning of a new phase of our life as its humble recipient. In Shin Buddhism, our responding gratefully to the Buddha-dharma thus finds perfect expression in the practice of *nembutsu*, effortlessly voiced in response to the kindness that has been shown us throughout our lives, but that we have come to appreciate only now.

3. *Realizing the state of selflessness in real terms.* The true treasure of the Saṅgha turns on the realization of the state of selflessness (*muga*), that is, acting unselfishly. In the Shōgyōji Saṅgha, perpetuated in memory of the Venerable Daigyōin, fifty to one hundred people gather every morning from nearby Taya houses or ordinary households to take part in the morning service and *Eza*, or Saṅgha assembly. These services and assemblies are held all year round without break. At the *Eza*, or Saṅgha assembly, where people listen to and learn from priests and lay people talking about their experience of the Buddha-dharma, the *nembutsu* followers, priests and lay people alike, give full expression to all that lies in their hearts, and come to resolve their problems through open and mutual discussion. Whether it is trouble at home or difficulties in society, everyone strives to look into oneself in critical self-reflection and to engage one another in dialogue to reach the root of the problem. This allows an atmosphere of selflessness to flourish quite naturally in the Saṅgha, bringing a fresh infusion of energy that enables us to be the master of our lives wherever we may go. It is through this active life of selflessness that we strive to set in place the

cornerstone of Inner Peace and harmony essential to World Peace.

As far as Buddhism goes, the awakening to our true self takes place in this state of selflessness. When history reveals to us its true face, in this spiritual state of selflessness we see ourselves reflected in it and recognize ourselves for what we truly are. When we learn to accept ourselves as we are, it enables us to open ourselves fully to others and share with them unselfishly as never before. It is through this state of selflessness that the world of Inner Peace and harmony we seek to attain reveals itself for the first time as a viable choice on the road to World Peace. *Hō-on*, our responding in gratitude to the Buddha-dharma, and *shukuzen*, the awareness of our past karma as "good," may differ as far as words go, but in fact they point to one and the same reality: the awareness of the absolute present that arises in us in the here and now putting our hearts at ease via our Other Power faith.

The Venerable Daigyōin leaves us with these final words. "Once we recognize that the cause of that terrible war lies squarely within ourselves, our mission, then, as we go out to celebrate the end of the war, is to make sure that we never have to engage in such struggle again. Our temple, the Shōgyōji, recognizes the cause of the holocaust wreaked by the atomic bombing [of Hiroshima and Nagasaki] as being deeply embedded in our own human karma, and our great mission in life is one and the same: to never let another such a holocaust happen ever again, and to produce, instead, a world of ultimate bliss on this earthly plane" (*One-page Dharma Message* (*Ichimai hōgo*)) § 1040; adapted). This sentiment of the Venerable Daigyōin issues from his especially being kindly led by Other Power to see the totality of his past karma as "good" (*shukuzen*). Its experience was one that naturally led him to take up the life of *nembutsu*, effortlessly responding in gratitude for the kindness thus shown him. This subtle flow of Buddha-dharma from the world of Awakening to the world of man and back again is well symbolized by the eternal strains of Gagaku music performed

from ancient times to the present. Such is the aspiration that the
Venerable Daigyōin sets forth that informs the Shōgyōji
Saṅgha's constant search for Inner Peace. In our daily life
inspired by the eternal truth of Other Power faith, what Shin
Buddhism calls *shinjin* emerges in an uninterrupted and constant
stream on the plane of history in real time and in real terms.

   In closing, we would like to express our sincerest thanks
to all of our Dharma teachers and friends who have devoted
themselves to the cause of World Peace. Today, more than ever,
our thoughts dwell on World Peace and it is important that those
who are independently working to achieve such a goal join
forces in fellowship and shared humanity to dedicate their lives
to this noble cause more effectively. As we recite the *nembutsu*
in humble gratitude, we offer up these thoughts to the Buddha
from the depths of our heart.

References

All That Has Been Done For Us (*Go-On*), Shōgyōji's in-house monthly
   journal published since 1952, succeeding the quarterly *Dharma Friend*
   (*Hōyū*) and the earlier *Record of My Encounter with That Light* (*Gushikō
   roku*) published from 1929.
Ekai Hōni Chronology (*Ekai hōni nenpyō*), 2007. Historical materials on
   Ekaini compiled in the Shōgyōji Archives.
My Encounter with That Light (*Gushikō*), two volumes. Source book for
   original Daigyōin material, edited by Sudō Kaneomi and Ekaini, and
   published in 1953.
One-page Dharma Message (*Ichimai hōgo*). Shōgyōji Archives, ed., *Ichimai
   hōgo*, or "One-page Dharma Message"; official edition; to be published.
   Covers the writings of the Venerable Daigyōin from 1938 to 1948. In
   1975, this same work edited by Reverend Takehara Chimyō et al was
   published as *Ichimai hōgo, Daigyōin goroku*. The new official edition
   improves on the earlier work in several different ways, primarily by
   being more comprehensive and better organized.
Record of a Lifetime of Sayings (*Goichidaiki kikigaki*). A record of the sayings
   of Rennyo Shōnin (1415–1499), the eighth leader of the Honganji
   lineage, who made the lineage into a major religious institution and
   propagated his teachings through word, letter, and deed.
Record of My Awakening of Faith (*Nyūshinroku*) first published in 1926,
   relates the spiritual awakening that took place in 1910. Compiled in
   Ekaini, ed., *My Encounter with That Light* (*Gushikō*), Vol. 1, Kyoto:

1963, pp. 1–31. The title word *Gushikō* is taken from the *Larger Sūtra*, where it refers to those who encounter the radiant light of Amida Buddha, a sign of true religious awakening.

Record of My Encounter with That Light (*Gushikō roku*), with an Introduction dated 9 June 1929, published August 1929. *Gushi roku* is the title of a small-format magazine, of which the August 1929 issue was the first. The entire magazine is reproduced in *My Encounter with That Light* (Gushikō), Vol. 2, 137–206.

Record of the Words of the Venerable Daigyōin (*Daigyōin goroku*). Shōgyōji Archives ed., *Daigyōin goroku*, or "A Record of the Words of the Venerable Daigyōin"; official edition; to be published.

Short Biography of Prince Shōtoku (*Shōtoku Taishi denryaku*). Compiled from early biographies of Shōtoku Taishi, it was published in two volumes in 1672 during the Tokugawa period.

Short Biography of the Venerable Daigyōin (*Daigyōin shōden*). A text appended to *One-page Dharma Message* (*Ichimai hōgo*); pp. 497–595 in the 1975 edition.

Solution to the Problems of Society (*Shakai mondai no kaiketsu*), 1929. Compiled in Ekaini, ed., *My Encounter with That Light* (*Gushikō*), Vol. 2, Kyoto: 1963, pp. 75–130.

Wheel of Light Knows No Limits (*Kōrin kiwanaku*): *Ekai hōbo bunshū* (*The writings of Dharma mother Ekaini*), a series of Shōgyōji monographs containing the writings of Ekaini, published between 1990 and 1992.

PEACE IN SHIN BUDDHISM AND PROCESS THEOLOGY[1]

Steve Odin

Introduction

This essay takes up the notion of transpersonal PEACE as a theme for East-West comparative philosophy and Buddhist-Christian interfaith dialogue, with a special focus on the ideal of Peace in Jōdo Shinshū, or True Pure Land Buddhism, based on the teachings of Shinran Shōnin (1173-1263), in relation to the organismic process theology and process cosmology of Alfred North Whitehead. Here I attempt to clarify that while Amida Buddha and the God of traditional Christian theology are very different, Amida and the God of Whitehead's process theology are strikingly similar notions. To begin with, it will be demonstrated that like Amida Buddha in Shin Buddhism, the God of process theology is not an omnipotent creator of the universe. Like Amida Buddha, the God of Whitehead's process theology is to be envisioned through the image of "care," so that for both traditions reality is compassionate or caring in nature. Fundamental to Whitehead's process theology is that God is "dipolar" and therefore has two natures: (1) the Primordial Nature which acts as a persuasive lure for all events to realize God's divine aims for them; and (2) the Consequent Nature, a repository which acts as the divine memory that saves all events everlastingly in the kingdom of heaven. Whereas the Primordial Nature of God has been compared to the Primal Vow of Amida by process theologian John B. Cobb, Jr., the Consequent Nature has been compared to the understanding of Dharmākara/Amida as a personification of the "Storehouse Consciousness" by John Yokota. Cobb even identifies the Name of Amida Buddha with Christ as the divine Logos or

---

[1] This paper was presented at the Ninth European Block Conference at Lausanne in September 2002. It was included and published in *The Pure Land*, n.s., 21 (December 2004): 57-87.

Word that incarnates into each occasion of experience through the grace of deity. After clarifying this Buddhist-Christian interfaith dialogue between Shin Buddhism and process theology, I argue that transpersonal Peace is the ultimate spiritual value derived from God in process theology as well as Amida in Shin Buddhism. Peace in Whitehead's process theology is similar to Buddhist nirvāṇa, insofar as it is not only a goal of civilization, but also an expanded awareness transcending the ego self whereby one achieves deliverance from the suffering and tragedy inherent in the perpetually perishing nature of impermanent events in the flux of interrelational existence. Finally, it is shown that for Whitehead's process theology, transpersonal Peace is not achieved through personal effort, but comes only as a "gift" of divine grace through the divine immanence of a caring God, just as for the Shin Buddhist teachings of Shinran, rebirth into the Pure Land of Peace is not achieved by "self-power" (*jiriki*), but only through a "gift" (*ekō*) received from the transformative grace of Amida Buddha's compassionate "Other Power" (*tariki*).

'Amida' in Shin Buddhism & the 'Dipolar God' of Process Theology

Various scholars have noted how out of all Buddhist schools it is Japanese Shin Buddhism which most nearly approximates Christian theism, just as Amida Buddha as the compassionate Savior of all sentient beings comes nearest to the Christian monotheistic idea of God. In response to the question, "Is Amida Buddha a Buddhist 'God'?" Kenneth Tanaka has given the following response:

> You could say that Amida is "God," but only if you define God as the dynamic activity of understanding (wisdom) and caring (compassion). But clearly, Amida is not a personal God who is 1) the creator of the universe, 2) a divine, transcendent being, 3) an omniscient (all knowing) being

who knows my daily activities, and/or 4) a judge who decides my final destiny.[2]

As indicated by Tanaka, Amida Buddha is not "God" in the sense of traditional Christian theology, wherein God is described as: (1) creator of the universe, (2) absolutely transcendent, (3) omniscient, and/or (4) a moralistic judge. However, none of the divine attributes enumerated by Tanaka is applicable to Whitehead's revolutionary concept of God. To begin with, against the traditional Christian theological conceptions of God, Whitehead argues that "the nature of God is dipolar. He has a primordial nature and a consequent nature."[3] While the dipolar God is absolute, transcendent, impassible (unfeeling), eternal, and unchanging in his Primordial Nature, God is also relative, immanent, sympathetic, temporal and changing in his Consequent Nature. (1) The most radical aspect of Whitehead's process theology is that God is not to be understood as divine Creator of the world, but rather, as a caring deity that aims to save all occasions in world-process: "He does not create the world, he saves it."[4] According to Whitehead's process theology, "God" is not the omnipotent creator of the universe, since the ultimate metaphysical category is "creativity,"[5] according to which all events in nature are self-creative, in that they arise through a process of *creative synthesis*, a dynamic activity of unifying the dynamic web of interrelationships into a novel event or occasion with beauty and value. (2) In his critique of the Judeo-Christian and Islamic traditions, Whitehead argues that dogmatic notions of God as an absolutely transcendent, omnipotent deity who creates the world *ex nihilo* by divine fiat, has long been a basic theological fallacy: "The notion of God as ... transcendent creator, at whose fiat the world came into being, and whose imposed will it obeys, is

---

[2] Kenneth K. Tanaka, *Ocean: An Introduction to Jōdo-Shinshū Buddhism in America* (Berkeley: Wisdom Ocean Publications. 1997), 153.

[3] A. N. Whitehead, *Process and Reality*, eds. David Ray Griffin & Donald W. Sherburne (1929; New York: The Free Press, 1978), 345.

[4] *Ibid*, 346.

[5] *Ibid,* 21.

the fallacy which has infused tragedy into the histories of Christianity and of Mahometanism."[6] (3) For Whitehead, as well as for Charles Hartshorne, John Cobb, and other leading process theologians, insofar as all events arise through a process of creative synthesis, they are spontaneous, emergent, and unpredictable, so that God cannot be "omniscient" in the sense of an infinite, unqualified knowledge that sees the outcome of all decisions made by occasions emerging in the present, or of future occasions that have not yet arisen into actuality. (4) Finally, Whitehead clearly rejects the image of God as a legalistic judge, lawgiver, or "ruthless moralist."[7] Instead, God is to be envisioned through the image of "care."[8] Hence, while traditional notions of the Christian God might be very different from Amida Buddha, Whiteheadian process theology provides a description of God that resonates deeply with the Shin Buddhist vision of Amida as a peaceful, gentle and caring deity that operates to forever lure all events toward realizing its divine aims toward value, beauty, goodness, truth, harmony, peace, and salvation. It might be said that the dipolar God of Whitehead's process theology functions like Amida as the Cosmic Buddha defined as a dynamic activity of wisdom and compassion.

(a) The 'Primordial Nature' of God and the 'Primal Vow' of Amida

The Buddhist-Christian interfaith dialogue between Shin Buddhism and Whitehead's process theology was initiated by John B. Cobb, Jr. in his groundbreaking work *Beyond Dialogue: Toward a Mutual Transformation of Christianity and Buddhism.* In this work Cobb endeavors to show various parallels between the "Primal Vow" as the working of the compassion of Amida Buddha's Other Power and the "Primordial Nature" of God in process theology: "Whitehead's account of the Primordial Nature

---

[6] *Ibid,* 342.

[7] *Ibid,* 343.

[8] *Ibid,* 346.

of God addresses the same feature of reality as that spoken of by Shinran as the primal vow of Amida. Both of these are remarkably analogous to ... accounts of the Word of God or Logos or Truth which is Christ."[9] He then goes on to make the bold declaration: "The conclusion from the above is that *Amida is Christ*. That is, the feature of the totality of reality to which Pure Land Buddhists refer when they speak of Amida is the same as that to which Christians refer when we speak of Christ"[10] (italics added). Here, it should be pointed out Cobb in agreement with the view of Nishida Kitarō (1870-1945), founder of the Kyoto school of modern Japanese philosophy, who likewise argues that the Name of Amida Buddha in the Shin Buddhist teachings of Shinran is to be identified with Christ as the divine Logos or Word of God in Christian theology.[11] The profound insight of Cobb is that Christ as the divine Logos or Word is itself the Primordial Nature of God, which incarnates into each and every occasion as the "initial aim" toward realizing maximum harmony and value, while moreover identifying the Logos or Primordial Nature with the Primal Vow of Amida. Whitehead describes the Primordial Nature of God as a "lure"[12] to realize value. For Cobb, the lure of God in his Primordial Nature is a theological equivalent to the Primal Vow of Amida, or as it were, the "call of Amida."[13] Elsewhere, Cobb refers to Whitehead's idea of Primordial Nature of God or Logos in its working as a divine lure prescribing initial aims, as "the call forward," and therefore describes God as "the One Who Calls."[14] For Cobb, the lure of God in his Primordial Nature as Logos or Word is therefore a Christian theological equivalent to the Primal

---

[9] John B. Cobb, Jr., *Beyond Dialogue: Toward a Mutual Transformation of Christianity and Buddhism* (Philadelphia: Westminster Press, 1982), 128.

[10] *Ibid.*

[11] Nishida Kitarō, *Last Writings: Nothingness and the Religious Worldview*, trans. D. Dilworth (Honolulu: UH Press. 1987), 195.

[12] Whitehead, *op. cit.*, 344.

[13] Cobb, *Beyond Dialogue: Toward a Mutual Transformation of Christianity and Buddhism*, 136.

[14] John B. Cobb, Jr., *God & the World* (New York: Wipf and Stock Publishers, 1998), 43-66.

Vow of Amida Buddha, or what he otherwise describes as the "call of Amida."[15]

Finally, Cobb argues for another similarity between Amida and the dipolar God, holding that the ultimate metaphysical category of creativity as an indeterminate formless activity of creative synthesis, is itself conditioned by the determinate forms of harmony provided by the Primordial Nature of God, just as the formless emptiness of Dharmakāya Buddha is conditioned by the Primal Vows of Amida (the Saṃbhogakāya Buddha) in Shin Buddhism: "It is the Primordial Nature which qualifies creativity in a way so strikingly similar to the qualification of the Dharmakāya by the primal vow. Just as the Primordial Nature of God is the primordial decision for the sake of all creatures, even more clearly the primal vow is made for the sake of all sentient beings."[16]

The depth of Cobb's penetrating interpretation of the Primal Vow in Shin Buddhism as the "*call* of Amida," can further be established by reference to the writings of Taitetsu Unno, a leading academic scholar and ordained minister of Shin Buddhism. In his introductory book about the Pure Land teachings of Shin Buddhism, Unno develops his understanding of the *nembutsu*, or vocal recitation of the Name of Amida Buddha of NAMU-AMIDA-BUTSU, as the "Name-that-Calls."[17] In his hermeneutics of Shin Buddhism, Unno asserts that *nembutsu*, the vocal practice of reciting the divine Name of Buddha, is to be interpretively translated into English as "the Name-that-Calls."[18] Unno states that the *nembutsu* is the Name that calls one to go beyond the ego-self and achieve their full possibility for enlightenment as an awakened human being.[19] Even though one calls to Amida through the *nembutsu*, at the same time, since the *nembutsu* is recited only

---

[15] Cobb, *Beyond Dialogue: Toward a Mutual Transformation of Christianity and Buddhism*, 136.

[16] *Ibid*, 131.

[17] Unno Taitetsu, *River of Fire / River of Water: An Introduction to the Pure Land Tradition of Shin Buddhism* (New York: Doubleday, 1998), 26-35.

[18] *Ibid*, 32.

[19] *Ibid*, 31.

through a gift of Amida's compassion, the *nembutsu* is ultimately to be conceived as the Name-that-Calls, that is, it is the beckoning call of Amida to transcend the ego-self through reliance on the compassionate Other Power grace of Amida Buddha. As Unno elsewhere asserts, "If I were to translate *nembutsu* into English, it would be the name-that-calls, for it calls us to awaken to our fullest potential to become true, real and sincere human beings."[20] Unno clarifies that the name-that-calls is an "Interpretative translation for *nembutsu*, NAMU-AMIDA-BUTSU, which is the beckoning call to human beings from the side of Amida Buddha to take leave of delusion and awaken to reality-as-it-is." [21] He further explains how according to the Shin Buddhist teachings of Shinran, "the saying of *nembutsu* is experienced as a call from Amida, but simultaneously it is our response to that call."[22] Again, "In Shin Buddhism, the ultimate goal of transformation occurs in the saying of *nembutsu*, NAMU-AMIDA-BUTSU ... the *nembutsu* is the flowing call of the Buddha of Immeasurable Light and Life, coming from the fathomless center of life itself, as well as our response to that call without any hesitation or calculation." [23] Since the *nembutsu* of NAMU-AMIDA-BUTSU is the name-that-calls, accordingly, the central practice of Shin Buddhism is that of "deep hearing" (*monpō*), or as it were, "deep hearing of the call of Amida."[24] Unno states, "Religiously speaking, deep hearing means that we have no choice but to hear and respond to the call of boundless compassion. It is through the name-that-calls that Amida Buddha gives us the ultimate gift of true and real life .... Thus, the invocation of the Name, NAMU-AMIDA-BUTSU, is ... a voicing of the call that comes from the bottomless source of life itself, the Buddha of Immeasurable Light and Life." [25]

From Unno's understanding of the *nembutsu* or vocal recitation of the Name of Amida Buddha of NAMU-AMIDA-BUTSU, as the

---

[20] *Ibid*, 24.
[21] *Ibid*, 257.
[22] *Ibid*, 5.
[23] *Ibid*, 23.
[24] *Ibid*, 19.
[25] *Ibid*, 52.

"Name-that-Calls," [26] one can thereby come to appreciate the profound significance of Cobb's interfaith dialogue between Whiteheadian process theology and Shin Buddhism. For it is Cobb's landmark contribution to have reformulated Whitehead's notion of the initial aim or lure toward perfection for self-actualizing occasions derived from the Primordial Nature of God or Logos as "the call forward" from the power of deity as the "One who Calls," while at the same time identifying this with the Primal Vow of Amida Buddha, understood as the "call of Amida."

(b) The 'Consequent Nature' of God and Amida Buddha as the 'Storehouse Consciousness'

(1) Although Cobb analyzes parallels between the Primordial Nature of God and the Primal Vow of Amida Buddha to save all sentient beings through the working of compassionate Other Power, he does not find any parallels between the Consequent Nature of God and Amida. Cobb argues that whereas the value-qualities realized by momentary events arising and perishing in the world of creative process function to influence and enrich the Consequent Nature of God, he sees no sense among Buddhists that dharmas contribute anything to Amida: "There is, in other words, nothing [in Shin Buddhism] comparable to what Whitehead calls the Consequent Nature of God." [27]

However, the significant contribution of John Yokota, a scholar of both Shin Buddhism and process theology, is to have demonstrated the profound relation between the Consequent Nature of God and Amida Buddha. More specifically, Yokota argues for a parallel between the Consequent Nature of God as the repository functioning to save all perishing events, and the nature of Dharmākara Bodhisattva/Amida Buddha as the "Storehouse Consciousness." Yokota rightly asserts, "The tradition [of process theology] is unanimous in its understanding of God as this final

---

[26] *Ibid*, 26-35.

[27] Cobb, *Beyond Dialogue: Toward a Mutual Transformation of Christianity and Buddhism*, 131.

and unifying repository of all events. God is the keeper of the past."[28] In Whitehead's process theology, when an event perishes, it then becomes a cause influencing all future events, thereby to acquire what he terms an "objective immortality." Yet with the passing of time, the causal influence of each passing event in its objective immortality would become dimmer and dimmer, gradually fading away into oblivion, if not for the functioning of the Consequent Nature of God. For according to Whitehead's process theology, the values realized by all events in fact do not fade away with the passage of time, because they are retained, stored and saved everlastingly in their full intensity and vividness as imperishable data in the divine memory: namely, the Consequent Nature of God as the collective repository of the past. Explicating the relevance of the Consequent Nature of God in process theology to Amida Buddha in Shin Buddhism, Yokota states, "As the [Buddhist] tradition develops, one encounters the notion of *ālayavijñāna* or the storehouse consciousness that is comparable to the collective unconscious. It is the storehouse of all karma.... It is interesting to note that the Shin Buddhist scholar Soga Ryōjin equated Amida with this storehouse consciousness."[29] Yokota here makes reference to the insights of the Shin Buddhist scholar Soga Ryōjin (1875-1971), a former president of Otani University, who endeavors to locate Pure Land Buddhism within the mainstream of the Mahāyāna Buddhist tradition by showing how Dharmākara Bodhisattva/Amida Buddha is the personification of the Storehouse Consciousness, the repository of all dharmas or karmic events.[30] Because of his compassionate Primal Vow that aims to save all sentient beings, Dharmākara Bodhisattva was to become Amida Buddha presiding over the Pure Land of Peace and

---

[28] John Yokota, "Understanding Amida Budda: A Process Approach," in *Toward a Contemporary Understanding of Pure Land Buddhism: Creating a Shin Buddhist Theology in a Religiously Plural World*, ed. Dennis Hirota (Albany, New York: SUNY Press, 2000), 91.

[29] *Ibid*, 95.

[30] Soga Ryōjin, "Dharmakāya Bodhisattva," in *The Buddha Eye: An Anthology of the Kyoto School*, ed. Frederick Franck (New York: Crossroad Publishing Co., 1982), 221-231.

Bliss. In his analysis of the name Dharmākara, Soga clarifies how the meaning of the Sanskrit word *ākara* (Jpn., *zō*) is "storage," so that Dharmākara (Jpn., *Hōzō*) is the "Dharma storehouse." [31] According to Soga, "Dharmākara Bodhisattva of Pure Land doctrine is synonymous with the Storehouse Consciousness, the *ālayavijñāna* of traditional Mahāyāna Buddhism." [32] He further asserts, "Many years ago I called the *ālayavijñāna*, this supraconsciousness in which all dharmas are stored, this 'storehouse consciousness,' Dharmākara consciousness." [33] Furthermore, Soga emphasizes not only that Dharmākara / Amida is the personification of the Storehouse Consciousness, but that the Storehouse Consciousness is itself the "Buddha Nature."[34]

I myself have developed parallels between Whitehead's Consequent Nature of God with both the Collective Unconscious of Jungian depth psychology as well as the Storehouse Consciousness of Buddhism, in my book about the microcosm-macrocosm conception of reality as a dynamic network of interrelatedness, interdependence, and interpenetration formulated both in Whiteheadian process metaphysics and Huayan (Jpn., Kegon) Buddhism. [35] However, from the perspective of Shin Buddhism, Yokota specifically clarifies how the Consequent Nature of God in process theology relates to Dharmākara Bodhisattva and his fully realized state as Amida Buddha, in his function as the Storehouse Consciousness. Yokota states, "As the discussion of objective immortality noted, it is in the incorporation into God of the entirety of an occasion in all its vividness and completeness that the evil of perpetual perishing is resolved. Amida too is seen as taking in the entire person in that the karma of that person is taken on by Amida in its entirety."[36] Yokota's point is that just as for Whitehead's process theology all events in

---

[31] *Ibid*, 228.

[32] *Ibid*, 223.

[33] *Ibid*, 228.

[34] *Ibid*, 225.

[35] Steve Odin, *Process Metaphysics and Hua-Yen Buddhism* (Albany: SUNY Press, 1982), 158-171.

[36] Yokota, "Understanding Amida Budda: A Process Approach," 95.

their objective immortality functioning as causes which condition all future events would gradually fade away if not for being fully retained, stored and saved in the Consequent Nature of God, likewise, the karmic influence of all dharmas on future events would also gradually fade away into insignificance if it were not for the working of Dharmākara Bodhisattva / Amida Buddha, who as the personification of the Storehouse Consciousness functions as the collective repository of the past which saves all dharmas in their full vividness and intensity.

(2) There is yet a further dimension to the parallel between the Consequent Nature of God in Whiteheadian process theology and Dharmākara / Amida in Shin Buddhism which needs to be explored. In Shin Buddhism, persons are saved through the compassionate Other Power of Amida Buddha upon rebirth in the Pure Land. Likewise, in process theology, all perishing events are "saved" [37] as they enter into the everlasting divine life of the Consequent Nature of God, explicitly identified by Whitehead as the Kingdom of Heaven. At the conclusion of his final chapter titled "God and the World" from *Process and Reality*, Whitehead propounds, "Thus the consequent nature of God is composed of a multiplicity of elements with individual self-realization .... This is God in his function of the *kingdom of heaven*" (italics added). [38] He continues, "The kingdom of heaven is with us today. The action of [this] phase is the love of God for the world.... What is done in the world is transformed into a reality in heaven and the reality in heaven passes back into the world ... the love in the world passes into the love in heaven and floods back again into the world." [39] Thus, here we find yet another convergence between Shin Buddhism and process theology: namely, the idea of salvation through rebirth in Amida's heavenly paradise as the Pure Land of Peace and Bliss, and Whitehead's soteriological notion whereby events are saved by passing into the everlasting life of the Consequent Nature of God as the Kingdom of Heaven.

---

[37] Whitehead, *Process and Reality*, 346.

[38] *Ibid*, 350.

[39] *Ibid*, 351.

(3) Although he does not discuss either Whitehead's process theology or the idea of Amida Buddha as the Storehouse Consciousness, nevertheless, Taitetsu Unno clarifies the deep spiritual meaning of this consequent function of the divine nature from the perspective of the Japanese Buddhist poetics of impermanence. Unno explains how the Buddhist teaching of "impermanence" (Jpn., *mujō*) was depicted in Japanese poetry of the Heian Period (794-1185) through the image of fleeting dewdrops. This Heian poetics of impermanence came to be known as *mono no aware*, the "tragic beauty" of perishing events in the flux of becoming. Unno goes on to say, "In this early period, the notion of impermanence had a negative tone, carrying a tone of sadness, regret, and pathos. But with the passing of time, it took on a more positive tone an encouragement to discover an enduring, unchanging reality beyond the phenomenal world."[40] Unno then illustrates this with a poem by the priest-poet Ryōkan (1756-1831), a Zen monk filled with the spirit of the Pure Land who wrote poems on Amida:

> If not for Amida's inconceivable vow,
> what then would remain to me
> as a keepsake of this world?[41]

Ryōkan encouraged people to follow the path of *nembutsu* to find salvation from the suffering of impermanence where all transitory events disappear like falling dewdrops by taking refuge in the everlasting Pure Land of Amida the Buddha of infinite Light and Life:

> Return to Amida
> Return to Amida
> So even dewdrops fall.[42]

---

[40] Unno, *River of Fire / River of Water: An Introduction to the Pure Land Tradition of Shin Buddhism*, 164.
[41] *Ibid.*
[42] *Ibid.*

Unno goes on to interpret the above poems from the standpoint of Shin Buddhism as follows: "Everything in our evanescent world constantly reminds us not to rely on passing, unreliable things, but to entrust ourselves to that which is timeless Immeasurable Light and Life that is Amida." [43]

The closest Western parallel to the Buddhist teaching of "impermanence" (Jpn., *mujō*) and the Japanese poetic ideal of *mono no aware* or the tragic beauty of impermanence is to be found in the process theology of A. N. Whitehead. At the conclusion of his chapter titled "Peace" from *Adventures of Ideas*, Whitehead holds that due to the immanence of God, which provides divine aims to be actualized by events, each occasion realizes some degree of beauty, or aesthetic value-quality. Yet the beauty realized by events is always a "tragic Beauty"[44] in that the aesthetic value-quality of each occasion perishes immediately upon becoming in the incessant flux of process as the creative advance to novelty. For Whitehead, the problem of tragic beauty arising from the ultimate evil of the perpetual perishing of events in the ever-changing flux of becoming is thus to be resolved through the concept of deity formulated in his process theism, according to which all perishing events are retained, stored, and saved everlastingly in all their vividness and intensity in the Consequent Nature of God. Likewise, the Japanese poetic ideal of the tragic beauty of transitory dharmas in the ceaseless impermanence of universal flux is overcome in the Shin Buddhist tradition through salvation by rebirth into the Pure Land of Amida Buddha. Hence, just as for Whitehead, the tragic beauty of perpetually perishing occasions in the stream of process is overcome through retention in the Consequent Nature of God as the Kingdom of Heaven, so for Shin Buddhism, the tragic beauty of impermanence is overcome through salvation by rebirth into the heavenly paradise of the Pure Land of Amida Buddha as the Storehouse Consciousness which saves all dharmas forevermore.

---

[43] *Ibid.*

[44] A. N. Whitehead, *Adventures of Ideas* (New York: The Free Press, 1933), 296.

'Compassion' in Shin Buddhism and 'Care' in Process Theology

One of the most significant points of contact between the frameworks of Whiteheadian process theology and Shin Buddhism is that both envision the divine nature of God / Amida as a caring or compassionate deity, just as both underscore how care, concern or compassion is rooted in the metaphysical structure of ultimate reality itself, insofar as it is not constituted by separate, independent, and unrelated substances, but rather, by dependently arisen dharmas or events co-originated from out of an interdependent matrix as a dynamic web of relationships in the flux of becoming. For Shin Buddhism, the nature of Amida Buddha is that of unconditional "compassion" (*jihi*) working through the call of Amida's *tariki* or "Other Power" as expressed by the "Primal Vow" (*hongan*) with its aim, or compassionate intent, to save all sentient beings. Describing the divine nature of Amida Buddha's salvific Other Power as boundless compassion, Taitetsu Unno therefore asserts, "The working of the Primal Vow, the compassion of the Buddha of Immeasurable Light and Life, is called Other Power." [45] Yokota explains both the compassionate nature of Amida Buddha's Primal Vow to save all sentient beings through the grace of Other Power as a call to compassion as well as the centrality of compassionate moral conduct based on a wisdom seeing the emptiness / openness of reality as interdependence:

> The whole point of the Buddhist analysis of reality with its emphasis on impermanence, becoming, openness / emptiness, and dependent arising is that it tells us that reality is like this so that we can act accordingly ... in short, we should act compassionately. We act compassionately because a world of openness and dependent arising is a compassionate world.... If compassion is the primordial

---

[45] Unno, *River of Fire / River of Water: An Introduction to the Pure Land Tradition of Shin Buddhism*, 36.

character of existence, then a personal center to existence is undeniable. Compassionate intent (the primal vow) is present and undeniable as well. [46]

Like the Shin Buddhist tradition, Whitehead's organic process metaphysics articulates a doctrine of concern, care, or compassion based on a metaphysics of interconnected, dependently arisen events that emerge from out of a relational web or network of causal interconnections in the dynamic, creative, undivided aesthetic continuum of nature. Although Whitehead does not use the language of emptiness *per se*, he does formulate the most comprehensive Western theory of interrelated events arising through *prehensions*, or sympathetic feelings of relations to all other events, which at once calls to mind the Buddhist doctrine of *pratītya-samutpāda*: dependent co-origination, interconnectedness, or relational existence. For Unno, this awareness of as a "vast network of interdependence" is itself the core of Shin Buddhism, [47] further emphasizing that, "Interdependence is an elemental truth. When one awakens to this fact, compassion that sustains us strikes us with full force, and we are made to respond to the world with the same compassion." [48] Whitehead's metaphysical principle of "universal relativity" functions as a generalized category expressing the interrelatedness, interdependence and interpenetration of all events. The principle of relativity states that "every item of the universe including all the other actual entities is constituents in the constitution of any one actual entity." [49] Again, the principle of relativity asserts that "every item in the universe is involved in each concrescence." [50] Indeed, Whitehead's principle of relativity is at once reminiscent of the Buddhist doctrine of *śūnyatā* (Jpn., *kū*) or "emptiness," which has been alternatively

---

[46] Yokota, "Understanding Amida Budda: A Process Approach,"211.

[47] Unno, *River of Fire / River of Water: An Introduction to the Pure Land Tradition of Shin Buddhism*, 141.

[48] *Ibid,* 142.

[49] Whitehead, *Process and Reality*, 148.

[50] *Ibid,* 22.

translated as "relativity" and "universal relativity" by the Soviet Buddhologist Th. Stcherbatsky.[51]

In Whitehead's organismic process metaphysics, the Buddhist theme concerning the "indivisibility of emptiness and compassion" is articulated in terms of what the former calls the "concern" structure of causal process and universal relativity, wherein each act of prehension, or "feeling of feeling," is itself comprehended as an act of "sympathetic concernedness." In the technical vocabulary of Whitehead's process cosmology, each dependently co-arising occasion or event is a unified *subject* arising through prehension, sympathetic feeling, or "concern" for all multiple *objects* of the past: "The occasion as subject has a 'concern' for the object. And the 'concern' at once places the object as a component in the experience of the subject with an affective tone drawn from this object and directed towards it."[52] Whitehead further states, "It must be directly understood that no prehension ... can be divested of its affective tone, that is to say, of its character of a 'concern'.... Concernedness is of the essence of perception."[53] This concern structure of causal process whereby events arise through their concern for every other event, is further clarified by his notion of "sympathy," or feeling of feeling, whereby each occasion arises through sympathetic feelings of its relationships to all other events.[54] Hence, for Whitehead, "concern" is a functional equivalent to compassion (deriving from the Latin verbal root *compassio* meaning "to feel with"), understood as sympathy or feeling of feeling. Like Buddhist compassion. Whitehead's concernedness involves sympathy with all phenomena arising out of the dynamic network of interrelationships.

Here, it should be further clarified how the dipolar God of Whitehead's process theology relates to the image of Amida Buddha. In Whitehead's process theology, God is not the

---

[51] F. Th. Stcherbatsky, *The Conception of Buddhist Nirvāṇa* (Leningrad: Public Office of the Academy of Sciences of the USSR), 42.

[52] A. N. Whitehead, *Adventures of Ideas* (New York: The Free Press, 1933), 176.

[53] *Ibid*, 180.

[54] Whitehead, *Process and Reality*, 162.

omnipotent creator of the universe, just as in Shin Buddhism, Amida Buddha is not understood as a divine creator, since all dharma events naturally emerge from out of the dynamic web of interrelationships through the causal process of dependent co-arising, the coalescence of a field of causal relationships. According to Whitehead's process theology, in its Primordial Nature, the dipolar God is a "lure for feeling" [55] not an authoritarian deity who rules by forceful coercion but a caring deity who lures events to achieve maximum depth of aesthetic value, beauty, harmony and peace through gentle persuasion. Whitehead rejects the images of God as an unmoved mover, an imperial ruler, or a ruthless moralist, and instead envisions a patient, tender and caring God who lures events to realize divine aims. He writes that in contrast to these other images, the origins of Christianity in Jesus suggest a new image of a caring God that "dwells upon the tender elements in the world, which slowly and in quietness operate by love."[56] Whitehead describes the divine care operating through the Primordial Nature of God in terms of the image of *tenderness*: "His tenderness is directed towards each actual occasion, as it arises."[57] Again, in his description of the Primordial Nature of God in its function as a lure toward value, Whitehead asserts that God is "the poet of the world, with tender patience leading it by his vision of truth, beauty, and goodness."[58] In its Consequent Nature, the dipolar God is a caring deity who saves all beauty achieved by creative events as everlasting value-qualities in the divine memory. Describing the cosmological function of God's Consequent Nature, Whitehead thus writes, "The image ... under which this operative growth of God's nature is best conceived, is that of a *tender care* that nothing be lost" (italics added). [59] Just as in his organic process cosmology Whitehead describes the "concern"[60] structure of interrelated events arising

---

[55] *Ibid*, 344.

[56] *Ibid*, 343.

[57] *Ibid*, 105.

[58] *Ibid*, 346.

[59] *Ibid*, 346.

[60] Whitehead, *Adventures of Ideas*, 180.

through the causal process of sympathy, or feeling of feeling, whereby an occasion emerges into actuality by sympathetically feeling its relations to all past occasions, so in his process theology he emphasizes that God's ultimate divine nature is that of "care." In his Primordial Nature, the care of God lures all events to actualize his divine aims for them to realize harmony, beauty and value, just as the Primal Vow of Amida's compassionate Other Power grace calls out to all sentient beings to achieve enlightenment, nirvāṇa, and rebirth into the Pure Land. The Consequent Nature of God as the Kingdom of Heaven is a caring deity that operates like the compassionate nature of Dharmākara / Amida as the Storehouse Consciousness which functions to save all sentient beings through rebirth in his heavenly paradise as the Pure Land of Peace and Bliss. Hence, both Whiteheadian process theology and Shin Buddhism envision the divine nature of God / Amida through the image of *care* or *compassion*, just as they view the metaphysical character of ultimate reality itself as caring or compassionate, due to the *concern* structure of existence itself as composed of dependently co-arisen events or dharmas emerging from out of their sympathy, or dynamic process of feeling the feelings of all past events, which have arisen out of the dynamic interconnected matrix of relationships in the flowing continuum of nature.

Divine 'Suffering' in Process Theology and Shin Buddhism

In the classical tradition of Christian theology, God is an unchanging absolute, characterized by attributes of transcendence, immutability, and impassibility, thus to be completely unaffected by events in process. By contrast, the Consequent Nature of God in Whitehead's process theology is a caring God who feels the feelings of all becoming and perishing events, and is thus forever changing, growing and evolving with the world-process as the creative advance into novelty. Above it was shown how Whitehead's dipolar God is to be conceived through the image of "care,"[61] just as the structure of ultimate reality itself is to be described as the "concern" structure of causal feelings,[62] whereby events emerge by their "sympathy," or feeling of relationships with all other events.[63] In opposition to traditional Christian theology, wherein one of the fundamental attributes of God in His absolute transcendence is that of "impassibility," or total absence of feeling as an unmoved mover, Whitehead clarifies how the Consequent Nature of God is a caring deity who by concern, prehension, or sympathy, comes to feel the feelings of all other events, and therefore also feels both the suffering and joy of all becoming and perishing events in the creative process. Whitehead therefore asserts, "God is the great companion the *fellow sufferer* who understands" (italics added).[64]

Thus far, the interfaith dialogue between Whiteheadian process theology and Shin Buddhism has not yet addressed the importance of this notion of "divine suffering" in both traditions. However, Professor Takeda Ryusei of Ryukoku University, an eminent Japanese scholar of both Jōdo Shinshū and Whiteheadian process theology, has clearly explained the Shin Buddhist notion of *duḥkha* (Jpn., *ku*) or "suffering" in his article titled "Pure Land Buddhist View of *Duḥkha*."[65] In this essay, Takeda explicates what he calls "the bodhisattva's compassionate practice of vicarious *duḥkha*" in Shin Buddhism.

> This dynamism of the bodhisattva's ceaseless 'de-substantializing' [self-emptying] is embodied as the universal creativity of Dharmākara Bodhisattva's Primal Vow, whose fulfillment is Amida Buddha's untiring dynamism of saving all sentient beings. The uniqueness of

---

[61] Whitehead, *Process and Reality*, 346.

[62] Whitehead, *Adventures of Ideas*, 176.

[63] *Ibid*, 180.

[64] Whitehead, *Process and Reality*, 351.

[65] Takeda Ryusei, "Pure Land Buddhist View of Duḥkha," in *Buddhist-Christian Studies* 5 (1985): 7-24.

Amida's compassion ... is the ultimate form of bodhisattva's vicarious *duḥkha*.[66]

Like Whitehead's God of care who acts as a "fellow sufferer" who understands, Dharmākara Bodhisattva / Amida Buddha is a compassionate deity who saves all sentient beings by feeling their suffering as its own through vicarious *duḥkha*. Although he does not explicitly refer to Whitehead in this essay, Takeda nevertheless shows the unmistakable influence of process theology by his use of Whitehead's distinctive technical term "ingression" when discussing the influx or incarnation of divine grace as a gift of faith from the Primal Vow of Amida Buddha's compassionate Other Power, thereby implying a parallel between the ingression, descent, or incarnation of grace from the divine immanence of the Primordial Nature of God, such as when he writes: "For Shinran, Buddha nature is faith. Faith is given by Amida to each being, and through this gift of faith the Buddha nature *ingresses* itself into each being" (italics added).[67] Again, he states, "Apart from the bodhisattva's actualization as *ingressing* his will into the actual existence of each being, the 'desubstantializing' [self-emptying] reality turns out to be so abstract that any sort of reference to it falls into delusive attachment to that reality itself, which is none other than its dogmatic substantialization."[68]

PEACE in Shin Buddhism and Process Theology

Imamura Yemyo (1867-1932), one of the earliest pioneer missionaries who transmitted Shin Buddhism to America, and the Bishop of Honpa Hongwanji Mission of Hawaii the first Buddhist temple in America, proclaimed a Gospel of Peace grounded in the Primal Vow of Amida to bestow the gifts of peace, happiness and salvation to all beings. In his essay "Democracy According to the Buddhist Standpoint," he writes:

---

[66] *Ibid*, 15.

[67] *Ibid*, 21.

[68] *Ibid*, 15.

"Peace! Peace!" is the universal cry; for this is the only condition in which we can realize our ideals of truth, goodness, and beauty. But we cannot have a permanent peace unless we have a thorough understanding as to the true signification of peace. [69]

Imamura concludes, "We cannot stop short of propagating *the gospel of true peace* based upon the Will-to-Save [Primal Vow] of the Buddha." [70]

The process theology of Whitehead similarly holds to a vision of God as having a Primordial Nature that out of concern aims to lure all events toward realization of peace, happiness, and salvation. For Whitehead, Peace is the ultimate spiritual value which comes as a gift of God's divine grace. As will be seen, the God of process theology is a poet of the world luring it toward his vision of beauty, goodness and truth, along with their unity in the supreme Harmony of Peace. Whitehead holds that the divine nature of God as well as the generic metaphysical structure of reality are revealed in an epiphany of the person, life, and teachings of Jesus Christ through his gospel of peace, love, and sympathetic care for all creatures. For Whitehead, as for Shin Buddhism, the realization of Peace as cosmic Harmony is both an ultimate goal of civilization, as well as an expanded transpersonal state of consciousness beyond the ego-self analogous to resolution of suffering through overcoming attachment to an ego-self in the Peace of nirvāṇa. Hence, in this final section, I want to clarify how both Whiteheadian process theology and Shin Buddhism culminate in a Gospel of Peace, including both the social ideal of Peace as the goal of civilization and the soteriological goal of an expanded consciousness transcending the ego-self in a cosmic Harmony of harmonies.

(1) *PEACE in Shin Buddhism*: The imaginative picture of Amida Buddha depicted in the three great maṇḍala images

---

[69] Moriya Tomoe, *Yemyo Imamura: Pioneer American Buddhist*, translated by Tsuneichi Takeshita, edited by Alfred Bloom and Ruth Tabrah (Honolulu: Buddhist Study Center Press, 2000), 87.

[70] *Ibid,* 108.

representing the three Pure Land scriptures, as magnificently reproduced in *The Three Pure Land Sūtras* by Inagaki Hisao, illustrate the serene countenance of Amida Buddha in his Pure Land of Peace and Bliss. This same tranquil and quiescent visage of Amida Buddha's sublimely calm expression is shown through such great religious art as the famous Daibutsu, or Great Buddha, located in Kamakura. Throughout the Pure Land scriptures, along with the writings of Hōnen, Shinran and other Japanese masters of Shin Buddhism, it is constantly repeated that the Pure Land of Amida Buddha is the realm of Peace, as imparted by a variety of technical Japanese terms in the lexicon of Jōdo shinshū, including *annyō* (Land of Peace), *annyō jōdo* (Pure Land of Peace), *annyō jōsetsu* (Pure Land of Peace), *annyō kai* (Land of Peace), *anraku bukkoku* (Buddha Country of Peace and Bliss), *anraku butsudo* (Buddha Land of Peace and Bliss), *anraku jōdo* (Pure Land of Peace and Bliss), *anraku koku* (Land of Peace and Bliss), *anraku kokudo* (Land of Peace and Bliss), and *anraku sekai* (World of Peace and Bliss) to list just a few representative examples.[71]

As noted by James Frederiks, for Shinran, Rennyo and the whole Jōdo shinshū tradition, "the true sign of saving faith came to be 'peace of mind' (*anjin*)."[72] Shinran's notion of *anjin*, or "peace of mind," is itself the criterion of true *shinjin*, or the state of openness and receptivity to the transformative grace of Amida Buddha's compassionate Other Power. Hence, in the writings of Shinran the faith-consciousness of *shinjin* is called the "peace-bestowing pure mind."[73]

In the *Kyōgyōshinshō* and other writings from his *Collected Works*, Shinran often quotes from the Pure Land scriptures about the Buddha's teachings on Peace. Thus, in *The Sūtra of the*

---

[71] Inagaki Hisao, *A Glossary of Shin Buddhist Terms* (Kyoto: Ryukoku University Research Center, 1995), 3

[72] James Frederiks, "Jōdo Shinshū's Mission to History: A Christian Challenge to Shin Buddhist Social Ethics," in *Engaged Pure Land Buddhism*, eds. Kenneth K. Tanaka and Eisho Nasu (Berkeley: Wisdom Ocean Publications, 1998), 56.

[73] Shinran Shōnin, *The Collected Works of Shinran*, 2 Volumes (Kyoto: Hongwanji, 1997), 1:171.

Tathāgata of Immeasurable Life, Amida Buddha declares, "I will benefit the world, bringing peace and happiness."[74] Again, "Such people as these, hearing the Buddha's Name, will be full of peace and obtain the supreme benefit."[75] For Shinran, these kind of scriptural passages declare Amida Buddha's Primal Vows (Jpn., *hongan*) to compassionately bestow infinite Peace on all who call out Buddha's Name while at the same time guaranteeing the effectiveness of reciting the Buddha's Name through the *nembutsu* of NAMU AMIDA BUTSU for rebirth into the Pure Land of Peace and Bliss. For Shinran, "practicing the saying of the Name alone" leads one to "birth in the Pure Land of peace."[76] Shinran further quotes the authority of Master Ciyun, "Only the *nembutsu* is quick and true as the pure act that brings one to the land of peace; therefore, practice it."[77] Moreover, Shinran underscores how rebirth into the "Pure Land of Peace" (*annyō jōdo*) through recitation of *nembutsu* itself spontaneously, effortlessly, and naturally springs forth as the expression of *shinjin*, faith. It is therefore asserted, "Swift entrance into the city of tranquility ... is necessarily brought about by *shinjin*."[78] Shinran remarks, "We see, therefore, that the realization described above is all the great benefit we receive in the Pure Land of peace, the inconceivable, perfect virtue of the Buddha's [Primal] Vow."[79]

The Primal Vow of Dharmākara Bodhisattva / Amida Buddha that aims to compassionately bestow Peace on all who recite his Name is cited by Shinran in such passages as follows: "When I attain Buddhahood, the sentient beings throughout the countless, immeasurable, inconceivable, numberless worlds throughout the ten quarters who receive the Buddha's majestic light and are touched and illuminated by it shall attain peace."[80] For Shinran, the realization of the pure mind of "enlightenment" is characterized by

---

[74] *Ibid*, 1:15.
[75] *Ibid*, 1:16.
[76] *Ibid*, 1:113.
[77] *Ibid*, 1:49.
[78] *Ibid*, 1:73.
[79] *Ibid*, 1:62.
[80] *Ibid*, 1:117.

the overcoming of "suffering" (*ku*) and the experience of divine Peace as the "gift" (*ekō*) of the saving grace of Amida's compassionate Other Power (*tariki*) received in the openness and receptivity of *shinjin*, faith. Shinran cites *The Sūtra of Immeasurable Life*: "The peace-bestowing pure mind (so termed) because (the bodhisattvas) eliminate all sentient beings' pain."[81] Again, "[T]hey follow the gate of compassion. They eliminate all sentient beings' pain and become free of thoughts that do not bring peace."[82] Shinran remarks, "The undefiled pure mind is in accord with the gate to enlightenment."[83] Also, "Enlightenment is the realm of purity that brings peace to all sentient beings."[84] In his commentary on these scriptural passages, Shinran further emphasizes that Amida Buddha's Primal Vows arise from the heart of "compassion" (*jihi*) and promise to eliminate the problem of suffering due to impermanence by bestowing Peace on all who recite his Name in the state of faith: "[Concerning compassion (*jihi*)], to eliminate pain is termed *ji*; and to give happiness is termed *hi*. Through *ji* one eliminates the pain of all sentient beings, and through *hi* one becomes free of thoughts that do not bring them peace."[85] The Pure Land is continually referred to as "the land of peace."[86] Shinran continues, "Thus we clearly know from the Tathāgata's true teaching and the commentaries of the masters that the Pure Land of peace is the true fulfilled land."[87]

(2) One of the most neglected categories in Whitehead's scientific process cosmology and Christian process theology is his notion of transpersonal Peace. Yet his idea of transpersonal Peace is not only the crown of his process cosmology and process theology; it is also the nearest parallel to the ultimate Buddhist goal of *nirvāṇa*, or Peace. The notion of Peace is therefore a central point of intersection between Whiteheadian process

---

[81] *Ibid*, 1:169.
[82] *Ibid*.
[83] *Ibid*.
[84] *Ibid*, 1:168-169.
[85] *Ibid*, 1:169.
[86] *Ibid*, 1:194.
[87] *Ibid*, 1:202.

theology and the Shin Buddhist idea of rebirth in Amida's Pure Land of Peace and Bliss, as well as its idea of the Peace of nirvāṇa as a gift of the divine grace of Amida Buddha. It might be said that both Amida Buddha in Shin Buddhism and the dipolar God of Whitehead's process theology represent the Peace-bestowing Buddha / Christ whereby there comes to be the *ingression*, influx, or descent of transpersonal Peace, as the divine aim toward cosmic Harmony in each dharma event through the grace or persuasive agency of divine immanence as the Primordial Nature of God, the Primal Vow of Amida. For Whitehead, Christian theology explains Christ as a revelation of God's persuasive agency in the world as a lure toward the divine aims of peace, love and sympathy: "The essence of Christianity is to appeal to the life of Christ as a revelation of the nature of God and the world."[88] Whitehead then describes the revelation of the life, person and teachings of Jesus Christ as occurring through "his message of peace, love, and sympathy." [89] In *Process Theology*, co-authors Cobb and Griffin write, "Christian Peace is an expansion of care for self to care for others. "[90] This statement underscores how in process theology there is a deep relation between God's function as bestowing Peace and the divine nature as care, concern, compassion, love, and sympathy.

Whitehead's most visionary book, *Adventures of Ideas*, concludes with a remarkable chapter entitled "Peace."[91] According to Whitehead, transpersonal Peace is not only the ultimate aim of civilization; it is also an expanded state of consciousness wherein the self is transcended in a cosmic Harmony. In Whitehead's process metaphysics of becoming and perishing events, suffering, pain, and tragedy are intrinsic to the dynamic evolutionary temporal process of creative advance into novelty: "Decay, Transition, Loss, (and) Displacement belong to the essence of

---

[88] Whitehead, *Adventures of Ideas*, 167.

[89] *Ibid.*

[90] John B. Cobb, Jr., and David R. Griffin, *Process Theology: An Introductory Exposition* (Philadelphia: Westminster Press, 1976), 140.

[91] Whitehead, *Adventures of Ideas*, 284-296.

Creative Advance."[92] And just as for Buddhism, deliverance from the "suffering" of impermanence is realized only in the Peace of *nirvāṇa,* so for Whitehead, salvation from the tragedy, pain, and suffering of existence as the perpetual perishing of momentary events in the flux of becoming, comes only with the immediate experience of transpersonal Peace, the Harmony of Harmonies: "The Adventure of the Universe starts with the dream and reaps tragic Beauty. This is the secret of the union of Zest with Peace: That the suffering attains its end in a Harmony of Harmonies. The immediate experience of this Final Fact ... is the sense of Peace."[93] Whitehead further describes his concept of Peace in a manner consonant with Buddhism when he writes: "Peace is the understanding of tragedy."[94]   Again, "The inner feeling (that) belongs to this grasp of the service of tragedy is Peace, the purification of the emotions."[95] The salvific transpersonal dimension of Peace is then indicated by Whitehead in a manner reminiscent of Buddhist *muga* (Skt., *anātman*), or no-self: "Peace is ... the width where the 'self' has been lost, and interest has been transferred to co-ordinations wider than personality."[96] Again, "Peace carries with it a surpassing of personality."[97] Moreover, "Peace ... is a broadening of feeling due to the emergence of some deep metaphysical insight."[98] Whitehead even identifies the immediate experience of transpersonal Peace as the "attainment of truth"[99] and with "extreme ecstasy."[100]

In *Process Theology* by John Cobb and David Griffin, the coauthors state, "To whatever extent our lives become aligned to God's ever-changing aims for us, we can have 'that Peace, which is the harmony of the soul's activities with ideal aims that lie

---

[92] *Ibid,* 286.
[93] *Ibid.*
[94] *Ibid.*
[95] *Ibid.*
[96] *Ibid,* 285.
[97] *Ibid.*
[98] *Ibid.*
[99] Whitehead, *Adventures of Ideas,* 292.
[100] *Ibid,* 289.

beyond any personal satisfaction.'"[101] They further clarify that, "it is the immanence of deity as a whole, with its Primordial and Consequent Natures, its creative and responsive love, which is the source of Peace: 'It is the immanence of the Great Fact including this initial Eros and this final Beauty which constitutes the zest of self-forgetful transcendence belonging to Civilization at its height .... The immediate experience of this Final Fact is the sense of Peace.'"[102] Through the caring persuasive agency of God's Primordial Nature as the divine lure, there is implanted in each dependently co-arising event an initial aim toward realizing the harmonic value qualities of beauty, art, adventure, and truth, as well as their unity in the supreme aim of Peace, the cosmic Harmony of harmonies: "The presence of God in us is divine grace.[103] It gives rise to adventure, and to art. To it we owe the beauty.... It works at all times in all people. The supreme gift is Peace, which is an alignment of ourselves with God's grace."[104] As again emphasized here, this aim toward Peace in each occasion derived from God's Primordial Nature as the divine lure is the functioning of grace, and the realization of Peace in each occasion as a result of this grace is itself the gift of God through Christ as the divine Logos which incarnates into each occasion. Cobb and Griffin therefore conclude, "Peace is the gift of Christ."[105]

Whitehead himself writes that, "The experience of Peace is largely beyond the control of purpose. It comes as a *gift*" (italics added). [106] Again, "Peace carries with it a surpassing of personality .... It is primarily a *trust* in the efficacy of Beauty.... The trust in the self-justification of Beauty introduces *faith*, where reason fails to reveal the details" (italics added). [107] For Whitehead, transpersonal Peace comes as a "gift" of grace ingressing as the divine immanence of God received through entrustment, or faith in

---

[101] Cobb and Griffin, *Process Theology*, 124.

[102] *Ibid*, 125.

[103] Cf. Whitehead, *Adventures of Ideas*, 205.

[104] Cobb and Griffin, *Process Theology*, 126.

[105] *Ibid*, 127.

[106] Whitehead, *Adventures of Ideas*, 285.

[107] *Ibid*.

the divine efficacy of God's ideal aims for each occasion. Thus, we arrive at a most remarkable convergence upon the idea of salvation from the suffering and tragic beauty of impermanent dharma events through a bestowal of transpersonal Peace by God / Amida in the framework of Whitehead's process theology and that of Shin Buddhism. For just as in Whitehead's process theology the realization of Peace is not attained by self-effort, but is only received as a "gift" of divine grace through faith by means of the divine immanence of God, so in Shin Buddhism based on the teachings of Shinran Shōnin, one attains salvation, enlightenment, nirvāṇa, and rebirth in the heavenly paradise of the Pure Land of Peace and Bliss, not through the efforts of "self power" (*jiriki*), but only as a "gift" (*ekō*) of the transformative grace of Amida Buddha's compassionate "Other Power" (*tariki*) realized in tranquil inwardness of *shinjin*, faith. It is in such a manner, then, that we have arrived at this vision of Amida in Shin Buddhism, and the dipolar God in Whitehead's process theology, as the caring and compassionate Peace-bestowing Buddha / Christ that forever guides and saves all events co-arising from the dynamic network of interrelationships in the ceaseless flux of becoming.

Bibliography

Doniger, Wendy. *Splitting the Difference.* Chicago: University of Chicago Press, 1999.

Cobb, John B., Jr. *Christ in a Pluralistic Age.* Philadelphia: Fortress Press, 1975.

___. *Beyond Dialogue: Toward a Mutual Transformation of Christianity and Buddhism.* Philadelphia: Westminster Press, 1982.

Cobb, John B., Jr., and David R Griffin. *God & the World.* New York: Wipf and Stock Publishers, 1998.

___. *Process Theology: An Introductory Exposition.* Philadelphia: Westminster Press, 1976.

Frederiks, James. "Jōdo Shinshū's Mission to History: A Christian Challenge to Shin Buddhist Social Ethics." In *Engaged Pure*

Land Buddhism. Edited by Kenneth K. Tanaka and Eisho Nasu. Berkeley, California: Wisdom Ocean Publications. 1998.

Hirota, Dennis, ed. *Toward a Contemporary Understanding of Pure Land Buddhism: Creating a Shin Buddhist Theology in a Religiously Plural World.* Albany, New York: State University of New York Press, 2000.

Inagaki, Hisao. *The Three Pure Land Sūtras.* Kyoto: Nagata Bunshodo, 1995.

____. *A Glossary of Shin Buddhist Terms.* Kyoto: Ryukoku University Research Center, 1995.

Ingram, Paul O. *The Modem Buddhist-Christian Dialogue: Two Universalistic Religions in Transformation.* Lewiston/ Queenston/Lampeter: The Edwin Mellen Press, 1988.

Kalupahana, David. *The Buddha and the Concept of Peace.* Sri Lanka: Vishva Lekha Publishers, 1999.

Moriya, Tomoe. *Yemyo Imamura: Pioneer American Buddhist.* Translated by Tsuneichi Takeshita. Edited by Alfred Bloom and Ruth Tabrah. Honolulu, Hawaii: Buddhist Study Center Press, 2000.

Nishida, Kitarō. *Last Writings: Nothingness and the Religious Worldview.* Tr. D. Dilworth. Honolulu: University of Hawaii Press, 1987.

Odin, Steve. *Process Metaphysics and Hua-Yen Buddhism,* Albany, New York: SUNY Press, 1982.

____. *The Social Self in Zen and American Pragmatism.* Albany: New York: SUNY Press, 1996.

____. *Artistic Detachment in Japan and the West.* Honolulu: University of Hawaii Press, 2001.

____. "Leap of Faith in Shinran and Kierkegaard." In *The Pure Land,* n.s., 19 (December 2002).

Stcherbatsky, F. Th. *The Conception of Buddhist Nirvāṇa.* Leningrad: Public Office of the Academy of Sciences of the USSR, 1927.

Shinran Shōnin. *The Collected Works of Shinran.* 2 Volumes. Kyoto: Jōdo Shinshū Hongwanji, 1997.

Soga Ryōjin. "Dharmakāya Bodhisattva." In *The Buddha Eye: An Anthology of the Kyoto School*. Edited by Frederick Franck. New York: Crossroad Publishing Co., 1982. 221-231.

Takeda, Ryusei. "Pure Land Buddhist View of *Duḥkha*." In *Buddhist-Christian Studies* 5 (1985): 7-24.

Tanaka, Kenneth K. *Ocean: An Introduction to Jōdo-Shinshū Buddhism in America*. Berkeley, California: Wisdom Ocean Publications. 1997

Unno, Taitetsu. *River of Fire / River of Water: An Introduction to the Pure Land Tradition of Shin Buddhism*. New York: Doubleday, 1998.

____. *Shin Buddhism*. New York: Doubleday, 2002.

Whitehead, A. N. *Adventures of Ideas*. New York: The Free Press, 1933.

____. *The Interpretation of Science: Selected Essays*. Edited by A. H. Johnson. New York: The Bobs-Merrill Company, 1961.

____. *Modes of Thought*. New York: The Free Press, 1981.

____. *Process and Reality*. Edited by David Ray Griffin & Donald W. Sherburne. 1929. New York: The Free Press, 1978.

____. *Religion in the Making*. 1926. New York: Meridian, 1974.

____. *Symbolism: Its Meaning and Affect*. New York: MacMillan, 1927.

____. *Science and the Modern World* (1925). New York: The Free Press, 1967.

Yokota, John. "A Call to Compassion: Process Thought and the Conceptualization of Amida Buddha." In *Process Studies* 23.2 (Summer 1994): 87-97.

____. "Understanding Amida Buddha: A Process Approach." In *Toward a Contemporary Understanding of Pure Land Buddhism: Creating a Shin Buddhist Theology in a Religiously Plural World*. Edited by Dennis Hirota. Albany, New York: SUNY Press, 2000.

____. "A Call to Compassion." In *Toward a Contemporary Understanding of Pure Land Buddhism: Creating a Shin Buddhist Theology in a Religiously Plural World*. Edited by Dennis Hirota. Albany, New York: SUNY Press, 2000.

REFLECTIONS ON THE ETHICAL MEANING OF SHINRAN'S TRUE ENTRUSTING

Victor Forte

The purpose here in examining Shinran's notion of *shinjin* or "true entrusting" is to consider first, how this teaching supports his assertions about attainment and second, the possible ethical implications given these assertions. My main philosophical interests are in examining the ethical meaning that results from the varying claims and descriptions of attainment that one encounters in Buddhist traditions. This would include not only what may result out of the contents of attainment, but also the ethical implications that might result from the *assumed possibilities* of attainment. In the case of Shinran (1173-1262 CE), both content and possibility are given such a unique and radical meaning that there may be no single figure in Buddhism who compares in his courage and vision to take the Dharma in a fundamentally new direction. Yet, as is often recognized in contemporary studies of his work, he has attracted little interest from Western scholars.[1]

---

[1] The most devoted Western scholar in the field has been Alfred Bloom. His classic early text on Pure Land Buddhism, *Shinran's Gospel of Pure Grace* (Tucson: University of Arizona Press, 1965) remains a highly regarded study. He continues to be the most recognized Western voice, recently editing two collections on Shinran - *The Essential Shinran: A Buddhist Path of True Entrusting* (Bloomington, Indiana: World Wisdom, 2007) brings together excerpts from a number of important primary Shin Buddhist texts, arranged according to different themes in Shinran's life and thought. *Living in Amida's*

This may be due to a number of factors – the mythic foundations of Shin Buddhism, the assumed similarities with Christianity, the apparent simplicity of the doctrine, the lack of consideration given to the teaching of emptiness. Regardless of the accuracy of these assumptions, Shin Buddhism does present a number of challenges in terms of the ethical meaning of its doctrine, and may warrant greater attention for this reason. For now, I would like to focus on a single paradoxical question concerned with Shinran's understanding of true entrusting and attainment: How might the ethical hopelessness of true entrusting make the ethical life possible?

One of the most striking features of Shinran's explanation of true entrusting is that he claims it is functionally operative only when there is a thorough and complete recognition of the impossibility of ethical action. He supports this claim with the assertion that the deep burden of karma we carry into the present existence provides the very ground for each and every action that arises out of our lives. For example, in the following verses from *Gutoku's Hymns of Lament and Reflection*, Shinran asserts the impossibility of good action:

> Each of us, in outward bearing,
> Makes a show of being wise, good and dedicated;
> But so great are our greed, anger, perversity, and deceit,
> That we are filled with all forms of malice and cunning.
>
> Extremely difficult is it to put an end to our evil nature;
> The mind is like a venomous snake or scorpion.
> Our performance of good acts is also poisoned;

Universal Vow (Bloomington, Indiana: World Wisdom, 2004) is a collection of essays from leading scholars and practitioners of Shin Buddhism. One cannot help but to notice that in this collection the great majority of contributors are Japanese, with only four Western writers besides Bloom contributing five essays among twenty-one total. Only one of the four is a scholar in Japanese studies, Galen Amstutz.

Hence, it is called false and empty practice.[2]

Making distinctions between good and evil actions are of no consequence since even what might be categorized as a good action arises out of karmic conditionality – so there is no agency associated with ethical choice, and no measurable progressive benefit that can come from action of any kind. These assertions would seem at first glance to be at odds with traditional Buddhist practice, given that it is commonly assumed that ethical practices are necessary in order to progress towards liberation. But if we look closely at the relationship between ethics and liberation in the foundational teachings of Indian Buddhism, we might find some precedence for Shinran's assertions, specifically in terms of the meaning of *puñña* and *kusala*, the two main categories of ethical activity found in the Indian canons. The way they are often distinguished is that *puñña* pertains to actions that accumulate karmic merit and lead to more auspicious rebirths, while *kusala* refers to actions that lead to liberation. This commonly held understanding of their meaning has brought about a fair amount of critical debate among Western Buddhologists concerning the relation between the two[3] – Do they represent two paths, *puñña* for laypersons and *kusala* for monks? Does the practice of *puñña* eventually lead to *kusala*, or does *puñña* possibly interfere on some level with *kusala*, or are they really just two ways of speaking about the same process?

Perhaps, one could argue that essentially *puñña* and *kusala* are both employed by Buddhist practitioners in order to lead to the formation of interior and exterior environments conducive to the

---

[2] See Dennis Hirota, trans., *The Collected Works of Shinran* (CWS) (Kyoto: Jōdō Shinshū Hongwanji-ha, 1997), *Gutoku's Hymns of Lament and Reflection*, I, 421, # 95-96.

[3] There has been an on-going discussion about this topic among contributors to the online *Journal of Buddhist Ethics*. An editor and co-founder of the journal, Damien Keown, initiated much of the interest in these teachings in his *The Nature of Buddhist Ethics* (New York: St. Martin's Press, 1992). A number of scholars writing in the *Journal of Buddhist Ethics* have contributed essays responding to Keown and adding their own interpretations of *puñña* and *kusala*, including L. S. Cousins, Abraham Velez de Cea, and Martin T. Adam.

achievement of liberation. [4] This would indicate then that the primary reason for engaging in ethical practices is to create the proper psychic conditions for attainment, whether that is the attainment of arhatship or Buddhahood. [5] To assert, as Shinran asserts, that all actions regardless of their apparent moral attributes are inherently evil is to essentially negate the practice of both *puñña* and *kusala*. True entrusting is nothing more than the forfeiting of these practices. This would seem to indicate a dramatic break from tradition, forming the basis for Shinran's distinction between self power and other power, or the path of the sages and the path of true entrusting. However, one could also say that it was never the case that *puñña* and *kusala* were understood as actually *leading* to liberation, even according to the Indian foundational teachings. The ethical practices always remain within

---

[4] This is my main position concerning the practices of *puñña* and *kusala*. Namely, ethical practices do not lead causally to liberation, but only provide the kinds of environments, internally and externally, which are conducive to liberation. By practicing the precepts and other ethical systems in the Buddhadharma, we reduce the amount of discord in our relationships and in our consciousness. In order to achieve the highest levels of concentration, our internal and external environments must allow for the possibility of reaching these states, however there is little evidence to conclude that such environments actually *cause* liberation. Nor do the canonical records of Indian Buddhism indicate that attainment occurs as a result of the removal of past karma – that is the way of the Jains. The way of the Buddha is to recognize the functional laws of causation and use them to one's benefit. Ethical behavior results mainly from a wise recognition of causation. Even in terms of merit, we achieve higher realms of existence that are less chaotic and violent, providing environments more conducive to the practices of meditation – this is the main benefit of *puñña*, not the pleasurable karmic rewards of merit making. The Buddha resided in Tuṣita heaven in his lifetime immediately before being born as Siddhārtha Gautama, the result of innumerable lifetimes of *puñña* cultivation, but the danger of rebirth in a heavenly realm is that the pleasures of such a life can impede spiritual progress as well. This distinction is illuminated in the story of the Buddha's religious journey when he rejects the attainment of the formless *jhānas* as liberation.

[5] One could argue that the main difference between the path of the arhat and the path of the bodhisattva is that the former limits the practice of *puñña* in emphasizing *kusala*, while the latter expands the practice of *puñña* to such a degree that the accumulation of merit leads beyond arhatship to Buddhahood.

karmic conditionality, and their main purpose is to lead to beneficial environments supportive of efficacious meditational states.[6]

By insisting that all action is bound to karmic conditionality and so always resulting ultimately in evil, Shinran was mainly attacking a common misrepresentation of the Dharma, namely that liberation is a direct result of human agency.[7] This is further emphasized in his argument that even *shinjin* originates from Amida's vow and not from the practitioner, so that attainment as true entrusting does not result from human agency either. Rather, it occurs as an awakening to one's full renunciation of progressive cultivation, a realization of the utter surrender of self power (Jpn., *jiriki*). This surrender, however, does not result in an eradication of one's karmic debt, but in the moment of a surrender of such depth and completeness, the karmic weight holding us in samsaric bondage is transformed into the good that makes the attainment of the Pure Land a possibility. According to Shinran:

> ...without the practitioner's calculating in any way whatsoever, all his past, present and future karmic evil is transformed into good. "To be transformed" means that karmic evil, without being nullified or eradicated, is made

---

[6] See the *Ambalaṭṭhikārāhulovāda Sutta* from the *Middle Length Discourses of the Buddha* (*Majjhima Nikāya*). When the Buddha teaches his son Rāhula about the benefits of reflecting on one's actions, he concludes by stating, "But when you reflect, if you know: 'This action that I have done with the body does not lead to my own affliction, or to the affliction of others, or to the affliction of both; it was a wholesome bodily action with pleasant consequences, pleasant results,' you can abide happy and glad, training day and night in wholesome states." See *The Middle Length Discourses of the Buddha: A New Translation of the Majjhima Nikāya*, trans. Bhikkhu Ñāṇamoli and Bhikkhu Bodhi (Boston: Wisdom Publications, 1995), 525.

[7] Nāgārjuna takes up this question in the *Mūlamadhyamakakārikā*, on the "Examination of Bondage," stating, "'I, without grasping, will pass beyond sorrow, and I will attain nirvāṇa,' one says. Whoever grasps like this has a great grasping. When you can't bring about nirvāṇa, nor the purification of cyclic existence, what is cyclic existence, and what is the nirvāṇa you examine?" See *The Fundamental Wisdom of the Middle Way: Nāgārjuna's Mūlamadhyamaka-kārikā*, trans. Jay L. Garfield (New York: Oxford University Press, 1995), 42.

into good, just as all waters, upon entering the great ocean, immediately become ocean water. [8]

If the ocean water represents the mind of Amida, then in surrendering one's agency of progressive ethical development, one participates in, or comes in contact with, the pure mind of wisdom and compassion personified in the identity of Amida Buddha. It is not as though karmic evil is somehow transformed into a karmic or meritorious good through true entrusting; instead, karmic evil is transformed into good through the realization of its utter intractability. The paradoxical result of Shinran's interpretation of Amida-inscribed Dharma is the assertion that the ethical life is made possible through the hopelessness of ethical action. In the recognition of the hopelessness of self-determined agency, one may experience a freedom grounded in humility and the shared human condition – the wisdom and compassion associated with Buddhahood is made known in the moment of true entrusting, in the defiled life of an ordinary human being through a receptive self surrender. So, it is in the sacrifice of *puñña* and *kusala*, in the sacrifice of ethics as meritorious, efficacious practice, that one's actions are purified as true compassion.

Attainment of the Pure Land as Non-Retrogression

Therefore, *shinjin*, according to Shinran, is attainment – not the promise of attainment in the next life, but the attainment of the Pure Land in the very moment of true entrusting. But what exactly is the meaning of this attainment? The writings of Shinran are quite clear that *shinjin* is the attainment of non-retrogression (irreversibility), [9] a traditional notion related to the path of the bodhisattva as it was described in the Indian *Prajñāpāramitā*

---

[8] *Notes on "Essentials of Faith Alone,"* CWS I, 453.

[9] For example, in *Lamp for the Latter Ages*, Letter 7, "You should understand that the moment of settling of those who entrust themselves to Tathāgata's Vow is none other than settling into the stage of non-retrogression, because they receive the benefit of being grasped, never to be abandoned." CWS I, 532.

Sūtras. [10] What these texts describe mainly is the attainment of non-retrogression, not the ultimate attainment of Buddhahood. Buddhahood, the apparent goal of the Mahāyāna vehicle, is to a certain degree, subverted in the foundational literature by placing greater emphasis on the intermediate goal of bodhisattvic non-retrogression. There is evidence of this emphasis in other Mahāyāna literature as well. Even Gautama Buddha plays a mere cameo role in the *Vimalakīrti Sūtra.* In the *Heart Sūtra,* the Buddha instructs Śāriputra to turn his attention to Avalokiteśvara Bodhisattva's practice of the Perfection of Wisdom, and in the *Larger Pure Land Sūtra* (Skt., *Sukhāvatī-vyūha;* Jpn., *Daimuryōjukyō*), it is the vows of Dharmākara Bodhisattva that provide the possibility for true entrusting. In this sense, non-retrogression is an attainment *without* attainment, an assured being-on-the-way towards an attainment that is coming, but not yet. In non-retrogression, the bodhisattva courses freely in *saṃsāra,* unfettered by preferences or views, employing skillful means, and continuing to accumulate the karmic merit required for Buddhahood.

From the Indian sources, non-retrogression is achieved in the 8th stage (*bhūmi*) of the ten stage progression to Buddhahood. [11] At this stage of development, achieved through innumerable lifetimes of dedication to the practice of the *pāramitās,* the bodhisattva has

---

[10] In the *Aṣṭasāharasrikā Prajñāpāramitā Sūtra,* it states, "Now those Bodhisattvas who have stood on the irreversible Bodhisattva-stage, ...they expound the perfection of wisdom for sons and daughters of a good family who are earnestly intent, who train themselves, and strive in the perfection of wisdom.... There are, on the other hand, countless beings who raise their thoughts to enlightenment, who strengthen that thought of enlightenment, who course towards enlightenment, and perhaps just one or two of them can abide on the irreversible Bodhisattva-stage! For full enlightenment is hard to come up to if one has inferior vigor, is slothful, an inferior being, has inferior thoughts, notions, intentions and wisdom." See *The Perfection of Wisdom in Eight Thousand Lines and its Verse Summary,* trans. Edward Conze (San Francisco: Four Seasons Foundation, 1973), 107.

[11] A systematic elaboration on the ten stages of the bodhisattva path is presented by Candrakīrti in his *Madhyamakāvatāra* or *The Entry into the Middle Way.*

attained such a high level of wisdom (*prajñā*), (perfected in the 6th stage), and skillful means (*upāya*) (perfected in the 7th stage) that achievement of liberation is understood as so close at hand, that final liberation must be resisted in order to eventually achieve Buddhahood. [12] Having attained non-retrogression, the attainment of Buddhahood may actually be several lifetimes removed from the present lifetime, but Buddhahood is nevertheless guaranteed. However, the attainment is only the attainment of the guarantee and so it is an attainment that is at the same time, a non-attainment. [13] Having attained the guarantee, this stage is recognized as the "perfection of the vow." It is in this space between the attainment of non-retrogression and the attainment of final liberation that the vow is achieved, and great compassion is made possible, since the guarantee of non-retrogression releases the bodhisattva from any possible remnant of self-concern, while still allowing for continued response to the needs of suffering beings.

But what is the non-retrogression that is achieved through true-entrusting? Rather than the result of innumerable lifetimes of progress, moving through the successive stages of the bodhisattva path, non-retrogression is achieved according to Shinran by

---

[12] According to Huntington, for example, "At this juncture in his practice, he would seem most susceptible to the temptation to withdraw completely from the net of relationships (were such an act possible) and to enter into unconditional peace and liberation from suffering for himself alone. Yet just when he might be prepared to turn away from the everyday, pain-filled world, there appears to him a vision of all the Buddhas who have traveled along this same path, and relying on their example, he is inspired to reaffirm his original vow to rescue all sentient beings from the suffering caused by spiritual ignorance and clinging." See C. W. Huntington, Jr., with Geshe Namgyal Wangchen, *The Emptiness of Emptiness: An Introduction to Early Indian Mādhyamika* (Honolulu: University of Hawaii Press, 1989), 101.

[13] Candrakīrti describes the 8th stage named "The Immovable" (*Acalā*) in the *Madhyamakāvatāra* by stating, "The wisdom of nonclinging does not abide in the company of any faults, and therefore at the eighth stage these impurities along with their roots are thoroughly eradicated. The afflictions have been extinguished, yet even though [the bodhisattva] is preeminent in the triple world, still he is unable to obtain the treasure of the [qualities] of the buddhas, which is limitless as the heavens." See Huntington, 186.

sacrificing the path, by fully accepting its impossibility. In a single moment of *shinjin*, one finds oneself in the 8th stage of the bodhisattva path, having never passed through the previous seven stages. But in both cases, the 8th stage is achieved through the perfection of the vow. In the case of the Shin Buddhist, the vow originates not from some previous lifetime of the practitioner, however distant the origins of taking up the path may have been, but from a primordial vow of Other-power (*tariki*), originating from an immeasurable mythic past, and preceding any and all volitional vows that could be traced to a personal karmic history. It is a vow of perfect purity because it functions independently of the conditioned necessities of all other forms of religious practice. There is no need here, for example, to somehow unbind oneself from the karmic traps of merit making by engaging in practices of merit transference, since the attainment of the vow in this case is completely unmerited! It occurs independently of any and all personal conditionality, and so is, according to Shinran, inconceivable.

> …with regard to Other Power, since it is inconceivable Buddha-wisdom, the attainment of supreme enlightenment by foolish beings possessed of blind passions comes about through the working shared only by Buddhas; (and) it is not in any way the design of the practitioner. [14]

Non-retrogression originating from Amida's vow also functions as a guarantee in the sense that it releases the practitioner of true entrusting from self-concern in the present life. Birth is attained in that moment, yet there remains the space left open between attainment of the vow and final attainment of Buddhahood, allowing for the possibility of the compassion of Amida to manifest itself within the earthly domain of a degenerated Dharma (*mappō*). But unlike the bodhisattva path of traditional Mahāyāna, the guarantee of Amida's vow promises Buddhahood in the very next life, so there is even less temporal

---

[14] *A Collection of Letters*, CWS I, 571, #10.

uncertainty than in the traditional bodhisattva path. One lives in the recognition that Buddhahood will be manifested in the proximity of one's next life, while still leaving open a space for compassionate activity within the present life. The narrowing of the space between non-retrogression and final attainment as promised by Amida concentrates the power of his compassion in the immediacy of a single human lifetime. In addition, unlike the path of the bodhisattva in the 8th stage of non-retrogression, compassion for the truly entrusting has no merit-making capacity whatsoever. In the case of the bodhisattva in the 8th stage there remains the necessity to build up huge stores of merit in order to eventually achieve Buddhahood. *Compassion is practice.* But those who have achieved non-retrogression through true entrusting are brought to compassion through the recognition of their own shared defilement and their gratitude towards the vow. Merit making has been completely forfeited. Even the continued recitation of the *nembutsu* is for Shinran an expression of gratitude, not an activity of merit making.

Shinran's Promise

The possibility and meaning of attainment in Shin Buddhism is dependent in large part on the radical interpretation of the original Pure Land texts offered by Shinran. The vow is not only Amida's promise, but it also is Shinran's promise as well. But how are we to measure Shinran's interpretation in terms of his actual understanding of the canon? Contemporary scholars seem divided on how far they are willing to take the mythic literalism of Shin Buddhist doctrine. The debate is centered on two related concerns, the literalism of the Pure Land and the particular form of Buddha-body attributed to Amida. [15] Based on the face value of the

---

[15] The two questions are interrelated. According to Shinran, is the Pure Land a literal destination for the truly entrusting, or can we simply equate the Pure Land with emptiness and Shinran's system as an example of skillful means, making the truth of emptiness accessible to everyone through a compelling mythical construction? If we accept the former, we might emphasize Shinran's recognition of Amida as a *Saṃbhogakāya* Buddha (Bliss-body) who resides in a

canonical sūtras, one could argue that the texts simply trace the story of a particular *Saṃbhogakāya* (Bliss-body) Buddha, Amitābha, who had established a Buddha Realm, one of many such realms in the cosmology of Indian Mahāyāna Buddhism. Japanese Shin Buddhism resulted ultimately from an imported Chinese cult that centered its practices on the canonical authority of the Pure Land sūtras. But how literal is Shinran's interpretation of the Pure Land? If we assume it is purely literal, then we must conclude that attainment through true entrusting and rebirth in a Western paradise was for Shinran, the necessary result for all Shin Buddhists in their recitation of the *nembutsu*. If not, then Shinran's Pure Land may be interpreted simply as a representation of traditional Dharmic doctrine (i.e., emptiness), customized to make accessible to the many what had been only available for the few.

According to Amstutz, for example, "Shinran's interpretation of the Pure Land mythos...short-circuited the mediating feature of conventional Buddhist religiosity....changing the Amida from a more or less physical, concretely visualized deity to a relatively abstract representation of perfected *pratītya-samutpāda*." [16] In Keel's *Understanding Shinran: A Dialogical Approach*, he, in a similar vein, states, "From the enlightened perspective, ... the story is nothing more than an expedient or temporary means (*hōben*) to lead ignorant and sinful beings to an enlightenment that, once realized, has no use for the expedient. The Pure Land story is for the enlightened of the Pure Land an 'unreal' means for realizing

---

Western Paradise. If we argue the latter, the identity of Amida can be more accurately equated with the *Dharmakāya* (Law Body) – reality itself, or suchness. This would mean that Amida is not a particular Buddha, but a representation of realization – the Buddhahood of all Buddhas. This is further complicated by the fact that the *Dharmakāya*, as interpreted by the early Chinese Pure Land practitioner, Danluan (476-542 CE) is based on a two-body theory, arguing that the *Dharmakāya* is expressed as both the "Dharma Body of suchness" and the "Dharma Body as compassionate Means." Shinran was also influenced by Danluan in his own interpretation of Amida's identity.

[16] Galen Amstutz, "Shinran and Authority in Buddhism," in *Living in Amida's Vow: Essays in Shin Buddhism*, ed. Alfred Bloom (Bloomington: World Wisdom, 2004), 146.

'reality.'"[17] In response to Keel, Gregory Gibbs states, "I would challenge Professor Keel to find any language in Shinran's writings compatible with the reductionistic view he takes of the Pure Land via concepts of "emptiness" and "skillful means."[18] Although Gibbs recognizes "these concepts are important and do occur in Shinran's texts," he also finds, "a tendency to assess Buddhist thinkers in terms of highly edited and homogenized versions of medieval scholastic Buddhist thought."[19] John Keenan observes a "neglect of emptiness" in Shinran's writings, arguing that the founder of Shin Buddhism placed the Mādhyamika in the path of the sages and "avoided it [the teaching of emptiness] like the plague."[20] He concludes that:

> Shinran will not allow the language of emptiness to swallow up the reality of Amida Buddha. He will not admit that the teaching of emptiness constitutes a meta-language in which all other teachings may be expressed and to which they may be reduced....Shinran was...emptying all theories indeed, even that of emptiness – a very traditional Mādhyamika move indeed![21]

One problem with these attempts to somehow determine an accurate interpretation of Shinran's true sense of the meaning of the Pure Land, is that in order to take such a position, Shinran would have to recognize himself as authoritative, which it seems to me he takes great pains to deny throughout his writings. [22]

---

[17] Hee-sung Keel, *Understanding Shinran: A Dialogical Approach* (Freemont, CA: Asian Humanities Press, 2000), 161.

[18] Gregory G. Gibbs, "*Understanding Shinran* and the Burden of Traditional Dogmatics," in *The Eastern Buddhist* 30. 2 (Summer 1998): 283.

[19] *Ibid.*

[20] John P. Keenan, "Shinran's Neglect of Emptiness," in *The Eastern Buddhist* 33.1 (Spring 2001): 10.

[21] *Ibid*, 13-14.

[22] For example, "Through hearing the *shinjin* of the wise, the heart of myself, Gutoku ("foolish/stubble-haired") becomes manifest. The *shinjin* of the wise is such that they are inwardly wise outwardly foolish. The heart of Gutoku is such that I am inwardly foolish." See *Gutoku's Notes*, CWS I, 587.

Although Shinran is engaged in interpretive and even polemical assertions throughout his works, these are grounded in recognition that he is only capable of receiving *shinjin* – his interpretations are primarily structured to refute his own authority, and prove his complete dependence on the vow. If he claims for example, that he does not have a single disciple, then the practice of skillful means would be both presumptuous and contradictory. Or in stating (as recorded in *A Record in Lament of Divergences*, Jpn., *Tannishō*) that he is not sure whether the *nembutsu* will send him to the Pure Land or to hell,[23] he certainly claims no textual authority. So his arguments are not designed necessarily to support a particular interpretive position, but to always follow the path of true entrusting. Following this path may have often been conscious and strategic, but his practice of *shinjin* was limited to the particulars of his own karmic predicament, and so he could not claim to be designing a path for others. From his point of reference the compassionate vow of Amida was established for him alone.[24] However, in openly recognizing his own complete dependence on the vow, it allowed him to share with his contemporaries an authentic awakening to human vulnerability and need.

---

[23] *A Record in Lament of Divergences,* CWS I, 622, #2.
[24] *Ibid,* 679, in "Postscript."

RE-IMAGINING SOCIALLY ENGAGED BUDDHISM

James Kenneth Powell II

This term "socially engaged" Buddhism makes reference to a false dichotomy: "socially engaged" and "Buddhism." One has only to think of the Buddha's own life to realize this. Universal education and health care were the principle of his community, powered by a democratic institution and strict rules to avoid corruption. Tolerance, restraint and mental stabilization along with abstinence from intoxicants and sex preserve and stabilize the lay and clerical communities alike.

The western meaning serves for the definition of idea "socially engaged." The western monotheisms focus as part of their nature on the community, society at large, while Buddhism engages the individual. For the Semitic monotheisms, the idea of the "Chosen People" is central. The surprising fact is that the society is comprised of individuals, and so for Buddhist political theory, engaging the individual in terms of education, ethics and altruism, through meditation and restraint, entails the larger interest in "social" ethics of the greater masses.

Specifically it is the Protestant idea of social action, mass revolt to oppose political oppression "by order of God" that is new to Buddhism. "God" is styled as a shepherd, thus leading sheep – the congregation. I suggest that the new context of this idea "socially engaged" Buddhism is the meeting of principally Calvinist social traditions with principally Zen Buddhism. It is then the task to decipher the social engagement of Buddhism via Asian evolutes from the influence of Protestant values through contact with the West. This task is the focus of this paper.

Each of the major Eurasian "families" of religions has a vertical and horizontal tradition with regard to not only social ethics, but arguably, in all spheres. In China, the hierarchical contrast of Confucianism with Daoism is clear. Hierarchically structured Confucianism provides social security, stability and order. Daoism suggests freedom for the individual, integration with unspeakable, "chaotic" nature and a mistrust of social hierarchies.

Again, the contrast of Hindu *varnasrama* the "color code" which the Portuguese first called the *casta* or "rank" social order contrasted with the "vertical" and egalitarian structure of the Buddhist Saṅgha is equally well-known. In the West, what is not so well-known are the pre-Christian Greco-Roman hierarchical social traditions modeling Zeus at the top with relative rankings in importance on down. The impact of these ancient traditions remains only subliminally upon our awareness of the Greek and Roman nature of the Eastern Orthodox and Roman Catholic churches. The hierarchy of these traditions is arguably a betrayal of the socially egalitarian ethics of Jesus and followers, but more on that to come. Both the Hindu and Greco-Roman traditions share origins in the ancient pre-historic Aryan perspective. The classic pantheon first appears in written form in Hittite literature, thence through Sanskrit, Greek and Latin among others, the multitude of Aryan light deities traverses the entire range of cultures from Iran (Aryan) and North India to Ireland (Aryaland).

To begin, let us note the fact of climate and culture as informed by Tetsuro Watsuji, who emphasized the priority of space with relationship to consciousness. To understand protestant ethics, one must travel back in time to the desert climates that produced the fearsome warrior deities of Babylon and related Middle Eastern cultures. The most ancient civilization and source of the world's alphabets, zodiac, legal codes is indeed Iraq. Without top-down command authority, irrigation and agriculture along the Tigris and Euphrates Rivers are unsustainable. Those at the top take the majority of water leaving none for the ancient cities of the delta. The *edin* as it is put in the Semitic Akkadian language, or "Eden" as it is known to the Bible, is that relatively small patch of green along the rivers. Beyond lay death and "un-God," soon to evolve into Satan, the Devil.

Students of the Bible know both that the founder of the Abrahamic traditions, the legendary Abraham, is said to have originated from Ur of ancient Iraq *circa* 1800 BCE at the time of the promulgation of the first known human legal decree from Hammurabi, King of Babylon. Some five centuries later, Abraham's people have allegedly become slaves in Egypt and we have with Moses, the egalitarian Ten Commandments *circa* the 13th century BCE. Unlike the law Code of Hammurabi, Mosaic Law applies to all alike, without a "fine for murder of a little man, public torture execution for the murder of a big man" as Hammurabi's Code puts it.

As again geography plays a role in the development of subsequent Israelite religion culminating in Judaism, the constant invasions heaped upon the inhabitants of Israel / Palestine evolve an awareness not only of freedom from slavery, but castigation of the great empires as abominations to Jehovah, the God of Moses. First the Babylonians, then the Assyrians, the Greeks and Macedonians, finally the Romans destroy the Temple and send the Jews into exile in Egypt.

With them travels the early messianic Jewish sect today known as Christianity. This perspective found its way among the slaves of the Roman Empire as it promised that "in Christ, there is neither slave nor free." The communist lifestyle of the early Christians is renowned. Their refusal to acknowledge the divinity of the Roman Emperor won them agonizing and tortured executions. In the end, the "slave perspective" prevailed and Roman Empire became Catholic through Roman and Eastern or Greek Orthodox traditions.

As the Roman Catholic Church in the remnants of a Western Roman Empire devastated by Hun and German invasions, served as the only glue left to hold society together through the so-called

"Dark Ages" of Europe. To corral the Germans, the hierarchy evolved within the church was employed in at first beneficent, then exploitative ways. In the beginning, a bishop or *episcopus* in the Greek was an "overseer" rather like the janitor and secretary of the early and slave church. At the end of the day, the bishop of Rome is ruler of all Western Europe. It is into this situation that the Protestant principle emerges.

I will say a great role model for the first *successful* Reformer of the Catholic church, Martin Luther, was Muhammad. By Martin Luther's day, Muslims had ruled Spain for some seven hundred years. The Arab Empire expanded so rapidly due to the fact of its explicit anti-slavery message as mercenary and slave armies of Byzantium and Persia deserted to the Muslims. Muhammad treated women as equals and harmed neither Christian nor Jew in his own life or for the most part, did his followers. Precipitating the Protestant Reformation, Turkish Muslim troops were "banging on the doors of Vienna" and the Pope and his military advisors also often serving as bishops – were scared. The Pope of Rome depended upon taxes from Western European peasants to "defend" Europe from the "infidel" Muslims.

Luther's insistence on translating the Bible into the vernacular German so all Germans could know it directly along with his opposition to the hierarchy of the Catholic church appealed to peasants to such a great degree, Luther's writings incited a massive peasant rebellion. Just as Muhammad is said to have "created" the Arabic language through his Qur'an, likewise is Luther considered to have "created" the German language through his translation of the Bible. His principle? The relative equality of all believers. This is the inspiration for the "protest" of Protestants. The protest is lodged at the hierarchy and like the anti-temple prophets of Israel and the anti-temple features of the life of Jesus, to rebel against "false priests", the unfair treatment of all and bowing to that "whor, Babylon" is an affront to God's intention for humans, created equally in the image of God.

Tragically, the wars that ensued as Europe was engulfed in civil war, Protestant versus Catholic war, resulted in the loss of many millions of lives. The Catholic Church, expanding not only against the Muslims of Spain and Portugal, expanded her power into the "New World" with the brutal enslavement and murder of untold millions of Native Americans as the Roman church once more modeled the Roman Empire. The Protestants of the north, while also conforming to a policy of cruelty to the natives, nevertheless established a democratic state among the thirteen colonies. The nature of Protestantism is to tend towards independence rather than universality *a la* the Catholics and thus, without a single denomination to dominate the new United States, but rather the multiplicity of contending Protestant sects, a nation without a king or a religion emerged, a first in history.

Having established the fact of protestant egalitarianism, I want to turn our attention to the fact of the historically socially engaged tradition of the Buddha. We know first of the rejection of the authority of the *Vedas* and the description of the caste system as mass hallucination or group delusion, and we know the Buddha rejected his crown, and we know of the democratic structure of the Saṅgha and of the Buddha's preference for the classic Indian democracies, notably the Vrji Republic. The relatively egalitarian social structure for women allowed them to escape the abusive husband or family and obtain an education in the Buddhist community. The early Buddhist depiction of the *Brahmin* as "greedy and deceitful" reminds one of the similar casting Protestants have of the Pope and his hierarchy. "The closer you get to Rome, the greater corruption you will find" goes an old Protestant saying.

We have in the instance of the Emperor Aśoka, edicts of toleration for all perspectives, the building of animal shelters, rest areas for common travelers, and the dissemination of Buddhism in all directions through his direction. As the Mahāyāna tradition emerges especially in the northwest of India, one finds the exaltation of the "defiled" merchant Vimalakīrti in relationship to the Buddha's most intellectual *bhikṣu* Śāriputra. The female Śrīmālādevī is exalted as purely realizing her Buddha Nature in what earlier would be deemed the "impure" female body. The *Lotus Sūtra* exhorts all to treat those of all perspectives equally, as they are all equally vehicles along the path to Awakening.

As Buddhism enters China, we see the clear conflict with hierarchical Confucianism, yet increasing merger with the "horizontal" socially egalitarian structure of Daoism. The anti-family attitude of Buddhism, its tendency towards the individual striving than the organization of "the masses" and the manner in which the role of Sage is now open to all equally, not to mention the attack on Confucian traditions five relationships, notably that women are subordinate to their husband – all this elicited the persecution of Buddhism from 842-845 after a heyday during which China's only female Emperor reigned, the Buddhist Empress Wu.

After the Confucian crackdown, one finds Buddhism principally alive among the peasants, some of who may simply hold out for the devotional path to Amitābha and hope for rebirth in *Sukhāvatī* or the "Happiness Realm" or simply wandered the woods as a Daoist-style Chan master. The sophisticated monasteries of Buddhism's Golden Age in China were finished. With the advent of China's domination by Mongols following hierarchical Tibetan religious advisors, we find the peasants rebelling against this domination establishing the Ming Dynasty through especially the actions of the White Lotus Society and its great appeal to women and the poor. The vast demonstrations and resistance culminated in ousting the hierarchically organized Mongol religious traditions governed by the lamas of the Sakya sect of Tibetan Buddhism.

We can note then again the appeal of this similar Buddhism, the so-called Pure Land *Sukhāvatī* tradition of Japan in the ministry of Shinran. He notes in a manner so eerily similar to that of Martin Luther, that Infinite Light Buddha Amitābha is nearer to the sinner than the pious. Luther's proclamation was to "sin boldly" that god could save the more. Both left the relatively elite monasteries, married and modeled householder life, valuing the common life over that of the monastic.

Each of these figures inspired extremist interpretations. Thomas Muenzer concluded from Luther's thought that the peasants should also rebel and overthrow the feudal lords. An estimated one hundred thousand peasants were massacred by the knights. Zenran, Shinran's son, was disowned in the end, for thinking that debauchery and lying were to be tolerated in Amitābha's grace. Clearly, to merge with Amitābha is to carry the sincere conviction that Amitābha or "Infinite Light" is everywhere, all the time and to be authentic and respectful of that. One should live as if there already. Perhaps we can somehow even go so far as to say that the social movements represented by Luther and Shinran go back to the most massive slave rebellion the world has ever known: Islam. The Turks had converted from Buddhism in its West and the North Africans had converted in Europe's East.

So, Buddhism has always been socially engaged. Engaged with the individual no matter his or her social status. The monotheisms of the West address the "mass-man" (and I mean "man"). Both Israelite and Indian traditions permeate their West and East respectively, through Judaism and Buddhism respectively. As each "horizontal" system enters the "vertical" and hierarchical systems, a mutual transformation occurs. New systems emerge. New vortices of inter-relationship take place as Judaism becomes Catholicism, and Buddhism becomes "Buddho-Daoism". A fine blend of coffee, don't you think? In the social sense then, Chan (Jpn., Zen; Kor., Seon) tradition has more in common with the Protestants of north Europe than with the Dalai Lama. The system in which he works is then, more akin to the Catholic / Orthodox systems.

To then consciously develop future strategies for peacemaking, we should all become cognizant of these patterns, these systems, these "fractalizations" as the *taiji* or "Universal Absolute" in Daoism. Thus to repeat and conclude: the insights of Daoism, Buddhism, Judaism, Islam and Protestantism can be utilized to restrain the hierarchical, vertical forces of Confucianism, Hinduism and the Roman Catholic / Greek Orthodox amalgam. Let's mix them together now!

BUDDHIST PROTEST IN MYANMAR: BASIC QUESTIONS

Ronald S. Green

Over the past year, many Americans have been puzzled and excited by news of events in Myanmar (also called Burma). [1] Images of monks with megaphones and raised fists challenge typical understandings of Asian Buddhists as portrayed in classrooms and media. As a result, the pro-democracy demonstrations by Buddhist monks in Myanmar have provided rich grounds for university discussions on such issues as modern Buddhist practices, socially engaged Buddhism and the application of classical Buddhist ideas to the alleviation of social inequities of the modern world. In hopes of contributing to the learning process this paper makes a basic examination of some of these topics with reference to the events in Myanmar and statements by those involved. It identifies a number of details Americans are likely to view as inconsistencies, such as the democracy leader's tendency to expound the virtues of Buddhist kingship.

In September 2007, Buddhist monks led the largest protest against the military government of Myanmar that country had experienced since the popular uprising of 1988 when 3,000 people

---

[1] In 1989, the Burmese military government officially changed the English version of the country's name from Burma to Myanmar, and the capital city from Rangoon to Yangon. These changes reflect the local names. Some groups opposing the government refuse to recognize the name changes.

were reportedly killed. Leading up to the events of September, a month earlier the government doubled the price of gasoline, triggering corresponding rises in the price of public transportation, rice and cooking oil in the impoverished country. Deep social economic suffering in Myanmar is well documented. In 2006, the UN Development Programme's Human Development Index sited a high infant mortality rate, short life expectancy, the serious threat posed by the HIV/AIDS epidemic, tuberculosis and malaria for ranking Myanmar 130 out of 177 countries in terms of development. In May 2007, the International Committee of the Red Cross (ICRC) issued a rare criticism by accusing the Myanmar government of abusing the rights of the people. The new burden imposed by the gasoline price hike was likely felt to be intolerable by many. Within days of the price increase, a pro-democracy demonstration of about 400 people took place in Yangon (also called Rangoon), the former capital and largest city of Myanmar with a population of six million. While the government quickly suppressed the protest, arresting numerous activists, smaller demonstrations continued around the country with the participation of a modest number of monks. On September 5, the military forcibly stopped a rally in the town of Pakokku, injuring at least three monks. This provoked public and monastic outrage since a large majority of the population in Myanmar is devoutly Buddhist and the hundreds of thousands of clergy members hold high stature in society.[2] At some point in life, most males in Myanmar become monks for at least a three-month period, usually as a child or just before marriage in order to learn social morals. Thus, the public has a very close connection to the 400,000 - 500,000 professional monks in the country of around 50 million people.

The next day, monks in Pakokku made a drastic if not heretical move by taking government officials hostage for a short time, demanding that the government issue an apology by September 17. After the deadline passed with no apology, monks began protesting daily around the country, their numbers increasing to tens of

---

[2] It is estimated that 89 percent of the Myanmar population is Buddhist, https://www.cia.gov/library/publications/the-world-factbook/geos/bm.html.

thousands. Reading this, Americans are very likely to ask a number of questions including the following: Were the protests, at least at first, about an apology? If so, what is the dharmic significance or importance of an apology? Why did the monks feel the need for an apology? Were egos and humiliation factors? Is so, how does that reflect on Buddhism? Were the protesters acting as individuals or truly as representatives of the clergy?

At this time, monks also refused to accept alms or perform religious services for members of the military and their families. In Myanmar, non-monastic Buddhists participate in the religion largely by earning merit for good fortune in this life and a better future birth by contributing materially to the well-being of monks.[3] The system of merit and demerit is believed by hundreds of millions of Buddhists worldwide. It provides an explanation for why a person is born in a particular situation. For example, the justification for an individual maintaining the wealth of his or her family in an overwhelmingly impoverished country, an individual's right to rule the country, or conversely, a baby being born with cancer, are all routinely explained by past-life karma accrued by earning merit or demerit. For this reason, it is of utmost importance to earn merit in this life. Thus, the Myanmar monks' refusal to accept alms from the military and their families affectively denied access to the merit system and so, according to the belief, to well-being. A question this raises among American university students concerns Buddhists taking vows to save all sentient beings or to provide spiritual aid to any person seeking it. Are monks obligated to accept alms and by refusing, were they in violation of a precept? Could the didactic purpose in the act ultimately help believers even more than accepting their donations would have? So far, no answers to these questions have been forthcoming. As time went on and monks persevered in their refusal to accept alms, donated food was left to rot in the streets. Despite widespread hunger in Myanmar, the population would not touch the food. This attests to both the popular support of the

---

[3] This idea of buying good fortune compares roughly to the Christian notion of giving tithe.

political cause of the monks and the belief in their spiritual efficacy. But in the eyes of the world, how does the failure to distribute the food in some way reflect on the monks?

On September 21, a group calling itself Alliance of All Burmese Buddhist Monks issued a statement saying the government is "the enemy of the people" and calling to the citizens of Myanmar to join the demonstrations. The group promised to continue the protests until they "wiped the military dictatorship from the land of Burma."[4] Regardless of the all-inclusive name of the group, apparently conservative temple elders were not part of the All Burmese Buddhist Monks. Almost certainly at the behest of the junta leaders of "The Saṅgha," the official government-supported Buddhist agency issued statements directing the apparently "junior monks" to return to the temples and confine themselves to "learning and propagating the faith."[5] It is possible the activist monks believed their actions were proof they had learned the faith and were propagating it to millions of media watchers. The Saṅgha's statement makes clear this is not the orthodox interpretation. Its directive was, however, largely ignored, again raising questions about violating monastic precepts. Can a monk properly disobey a directive of a senior priest? Urging the senior monks to control the protesters also attests to government attempts to nonviolently avert the public relations disaster, if not the expenditure of lives armed suppression would involve. On the other hand, some viewed the senior monks' silence up until the point of probable government coercion as indication of support.

In Yangon on September 24, monks gathered in mass to pray at Shwedagon, the world renowned Golden Pagoda in Yangon, before marching in protest. Afterwards, monks led a demonstration by the house of Aung San Suu Kyi, leader of the opposition party, the National League for Democracy (NLD), who has been detained under house arrest for 12 of the last 18 years. Some monks chanted

---

[4] BBC News, October 2, 2007, http://news.bbc.co.uk/go/pr/fr/-/2/hi/asia-pacific/7010202.stm.

[5] *New York Times*, September 24, 2007.

"Release Suu Kyi." Suu Kyi has written numerous articles in support of Burmese Buddhism and is a celebrated activist for democracy. By coming to her house, Monks further linked the protests to the desire for a change of political regimes and particularly to democracy. Suu Kyi's party won a landslide victory in the country's 1990 general election. Afterwards the military leaders voided the election and placed Suu Kyi under house arrest. When she spoke to demonstrators in September, it was the first time she had appeared in public since 2003.

Initially, public response in Myanmar was meager, perhaps due to fear of government reprisal. Within a few days, however, the number of marchers grew as photos and film appeared spotlighting the cause in the international media. Dramatic footage, apparently taken on cell phones or sent out via the internet, showed the world protesters from the general public lining both sides of a road, shielding thousands of orchid-robed monks from possible military violence. On September 25, the *New York Times* published a picture likely surprising to its audience. It showed a monk holding a megaphone in his left hand and his right fist raised above his head. The caption told readers the young monk was shouting slogans during a protest against the military government. Behind him, non-cleric protesters carried a sign saying, "Sufficiency in food, clothing and shelter, national reconciliation, freedom for all political prisoners." This sign does not mention democracy as the way of achieving these demands.

During the first days, military leaders allowed the protests to proceed without overt interference. As the number of protesters grew for a week, the government issued a warning that they were poised to "take action." On September 25, police used pickup trucks with loudspeakers in Yangon and Mandalay to order protesters to disperse. A curfew was issued and troops were stationed on the streets to suppress further demonstrations. The government may have made efforts to stop cell phone and internet pictures from leaving the country, as reported by *Irrawaddy*, the pro-democracy and pro-Buddhist opposition news agency of Myanmar, headquartered in Thailand. *Irrawaddy* maintained news and pictures of the events and became a major source for information on the protests. Despite government efforts, international television stations broadcasted pictures of the police using batons and tear gas on monks.

Public violence reached a peak on September 27 as the military opened fire with automatic weapons to disband the protesters. Media sources published ominous photographs of recently emptied streets littered with sandals discarded in haste. These were guarded by uniformed military personal equipped with helmets and rifles. Around this time, the *Irrawaddy* website went down, sparking allegations of government tampering. By the government's account, a dozen people had been killed, including a Japanese journalist.[6] Dozens more were wounded and over 2,000 people were arrested.[7] Afterwards, news agencies reported monks were conspicuously absent as police officers stood armed in the hallways of otherwise deserted monasteries usually abuzz with tourists and the faithful.

In response, the US imposed further sanctions on the military leadership of Myanmar and President George W. Bush condemned the violence. It should be noted that the United States has vested interest in seeing the junta topped and a more market-friendly and politically controllable regime established. China, considered Myanmar's closest ally, made public statements calling for restraint of violence. Other than this, along with Russia and India, China maintained its usual stance of noninterference. Americans are likely to note that while China is willing to use force against activist monks in Tibet and pro-democracy demonstrators in Tiananmen Square, they are also concerned with appeasing the US and maintaining a pleasant façade for trading partners and potential

---

[6] Japanese Foreign Minister, Masahiko Komura claimed video footage appeared to prove photo journalist Kenji Nagai was deliberately shot and the perpetrators should be held accountable. "9 Killed in the 2nd Day of Myanmar Crackdown," Associated Press, September 27, 2007. The Myanmar *The New Light of Burma* newspaper alleged the death was accidental.

[7] Ibrahim Gambari's report to the UN Security Council, available through BBC News, http://www.bbc.co.uk/mediaselector/check/player/nol/newsid_7030000/newsid_7030400?redirect=7030407.stm&news=1&bbwm=1&nbram=1&bbram=1&nbwm=1&asb=1.

tourists. During the Myanmar incidents, the time of the 2008 Olympic games was approaching in China.

On September 30, the UN's special envoy to Burma, Ibrahim Gambari, met with military leaders and paid a rare visit to Aung San Suu Kyi. In his report to the UN security council, Gambari said, "Of great concern to the United Nations and the international community are the continuing and disturbing reports of abuses being committed by security and non-uniformed elements, particularly at night during curfew including raids on private homes, beatings, arbitrary arrests and disappearances."[8] As a part of his official mission, Gambari urged government leaders to open talks with Aung San Suu Kyi. As a result, Senior General Than Shwe offered to meet with her, even though it is reported he did not allow people to even mention her name in his presence.[9] Later Suu Kyi voiced disappointment in meetings with government representatives.

Since the protests, the government of Myanmar has stepped up its "Road to Democracy" plan including drafting a new constitution, which was ratified in May 2008. However, pro-democracy opponents of the constitution argue it does little more than solidify the military's position as national leaders while formally excluding Aung San Suu Kyi. The NLD mounted a campaign to persuade the public to vote "no" to the constitution. In addition, the government plans to hold a national election in 2010 but rejected the UN's offer to monitor the process. Currently, Aung San Suu Kyi is prohibited from holding government office. A law forbids anyone having the ability to hold legal citizenship in another country from so doing. Suu Kyi was married to a British academic and is therefore disqualified.

Meanwhile, in December 2007, the US government sent another political message of disagreement with the government of Myanmar when the House of Representatives voted unanimously to award Aung San Suu Kyi the Congressional Medal of Honor,

---

[8] *Ibid.*

[9] BBC News, October 9 2007, http://news.bbc.co.uk/2/hi/asia-pacific/7033911.stm.

America's top civilian honor. Past recipients include George
Washington, Martin Luther King, Jr., and the fourteenth Dalai
Lama Tenzin Gyatso. Suu Kyi was also a recipient of the 1991
Nobel Peace Prize. In May 2008, a devastating cyclone hit
Myanmar. The government of that country refused to grant
humanitarian workers free access to those in need. The world
watched in anguish as the death toll rose. As the US publicly tried
to persuade the junta to open its doors to relief workers, it may
have only damaged such efforts by officially awarding the Medal
of Honor to Aung Sang Suu Kyi at the time.

Buddhism and Politics in the History of Myanmar

The Golden Pagoda (Shwedagon) is the most outstanding and
famous structure in Yangon. Although historians estimate it was
built between the 6th and 10th century, legend says it dates from
before the Buddha was born. This might reflect the possibility that
the area was considered sacred before it became associated with
Buddhism. Buddhist pagodas or stūpas of Asia generally contain
important relics. This may be the physical remains of a master, a
central sūtra, or in the case of the most revered stūpas, a relic of the
historical Buddha such as a small bone fragment. Shwedagon
allegedly contains six hairs of the Buddha and other relics.
Because of this, it has been considered by many over the centuries
the most sacred space of Myanmar.

Americans are often surprised to learn of the long association
of politics and Buddhism throughout Asia. For many centuries in
Myanmar, political figures have made use of the sacred
identification of Shwedagon as well as the mass support for
Buddhism generally. In 1057, King Anawrahta founded the first
unified Burmese state and is said to have introduced Theravāda
Buddhism to the country. He is also reputed to have fought Mons
in order to capture the Tripiṭaka, the collection of Buddhist
scriptures. After coming to power, he set about building or
restoring Shwedagon. Over time, "Stūpa Builder" became an
honorific title. Monarchs and the general public put much effort
into building temples and thereby were said to gain merit.

Likewise, rulers and monastics benefited by mutual support.[10] This continued throughout the history of the country.

In 1852, the British came to occupy Myanmar, as they did India and other areas of Asia around this time. Recognizing Shwedagon as an important strategic point, the British captured the temple grounds and held it under guard by military forces until 1930. This caused much anxiety among the population and has been called "a form of psychological torture."[11] Shortly after a section of the temple was allowed to reopen, anti-colonial groups formed nearby. At the outbreak of WWII in 1939, Buddhists asked the British to not use Shwedagon as a fortress.

During British colonization of Asia, China, the giant power of the region, was defeated and forced to accept unequal trading agreements. As Asian countries fell to European powers, Japan somehow managed to defeat Russia, considered perhaps the strongest of those powers. As a result, it appeared to some that Japan might hold the key to Asian liberation from imperialist forces. For this reason, during the British occupation of Myanmar, an anti-colonial militant group led by a man named Aung San left the country to seek military help from Japan in defeating the British. The group was trained by the Japanese and formed the Independence Army, led by General Aung San. In 1942, Aung San became a national hero when, alongside the Japanese Army, the Independence Army defeated the British. His victory was to be bittersweet however, as now the Japanese assumed the role of occupiers. Undeterred, Aung San made an unimaginable move by asking the British to help him defeat the Japanese. Stunned by the devastation of WWII and withdrawing from their occupation of Asia, the British softened its attitude towards the country. In 1945, the British together with General Aung San's Liberation Army freed Myanmar from Japanese occupation. General Aung San announced independence of the country at a huge gathering held at Shwedagon. Two years later, he was assassinated by political

---

[10] See Penny Edwards, "Grounds for Protest, Placing Shwedagon Pagoda in Colonial and Postcolonial History," *Postcolonial Studies* 9.2 (2006): 197-211.

[11] *Ibid,* 205.

opponents, but not before fathering Aung San Suu Kyi, who would become the leader of the National League for Democracy by virtue of her father's fame.

After suffering through more than a decade of political instability, a military coup took place in 1962. At that time, a single-party government was established and a ban on independent newspapers went into place. Though much turmoil and poverty has persisted, the government has remained in power. In 1987, the country's currency was devalued and many people lost their savings, triggering widespread anti-government sentiments. At Shwedagon in 1988, Aung San Suu Kyi addressed a crowd of 500,000, demanding the instatement of democracy. Following this, the 8888 movement occurred (August 8, 1988) and thousands were killed in anti-government riots. As a result, The State Law and Order Restoration Council (Slorc) was formed and thousands were arrested. Shortly afterwards Burma was renamed Myanmar and Rangoon renamed Yangon. In 1989, National League for Democracy leader Aung San Suu Kyi was put under house arrest. In numerous articles and statements, she has consistently voiced her support for Buddhism and democracy, sometimes using the notion of Buddhist kingship as the model for righteous and democratic governing. From the point of view of "American democracy," these ideas are likely to appear widely incongruous. A different type of question comes to mind from the opposite direction. Is the very nature of Buddhist institutions, as they have developed historically, more like a kingship than a democracy? This question points to the hierarchal structure of the master-disciple relationship prevalent on many levels of organization of the saṅgha, which is anything but democratic. If so, coupled with centuries of Asian history does this religious structure make it more likely that Buddhists and Buddhist-oriented leaders such as Aung San Suu Kyi will think about politics in terms of a kingship rather than a democracy? More importantly, can Buddhist leaders' courtship of democracy be viewed as General Aung San's wooing of first the Japanese and then the British, as expedient means to throwing off the present evil but not meant for a long-term commitment?

Three explanations of Buddhists' interest in democracy

Why are Buddhists interested in propagating democracy? Typically, references to promoting democracy are found in the context of broader treatments of socially engaged Buddhism. Most writings on socially engaged Buddhism do not mention democracy and it may or may not be a major objective of the larger movement worldwide. To answer the question, it may be helpful to look at the wider treatment of why Buddhists are sometimes social activists.

Socially engaged Buddhism literature, socially engaged Buddhists and other writers offer three main explanations. [12] Perhaps the most common of the three explanations connects social activism to a central goal in Buddhism, if not *the* central goal of Buddhism: the alleviation and ultimate ending of suffering. Second, Buddhist work for social change is sometimes explained through the related but not identical idea of *dāna*, charity. A third explanation comes from the Mahāyāna "Bodhisattva Ideal," again related to the first two but not identical. Some of the literature appears to be unconcerned with or perhaps does not recognize these three as separate and there could be ideological and practical advantages in that. For example, describing the Mahāyāna Bodhisattva Ideal as expressing the Four Noble Truths circumvents the necessity of further ideological justification of that Ideal. Practically, this would validate acting according to that Ideal. However, there may also be internal contradictions and other potential problems in combining the three explanations. Even if we only take these as rough bases for explanation by these writers alone, a number of issues need clarification for understanding their position on the relationship of Buddhism and democracy.

---

[12] Although these three can be found as the main explanations in the larger body of literature on socially engaged Buddhism, for the sake of the present study my sample will be the articles published in the last three years by Blue Pine Books in their four serial books on socially engaged Buddhism. These explanations are pervasive in writings on socially engaged Buddhism whether or not they equally encompass the rationale of activists.

We should begin by examining the first explanation to see if striving for democracy is related to the central goal in Buddhism, the alleviation and ultimate ending of suffering. The main theme of the Buddha's Four Noble Truths, perhaps the most basic doctrinal statement in Buddhism, deals with suffering (*dukkha*). The end of suffering is revealed in the Third Noble Truth, to end suffering one must end desires. The Fourth Noble Truth says the way to end suffering is by following the Eightfold Path. The Eightfold Path begins with the necessity of Right Understanding. Right Understanding is specifically the understanding of the Four Noble Truths, suffering, the cause of suffering and the path to end suffering. This understanding is necessarily based on individual attainment. In contrast, socially engaged Buddhists' goal of alleviating suffering is not only self-directed but directed towards others who may, according to Buddhist understanding, be at lower levels of attainment, due primarily to merit and birth. On the other hand, it is widely held among Buddhists that self-attainment may be the best means of helping others. A model can be found in Siddhārtha's abandoning the obligations to his family for meditative pursuits in the forest. Although this act appears to be selfish, according to the story, Siddhārtha's subsequent achievement of Buddhahood brought the path of salvation from suffering to the world, a greater good for his family and others. The implication seems to be an individual's self-attainment is the best and perhaps the only way to end suffering of self and others. After all, the Buddha did not return to the palace in order to establish a Buddhist monarchy, much less a democracy. On the other hand, by numerous canonical accounts, Buddhism appears to oppose the Brahmanical caste system. Yet, belief in the equal ability of all individuals to attain enlightenment, albeit, according to some traditions this is true only after many rebirths, is not democracy. There is no vote on who becomes a leader or a Buddha. Even though not caste-dependent, this is still considered to be a matter of birth combined with individual effort. While capitalism theoretically holds to a hierarchy based on individual achievement, democracy does not.

All three of these explanations of why Buddhists are interested in propagating democracy are concerned with alleviating or ending suffering. But, according to Buddhist doctrine, is all suffering always bad? Alternatively, is at least preliminary suffering necessary for later attainment and indeed inescapable for those of lesser attainment? Is it not considered righteous punishment from the perspective of merit? When considering what might be called Buddhist theodicy, perhaps more so than suffering, ignorance might be called evil. Yet labeling ignorance, which is at least the cause of suffering if not suffering itself, evil, potentially misses the point that ignorance and suffering are the human condition. A notion shared by many Indian religions is that austerities and self-mortification are spiritually beneficial. While the Buddha proclaimed the Middle Path between austerities and materialism, there may remain a sense in which suffering is good in that it leads to striving for overcoming it. [13] *The Awakening of Faith*, a Mahāyāna text extremely influential in the development of a number of traditions of East Asian Buddhism, says, "Ignorance does not exist apart from enlightenment."[14] The basic problem for humanity, according to this text, is not that we must overcome suffering by political means, but that we must overcome its cause by realizing ignorance is an illusion and enlightenment is our intrinsic state. Mahāyāna Buddhism, particularly as it developed in China, appears to emphasize liberation, the Third Noble Truth, more than suffering and ignorance found in the First and Second Noble Truth. [15]

Similar questions arise in relation to the second explanation of why Buddhists are engaged in the propagation of democracy. Is the struggle for democracy *dāna*, charitable offering? If suffering

---

[13] There is a circularity to this argument in that if there were no suffering there would be no need to overcome it.

[14] Yoshito S. Hakeda, trans., *The Awakening of Faith* (NY: Columbia University Press, 1967), 41.

[15] This is perhaps owing to the influence of Daoists and other Chinese philosophers such as Mencius who are said to view the "human condition" in "positive" terms in contrast to the view found in Indian religions that the basic human condition is ignorance and suffering.

helps people overcome ignorance, alleviating suffering cannot be
dāna. If suffering is not socio-political but a deep part of the
human psyche, then offering democracy as *dāna* cannot alleviate
human suffering. Then how can it be a merit-building gift? Merit-
building gifts are typically those that support the clergy. *Dāna*
furthers individuals on the path to enlightenment. Is democracy
believed to further people on the path to enlightenment? If so, how
can it since political suffering is not the issue?

Whether suffering can be said to be bad or good, according to
the Four Noble Truths it is inevitable for humans who do not
understand its cause and follow the path to its destruction. It may
be objected that the articles on socially engaged Buddhism in
question do not claim that democracy will end suffering but will
alleviate some of its harshness. Based on the actions of socially
engaged Buddhists, such severe conditions apparently are not
considered necessary for bringing individuals to the truths of
Buddhism. In the context of Buddhism, we can think of at least
two explanations of why severe conditions would not help
individuals gain enlightenment. First, attainment is based on birth
and rebirth, largely dependent on merit and demerit in the present
and past. Two objections to this view being related to democracy
are offered here. An individual's suffering and understanding of it
is decisive as motivation for building merit. And, in this view,
suffering is righteously applied for past life deeds.

A second explanation of why severe conditions would not help
individuals gain enlightenment is that *dukkha* is not suffering in the
political sense or not only in the political sense. Instead, Right
Understanding is a philosophical or loosely "religious"[16] revelation
about the basic human condition beyond political concern.
According to this interpretation, if it were possible to build a
utopian political society wherein the basic needs of all people were
met, there would still be suffering in the Buddhist sense.
According to doctrine, Buddhist attainment, if not enlightenment,

---

[16] I use the term guardedly in this particular context in deference to many
Buddhists who say Buddhism is not a religion. In other contexts, we find most
elements associated with Buddhism as practiced by the majority of people in
Myanmar and the world may be termed "religious" as commonly understood.

is the only way to end this kind of suffering. This explanation is somewhat ideologically satisfying. However, it is not pervasive in the socially engaged Buddhism literature on democracy. For our purpose, this fact necessitates further elucidation. Most importantly, if *dukkha* is not political suffering, then the Four Noble Truths cannot be given as a reason for socially engaged Buddhists' struggles for democracy.

We will return to the third explanation of Buddhists involvement in propagating democracy below.

Possible incompatibilities of Buddhism, Democracy, and Capitalism

In considering the view that Buddhism engages in the struggle for democracy as a way to alleviate suffering, in addition to questioning the idea of suffering, we should ask if democracy alleviates suffering and if it is the best means or even the most expedient means of achieving this goal. If democracy can alleviate suffering in one situation, can that be universalized? An argument sometimes forwarded by those anti-democratic forces in power is that democracy is not right for Asia. Aung Sang Suu Kyi specifically rejects this argument out of hand, perhaps rightly but without explanation. [17] That aside, for our purposes, a part of reflecting on the "best means" for alleviating suffering must be about whether democracy and what accompanies it can be suitable morally or otherwise in terms of Buddhism.

In this vein, several comments might be made concerning broader implications of the relation of Buddhism and democracy, the role of religion and politics. In America, there is a widely held belief in the notion that there should be a hard separation of church and state as directed by the US Constitution. The First Amendment to the constitution prohibits the establishment of a national religion. In contrast, Aung Sang Suu Kyi holds up the Buddhist Chakravartin king as the ideal model for the leader of Myanmar

---

[17] Aung San Suu Kyi, *Freedom from Fear* (NY: Penguin, 1995), 167.

democracy. [18] While the US Constitution does not prohibit a religious leader from assuming government power, it does prohibit the formation of a national religion. The idea of the separation of church and state might commonly be misinterpreting as implying religion has no business in politics. However, according to the Constitution and subsequent Supreme Court interpretation, the principle only addresses the opposite: that state may not restrict religion or the rejection of religion. Nor may it support one religion more than another. In America, some feel the separation of church and state is at times opposed by fundamentalist Christian organizations seeking to establish a theocracy. Theocracy is typically seen as the antithesis of democracy. Like the Christian theocracy, the Buddhist version would not necessarily see the government leader as a deity, but as one who is the most direct link to divine beings or teachings. Suu Kyi describes the social contract involved in the Buddhist kingship but the underlying assumption remains the king's position was accomplished by virtue of past merits and favorable birth. While birthright is indeed the dominant means by which the American capitalist class is renewed, and the capitalist class is arguably the ruling class, that aspect of society is anti-democratic.

If, on the other hand, Suu Kyi means to say the Buddhist kingship is not a true model for a democratic country but some features of it may be applicable, she fails to make this point. Instead, she argues the Buddhist king is chosen by the people and only remains in the royal position if he (there is no mention of the possibility of 'she') fulfills the terms of the social contract, specifically providing just rule. With much trepidation, the question arises as to where in the history of any country of the world this elected Buddhist king is found. Incredibly but predictably, she points to King Aśoka (304-232 BCE) as her ideal exemplar. [19]

---

[18] *Ibid*, 172.

[19] She also mentions King Vessantara in this regard, a mythical previous incarnation of the historical Buddha from *Jātaka* tales and much celebrated in Theravāda countries (*ibid*, 173).

Aśoka is often referred to in Buddhism, particularly Theravāda Buddhism, as the ideal ruler. Likewise, in the literature of socially engaged Buddhism Aśoka is mentioned prominently in this regard. However, far from being elected by the masses to rule justly, Aśoka came to power by leading armies in the most brutal violence ever perpetrated on the Indian subcontinent until his time. Aśoka is attributed with uniting India as a large country. He achieved this by military imperialism against the kingdoms of the region in succession. Expediently, only after accomplishing this goal did he proclaim Buddhism as the national religion, and the Buddhist precept of non-killing to be the law of the land. This effectively made it illegal for potential dissenters to raise armies against his universal rule. Aśoka spread this and other advantageous Buddhist precepts as edicts inscribes on pillars placed throughout the land and beyond. He also built stūpas and temples to propagate his version of Buddhism and held councils to remove "heretics" from the fold. A heretic would have been anyone who professed a Buddhist view contrary to his orthodoxy. Having shaped orthodoxy in Buddhism and spread this hegemony beyond his borders into Southeast Asia, it is little wonder that Aśoka is held up in those countries as the ideal ruler. To outsiders, however, there can be much consternation in presenting an imperialistic king as a benevolent ruler because he became "Buddhist." At a much simpler level, one might assume that Americans would be opposed to a religious leader on the grounds of fanaticism. However, the American pop cultural appeal of the Dalai Lama and Buddhism in general suggests openness to this.

Another relevant point in regards to the Buddhist notion of the Chakravartin king can be made by reference to the life story of the Buddha. Stories of the Buddha's life are common among traditions and are found in many scriptures and writings. In the second century CE, the Sanskrit poet Aśvaghoṣa compiled a number of these stories and produced the canonical *Buddhacarita*. Accordingly, when Siddhārtha was born, a seer came to the palace and predicted he would become either a Chakravartin king or a Buddha. Upon hearing this, King Śuddhodana is delighted that his son may extend his own worldly ambitions beyond his dreams.

However, against his father's wishes, Siddhārtha becomes a Buddha, thus bringing salvation to the world. The story relates the way to overcome suffering is the Eightfold Path and portrays the Buddha as explicitly rejecting the way of the Chakravartin.

While the reverence for Aśoka is particularly widespread among Theravāda Buddhists, in Mahāyāna literature the Bodhisattva is endowed with supra-rational abilities and often acts socially based on this special wisdom. For this reason, it is assumed that an incarnation of a Bodhisattva, such as the Fourteenth Dalai Lama, would be the ideal ruler. This returns us to the third explanation of why Buddhists are interested in social engagement and propagating democracy: the Mahāyāna "Bodhisattva Ideal." Perhaps embarrassed today by the notion that a Bodhisattva has divine abilities or focusing on parts of scriptures likely to appeal to modern listeners, in contrasts to canonical descriptions, socially engaged Buddhist tends to emphasize the relatively ordinary abilities of the Bodhisattva. Even so, the extraordinary nature of such a being might be unavoidable. An example of the abilities of a socially engaged Bodhisattva appears in a story found in the *Skill-in-means Sūtra* (*Upāyakauśalya*), important in Tibetan Buddhism. The story takes place on a ship and tells of a Bodhisattva who has special insightful wisdom received metaphorically from the dragon king. Because he knows through supra-rational means that aboard the ship is a thief who will kill five hundred people, the Bodhisattva acts quickly and kills the thief. It is, of course, in violation of Buddhist precepts and principles to take life. However, according to the story the Bodhisattva accrued merit for this deed, in part because he was willing to sacrifice his future favorable rebirth by killing and so paradoxically secures a good rebirth.[20] The implication of this is that a Bodhisattva may act outside the guidelines of behavior prescribed in Buddhist precepts when acting in accord with supra-rational insight. Chinese Chan and Japanese Zen Buddhist texts

---

[20] Mark Tatz, trans., *The Skill in Means Sūtra* (Delhi: Motilal Banarsidass, 1994), 73-74. Variations are found in the *Yogācārabhūmi-śāstra* and in T.3.156.161b13-162a6.

contain numerous examples of masters with high attainment breaking precepts for unknown higher purposes.

As with the potential for harm in the Christian theocracy, this Buddhist belief opens to the door to justifying such actions as the "righteous war," which would be similar to killing the thief. Indeed, the Bodhisattva leader might have no boundaries whatsoever, since the ordinary person's understanding of the precepts or civil laws can be overridden by "wisdom" and "skill-in-means." Not only is this contrary to democracy, but it potentially, if not inevitably, leads to a tyranny of the Bodhisattva. In light of this, if there could be a Bodhisattva leader or even a Chakravartin king, would that be desirable? To state the point mildly, one problem with using the Bodhisattva as an ideal model for governing is that based on history, the existence of supra-rational insight applicable to governing modern nations is highly unlikely. Although Aung Sang Suu Kyi might not support the Mahāyāna Bodhisattva for president, her idea of the Chakravartin king is no less radical. Maybe her point is not that Buddhist kingship involves supra-rational insight but that it is the "best means" for alleviating suffering. If so, why is she the leader of the democracy movement and party?

In terms of the role of socially engaged Buddhism, it may also be useful here to consider not only the dynamic between religion and politics, but also among religion, politics and economic systems. In many modern purported democracies such as the US, there can be said to be a tension between capitalism and democracy. To mention a few of the many aspects of this tension, in US capitalism, for example, roughly ten percent of the population control eighty percent of the wealth although democracy holds that all people are equal in some ways. One of the ways American democracy holds this is in the supposed equality of individual political votes. Suu Kyi supports this view by telling of the democratically chosen Chakravartin king. In elections, it is in the economic interests of those who control wealth to use some of that affluence to choose and financially back politicians who will champion favorable causes for their group, potentially to the economic detriment of the majority. Theoretically the majority has the ability to reject such a candidate.

However, due to such influences as wielded by capitalist-controlled media and the overwhelming prevalence of the two-party system, seemingly unbeknownst to the majority, politicians may not be playing on a leveled political field. In addition, in the US version of a representative democracy, the popular vote may not count as much as the electoral vote in an election. Meanwhile, electoral voters were likely chosen to represent the capitalist class, coming into their positions by virtue of the system mentioned above in connection with the financial backing of the wealthy.

Our basic human condition may be pervasive dissatisfaction caused by perpetual desire as stated in the Noble Truths. However, in late capitalism, our desires are not our own in form, but take the shape of commodities sold to us through the media by business for profit. The same is true of our supposed choices in democratically elected leaders, who are in fact groomed and marketed to us by capitalists who profit from and control their reigns. In the marketing of both types of products, it is in the material interests of those profiting from their sales to perpetuate desire and manufacture ever increasing want. This is basic to the system and antithetical to the goal Buddhism as expounded in the Four Noble Truths.

Because of the widespread relationship between capitalism and democracy, it becomes important in this discussion to simultaneously ask what Buddhism's role should be in dealing with each. In our specific example of Myanmar, a major consideration becomes whether the ostensive drive to adopt some form of a Euro-American version of democracy also includes the implementation of those countries' version of capitalism. In Myanmar's drive for "democracy," does accepting the praise and support of Europe, America, Australia, Japan and perhaps even the UN, imply a willingness to also accept the democracy-accompanying capitalism of those countries? Such a question was likely behind the junta's reluctance to accept humanitarian aid after the cyclone in May 2008. If not in that case, there can be little doubt that such actions as the US awarding the Medal of Honor to Aung Sang Suu Kyi is no less than a strike at the economic system, not just the political system in place in Myanmar, in hopes of establishing trade relations more favorable to the US economic elite. Although Myanmar can see centuries of malevolent results of alliances between impoverished Asian countries and rich capitalist nations, ultimately, faced with the global economy, they may have little choice in the matter. If so, what will be the role of Buddhism in bringing it about, preventing it, or keeping it under control? This consideration is as important today as it should have been for General Aung Sang when asking Imperial Japan for help in ousting the British and the British for help in ousting the Japanese.

A final explanation for Buddhist social engagement comes from the canonical notion of dependent origination. This explanation is given, for example, by Venerable Daewon Ki as a reason for dedicating his temple to peace.[21] The idea is found in early scriptures, Abhidhamma literature and many later writings of Zen and other traditions of Buddhism. In short, the theory states that nothing exists in isolation and the existence of each constitute of the world is dependent on something else. This assumption leads to a belief that beneath the basic illusion that constitutes ignorance, all people are fundamentally connected and joined as the same. For this reason, the individual ego should be rejected as ignorance. This idea is well known among students of World Religions looking at the basics of Buddhism. It is seen as providing a basis for moral actions by assuming if we harm another we are harming ourselves. But, can it be connected with the Buddhist pro-democracy movement? Certainly, there is the implication of some degree of equality among people since we are all connected to the sufferings and exaltations of one another and in fact, the idea of "another" is deemed invalid. However, perhaps this very fact also invalidates the notion of individualism inherent in democracy as it certainly does in regards to capitalism. Taken to this extreme, it also challenges the assumptions of the individual merit / demerit system.

In dealing with our topic, this paper has skirted the most likely question to be raised by American students. We will conclude with

---

[21] Chanju Mun, ed., *The World is One Flower* (Honolulu: Blue Pine, 2006), xxxvii.

it now, as it is a central consideration for socially engaged Buddhism and is taken up by a number of contributors to this volume. Is it antithetical to Buddhism to perpetuate factional politics? By so doing, are the monks in Myanmar responsible for continuing that aspect of their own suffering and that of others they should be leading away from it?

VIRTUE, AND VIOLENCE IN THERAVĀDA AND SRI LANKAN BUDDHISM

Eric Sean Nelson

1. Introduction[1]

The English word ethics stems from the Greek word "ethos" that signifies a way of life or art of living. Ethics concerns human actions, behaviors, and practices, in particular how we *ought* to treat others and ourselves. In the western philosophical tradition, to speak schematically, there are two major forms of approaching ethics. On the one hand, one form of ethical theory consists of the rule based on ethics found in the deontological ethics of intention and duty, and the other the utilitarian ethics of evaluating actions in terms of their consequences. Virtue ethics and other varieties of context-based ethics, on the other hand, emphasize the individual and communal cultivation of virtues through role models and exemplars and their appropriate and flexible application to the situation. The ethical is not assessed by the intentions and consequences of actions but by how these and other elements fit into a concrete way of life as a whole.

---

[1] I would like to thank Ronald Green for his comments and suggestions for improving the argument and style of this paper. I am also thankful to Namita Goswami and Lori Witthaus for their thoughts on an earlier draft presented at the Association for Asian Studies. This early short version appeared as "Virtue, Violence, and Engagement in Theravāda and Sri Lankan Buddhism," *SACP Forum for Asian and Comparative Philosophy* 23.47 (Fall 2006): 192-216.

Recent scholarship, in particular Damien Keown's pioneering works on Buddhist ethics, has seen the development of the claim that Buddhist ethics is a variety of "virtue ethics." [2] That is, according to Keown, "Buddhist ethics is aretetic: it rests upon the cultivation of personal virtue in the expectation that as spiritual capacity expands towards the goal of enlightenment ethical choices will become clear and unproblematic." [3] Virtue ethics is a contemporary approach to morality that resorts to the moral paradigm developed by Aristotle. Aristotelian ethics emphasizes the cultivation of individual virtues and the political community in order to promote human flourishing or happiness in the broadest sense. Keown argues for an interpretation of Buddhist ethics "based on the Aristotelian model, or at least one understanding of it." Keown continues, "The parallel between Buddhist and Aristotelian ethics is, I believe, quite close in many respects. Aristotle's ethical theory appears to be the closest Western analogue to Buddhist ethics, and is an illuminating guide to an understanding of the Buddhist moral system." [4]

In this paper, I will examine the role of virtue ethics and violence in traditional Theravāda and contemporary Sri Lankan Buddhism. Despite the limits and problems of applying the virtue ethics model – especially in its Aristotelian form advocated by Keown – to Buddhist ethics, I contend that the virtue ethical elements of Theravāda Buddhism help clarify issues of war and violence as well as compassion and peace in a country such as Sri Lanka (the former British colony of Ceylon). The Sri Lankan people, both Sinhalese and Tamil, have suffered from approximately three decades of civil war, ethnic strife, and terrorism. An end to this conflict between the mostly Buddhist Sinhalese and predominantly Hindu Tamils is still not in sight.

The issues revealed by the relation between Buddhism, politics, and violence in South Asia should serve as a caution to and a

---

[2] Damien Keown, *Buddhist Ethics: A Very Short Introduction* (Oxford: Oxford University Press, 2005), 25; and *The Nature of Buddhist Ethics* (Basingstoke: Palgrave, 2001), 2.

[3] Keown, *The Nature of Buddhist Ethics*, 2.

[4] *Ibid*, 21.

source of self-reflection for the contemporary project of socially engaged Buddhism. Given (1) the everyday logic of being absorbed in circumstances and making exceptions for one's own actions and inactions; (2) the possibility of acting from the condition of exception and emergency (as being the norm and the typical rather than the extraordinary and atypical); and (3) the customary division between friend and enemy, native and foreign, ethical and social norms and practices can be used to reproduce and intensify rather than dismantle and resolve social conflicts. This is true even of an ethics that is well-intentioned and altruistic, such as perhaps the canonical Theravāda ethics of loving kindness (*mettā*), generosity (*dāna*), and compassion (*karuṇā*), if it obeys instead of confronting this logic of conflict.

Consequently, despite the many merits of the recent revival of the ethical and religious in contemporary thought and culture, the related privatization of social-political issues into private ones of charity and compassion can result in an ideological blindness to and a perilous one-sidedness in addressing issues of social justice. That is, the ethical requires an understanding of and concern with society beyond individual attitudes, intentions, and virtues if it is not to become an unethical and abstract cult of virtue or misused in the name of various particular religious, moral, national, and ethnic identities. To this extent, ethics in general and in Buddhism needs to be more than the virtue ethics of individuals and communities, i.e., more than an ethics of individual and social virtues in order to be both open and responsive to encountering others as well as critical of its own self-distortion, if ethics is a response to rather than an excuse for the underlying logic of conflict, violence, and war that so often dominate human relations.

2. Buddhism and Virtue Ethics

Morality, meditation, and wisdom constitute the three-fold basis of Theravāda Buddhist practice. As the foundation and prerequisite of the path, the moral life (*sīla*) is the first part of Bhadantācariya Buddhaghosa's great commentary *Visuddhimagga* and it is described by the Buddha as the foundation on which the path is built.[5] Theravāda Buddhist ethics is considered a variety of virtue ethics, which considers the effects actions have on one's general condition or way of life as a whole, because it emphasizes: (1) morality (*sīla*) as a way of life rather than a system of rules, (2) the cultivation of morality through precepts and as perfections and virtues, (3) moral psychology, which is richly developed in the Pāli *sutta*s and commentaries, and (4) the need for skillfulness, fittingness, and appropriateness in applying morality to the situation.[6] Although Theravāda ethics differs from the Aristotelian paradigm of virtue ethics, such as its focus on the actual and concrete suffering of the other and of all sentient beings, it remains comparable in some ways to Aristotelian and Confucian ethics in stressing the need for the cultivation of an apt ethical discernment that is responsive to the context through the appropriate enactment of morality.

There are aspects of the Pāli canon that clearly evoke Aristotelian virtue ethics, as when the Buddha described the moral life constitutive of the Buddhist path as a "noble aggregation of

---

[5] Bhadantācariya Buddhaghosa, *The Path of Purification*, tr. Bhikkhu Ñāṇamoli (Seattle: Buddhist Publication Society Pariyatti Editions, 1999); and *Numerical Discourses of the Buddha*, tr. and ed. Nyanaponika Thera and Bhikkhu Bodhi (Walnut Creek: AltaMira Press, 2000) is a selective translation of the *Aṅguttara-nikāya* (hereafter cited as AN), AN XI.1, AN XI.2.

[6] The view that Mahāyāna involves a kind of virtue ethic has been more extensively developed, especially given the claim that the Bodhisattva's compassion can override rules. Arguments for Zen and Mahāyāna virtue ethics are found in Simon P. James, *Zen Buddhism and Environmental Ethics* (Aldershot: Ashgate, 2004) and David E. Cooper and Simon P. James, *Buddhism, Virtue and Environment* (Aldershot: Ashgate, 2005).

virtues" involving a "faultless happiness." [7] Here we see an emphasis on the cultivation of virtues, their complementary unity in producing a balanced way of life, and the happiness that this entails. For the Buddha, the self-interested concern for one's own welfare leads one to develop a goodness that involves its own kind of well-being. [8] Likewise, the Buddha's emphasis on moral appropriateness instead of ethical absolutes and skillfulness in relation to the situation and context is a characteristic of virtue ethics. Nevertheless, Keown's argument for the parallel between Buddhist and Aristotelian ethics is problematic given that Aristotle's *phronesis* (prudential judgment or sense of appropriateness) is primarily an aristocratic mastery, an accomplishment of the patriarchal householder and active citizen, whereas Buddhist moral skillfulness (Pāli: *kusala*) transcends the *ekos* and *polis* to a kind of freedom in relation to people and things. [9] This is not the freedom of indifference but of compassion (*karunā*, the core virtue) as a spontaneous responsiveness constituted by instead of transcending the ethical. Such freedom evokes one aspect of a different variety of ancient Greco-Roman virtue ethics – the cosmopolitanism of the Greco-Roman Cynics and Stoics. Rather than restricting the ethical to the polis, the political community, the Hellenistic and Roman Cynics and Stoics argued for the moral community of humanity, advocating a universal rather than particularistic "virtue ethics." [10] Likewise in Buddhism, the ethical is not limited to the national community or even the human, as ethical responsiveness extends to all sentient beings and to the world itself. This suggests a kind of Buddhist

---

[7] MN I. 269; translation in John J. Holder, ed. and tr., *Early Buddhist Discourses* (Indianapolis: Hackett Publishing, 2006), 70.

[8] SN III.4. Most passages cited from SN can be found in the following incomplete translation: *The Sutta-Nipata*, tr. H. Saddhatissa (Surrey: Curzon, 1994).

[9] Keown, *op. cit.*, ch.8.

[10] Martha Nussbaum criticizes the reduction of virtue ethics to the communitarian model of Aristotelian ethics, contending that Stoicism offers a more humanistic and universalistic model in "Kant and Cosmopolitanism," in James Bohman and Matthias Lutz-Bachmann, eds., *Perpetual Peace: Essays on Kant's Cosmopolitan Ideal* (Cambridge: MIT Press, 1997), 46.

world-community (*cosmo-polis*), which is further supported in the ideal of the *cakkavatti* as a universal and inclusive wheel-turning monarch. The wheel-turning monarch conquers through law rather than violence ("stick or sword"), instituting peace and fairness for all.[11]

Whereas appropriateness is secondary to principle in rule-based ethics and to command and law in the legalism of command theory, virtue and context-oriented ethics is defined by the recognition that appropriateness is not accidental but constitutive of the ethical. Ethical life calls for the development of moral sensibility or judgment, since the richness and complexity of life cannot be adequately articulated and addressed through an abstract system of mechanical rules or rigid commands. Some might object that Buddhism has no ethics but only calls for a non-moral meditative insight into the causality of karma. This view of karmic determinism is clearly false, as I have argued in more detail elsewhere.[12] For the Buddha, as he is said to state repeatedly throughout the *Sutta-nipāta*, the path is intrinsically ethical although morality alone is insufficient for liberation.[13] Buddhism is about deeds rather than rules and rites.[14] One should focus on moral conduct, virtue and responsibility instead of the fate or destiny of caste or birth;[15] since there is no shelter except the actual good we have done.[16]

Given that family resemblances and analogies do not entail identity, it is important to resist conflating Buddhist with other varieties of virtue ethics such as Aristotle's. This context-sensitive and flexible responsiveness articulated in Buddhism is not based in political prudence, interpreted as discriminatory judgment, and the

---

[11] DN I.89, DN III.59. *Dīgha Nikāya*, translation available in *The Long Discourses of the Buddha*, tr. Maurice Walshe (Boston: Wisdom Publications, 1995).

[12] E. S. Nelson, "Questioning Karma: Buddhism and the Phenomenology of the Ethical," in Charles Prebish, Damien Keown, and Dale S. Wright, *Revisioning Karma* (*Journal of Buddhist Ethics* 14 (2007)): 353-373.

[13] SN IV.898.

[14] SN II. 249-250.

[15] SN I. 136-140, III. 462, III. 648-650.

[16] AN III. 51.

hierarchy of social relations legitimated by Aristotelian ethics. Buddhist social ethics is often interpreted as being more republican and egalitarian, due to the Buddha's historical origins and message. [17] Ideally, Theravāda Buddhist virtues are oriented towards a mindful loving-kindness that is developed and disclosed in practices of morality, mediation, and wisdom. The primary example of such mindfulness is the Buddha himself as the embodiment of a purely skillful and spontaneous ethical responsiveness towards all beings. This openness and situatedness also opens up possibilities for misunderstanding and misapplication when the person acts, speaks, and thinks without mindfulness. The lack of mindfulness might generate the conclusion that the first precept of non-harm (*ahiṃsā*) can be bracketed in the name of another good such as the protection of Buddhism. Such a perspective is found in utilitarian interpretations of Buddhist ethics, where the lives of the many might outweigh one life, and in the phenomenon that has been described as "Buddhist fundamentalism" by Tessa J. Bartholomeusz and Chandra Richard de Silva.[18] However, this phenomenon is more aptly described as the nationalistic and communalistic use (or cooption) of Buddhism, since it is not based in the authority of the Pāli Canon, and insofar as the word fundamentalism usually entails a return to and literal reading of a canonical or sacred text rather than a radical departure from it.

The majority of the Buddhist *sutta*s forbid violence and war, with some interesting exceptions, calling for non-attachment even ultimately to Buddhism itself. Such non-attachment is often conflated with indifference. Critics of Buddhism often confuse non-attachment and indifference, conflating a stereotypical view of Stoicism (with its supposed repression of the emotions for the sake

---

[17] David J. Kalupahana, *Ethics in Early Buddhism* (Honolulu: University of Hawaii Press, 1995), 100-101; and Etienne Lamotte, *History of Indian Buddhism: From the Origins to the Saka Era* (Louvain-la-Neuve: Université catholique de Louvain, Institut orientaliste, 1988), 10.

[18] This expression is developed in Tessa J. Bartholomeusz and Chandra R de Silva, eds., *Buddhist Fundamentalism and Minority Identities in Sri Lanka* (Albany: SUNY Press, 1998).

of virtue and the equanimity of *ataraxia*) and Buddhism (which calls for recognizing, working with, and transforming emotions).[19] Another critique would reduce Buddhism to the opposite of indifference – egotistical self-satisfaction and joy in oneself.[20] Yet it is clear from the Pāli canon that the Buddha is never portrayed as advocating moral indifference to the fate of others. On the contrary, the noble person is: "One who is devoted to one's own welfare and cultivates the virtues, while at the same time [being] devoted to the welfare of others by causing others to cultivate their virtues."[21] From a perspective that is critical of the popular or political uses of Buddhism, which seem to contradict Buddhist teachings, the treatment of Buddhism as a reified cultural identity and exclusive possession that excludes others and justifies hostility toward them is at odds with its moral content. This politicized Buddhism seems to contradict the explicit call for taking up others well-being, and in particular, its universalism and cosmopolitanism that extends to humanity and indeed the entirety of sentient life. The violent promotion of Buddhism as a particular way of life conflicts with the very practice and aim of that way of life. This problematic nexus between Buddhism and the political is as much an issue for contemporary Buddhism, including "engaged Buddhism," as it is for its traditional forms.[22]

---

[19] For a more nuanced approach to the emotions in Stoicism, see Nussbaum, 44-45.

[20] See Elizabeth Harris, who has an interesting analysis of such claims in "Buddhism in the Media," in Karma Lekshe Tsomo, ed., *Innovative Buddhist Women: Swimming against the Stream* (London: RoutledgeCurzon, 2000). The implausible view that Buddhism aims at a stereotypical "Stoic indifference" excluding possibilities for transformation is also found in other figures, such as Gillian Rose's critique of what she calls Levinas' "Buddhist Judaism," in *Mourning Becomes the Law: Philosophy and Representation* (Cambridge: Cambridge University Press, 1996), 37-38.

[21] Kalupahana, *op. cit.*, 76.

[22] For a survey of the relations between Buddhism and political institutions and movements in recent Asian history, see the essays gathered in Ian Harris, ed., *Buddhism and Politics in Twentieth-Century Asia* (London: Continuum, 1999). On the many problems of engaged Buddhist interpretations of Buddhist ethics, see Christopher Ives, "Deploying the Dharma: Reflections on the

Utilitarian and contextualist readings imply that in some cases moral agents are justified in sacrificing their own virtues and the goods and lives of others for the sake of a greater good. For instance, in common dilemmas from moral philosophy, agents might be justified in killing one person who would otherwise kill hundreds or thousands. The argument that it is legitimate for the first precept demanding *ahiṃsā* to be suspended under limited exceptional circumstances, i.e., in order to assimilate some forms of self-defense, is itself conditional, since it is clear from the *sutta*s that karmic responsibility is unavoidable for killing. One is always culpable for killing, although one might be considered more or less culpable.[23] Violence only creates more violence and, no matter how necessary or legitimate it seems, always has its consequences such that the end cannot cleanse or sanctify the means. But even given this understanding, individuals and groups have felt compelled for various reasons to engage in violence, and with some justification in cases of compassion for the greater good, as in the *Jātaka* narratives when the Bodhisatta (Skt., Bodhisattva) saves the tiger by allowing it to eat him or the ship-captain kills one in order to save many, or for the sake of self-defense.[24] As Peter Harvey notes, despite any moral dilemma: "Most lay Buddhists have been prepared to break the precept against killing in self-defense, and many have joined in the defense of the community in times of need."[25]

Reflection on the history of South and South-East Asia illustrates that the Buddha's commitment to non-harm and non-violence has often been in tension with political institutions that have never abandoned the right to use force and established social

---

Methodology of Constructive Buddhist Ethics," in *Journal of Buddhist Ethics* 15 (2008): 23-44.

[23] Hammalawa Saddhatissa, *Buddhist Ethics* (Boston: Wisdom Publications, 2003), 60.

[24] On compassionate killing, see Peter Harvey, *An Introduction to Buddhist Ethics* (Cambridge: Cambridge University Press, 2000), 135. H. Saddhatissa introduces the self-defense of the community through a comparison with Plato's *Republic* (*Ibid*, 114), although violence is simultaneously seen as a condition of decline (*Ibid*, 120, 124).

[25] Peter Harvey, *op. cit.*, 255.

practices involving the mistreatment of other humans and animals. The idea that *ahiṃsā* is a primary virtue has coexisted with its repeated violation. Since the canonical virtue of *ahiṃsā* can be overridden by the weight of circumstances in societies that have claimed to promote the *Dhamma*, it is worthwhile to consider the logic at work in the justification of internal coercion and external war. This raises the question of whether violence is inherently incompatible with the *Dhamma*, as the Buddha is generally portrayed as advocating, or whether there is a "Buddhist just war theory" based on other canonical sources and non-canonical popular "lived" practices and ways of reasoning? Although Ananda Abeysekara denies this apparent paradox by arguing that Buddhism cannot be separated into an authentic philosophical discourse stemming from the Buddha and popular violence, since they are contingent and constructed categories, this paradox cannot be evaded if Buddhism does not only consist of practices but normative claims that can potentially problematize those very practices.[26]

3. Virtue and Engagement

In many senses, Buddhism is inherently ethically engaged. Buddhism is about practices and a way of life, and the Buddha called for the appropriate practice of the virtues.[27] Compassion, generosity, and loving-kindness are primary Theravāda virtues. These are genuinely altruistic and other-oriented since they are ultimately not done out of any "need" but out of freedom.[28] Although Richard Gombrich is correct when he asserts that the Buddha's primary goal was not social reform but spiritual liberation,[29] the historical Buddha remains an ethical model and exemplar who confronted social injustices, such as caste hierarchy

---

[26] See his *Colors of the Robe: Religion, Identity, and Difference* (Columbia: University of South Carolina Press, 2002), 204.

[27] SN I. 73.

[28] SN I. 25.

[29] Richard Gombrich, *Theravāda Buddhism* (London: Routledge, 1988), 30, 68.

and the exclusion of "untouchables," and the social pathologies of violence and war. He did not do so because he was commanded to do so to avoid punishment by a divine being, but because of an insight into the moral nexus of *kamma* (karma), which as moral is never simply a predetermined fate or destiny.[30] He is described as responding immanently from out of his own condition to the concrete suffering of others. Although the Buddha's initial encounter with the suffering of others can be interpreted as reflecting his concern about suffering the same afflictions, as being self-interested, it is still his being affected by the other's suffering – the disquiet, sickness, old age, and death of others – that set him on the path of awakening.[31] This encounter with and uncalculated response to suffering provided the basis for *kamma* becoming ethical and the universe a basically moral arena in early Buddhism.[32]

It is sometimes argued that "socially engaged Buddhism" is a relatively new and western inspired phenomenon. First, this claim presupposes that something else is meant by "engagement" than traditional forms of Buddhist ethical engagement for sentient life. Second, this claim is inaccurate insofar as engaged Buddhism is not merely a contemporary western construct insofar as there are qualities in traditional Buddhism allowing contemporary western redeployments. Third, whereas "Western" interpretations often focus on the individualism of Buddhism, and there are elements emphasizing working for one's own salvation, Asian Buddhists have interpreted *kamma* as inherently social. *Kamma* inherently binds one to others, forming a network of freedom and fate, and responsibility extends beyond the immediacy of the moment into the past and future of this and other lives.[33] Further, a number of

---

[30] I develop this argument concerning the moral character of karma in "Questioning Karma," 353-373.

[31] On the general importance of feeling, affective response and moral sentiment in Buddhist thought and practice, see Keown, *The Nature of Buddhist Ethics*, 68-78.

[32] Gombrich, 69.

[33] On the social character of karma and responsibility, see Jonathan S. Walters, "Communal Karma and Karmic Community in Theravāda Buddhist

Eric Sean Nelson

contemporary ethical issues such as the moral status of animals and the environment are arguably more fully articulated in Buddhist than in traditional western discourses.[34] The modern focus on social activism and engagement is motivated by enlightenment ideas of liberty, equality, and fraternity and the social movements of the nineteenth and twentieth centuries. As varied responses of historical agents, who can interpret and engage their contexts and are not the mere passive product of colonial hegemony, anti-colonial liberation struggles involve a multiplicity of traditions and inspirations that are more than their Western and Christian sources.

Socially engaged Buddhism, inconceivable without its Asian sources, brings traditions of Buddhist ethical reflection to bear on contemporary moral and social issues. If ethical insights of the *Dhamma* are needed in a world that all too readily resorts to intolerance, persecution, and violence, then vigilance concerning the possible dangers (whether to non-Buddhists or to Buddhists themselves) of inappropriately and unskillfully engaging Buddhist ethics remains vital to such engagement for peace, social justice, and the common welfare. These dangers are apparent in the history of Asian Buddhism and should serve to stimulate Western

---

History," in J. C. Holt, J. N. Kinnard, and Jonathan S. Walters, *Constituting Communities* (Albany: SUNY Press, 2003), 9-39, see especially 10, 18, 28. According to Walters, the notion of rebirth in Sri Lankan popular Buddhism only deepens one's sense of responsibility for others and the social character of karma. My relations with others are unavoidable, given that I am bound to them not only in this life but in others as well. The suffering that I ignore today, because I believe the other person deserves that suffering because of past deeds, will become part of my own suffering.

[34] The notion of social engagement said to be lacking in traditional Buddhism is not so much a traditional Christian idea, which is not necessarily altruistic or purely ethical in the Kantian sense since charity is done for the reward of salvation rather than purely for its own sake, as it is a modern one emerging from the moral and political thought of the enlightenment. Compare Rita Gross's discussion of the claim that Christianity is the source of socially engaged Buddhism in *Soaring and Settling: Buddhist Perspectives on Contemporary Social and Religious Issues* (New York: Continuum, 1998), 13-18. No doubt, the encounter between East and West has promoted contemporary engaged Buddhism, yet this would have remained unlikely if it did not have a basis within Buddhism itself.

reflection on the character and potential consequences of moral and political engagement.

The first danger is the possibility of the *Dhamma* being appropriated by and limited to a political program such that it becomes part of the ideological legitimation of problematic political practices and institutions. One is unlikely to critically engage a political order with which one is complicit. In engaging politics, Buddhism – like any other philosophy, religion, or way of life – risks becoming an instrument of the state or a party. Providing an ethical basis for action, and morality is the basis of practice[35], entails establishing a foundation for the justification and legitimation of action, although living morally is distinguished from being attached to and anxious about right and wrong as viewpoints. [36] On the one hand, this makes ethics and moral judgment possible. On the other hand, it opens up the danger of losing the ethical in its very institutionalization. There are numerous historical examples that show how moral values and ideals are used to excuse horror such that peace becomes war, justice turns into injustice, humanitarian compassion justifies violence, and freedom is turned into tyranny. Connections with the state, the military, political parties and economic powers have at times morally compromised Buddhism and can do so again in the future. This is not without its rationale within Buddhism, which often – analogously to the Christian two kingdom doctrine of the earthly and divine kingdoms – either accommodated itself to the state or left it to its own devices. [37]

Social engagement or activism, which counters tendencies toward the privatization of moral questions, is by itself an insufficient condition or criterion for addressing structural and institutional social-political issues that concern issues of power, justice, and equality that involve more than the intentions and good will of individual agents. [38] Buddhism should not be reduced to

---

[35] DN I. 206.

[36] DN I. 26.

[37] See Gombrich, 70 and 116.

[38] Ives makes the important point that Buddhist ethics addresses individual suffering and the individual's response to suffering more than it does the social-

engagement because it is "other-worldly" but insofar as engagement blinds one to the need for mindfulness and comprehension (*saṃpajāno*) in general and comprehension of suitability (*sappaya saṃpajāno*) or the "art of practicality" in particular. This art involves skillfulness and appropriateness in the choice of the right means (Pāli, *upaya-kusala*; Skt., *upāya-kauśalya*) for the right situation at the right moment, which Mark Siderits translates as "pedagogical skill" and Jan Nattier more broadly as "tactical skill."[39] This virtue is one that the Buddha preeminently exemplified.

Although the *Dhamma* is oriented towards peace, moral responsibility and compassion, a second danger can be seen in attempts to use Buddhism to justify violence and war. The various forms of Japanese Buddhism, subordinated to the interests of the Imperial state and state-Shinto after the persecutions of the Meiji era, became part of a militaristic system of justifying expansion, colonization, and war.[40] It was the reduction of the *Dhamma* to socio-political interests that legitimated acting contrary to the *Dhamma*. Distinguishing "reactionary" and "progressive" engagement by itself does not resolve this issue. Imperial Japan's political and militaristic use of Buddhism and the support of aggressive war by the majority of Japanese Buddhists are one powerful example employed by critics of the social role of Buddhism such as Brian Victoria.[41] Yet this question can be raised in contemporary contexts. There are Buddhists who actively work for the non-violent resolution of the Sinhalese-Tamil conflict, for example the Buddhists involved in *Sarvodaya Shramadana,* while

---

political diagnosis of suffering in Ives, "Deploying the Dharma: Reflections on the Methodology of Constructive Buddhist Ethics," 35.

[39] Mark Siderits, *Buddhism as Philosophy: An Introduction* (Indianapolis: Hackett Publishing, 2007), 58; and Jan Nattier usefully explores the different senses of "tactical skill," involving more than teaching or pedagogy, in *A Few Good Men: The Bodhisattva Path according to The Inquiry of Ugra* (Honolulu: University of Hawaii Press, 2003), 154-156.

[40] The extent of this complicity and active engagement has become apparent from the work of Brian Daizen Victoria, *Zen at War* (Lanham: Rowman & Littlefield, 2005) and *Zen War Stories* (London: RoutledgeCurzon, 2003).

[41] *Ibid.*

other Buddhists have played a significant role in intensifying and participating in the conflict. [42] We can thus find at least two conflicting models of socially engaged Buddhism in contemporary Sri Lanka, one "for peace" and the other "for war."

What lessons should be drawn from uses of Buddhism that seem morally problematic or unvirtuous by Buddhist ethical criteria? Are there sources within Buddhist teaching, as Brian Victoria has argued of Zen and Tessa Bartholomeusz of Sri Lankan Theravāda, which potentially legitimate violence and war?[43] The first precept, or first moral rule, of Buddhism seems clear: I undertake the precept to refrain from destroying living creatures (*Panatipata veramani sikkhapadam samadiyami*). The first precept of *ahimsā*, a vow taken to dedicate oneself to non-harm and non-violence, does not seem a promising start for justifying violence and yet it is not the case that individuals and groups claiming to be Buddhist have never engaged in violence. One can blame this on the imperfection of human character, and accordingly people often distinguish the pleasant ideal from the unpleasant reality. This separation of norms and practices, besides being dualistic, precludes critical discussion and leaves unanswered the question of whether there are possible sources within Buddhist teaching for departing from the moral demand of *ahimsā* to not harm sentient beings.

4. Virtue, Violence, and War

Through hatred, hatred is never overcome; through non-hatred, hatred is always overcome – this is the eternal law. [44]

The obligation to cultivate compassion, loving-kindness, respect, and reverence for all human and sentient life does not

---

[42] For a brief account of the *Sarvodaya Shramadana* movement in relation to Buddhist ethics, see Harvey, 225-234.

[43] Brian Daizen Victoria, *Zen War Stories* and Tessa J. Bartholomeusz, *In Defense of Dharma: Just-War Ideology in Buddhist Sri Lanka* (London: RoutledgeCurzon, 2002).

[44] *Dhammapada*, verse 5.

seem a hopeful beginning for the justification of war. The argument that it is better to suffer harm than to do harm appears less auspicious for legitimating violence of any kind. Buddhists and non-Buddhists alike often take for granted that there is no legitimate Buddhist justification of war much less a Buddhist tradition of just-war theory. To use violence is to betray the Buddha's teachings: "There is a person who abstains from the destruction of life; with the rod and the weapon laid aside, he is conscientious and kindly and dwells compassionately towards all living beings."[45]

There are noticeable historical exceptions to the obvious interpretation of the Buddha's first precept demanding non-harm. Traditional Buddhist kings have raised and used armies. Buddhist monks have developed and used martial arts. In Medieval China and Japan, monks have justified killing, carried weapons, formed armies, and been involved in rebellions.[46] Tibetan Buddhism tells of a future king who will militarily liberate them from external oppression in the stories associated with Shambhala and the *Kalachakra Tantra*. Japanese Buddhists supported the expansion of imperial Japan. There are questionable relations between Buddhists and the military in countries such as Burma and Thailand. Currently in Sri Lanka, Theravāda monks and laity have been implicated in persecution and violence in the Sri Lankan ethnic conflict and civil war.

Because of (1) the Buddha's rejection of violence and war as a legitimate means of achieving one's ends and (2) the long history and dedication to peace and non-violent social change in the Buddhist tradition, it is important to reflect on these historical exceptions. The powerful ethical character of Buddhism can be seen from the Buddha's critique of war, violence and social injustice to more contemporary movements as diverse as the Vietnamese peace movement of the 1960's, the Tibetan struggle

---

[45] AN, X, 206, also compare AN, IX, 7.

[46] A classic article on such issues in East Asia is Paul Demiéville, "Le bouddhisme et la guerre. Post-scriptum a l'«Histoire des moines guerriers du Japon» de Gaston Renondeau," *Mélanges publiés par l'Institut des Hautes Etudes chinoises*, Tome I, Paris, 1957, 347-385.

for religious freedom, the Burmese pro-democracy movement, and in Sir Lanka the lay *Sarvodaya Shramadana* movement for peace, communal self-help, and popular empowerment.

Counterexamples to what is often considered normative Buddhism, which was a plural and contested Asian "construct" before it was a western one, implicitly reveal the moral character of Buddhism in limiting and countering the drive to hatred, violence and war by the very fact that violence is deeply problematic in Buddhism. Those claiming to be Buddhists who engage in war are forced to appeal to the limited and contested (in Buddhist thought) idea of self-defense or to a questionable antinomian non-attachment to the ethical core of Buddhism itself – loving-kindness and compassion. Although one cannot and should not expect to exclude all possibilities for self-defense and especially non-violent resistance, practices contradicting this minimalist idea reveal that other motives and self-deception can be at work. Rather than there being a general "antinomianism" or "nihilism" inherently at work in Buddhism, as Brian Victoria contends, the problem lies in the ambiguity about moral appropriateness, including skillful means and skillfulness in Buddhism. Buddhist ethics does not advocate the application of one single rule or principle that is eternally and universally valid in all cases but involves ethics understood as (1) appropriateness, (2) a way of life, and (3) part of the way.[47] Although it is not the end or entirety of the Buddhist path, morality is its necessary prerequisite.[48]

Because of the virtue-ethical and context-sensitive character of Buddhism, a number of Buddhists and non-Buddhists suggest that there is a condition that transcends ethics, even understood as ethical virtues and appropriateness. One abandons morality, just as one abandons the raft that gets one to the other side of the river. Yet going beyond good and evil as unconditional absolutes and as

---

[47] For a recent argument in favor of principles in Buddhist ethics, see Ives, "Deploying the Dharma: Reflections on the Methodology of Constructive Buddhist Ethics," 30-34.

[48] AN, XI, 1-2. This point is developed in Gombrich, 74, 89; and Keown, *op. cit.*, 50-53.

discriminatory attachments does not entail transcending ethics as one's way of existing or dwelling. The art of suitability and skillfulness is not unethical in being anti-essentialist, as it directs the mind to considering the context and the level of understanding of oneself and others. This prudential context-sensitivity has and can be misunderstood as an excuse for unethical behavior among some Buddhist individuals and groups. Buddhist ethics at its simplest levels appeals to prudential self-interest, especially through the popular logic of merit and merit transfer that is the dominant form of popular Buddhist practice in Sri Lanka;[49] yet continuing to act out of self-interested motives is canonically considered only the lowest level of moral action.[50] Egotistical self-interest and attachment to one's own individual or group superiority undermines the basic equality of sentient beings that is asserted in the Buddhist tradition as well as the fundamental practices and virtues of loving kindness (*mettā*), generosity (*dāna*), and compassion (*karuṇā*).

It is fair to say that Buddhism does not endorse the use of violence. Still it is untrue that Buddhists – or at least individuals and groups claiming to be Buddhists and engaging in at least some of the practices associated with Buddhism – never engage in acts of war, hatred, and conflict. This is no doubt caused by human imperfection. Nevertheless, it should not just be accepted as human imperfection, since such actions always involve accruing *kamma* (karma) and Buddhism insists that beings strive for and realize universal wisdom and compassion. The Buddhist emphasis on non-attachment, including to itself, and developing universal compassion and self-criticism, especially of inadequate understandings of Buddhism, demands a greater emphasis on and means to critique one's own behavior towards others. The aggressive and brutal colonialism justified by Japanese Buddhists, the right-wing rhetoric and practices of some Sri Lankan monks and laity, and the connections between Buddhism and the military

---

[49] Gombrich, 78; and H. L. Seneviratne, *The Work of Kings: The New Buddhism in Sri Lanka* (Chicago: University of Chicago Press, 1999), 348.

[50] Kalupahana, 76.

discriminatory attachments does not entail transcending ethics as one's way of existing or dwelling. The art of suitability and skillfulness is not unethical in being anti-essentialist, as it directs the mind to considering the context and the level of understanding of oneself and others. This prudential context-sensitivity has and can be misunderstood as an excuse for unethical behavior among some Buddhist individuals and groups. Buddhist ethics at its simplest levels appeals to prudential self-interest, especially through the popular logic of merit and merit transfer that is the dominant form of popular Buddhist practice in Sri Lanka;[49] yet continuing to act out of self-interested motives is canonically considered only the lowest level of moral action.[50] Egotistical self-interest and attachment to one's own individual or group superiority undermines the basic equality of sentient beings that is asserted in the Buddhist tradition as well as the fundamental practices and virtues of loving kindness (*mettā*), generosity (*dāna*), and compassion (*karuṇā*).

It is fair to say that Buddhism does not endorse the use of violence. Still it is untrue that Buddhists – or at least individuals and groups claiming to be Buddhists and engaging in at least some of the practices associated with Buddhism – never engage in acts of war, hatred, and conflict. This is no doubt caused by human imperfection. Nevertheless, it should not just be accepted as human imperfection, since such actions always involve accruing *kamma* (karma) and Buddhism insists that beings strive for and realize universal wisdom and compassion. The Buddhist emphasis on non-attachment, including to itself, and developing universal compassion and self-criticism, especially of inadequate understandings of Buddhism, demands a greater emphasis on and means to critique one's own behavior towards others. The aggressive and brutal colonialism justified by Japanese Buddhists, the right-wing rhetoric and practices of some Sri Lankan monks and laity, and the connections between Buddhism and the military

---

[49] Gombrich, 78; and H. L. Seneviratne, *The Work of Kings: The New Buddhism in Sri Lanka* (Chicago: University of Chicago Press, 1999), 348.
[50] Kalupahana, 76.

of the situation itself. This raises the question of whether the first precept can be outweighed at times by other considerations such as utilitarian considerations of sacrificing one life in order to save multiple lives. Can one then in exceptional circumstances destroy or allow one life to be destroyed in order to save the lives of a community or multitude of individuals?

This reasoning about exceptions and the force of necessity is not only an abstract and speculative question. It has occurred within Buddhist historical traditions and has given birth to a Buddhist tradition that has been likened by some scholars to western "just-war theory." Just war theory seeks to explain the circumstances under which it might be legitimate or at least necessary to take life in armed conflict. Whereas scholars of Theravāda such as Damien Keown have argued that killing can sometimes be a legitimate response to suffering, other scholars such as Rupert Gethin have rejected this argument since it does not address *dukkha* as a reality that must be understood and worked through rather than suppressed. [55] The issue is not that people claiming to be Buddhists at times engage in violence and war in the name of self-defense. It is difficult if not impossible to demand the saintliness according to which it is illegitimate to defend one's parents, family, friends or community under any circumstances. The problem is the "slippery slope," i.e., when and how this reasoning can go wrong and become an ideological excuse for morally illegitimate violence and war.

The expression "skill in means" or "skillful means" (Skt., *upāyakauśalya*; Pāli, *upayakusala*) is a basic Mahāyāna concept, developed in the context of the compassion and wisdom of the Bodhisattva, and rarely found in the Pāli canon. The roots of this expression, both *upaya* ("way, means, or resource") and in particular *kusala* ("skillful, profitable or expedient," often used as equivalent for "good, moral, or wholesome"), are present in the

---

[55] Gethin develops this claim against Keown's position in "Can Killing a Living Being Ever Be an Act of Compassion? The Analysis of the Act of Killing in the Abhidhamma and Pāli Commentaries," in *Journal of Buddhist Ethics* 11 (2004): 168-202.

Pāli Canon.[56] *Upaya*, the ability of the Buddha to teach at different levels according to the understanding of the recipients, is restricted to the Buddha. *Kusala* – skillfulness and wholesomeness as opposed to unskillfulness and unwholesomeness – in action, thought, and word is advocated for all following the path in Theravāda Buddhism. [57] The use of a number of expressions indicating different abilities and capacities requiring appropriateness and skillfulness – such as *kusala, sappaya, upaya,* and *yoniso manasikārā* (wise or appropriate attention), *ugghatitaññu* (swiftness of understanding), *patisambhida* (the knowledge to appropriately discriminate things) – can be seen in the Pāli Canon.

For the Buddha, in the *Sangiti Sutta* of the *Dīgha Nikāya*, there are "three kinds of skill: skill in progress, skill in regress, and skill in means" (*tini kosallani: aya kosallam, apaya kosallam, upaya kosallam*).[58] The use of *upaya kosallam* in this context shows that skillful means is not foreign to the sense of skillfulness in the Pāli Canon and that it is not limited to the Buddha, at the same time as the Buddha perfectly embodies such skillfulness. [59] Skill in the Buddha's discourses does not seem to mean casuistry, cleverness or a merely calculative pragmatic prudence that is more political than ethical. It is an art that cultivates a moral ability and insight consisting of appropriately applying the *Dhamma* to the situation.

---

[56] For instance, DN I. 163-165. Two excellent accounts of the history and concept of skillful means in Mahāyāna Buddhism are those of Thomas Kasulis, who traces *upāya* back to the Abbhidharma, *Skillful Means: The Heart of Buddhist Compassion* (Honolulu: University of Hawaii Press, 2001) and Michael Pye, *Skilful Means: A Concept in Mahāyāna Buddhism* (London: Routledge, 2004). Also see Keown, *op. cit.*, 157-162.

[57] On skillfulness (*kusala*) as an equivalent term for morality in Theravāda Buddhism, see Gombrich, 62. On the basic role of *kusala* in the Pāli canon, see Harvey, 42-49.

[58] *DN* III.220. *The Long Discourses of the Buddha: A Translation of the Dīgha Nikāya*, trans. Maurice Walshe (Boston: Wisdom Publications, 1995), 486, translation modified.

[59] Michael Pye stresses the continuity between pre-Mahāyāna and Mahāyāna Buddhism and the importance of skillful means for Buddhism in general in Pye, ch. 7.

This is confirmed by another reference to the aptness of skillfulness in the *Nava Sutta* of the *Sutta-nipāta*, where it is said that the one who knows *Dhamma* is like the skillful boatman who is able to ferry others across a dangerous river. [60] Here again appropriateness is explained as being like an art or craft such that it is not simply the mechanical application of an abstract principle.

In another passage, understanding what is fitting and skillfully attending is the basis of wisdom. [61] In the *Avijjā Sutta*, skillfulness is associated with knowing and ignorance, when the Buddha is said to discuss how ignorance leads to unskillful qualities and knowing to skillful ones. [62] In *The Group of Ones*, appropriateness and skillfulness are interconnected such that both are essential to the path: "A *bhikkhu* who attends appropriately abandons what is unskillful and develops what is skillful." [63] This use of "skillful," which points to the cultivation of spontaneous activity as in learning a craft to the point where it becomes second nature, is not accidental to the Buddha's discourses.

Not only morality but also meditation is often compared to a skill that requires development. For example, in the *Aṅguttara Nikāya*, the Buddha said: "Just as monks, an archer, or his apprentice might practice on a straw man or a pile of clay, and thereby later become a long-distance shot, an impeccable marksman who can fell a large body, just so it is with a monk who reaches the destruction of the taints in dependence on the first *jhana*." [64] This sense of skill provides a partial basis for the later Mahāyāna reinterpretation and extension of skillfulness (*kusala*) as skillful means or skill in means (*upāya-kauśalya*). In early Mahāyāna texts such as the *Skill in Means Sūtra* (*Upāyakauśalya Sūtra*), and canonical texts such as the *Lotus Sūtra*, morality is

---

[60] SN II.8.

[61] MN 9. *The Middle Length Discourses of the Buddha: A Translation of the Majjhima Nikāya*, tr. Bhikkhu Ñāṇamoli (Boston: Wisdom Publications, 1995), 93.

[62] SN XLV.1, also compare SN XLIX.1.

[63] *Itivuttaka*, 16.

[64] AN IX.35, also see AN IX.36 not included in this translation: *Numerical Discourses of the Buddha*, 235.

fully absorbed into or subordinated to compassion such that the compassion of the Bodhisattva transcends the cultivation of the precepts considered as rules or virtues.[65]

Insofar as Theravāda ethics, like most Buddhist and many forms of non-Buddhist ethics such as Aristotelian and Confucian, is a form of virtue ethics, it faces the issue of appropriate action. If this is the case, then acting *from* the precepts, and the *Vinaya* in general, cannot be reduced to legalistic external conformity with them. Codes, precepts, and rules demand the ability to distinguish between the hypocrisy of breaking them for one's own advantage and the moral insight to adopt them to circumstances. For example, a Sri Lankan *bhikkhu* should not possess money, yet it might not be inappropriate for him to carry money for purposes that are difficult to avoid such as for bus fare to get across town.[66] Rules cannot be mechanically applied but require the skillful application of the *Dhamma* in acting in the proverbial right way at the right time in the right place.[67] A third source of the use of skillfulness in contemporary Theravāda Buddhism would be from the growing knowledge of Mahāyāna traditions of interpretation.

Is the Buddhist notion of skillfulness too open or ambiguous such that it can possibly justify unethical behavior in the name of a greater good? Can it potentially be used to justify behavior contrary to the basic ethical principles of Buddhism such as the Buddha's critique of violence and war? This question of skillfulness seems a more basic issue than that of ethical antinomianism and nihilism developed in some western critiques of Buddhism, since context-sensitive appropriateness would provide the justification for going "beyond good and evil" and other such expressions.[68] This is not only a potential problem in

---

[65] *The Skill in Means Sūtra* (*Upāyakauśalya Sūtra*), tr. Mark Tatz (New Dehli: Motilal Banarsidass, 2001).

[66] On the strict canonical prohibition of money and ways of lessening it, see Gombrich, 103. Also note Harvey, 203-205.

[67] Keown, *op. cit.*, 47-48.

[68] On the Western philosophical reception of Buddhism focusing on issues of nihilism, see Roger Pol Droit, *The Cult of Nothingness: The Philosophers and the Buddha* (Chapel Hill: University of North Carolina Press, 2003).

Zen or Mahāyāna but in all Buddhism, given that the issue of appropriateness is already significant in the Pāli Canon and in contemporary Theravāda Buddhism.

6. Buddhism and Conflict in Contemporary Sri Lanka

To turn now to a "case study" of the relation between Buddhist ethics and violence, I will consider the long-running civil war in Sri Lanka. The Sri Lankan conflict has its origins in the development of Sinhalese nationalism in response to British colonialism and during the post-war independence movement. The British played off Sinhalese and Tamil interests and sentiments in order to retain power during the colonial period, much as they did in their other colonies. The postcolonial period saw the deepening of various narratives of ethic self-identity among both the Sinhalese and the Tamil populations. Successive democratically elected Sri Lankan governments have reflected the interests and aspirations of the Sinhalese, contributing to Tamil sentiments of disentitlement. The resulting episodic civil war has killed over 65,000 people since the 1980's.

The ethnic conflict has occurred between a series of elected governments, led by various parities from the right to the left who have been supported by the mostly Buddhist Sinhalese majority, and the terrorist – insofar as suicide bombings, assassinations, eliminating all Tamil rivals, etc., are terrorist – and or self-described "liberation" organization Liberation Tigers of Tamil Eelam (LTTE) organization based in the mostly non-Buddhist Tamil minority. [69] The best option for both sides would be a

---

[69] Recent accounts of the LTTE's uses of terrorism include: Ami Pedahzur, *Suicide Terrorism* (Oxford: Blackwell, 2005), 70-88; Kingsley de Silva, "Terrorism and political agitation in post-colonial South Asia: Jammu-Kashmir and Sri Lanka," in Ramesh Thakur and Oddny Wiggen, eds., *South Asia in the World: Problem-Solving Perspectives on Security, Sustainable Development, and Good Governance* (Tokyo: United Nations University Press, 2004), ch. 7; and Shri D.R. Kaarthikeyan, "Root Causes of Terrorism? A Case Study of the Tamil Insurgency and the LTTE," in Tore Bjørgo, ed., *Root Causes of Terrorism: Myths, Reality and Ways Forward* (London: Routledge, 2005), ch. 10.

peaceful resolution and mutual cooperation, which seems presently unlikely. On the one hand, there is much to criticize in the Sri Lankan government and Sinhalese nationalists, from people who claim to be conserving and defending Buddhism and its role in Sri Lankan life to socialist populists, who have flamed the passions of war. On the other hand, the legitimate grievances of the Tamil population are used to support an authoritarian, nationalistic, and violent organization.[70]

Representatives of "engaged Buddhism" and "critical Buddhism" want to free Buddhism from what they describe as its traditional complicity with unjust social and political institutions and practices. They frequently point to Imperial Japan and the current conflict in Sri Lanka as primary examples that prove traditional Buddhism's complicity with violence, exploitation, and domination.[71] This argument appeals, in the case of Sri Lanka, to the fact that some Theravāda Buddhist monks and laity have been implicated in violence and calls for violence against the LTTE and / or the Tamil population. Any adequate consideration of this conflict begins to reveal the need for a more nuanced and differentiating approach to the question of what role Buddhism plays in the current conflict. This conflict raises two significant questions: (1) What is the role of Buddhism in promoting the conflict? (2) What are the arguments for and against the justice of war in the Buddhist traditions of Sri Lanka? The second question can be made more exact in the following terms: What possible

---

[70] Although some justify the violence of the Liberation Tigers of Tamil Eelam as a legitimate response to Sinhalese nationalism, it should be kept in mind that the LTTE, according to some observers, is "just as fanatically committed to a particular authoritarian agenda as the JVP and just as strongly nationalist. The Tamil Tigers' compulsive resort to terror has earned them, too, a justifiable comparison to the Khmer Rouge." (p. 97). See K. M. de Silva, "Sri Lanka: Surviving Ethnic Strife," *Journal of Democracy* 8.1 (1997): 97-111.

[71] For example, see Brian Victoria, "The Reactionary Use of Karma in Twentieth-Century Japan," in *Revisioning Karma*, 404, 427. This position is part of the "critical Buddhism" movement especially active in relation to Japanese Buddhism; see Christopher Ives, "What's Compassion Got to Do with It? Determinants of Zen Social Ethics in Japan," in *Journal of Buddhist Ethics* 12 (2005): 39-43.

justifications of violence are there in (i) the Pāli Canon, (ii) tales
about Aśoka – who has both righteous and violent traits[72] – and the
universal wheel-turning monarch (*cakkavatti*), (iii) postcanonical
Sinhalese narratives of kingship and nation such as the
Mahāvamsa,[73] and, finally, (iv) contemporary postcolonial Sri
Lankan Buddhism?

In the remainder of this paper, I will sketch out a possible
answer addressing a few aspects of these questions. One strategy is
to analyze Buddhist ideas in the context of western just-war and
ethical theory and conclude that Buddhism as it informs the
"popular" actions and practices of living Buddhist communities is
more complex than its normative or "elite" ideal. Buddhist lands
do not only involve traditions of nonviolence and loving kindness.
They also have had a long history of thinking about and engaging
in internal and external physical conflict. That is, wars from which
reasoned as well as opportunistic assertions of the possible justice
or unfortunate necessity of war can emerge. Buddhism privileges
non-violence *while at the same time* self-described Buddhists have
justified and engaged in war under certain conditions.

Buddhism is a diverse set of norms and practices; and this
diversity is also true of Sri Lankan Buddhism where one can see
three approaches to the question of war. First, there is a position
that Tessa J. Bartholomeusz and Chandra Richard de Silva call
Buddhist fundamentalism.[74] Yet fundamentalism suggests a return
to the fundamentals of Buddhism, which in this case would mean
to renounce violence as a means. As Mahinda Deegalle argues this
position is not so much Buddhist as it is Sinhalese nationalist,
which appropriates Buddhism as a symbol of Sinhalese heritage

---

[72] John S. Strong, *The Legend of King Aśoka* (Princeton: Princeton
University Press, 1983), 40-41.

[73] *The Mahāvamsa: The Great Chronicle of Sri Lanka* (Berkeley: Asian
Humanities Press, 1999). For a detailed account of the legacy of the
Mahāvamsa, see Steven Kemper, *The Presence of the Past* (Ithaca: Cornell
University Press, 1991).

[74] See the book edited by Bartholomeusz and de Silva.

and identity.[75] This raises the interesting question whether there is actually such a thing as religious fundamentalism. Many movements labeled as fundamentalist seem to be more about the use of the religious for nationalistic economic and political interests. The nationalist and "just war" positions can both appeal to the *Mahāvamsa*, which describes the Buddha's legendary visits to Sri Lanka and the military victories of ancient Sinhalese Buddhist kings against invading Hindu Tamils.[76]

The nationalists explicitly demands that the Sinhala-Tamil conflict must conclude not only with the defeat of the LTTE but also with the restoration of a unified and fully Sinhalese and Buddhist Sri Lanka. Their argument for war generally follows a three step legitimation of anti-Tamil sentiment: (1) Sinhala and Buddhist identity constitute a unity that is radically distinct from the Dravidian Hindu Tamil interlopers from South India; (2) Sri Lanka is the island of *Dhamma* (*dhammadvipa*) ordained by the Buddha himself (during his three apocryphal visits) for Buddhism such that the whole island is a sacred relic of the Buddha's and the loss of its integrity would destroy this legacy; and (3) the justice of a defensive war for the *Dhamma* justifies the preservation of Sri Lanka in its unity as a majority Sinhalese Buddhist nation through military action against the Tamils, identified with the invading *damila* of the medieval epics, thus associating the present dispute with past threats as well as the fear of tiny Sri Lanka being submerged in the vastness of India. Bartholomeusz contends that it is paradoxically Buddhist beliefs about pacifism – i.e., that Buddhists are more fair, tolerant, and peaceful – that leads Buddhists to differentiate themselves from others and turn to

---

[75] Mahinda Deegalle, "Theravāda Attitudes towards Violence," in *Journal of Buddhist Ethics* 10 (2003). Also compare Gombrich, 141-142; and Harvey, 255-260.

[76] On the question of *The Mahāvamsa*, nationalism and mythic violence, see John Clifford Holt, *The Buddhist Viṣṇu* (New York: Columbia University Press, 2004), 63-65, 93-94, 266-267. Also note the descriptions in Gombrich, 141-142; and Harvey, 255-258. Steven Kemper also emphasizes the role of colonial and other westernizing forces in the creation of modern Sinhalese nationalism in Kemper, 196-214.

violence to protect that very ideal. The perceived need to preserve endangered Buddhist peacefulness creates the conditions for violence. [77] Yet Buddhism is not so much the cause of such attitudes as it – or rather its surface historical facticity as uniquely Sinhalese – is instrumentally incorporated into conservative Sinhalese discourses and, more generally, the Sinhalese side of the "ethnic outbidding" that Neil DeVotta characterizes as a cancer eating away at Sri Lankan political life. [78]

The second range of views might be characterized as the moderate justification of the use of force, and maintains the justice of undertaking "defensive military action" against insurgencies even if the insurgents draw on some legitimate grievances. The war is interpreted as the defense of the territorial integrity and peace of the nation, as a proper function of the modern secular state, and/or the defense of the nation's endangered Buddhist identity. This model appeals to the conventional model of international law and its account of the justice and limits of war as well as to Buddhist principles such as maximizing well-being. Assuming one is attacked, and if common well-being outweighs the well-being of the attacker, it is then justifiable to defend oneself, one's parents and family, one's fellow citizens, including if it involves violence and killing. This argument is of course reasonable, and self-defense is not without its pragmatic justification and traditional authority. The problem is that such arguments often move imperceptibly from the exceptional justification of minimal violence under "conditions of necessity" to the ideological normalization of the state of war. Violence, once it is justified as an exception, becomes the norm from which there seems no escape. The ethical loses its normative and critical force and becomes part of the social reproduction and intensification of conflict rather than a medium of its resolution.

There are multiple strategies used by Sri Lankans to answer the question of how Buddhists can justify engaging in conflict and war.

---

[77] Bartholomeusz, 16.

[78] Neil DeVotta, "Liberalism and Ethnic Conflict in Sri Lanka," *Journal of Democracy* 13.1 (2002): 83.

Some stress the unfortunate necessity of military action despite its negative karmic consequences. Others, perhaps motivated by the need for a more inspirational message, suggest that righteous war (i.e., one with a morally legitimate goal and fought in an honorable fashion with morally acceptable means) has meritorious karmic consequences. Both strategies presuppose that the precept of nonviolence is a prima facie rather than an absolute duty such that nonviolence is a first duty that can be overridden under certain circumstances as a last resort.[79]

Theravāda ethics, especially when it is interpreted textually through the Pāli Canon, places absolute value on acting out of compassion and avoiding harm. In practice, Sri Lankan Buddhists reason with a plurality of context-sensitive prima facie duties. The precept against violence is not absolute and can be overridden by more pressing obligations such as defense of one's parents, country, or the *Dhamma*. The Buddha's account of moral skillfulness suggests, according to this reading, the use of practical judgment or a sense of appropriateness to apply moral principles to the situation. The Buddha's precepts are primary and conflicts between precepts require contextual reasoning that employs considerations that some have compared with utilitarian (maximizing compassion and minimizing suffering) and others to virtue ethical (the effects actions have on one's condition) reasoning. In this way, Buddhist ethical reasoning is used to justify violence for the sake of nonviolence and the Sri Lankan government's claim to wage "war for peace." The justification of war requires the fulfillment of certain conditions comparable to Christian and western just war criteria. A number of Sri Lankan Buddhists, in line with traditional justifications of war in the Buddhist kingdoms of South-East Asia,[80] appeal to the Hindu *Bhagavad-Gītā* and the Pan-Indic idea that the ruler (*rāja*) and warriors (*kṣatriya*) fulfilling their military duties are exempt from *ahiṃsā*.

---

[79] Bartholomeusz, 26-29.

[80] See Trevor Oswald Ling, *Buddhism, Imperialism and War: Burma and Thailand in Modern History* (London: G. Allen & Unwin, 1979).

Historically numerous leaders and societies claiming to be Buddhist have had armies, police forces, prisons, etc., with actual weapons and the possibility of using them. This is based in Pan-Indian ideas about kingship and in several Buddhist traditions. In the Pāli canon, the Buddha abandoned becoming a universal wheel-turning monarch in order to become liberated. This prioritized liberation, and the renunciation of violence and harm that is essential to its realization, yet at the same time was interpreted as giving a derivative or secondary legitimacy to political leadership. Such monarchs are portrayed as universally wise and generous but do not abandon the state's monopoly on force. This model of righteous kingship is the basis for the Buddhist warrior-kings of the *Mahāvamsa* that continue to have national appeal.

Popular Sri Lankan Buddhism incorporates a tacit "just war theory" according to which war is justifiable when fought with the appropriate intent and means. The Sinhalese supporters of war appeal to such ideas of the legitimacy of defensive war, which is defined by the compassionate intention to protect rather than the negative motivations of anger, greed or hatred. It is interesting that "militant Sinhalese nationalists," insofar as they still claim to operate within the framework of Buddhism, frequently appeal to a widener or more extensive notion of defensive war (such as the unity of "Buddhist Sri Lanka" as a whole) since canonical Buddhism provides no basis for offensive or aggressive war. [81] Buddhism does not have the tradition of offensive "holy war" and, since motivation and intention are more important than external ritual and obedience, there is no basis for war to convert others by force even for their own good – which leaves open the question of the tacit violence or implicit coercive power of education, socialization, and the socio-economic reproduction of society.

The first militant nationalistic and second moderate pro-war Sinhalese positions described above are differentiated by the portrayal of what is being defended and what means are justifiable. This remains an active question given the fragility of peace, the

---

[81] Bartholomeusz, 121-123.

continuation of death and destruction, the conflicting assertions about the "righteousness" of each side, and the competing claims about the justice and injustice of military action.

Finally, in a third type of position, there are Sri Lankan Buddhists who reject all and any violence as an impediment to *nibbāna* (*nirvāṇa*) and who have been prominently engaged in promoting the peace process and reconciliation. Bartholomeusz contends that this must be a consequence of giving the first precept of *ahiṃsā* a deontological status. That is, it is a universally valid principle and duty that is applicable regardless of circumstances and has no exceptions. The Buddha does not claim that violence is only sometimes wrong but that violence, no matter how righteous, always produces more violence; and warriors, no matter how virtuous, always suffer the consequences of war. However, the Buddhist precepts do not have to be interpreted according to the model of rule based ethics, or applying a conceptual principle to all cases, in order for Buddhists to unconditionally reject war. The most appropriate skillfulness may well generally result in the rejection of violence and war given its personal costs and karmic consequences. This position is adopted by the majority of Sri Lankan intellectuals, such as Walpola Rahula, who wrote in 1959 that "Violence in any form, under any pretext whatsoever, is absolutely against the teaching of the Buddha."[82]

According to the Buddha, "Conquest begets enmity; the conquered live in misery; and the peaceful live happily having renounced both conquest and defeat."[83] This position is in fact the only consistent one with the Pāli Canon, if not later non-canonical Sinhalese texts such as the *Mahāvamsa* that are also historically significant in shaping Sinhalese self-interpretations of their own identity and the possibility – albeit limited and tenuous – of a Buddhist theory of "just war." This difference shows the value of not reducing the normative dimension of Buddhism to its popular manifestations, and of not minimizing canonical texts and the

---

[82] Walpola Rahula, *What the Buddha Taught*, revised edition (New York: Grove Press, 1974), 5.

[83] *Dhammapada*, verse 201.

"philosophical" dimension of Buddhism in the face of its "violent" lived reality.[84] Since norms and exemplars are richly embodied in images and narratives, the distinction between normative claims and actual practices does not entail the reduction of Buddhism's symbolic dimension to an impoverished rationalized shadow. Exemplars and norms often serve a critical, regulative, and self-reforming function, providing a textured fabric and context to which individuals can appeal so as to engage their circumstances and practices differently. If it is illegitimate to isolate and reify supposedly "elite" normative or canonical Buddhism on the authority of "anti-essentialism," it seems similarly problematic to eliminate all normative and regulative claims in the name of "popular practices."

7. Conclusion: Virtue and Violence

The Sri Lankan conflict is not exclusively a question of one individual's insight and virtue in my estimation. If it was, it would not be at such an impasse. It is a structural crisis that requires a political solution that has to rely on a plurality of ethical, religious, and social possibilities and voices. My claim here contradicts current tendencies that (1) seek to privatize social problems into issues of personal virtue or (2) reduce the plurality of public life to one vision of the good life and/or religious redemption. To the degree that Buddhism shares these features, which are appropriate given its primary goal of spiritual liberation, it is insufficient by itself to resolve structural social-political crises to the degree that these require critical and empirically-oriented social research and transformation. Like other ethical and religious ideals, Buddhism can become a constituent part of social ills, if the Buddhist does not recognize the independent and plural structural qualities of social-political life. Nonetheless, despite these limits, it still offers a valuable response to the question. Because of its responsiveness to the suffering of others as well as its self-critical, non-coercive and egalitarian character, Buddhism provides a powerful and

---

[84] Compare Bartholomeusz, 110.

cogent individual way of life. And, as such, it can contribute to the resolution of conflict and suffering.

The conclusion that Buddhism is not the primary cause of the Sri Lankan conflict and can be part of its peaceful resolution is not a new thesis. P. D. Premasiri reasonably concludes that there is no place for righteous war within Pāli Buddhism: "the idea of a just or righteous war (*dharma yuddha*) involving the use of weapons of war and violence is conspicuously absent in the Buddhist canon. The Buddha countered the prevailing belief that soldiers of war who fight for a cause could, as a consequence of their rightful performance of duty, aspire to attain a heavenly rebirth if they succumb to their injuries while in combat. The Buddha states in the Pāli canon that one who fights a war does not generate wholesome thoughts but thoughts of malice and hatred, which are absolutely unwholesome. Therefore, their future destiny will be a woeful one, which is in accordance with their unwholesome *kamma*."[85]

According to my argument, Buddhism shares some of the potential problems of other varieties of virtue ethics. In particular, (1) moral appropriateness and skillfulness can become a potentially dangerous doctrine legitimating unethical behavior and (2) the ethics of individual self-cultivation of character can become ideologically complicit with systems of exploitation and domination. First, skillfulness can be reduced to an instrumental manipulation of means without regard for the quality of the ends, such that it is removed from its ethical context of loving-kindness, generosity, compassion, and *ahiṃsā*. Second, the privatization of the ethical separates questions of character from the reproduction of social-political systems, such that the moralist as well as the ideologue appeals to the good intentions of individuals without regard for underlying relations of power. Socially engaged Buddhists ought to be mindful of both issues if they are to counter the potential betrayal of the moral core of the *Dhamma* through individual practices and social-political institutions. These possibilities cannot be excluded *a priori* and indicate the need to

---

[85] P. D. Premasiri, "The Place for a Righteous War in Buddhism," in *Journal of Buddhist Ethics* 10 (2003).

be vigilant in cultivating and practicing the art of ethical appropriateness and skillfulness.

Like other forms of context-sensitive ethics, Buddhist ethics cannot be reduced to the mechanical application of one principle or universal rule, such as John Stuart Mill's principle of utility or Kant's categorical imperative. Whereas rule-based ethics requires the appeal to and application of a general principle to particulars, context-based ethics appeals to a concrete and existential way of living as a whole. This whole involves the interdependence of self and others as well as self and world.[86] In this context, even the first and most basic precepts of non-harm and non-violence (ahiṃsā) cannot be taken as unconditional or absolute if they cause more harm than not. This is why the taking of life in conflict or war is discouraged, especially because of their negative motivations and consequences, yet not absolutely forbidden in Pāli and Sri Lankan Buddhism. Likewise, vegetarianism is not taken as an absolute in the Pāli canon or in Theravāda countries. The Buddha rejected making it an unconditional duty or obligation, as one is more or less culpable for eating meat or even killing an animal given (1) the sentience/insentience of the being killed, (2) the motivation or intention involved in killing the animal (e.g., hunting for food as opposed to killing for employment or sport), (3) the amount of suffering produced by the action, and (4) the directness and indirectness of one's involvement in the killing of the animal.[87]

Instead of being an absolute independently existing command or obligation, morality is seen as a conditional and dependently arisen ethical mode of comportment. It is a situational and responsive disposition from which one can ethically respond to the diversity of concrete circumstances. Without this ethical orientation and context, a decontextualized notion of skillfulness – and appropriate judgment in general – can and has been used to justify violence and war in ways that run contrary to the Buddha's

---

[86] Note that interdependence by itself is not an ethical claim and Buddhist ethics entails some forms of ethical independence, as argued in Ives, "Deploying the Dharma: Reflections on the Methodology of Constructive Buddhist Ethics," 24-25.

[87] Compare Harvey, 159-162.

teachings. If my argument is valid, then moral skillfulness and appropriateness can legitimately be used to justify less morally problematic and culpable forms of violence such as self-defense and perhaps humanitarian intervention to prevent genocide. As a consequence, it provides a limited and conditional Buddhist just-war-theory such that Theravāda countries can legitimately have armies and police forces and still be considered Buddhist. Yet, these uses are circumscribed, and such reasoning cannot consistently be used to justify aggressive violence or war motivated by anger, craving, hatred, or attachment. From this perspective, there is much to criticize in these lands and their history. Nonetheless, if the realization of *Dhamma* right here in this life is not to be completely betrayed by worldly calculations, then even such a pragmatically reasonable position goes too far or risks too much. Despite actual and potential problems with Buddhists, who would like but have not yet realized the *Dhamma*, it remains a commendable virtue of Buddhism that it provides the means to rigorously question violence and war as well as demanding the proper cultivation of the skillfulness and insight to do so. Such insight means that one is not only attentive to what others do but more importantly to one's own activities and disposition, even more when one has the self-satisfaction of it seeming most sensible and decent.

A DIALECTICAL ANALYSIS OF THE CONCEPTION OF "SELF INTEREST MAXIMIZATION" AND ECONOMIC FREEDOM

Mathew Varghese

Through this paper, I am not trying to criticize the economic development models of today or suggesting an alternative methodology for managing wealth and resources. Here my effort is to understand the conception of economic freedom that each and every individual must be free economically to be a part of the community and live in harmony with it. Economic freedom should be viewed as an important aspect of life which could provide an answer to one of the important Socratic questions, "how should one live?" This query can be approached in many ways and one way I wish to pursue in this paper is through economic freedom, from the Buddhist context, as one aspect of human freedom that one seeks to achieve as a purpose of life. In that perspective, to reveal this conception clearly, I wish to use the Mādhyamika dialectics to identify the implicit dangers in pursuing some contextually constructed theoretical models vehemently without evaluating the consequences for solving one of our perpetual worries of life as an end in itself.

We live in a world where the idea of economic freedom has taken the central place in our thinking and put all our efforts into achieving greater economic power, presuming that it is the most efficient way for bringing greater values and an ultimate meaning to life. In fact, this idea, in the contemporary period, has shaken the world with a big bang. The wealthy nations or people are trying hard to control the power they have acquired from being wealthy, whereas the poor nations and people try to catch up with the wealthy nations by imbibing their ideologies and methods. In the market-driven economy of today, economic thinking is based on large scale production and maximum consumption. In this process of finding economic freedom and perfect richness for everyone, we consider that the procedure of creating more wealth is important in pursuing our desires and dreams to the maximum, for being a part of the consumerist society, so that more wealth can be produced and distributed. The negative side of this win-win situation may be that we could be completely using up all our resources and the world could be turning into a big waste basket. There is no simple solution to this problem from our present way of thinking and understanding as we base our thinking on knowledge and judgment conditioned by our desires. Mādhyamika dialectics allows us to reevaluate the validity of the epistemological sources and suggest solutions from the problems itself.

The Aspect of *Self Interest Maximization*

As an example, today one of the most used concepts for economic theories is "self interest maximization," which presumes that the foremost instinct motivating an individual to engage in any economic activity is self interest. Accordingly, the effective application of motivated self interest is the best factor for promoting growth in the economy and society is greatly benefited from the individualistic attitude toward desire fulfilling. For the perfect deployment of this method, one needs to make decisions using rational, technical, and innovative methods without giving space for moral or ethical concerns. Those human concerns in fact may act detrimental to the effective functioning of the modern economic system. J. S. Mill explained the requirement of a person engaging in economic activity with a quote from Dante, "Abandon all friendliness, you who enter!" Everyone who sets to engage in an economic activity should act like one who is committed to accomplishing a mission: that of maximizing wealth.

Adam Smith, who introduced this concept, was a professor of moral philosophy at the University of Glasgow. The following, from his book, *An Inquiry into the Nature and Causes of the Wealth of Nations*, is one of the favorite quotes for economic theorists: "It is not from the benevolence of the butcher, the brewer, or the baker, that we expect our dinner, but from their regards to their own interest. We address ourselves, not to their humanity but to their self-love, and never talk to them of our own necessities but of their advantages." We can see here that the 'self love' or 'self interest' to earn money and to achieve economic freedom that motivates a butcher to sell meat, and all other aspects connected with his life is subservient to this self instinct. In fact, this idea, according to noted economist Amartya Sen, is misinterpreted from what Smith actually wanted to explain. He wanted to explain the conception of self love from the context of *stoic philosophy*, that a human being's self interest involves discharging responsibility as an honest member of the community lived in. The self interest of the butcher, in this view, does not only involve earning money by selling meat. The butcher wants to see that those who have bought the meat have a good dinner. Here, the self love involves earning money and helping others to carry on with their lives. In the Buddhist context, one could carry out karma that would lead to freedom from sufferings. There is a huge space here for ethical and moral attitude (*dharma*) when engaging in the activity of finding economic freedom.

The Buddhist thought in this regard comes from the advice of the Buddha on right livelihood and the classical Indian philosophical thought which considers wealth (*artha*) as an important aspect that gives completeness to human life.[1] Indian thought considers the human life in this world as a quest to find liberation (*mokṣa*) in *artha*, *kāma* and *dharma*. The meaning of these terms relevant to this discussion is *artha* (wealth); *kāma* (love, passion, desire, etc.);[2] *dharma* (moral direction, ethical

---

[1] Theodore Stcherbatsky, *The Conception of Buddhist Nirvāṇa* (1968; reprint, New Delhi: Motilal Banarsidass, 1999), 62.

[2] In Buddhist philosophy, the desire prompted by ignorance is condemned, while the natural enthusiasm, passion, desire and love are accepted as esteemed human values. See Aryadeva's *Cittaviśuddhiprakaraṇa* edited from Tibetan and Sanskrit sources with introduction and the full text in Sanskrit by Prabhubhai Bhikhabhai Patel (Calcutta: Visva-Bharati, 1949), verse 42:

durvijñaiḥ sevitaḥ kāmaḥ kāmo bhavati bandhanam /
sa eva sevito vijñaiḥ kāmo mokṣaprasādhakaḥ //

duties, etc.) are the main motivating aspects of human life.[3] In the thoughts of contemporary economic thinkers, *kāma* represented by self interest maximization is the major motivating factor for achieving *mokṣa* (perfect happiness by winning wealth) while *dharma* is the most de-motivating factor and should be controlled. Amartya Sen joins with the Buddhist thinkers when he explains further about what Adam Smith wanted to say concerning moral considerations: "The misinterpretation of Smith's complex attitude to motivation and markets, and the neglect of his ethical analysis of sentiments and behavior, fits well into the distancing of economics from ethics that has occurred with the development of modem economics. Smith did, in fact, make pioneering contributions in analyzing the nature of mutual advantage exchanges, and the value of division of labor, and since these contributions are perfectly consistent with human behavior *sans bonhomie* and ethics, references to these parts of Smith's work have been profuse and exuberant." It is very explicit that individuals should not make it one whole life's purpose just winning wealth as similar to the case of contemporary economic thinkers.

Why are modern economists' views not sustainable? In fact, modern economists wanted to create a perfect economic system where generating wealth was the main concern and also to create a mathematical model to propitiate it. There is an accepted presumption in the contemporary world that the scientific method evolved in the modem period is valid eternally in explaining the phenomenal world and it could show us practical ways to find solutions to any problems.[4] The problem of scientific method is

---

The objects of desire and its enjoyment, for an unwise (ignorant) person, could become a source of bondage (*bandhanam*); the same object of desire and its enjoyment, for a wise person, becomes a source of liberation.

[3] Theodore Stcherbatsky, 62.

[4] Philosophers and thinkers in the last century wanted to introduce a kind of universal scientific method. The presumption is that the scientific method provides a certain amount of certainty and clarity and that certainty is applicable to each and every aspect of human life. See Ledwig Wittgenstein, *Philosophical Investigations*, 2nd edition (Oxford: Blackwell, 1959), 18. In the case of economics in the 18th century, the leading thinkers wanted to introduce

that it bases its judgments only from the humanly cognizable knowledge sources where human wisdom on anything is subservient to this perfectly alluded knowledge.

Here also the scientifically alluded 'self interest maximization' could solve all our problems of earning livelihood and beyond. Since the focuses of all our activities are motivated for maximizing as much wealth as possible, we consider everything in the world, especially the sources from which we draw wealth, as income rather than capital. The guiding logic might be that those sources are huge bounties that never perish. We need only to find means to exploit them as quickly and efficiently as possible. The butcher would be killing as many animals as possible to show a huge profit in his books without concern for the future of the resource. There is a difference between considering something as a capital and as income. [5] In practical wisdom (*prajñā*), capital should be maintained and protected and only a part of it can be used as income. In modern times, we are using the land, the natural resources, the environment, and the human resources with the presumption that the maintenance and upkeep of them are taken care of by some invisible force. The classical wisdom on such things gives way to human greed and huge desires. [6] We are actually perfectly rational and cool headed in these matters, but we expect an unseen force will take care of anything that might go wrong. This is the modern conception of God. The idea of such a God is relevant only if the scientific or analytical method we depend on fails us.

Staying with the example of the butcher, the butcher unconcerned about what happens with the meat sold kills as many

---

Newtonian methods to economics. See Todd Buchholz, *New Ideas from the Dead Economists* (New York: New American Library, 1989), 121.

[5] E. F. Schumacher, *Small is Beautiful* (New York: Harper & Row, 1973), 9.

[6] With the progress of modern economics and lifestyle thereof, human greed has taken the primary position of all human activities. The system otherwise is trying to encourage human greed for more and fear if that is not achieved. See Schumacher, 17.

animals as possible and eventually sells the butcher shop to a company and either becomes an employee of that company or gets a lot of money to do whatever was dreamed of. But what might be his biggest dream? The negative effect of this action is that the butcher looses almost everything mostly his identity. He soon understands that the money he earned has no special value for him. The other negative effect he may confront, which happens in most cases, is that butcher loses his job as the share value of the company that brought his butcher shop might go down and eventually go bankrupt. In both cases, the butcher would face a debasement of ethical life. He may have lost his social life and family as his children may not regard him highly and his wife may run away in pursuit of the maximization of her own interest. Mādhyamika dialectics sees this problem of the butcher as the problem of knowledge and judgment.[7]

The Buddhist View on Knowledge and Judgment

The advice given by the Buddha to his Brahmin friend Kūdadanda on the query on the right sacrifice is that the king should make sure that the capital is distributed properly with people who engage in different type of jobs, so that the money would multiply through more production and people could have comfortable lives without looting or creating political problems.[8]

---

[7] The Buddhist conception of understanding the phenomenal realities is in fact different from the conception of the modern theorists in this regard. Buddhism confutes the conception that it is possible to understand the phenomenal world with the help of a theory or a method. In the *Brahmajāla sūtra*, the Buddha criticizes the views that promote theoretical viewpoints and concludes that it is difficult to understand the world from the limitations set by a theory. In other words, the theoretical understanding of the phenomenal world basically originates from our expectations and preferences rather than what actually happens. See *sutta* 1 in Maurice Walshe's *The Long Discourses of the Buddha: A Translation of the Dīgha Nikāya* (Boston: Wisdom Publications, 1995).

[8] Brahmin, once upon a time there was a king called Mahāvijita. He was rich, of great wealth and resources, with an abundance of gold and silver, of possessions and requisites of money and money's worth, with a full treasury and

The Buddha advised that the king should use his *prajñā* (wisdom) in making decisions in relation to human life. He should see that he will not waste huge amount of resources as in the case of traditional knowledge based Vedic sacrifices that may, according to Buddha, not help bringing the expected harmony in the society.[9] The knowledge we use to form our judgments is normally inadequate and it is contextually determined. On the other hand, *prajñā* invokes our understanding faculties more effectively so that one is able to see reality properly. The meaning of *prajñā* is that it brings forth reality as it is (*prajñāyathābhūtam artham prajānāti*). It is considered that the functional *prajñā* puts an end to the normal human ignorance.[10]

The aspect of human nature that we depend on expectations and configure from what is available to us something that will liberate us from all our problems is elaborately discussed in

---

granary. And when King Mahāvihita was musing in private, the thought came to him: "I have acquired extensive wealth in human terms, I occupy a wide extent of land which I have conquered. Suppose now I were to make a great sacrifice which would be to my benefit and happiness for a long time?" And calling his minister-chaplain, he told him his thought. "I want to make a big sacrifice. Instruct me, Reverend Sir, how this may be to my lasting benefit and happiness." The Chaplain replied, "Your majesty's country is beset by thieves, it is ravaged, villages and town are being destroyed, the country side is infested with brigands. If your Majesty were to tax the region, that would be the wrong, that would be the wrong thing to do. Suppose Your Majesty were to think, "I will get rid of this plague of robbers by execution and imprisonment, or by confiscation, threats and banishment," the plague would not be properly ended. Those who survived would later harm Your Majesty's realm. However, with this plan, you can completely eliminate the plague. To those in the kingdom who are engaged in cultivating crops and raising cattle, let Your Majesty distribute grain and fodder; to those in trade, give capital; to those in government service, assign proper living wages. Then those people, being intent on their own occupations, will not harm the kingdom. Your Majesty's revenues will be great, the land will be tranquil and not beset by thieves, and the people, with joy in their hearts, will play with their children, and will dwell in open houses. See *sutta* 1 in *The Long Discourses of the Buddha: A Translation of the Dīgha Nikāya.*

[9] The Vedic sacrifices were performed based on traditional knowledge which had been handed over down to him by the king's forefathers.

[10] Stcherbatsky, 45.

Mādhyamika philosophy and it can suitably be applied to our topic. It is our wild desire that makes water visible in a mirage (when one is going in a desert, mad thirst for water manifests as water in the mirage). [11]

The economic theorists generally jump to gestalt water in the mirage (in the theories) and take us to that illusory water. [12] We may feel satisfied and also could feel a sense of victory but in fact like the one who chases the mirage those theories are not redeeming us but are putting us in a state of total confusion and misery. To explain this aspect more clearly, a person in the same desert, travelling in air-conditioned comfort and looking at the horizon, may see the mirage but may not necessarily expect water there or see it as an oasis. Mirage may appear as an interesting topic for him. Expecting water in the mirage is certainly a motivating factor for a desert traveler to find a real oasis, but no one can say that is the only motivating factor.

Nāgārjuna introduces the reason for confusion from these words: (dūrādālokitaṁ rūpamāsannair dṛśyate spuṭam / marīciryadi vāri syāddāsannaiḥ kiṁ na dṛśyate //) Normally the forms seen at far are clear when viewed from close proximity but why water seen in the mirages are not identified clearly by those nearby. [13] When we go close to the mirage, it moves away from us. The human mind has the tendency to infer ideas from such logical

---

[11] mṛgatṛṣṇājalaṁ nocchedo na ca śāśvatatā matā /
vastuśūnyaṁ jagat sarvaṁ marīpratimaṁ matam//

Similar to the vision created of wild desire, where there is no annihilation or no eternity (in this world), it is said of material objects in this world, all are like a mirage.

[12] The Buddhist notion of prajñā similar to the conception of śūnyatā explains that external empirical realities are essentially śūnya. The so-called realities of the phenomenal world are manifested because of our choices and expectations (kalpana). In the case of economic theorists, the idea of "self interest maximization" as the basic mode of human relationship, evolving from the expectation that generating more wealth creates a comfortable life for everyone, is an expectation and conceptual construction.

[13] Objects seen at far distance are revealed clearly when we go near to them, but things like the ocean of a mirage cannot be seen even when we go near to it.

sources or premises, if we desire for things that may come in the
purview of such sources. We can see a dialectic situation arising
here that certain objects or things can be experienced with clarity
when we approach near to them; and while certain things like
mirage water cannot be experienced clearly, when we go near to
them. In fact, they move further away on nearness. In this case, the
desert traveler's frustration increases and his actions become
absolutely illogical even though he is adamant in holding to certain
logical methods.

This dialectical situation is explained, using another example
by Nāgārjuna: *na niruddhān nāniruddhād bījād aṅkurasaṁbhavaḥ
/ māyotpādavad utpādaḥ sarva eva tvayocyate //* [14]

We cannot explain clearly the process of the origin of a sprout
or a tree in the pure rational sense. It is logically difficult to infer
that a sprout is originated from a destroyed seed, at the same time
one cannot declare that it is not originated from a destroyed seed,
or not originated from a seed. If we try to re-rationalize this
process of origin with the help of a theory, we must accept that the
originated sprout comes from an illusion.

Position of Mādhyamika Dialectics

From this discussion, it is clear that we are like the desert farer
who stands in the middle of the desert and hopes that water is there
in the mirage and when we go close to it, the mirage moves away
from us further, but still we expect the mirage to be real and move
further with it. It is important for us to understand the conception

---

[14] *vinaṣṭāt kāraṇāt tāvat kāryotpattir na yujyate/
na cāvinaṣṭāt svapnena tulyotpattir matā tava //*

or

*na niruddhān nāniruddhād bījād aṅkurasaṁbhavaḥ /
māyotpādavad utpādaḥ sarva eva tvayocyate //*

The origin of a sprout is not from a destroyed seed or from a nondestroyed
seed. You said that everything is originated from a manifested magical illusion.

of a sprout and its intrinsic relationship with the seed, but our vision is always mired by the illusion (*vikalpa*) with the perceptual knowledge of what we see at the horizon or the seed as the original cause of the sprout as real. There are schools of philosophy that consider that the seeds are the ultimate cause of sprout and theorize accordingly. Their theories may be partially true but they are not at all in a position to make a pure theory for the existence of the sprout because the sprout vanishes quickly into a seedling and then to a tree, making theorizing more difficult. But again here we are not confuting the existence either of the seed, sprout, nor the seedling. Our effort here is to see that the process of change is understood properly when we talk about a tree or the system as a whole. On the other hand, if we fail to see the actual process of changes, we fall into the trap of conceptual constructions (*vikalpas*). In this context, Buddhist philosophy introduces the conception of *śūnyatā* as an analytical tool. One of the most impressive and inspiring explanation given by Nāgārjuna on the conception *śūnyatā* is: *sarvasaṁkalpanāśāya śūnyatāmṛtadeśanā / yasya tasyām api grāhas tvayāsāvavasāditaḥ //* The direction given by *śūnyatā* is like *amṛta* (the curative property of *amṛta*) that it removes all the illusory imaginations. On the other hand, if one were to get hold of this concept, he would sink himself into it.

Mādhyamika dialectics [15] would view the topic discussion in such way that like a desert traveler who is thirty for water and looking for a place to rest, the economic theorist with the support of scientific thinking would configure that the economic freedom they are looking at is there in the mirage (from the inferential examples of 'objects seen at far' and 'the origin of sprout from seed.' Such economists would have us believe that travelling in the

---

[15] In Mādhyamika dialectics, the conception of *śūnyatā* is meant to help us to view the actual as the way it exists without falling into the abysmal depth of the confusions created by conceptual constructions. The *śūnyatā* functions as a dialectical tool that could help us to understand the real situation as it is, such as the question of seed or no-seed or the reality of mirage or its non existence. In those cases, the *śūnyatā* never confutes with the idea of the causal value of the seed but would not conclude that the seed causes a sprout necessarily. It takes a lot of things into account when it has to announce this causal relation.

desert with all our effort could get us to the goal of finding the oasis of happiness and plentitude. In this process, we take the examples of life with the analogy of the origination of a sprout from the seed or the Smithian position on self interest (self love) alone as the driving force for us to reach the goal for each individual to contribute to the welfare of the social economy.

It is none of those theorists who propagated the idea of self interest maximization as the basis of human transactions and engagements was aware of the context in which Adam Smith originally envisioned this idea that there are a lot of human concerns and moral considerations backing the notion of self interest. The real challenge before those theorists was to find a scientifically functional theory that could be applicable everywhere. In that sense, they used the knowledge from the quotation by Smith as common knowledge that could be applicable and which could give sound judgments. In this situation, normally people take the example of the relationship between seed and sprout without considering the other aspects relating to it. Knowledge of this kind is necessary for making judgments that are in demand, as in the case of water and a place to rest for the desert voyager. The scientific mode of thinking requests us to look forward and move forward since analytical knowledge considered a savior.

The problem of knowledge and judgment in dialectical situations is actually the course of such confusions in the world. For understanding this aspect better, we can find an impressive observation by Nāgārjuna in which he concludes that: *yaḥ pratityasamutpādaḥ śūnyatāṁ tāṁ prakaṣmahe/ sā prajñāptir upādāyā pratipat saiva madhyamā //* (Here everything that is originated dependently is revealed as *śūnyatā*; and that which is dependent on *prajñā* is seen in way of the middle – the way of the middle path.)

The explanation to this verse in my opinion is that we can use for understanding the real nature of phenomenal realities that implicitly reveal the implicit dependent nature of each phenomenon. In that sense, *śūnyatā* and *prajñā* serve the same function of revealing the actual situation without falling into the problem of conceptual construction.

The butcher who sold his butcher business did the same thing. He followed the knowledge made available to him by the economic theorists and created a conceptual world (*vikalpa*). He did not realize that the freedom he was seeking was available if he were to satisfy all three adjuncts of life: *artha*, *kāma*, and *dharma* for *mokṣa*. Or as Adam Smith wanted to say, we enjoy when we discharge our moral obligations as human beings. When we earn enough wealth and when we have satisfied our urge by earning, we want to be ethical. The butcher may now want a reversal of things that may not happen for him, but the conception of *śūnyatā* or *prajñā* helps one to view the problem and take corrective decisions.

PEACE THROUGH MORAL LIFE: AN ANALYSIS BASED ON EARLY BUDDHIST DISCOURSES

Y. Karunadasa

Peace through moral life – to some this may appear pretty obvious with no need for analysis; and to others, as an old-fashioned approach to the solution of a perennial problem. However, we would like to submit that at the bottom of all social problems, there looms a moral crisis as well – often masqueraded under more trendy labels. The moral problem therefore calls for our serious attention, for no sensible person can ignore the need for a moral basis for all inter-personal relations as the surest guarantee for ensuring peace. As an Indian classic observes, it is man's higher moral sense that marks him off from the lower species of evolution.[1] This could also be understood more as a prescription than as a description, as exhortation as to how man should conduct himself. For man has within him the potential and the wherewithal either to elevate himself to the highest levels of moral perfection or to descend down to the lowest depths of moral depravity. It is in this context that we would like to submit for your consideration the early Buddhist teaching on the moral life and its relevance to us today in promoting peace at all levels.

---

[1] Cf. *Dharmo hi tesaṁ adhiko viseso, dharmena hinaḥ pasubhiḥ samaṇaḥ* (*Hitopadesa*).

We must begin by saying that early Buddhism is an out-and-out ethical religion with an ethical idea as its final goal. It makes no distinction, therefore, between the religious and the moral life. What is morally reprehensible is not sought to be justified even on religious grounds. Accordingly, all Buddhist observations on politics and economics, on social institutions and inter-personal relations, take into consideration the primacy of the moral life and the need for a moral foundation of society. Buddhism also believes that the efficacy of a moral view of life should depend on the validity of the worldview, which serves as its *raison d'etre*. This explains why the practice of the Buddhist moral life begins with *sammā diṭṭhi* or right understanding. The reason behind this is that a proper way of life should begin with a proper view of life. The practice of the moral life must have as its rationale a worldview involving a proper interpretation of our internal and external experience.

The early Buddhist worldview could be described as a critical response to two other worldviews that, according to the Buddha, have a tendency to prevail throughout the history of the man's intellectual thought. Thus, addressing Kaccayana, the Buddha says, "This world, O Kaccayana, generally proceeds on a duality of the belief in existence and the belief in non-existence.... All exists, Kaccayana, that is one extreme. Naught exists, Kaccayana, that is the other extreme. Not approaching either extreme the Tathāgata teaches you a doctrine by the middle way."[2]

The reference is clearly to *sassatavāda*, the belief in permanence or eternalism and *ucchedavāda*, the belief in annihilation; in other words, to the belief in Being (*bhūta-diṭṭhi*) and the belief in non-Being (*vibhava-diṭṭhi*).[3] It is against these two worldviews that the early Buddhist problems are continually directed and it is by demolishing them that Buddhism seeks to construct its own worldview. This explains why the early Buddhist doctrines are presented in such a way as to unfold themselves or

---

[2] *Saṃyutta-nikāya* (= S.), PTS, II, 17.

[3] See, e.g., *Dīgha-nikāya* (= D.), PTS, I, 13; III, 108, 212; *Aṅguttara-nikāya* (=A), PTS, I, 83; S. II, 20; III, 99, 182; IV, 400.

follow as a logical sequence from a sustained criticism of *sassatavāda* and *ucchedavāda*. This particular context is sometimes explicitly stated, sometimes, taken for granted. The conclusion suggests itself, therefore, that it was as a critical response to two mutually exclusive worldviews that Buddhism emerged as a new faith amidst many other faiths.

What exactly does Buddhism mean by *sassatavāda* and *ucchedavāda* and why does Buddhism consider itself as a critical response to their mutual opposition? If we go by the early Buddhist discourses, *sassatavāda* is the worldview which seeks to explain the human personality by positing a soul entity which is distinct from the body. [4] What seems to be emphasized here is the distinction between a permanent metaphysical self and the perishable physical body. By implication, this means that man's true essence is to be found, not in the perishable physical body, but in the permanent metaphysical self. Since this soul-entity was also conceived as something eternal, this particular worldview came to be referred to in the early Buddhist discourses as *sassatavāda* or eternalism. [5] All the Indian religions current during the time of the Buddha, whether they arose as a linear development of the Vedic thought or as a reaction against it, seem to have subscribed to this particular theory of the human personality. We may then introduce this religious or spiritual view of life as the theory of metaphysical self. From the Buddhist point of view, therefore, all religions, past or present, which advocate the belief in an eternal / immoral self-subsisting spiritual entity are but different versions of *sassatavāda* and are therefore subsumable under this generic term.

On the other hand, *ucchedavāda* is the worldview which considers itself as a reaction against *sassatavāda*. Therefore, instead of positing a metaphysical soul-entity different from the physical body, it identifies the physical body itself as man's soul entity. [6] What is emphasized here is not the duality but the identity of the soul and the body. [7] By implication, this means that man's

---

[4] See e.g., D. I, 57, 188; S. IV, 392 *ff*; M. I, 157, 426; A. V, 31, 186, 193.

[5] See n. 3.

[6] D. I, 34, 35.

[7] See e.g., D. I, 157, 188; II, 333, 336; S. IV, 392 *ff*.

true-essence is to be found, not in an elusive metaphysical self, but in the empirically observable physical body. Since this physical self is something that gets annihilated at death, with no prospect of post-mortal existence, this particular worldview came to be referred to in the early Buddhist discourses as *ucchedavāda* or annihilationism. [8] The various schools of materialism current during the time of the Buddha seem to have subscribed to this theory of the human personality. We may, then, introduce this materialist view of life as the theory of the physical self. From the Buddhist point of view, therefore, all forms of materialism, past or present, which advocate the theory of the physical self, are but different versions of *ucchedavāda* and are therefore subsumable under this generic term.

Thus, the Buddhist critique of *sassatavāda* and *ucchedavāda* is the Buddhist critique of the spiritual and the materialist views of existence which, according to Buddhism, persist throughout the history of human thought. From the Buddhist point of view, both views are but two different versions of *ātmavāda*, the belief in a soul. The difference is to be seen between a soul that is spiritual and eternal and therefore which survives death, on the one hand, and a soul that is material and temporary and which therefore gets annihilated at death, on the other.

If Buddhism dissociates itself from *sassatavāda*, this means that it does not recognize a spiritual soul entity impervious to change. This may also be understood as the denial of any kind of spiritual substance in man which relates him to some kind of transcendental reality serving as the ultimate ground of existence. This is where Buddhism sets itself off from all spiritual ideologies which postulate an Absolute, either in the form of a personal God or an impersonal Godhead, as the *raison d'etre* of our world of internal and external experience. This characteristically Buddhist position has enabled Buddhism to focus its attention on man and his present predicament rather than on an ineffable Absolute. This explains why there are more psychological observations in Buddhism than metaphysical speculations, anthropology instead of

---

[8] See n. 3.

theology. It also explains why Buddhism considers that exalted humanity is a better ideal than elusive divinity. On the other hand, if Buddhism dissociates itself from *ucchedavāda*, this means that the human personality is not a pure product of earth awaiting to be annihilated at death, but an uninterrupted congery of psycho-physical phenomena which does not terminate at death, with the dissolution of the body. Although Buddhism does not agree completely with *sassatavāda*, it does not deny survival (*punabbhava*), moral responsibility and moral retribution (*kammavāda*).

If Buddhism transcends the perennial conflict between *sassatavāda* and *ucchedavāda*, it does so through its doctrine of dependent origination (*paticcasamuppāda*) or the conditionality of all phenomena (*idap paccayatā*).[9] This is the Buddhist doctrine which serves as a foundation for all other Buddhist doctrines. Hence, the Buddha says that one who has an insight into the fact of dependent origination has an insight into the very heart of the *Dhamma*.[10] The Buddha himself defines it as the Middle Teaching,[11] because it transcends the eternalist and the annihilationist ideologies (*sassatavāda* and *ucchedavāda*) whether they manifest themselves as "*sabbam ekattam*" or "*sabbam puthuttam*".[12] The first is the monistic view which reduces existence to a common ultimate ground. The second is the opposite pluralistic view which reduces existence to a concatenation of discrete entities.

The Buddhist critique of ideologies, it may be noted here, takes into consideration their psychological motivation as well. The theory behind this is that our desires and expectations have an impact on what we tend to believe in. According to the Buddhist diagnosis of the psychology behind *sassatavāda* and *ucchedavāda*,

---

[9] For a comprehensive account and critical analysis, see David J. Kalupahana, *Causality: The Central Philosophy of Buddhism* (Honolulu: University of Hawaii Press, 1975).

[10] M. I, 190.

[11] S. II, 17.

[12] S. II, 77.

the former is due to craving for being (*bhava-taṇhā*),[13] i.e., the desire to perpetuate the individual self into eternity, the desire for immortality; and the latter is due to the craving for non-being (*vibhava-taṇhā*),[14] the desire to get completely annihilated at death. For by denying survival, *ucchedavāda* provides us with a theoretical justification to lead a life without being burdened by sense of moral responsibility and tormented by the fear of moral retribution. Therefore, it abhors any prospect of after-death existence and it is this psychological resistance, if our interpretation is correct, that encourages the desire for complete annihilation at death. Thus, according to Buddhism, the mutual conflict between *sassatavāda* and *ucchedavāda* represents, not only the perennial conflict between the spiritual and materialist views of existence, but the human mind's oscillation between two deep-seated desires.

From what we have observed so far, two things should become clear: The first is that *sassatavāda* is the Buddhist term for all religions, past or present, which advocate the theory of the metaphysical self. The second is that *ucchedavāda* is the Buddhist term for all forms of materialism which, while advocating the opposite theory of the physical self, reject all religions including Buddhism. Thus, the Buddhist critique of these two worldviews brings into focus Buddhism's own worldview.

If the Buddhist worldview transcends the mutual opposition between *sassatavāda* and *ucchedavāda*, it also transcends the mutual opposition between their practical manifestations. For *sassatavāda*, the physical frame in which the elusive soul is encased is not an instrument but a veritable obstacle for the soul's deliverance. What prevents its upward journey is the gravitational pull of the body (sense-pleasures). Hence, deliverance of the self, its perpetuation in a state of eternal bliss, requires mortification of the flesh. This is what came to be referred to in the early Buddhist discourses as *attakilamatha-anuyoga* or self-mortification.[15] It

---

[13] D. III, 212, 216; S. V, 432; Vin. I, 10.

[14] *Ibid.*

[15] See D. III, 113, S. IV, 330; Vin. I, 10.

must, however, be mentioned here, this can have different levels in different religions depending on the way they define the relation between metaphysical soul and the physical body. Nevertheless, the subordination of the latter to the former implies where the direction and the emphasis are. It logically leads to the theoretical justification of ascetic practices as a means to self-perfection. On the other hand, since *ucchedavāda* identifies the self with the physical body, man's aim in life, during his temporary sojourn here on earth, cannot be the rejection of sensual gratification in the pursuit of a higher spiritual ideal. If anything, it could be just the opposite. This is what came to be referred to in the early Buddhist discourses as *kāmasukhallika-anuyoga*.[16]

According to the Buddhist assessment, what is wrong in self-mortification is that it considers the physical body not as a useful instrument but as an obstacle to mental culture. "Here the error lies in taking the body to be the cause of the bondage when the real source of the trouble lies in the mind – the mind obsessed by greed, aversion and delusion."[17] The mortification of the body is not only futile (*anatthasaṃhita*) but fraught with suffering (*dukkha*) and is therefore ignoble (*anariya*).[18] It amounts to the impairment of an instrument which is necessary for mental culture. This approach may be due to a genuine aspiration for moral perfection. In point of fact, the Buddha was less critical of self-mortification than sensual indulgence. This explains why although the latter is criticized as lowly (*hīna*), vulgar (*gamma*), and secular (*pothujjanika*), the same criticism is not extended to the former.[19] The implication seems to be that *sassatavāda* which serves as the theoretical background of self-mortification does not lead to the complete collapse of the moral life. It is not subversive of the higher ideals of human culture. For it recognizes a spiritual source in man and therefore the moral foundation of society. In fact, according to Buddhism, all

---

[16] *Ibid.*
[17] Bhikkhu Bodhi, *The Noble Eightfold Path* (Kandy: Buddhist Publication Society, 1984), 10.
[18] Vin. I, 10.
[19] *Ibid.*

religions are but different forms of *kammavāda*,[20] for they all
advocate the practice of the moral life. However, Buddhism adds
this provision, *kammavāda* or the advocacy of the moral life
becomes futile if it does not lead to *kiriyavāda* the advocacy of the
efficacy of moral acts, and this in turn, to *viriyavāda*, the advocacy
of the role of the human effort.[21] These are the three main pillars
on which Buddhism builds its own edifice of the moral life. And it
was by taking these into consideration that the Buddha criticized
the other-versions of *kammavāda* prevalent during the day.

Sensual indulgence, which is the other extreme and which has
a materialist view of life as its theoretical background, is from the
Buddhist point of view, more unsatisfactory. It is based on the
mistaken view that the path to happiness lies in the continued
gratification of the desire for sensual pleasure, the titillation of the
senses as the only means to happiness. From a moral point of view,
what is undesirable about this approach is that it encourages the
satisfaction of self-centered desires and ego-centric impulses. That
this way of life gives pleasure is undeniable, but "the enjoyment is
gross, transitory and devoid of deep contentment."[22] The Buddhist
critique of gratification in sensuality as a means to happiness has
much relevance to us today when secularism has set up
consumerism as a goal in itself. Alcoholism, drug addiction,
juvenile delinquency, sexual violence, and the appeal of cults
which promise immediate relief from boredom, besides many
others, are the symptoms of a worldwide malaise which finds no
signs of abatement. At the bottom of all this is the mistaken quest
for the conquest of happiness through continued indulgence in
sensuality. It fails to take into consideration "the principle of
diminishing returns which operates in the mere gratificatory quest
for happiness."[23]

It is in the context of this Buddhist critique of the two extremes
of self-mortification and sensual indulgence that the Buddhist

---

[20] Cf. S. II, "Nidāna-vagga."

[21] Cf. S. "Nidāna-vagga," A. I, 62; D. I, 115.

[22] Bhikkhu Bodhi, *op. cit.*, 10.

[23] K. N. Jayatilaka, *The Principles of International Law in Buddhist Doctrine* (Leydon: Sijthoff, 1967).

teaching on the moral life assumes its significance. Its description as the middle way (*majjhimā paṭipadā*) shows that it is aloof, or sets itself off, from both extremes. This does not mean that what Buddhism calls the Middle Path is a compromise between the two extremes or their admixture. It is their avoidance in two, the transcendence of their mutual opposition. The words used are "*ubho ante anupagamma*,"[24] meaning "without entering into either of the two extremes." The Middle Way is another expression for the Noble Eightfold Path that, in the words of the Buddha, "gives rise to vision, gives rise to knowledge, and leads to peace, to direct knowledge, to enlightenment, and to *Nibbāna*."[25]

If the Noble Eightfold Path begins with *sammā diṭṭhi* (right view), this means that the practice of the moral life should be based on a right view of actuality, our world of internal and external experience. The first path-factor thus serves as a guide to all other path-factors. The importance of right view lies in the fact that our perspectives on the nature of actuality condition all our actions and value-orientations. Therefore, the ideational framework through which we perceive the world has a direct impact on the way we make our choices and goals and on how we seek to actualize them. Whether we express our views and beliefs in public or whether we keep them to ourselves, they have a direct bearing on the way we conduct ourselves in our individual and social life. Hence, the Buddha says that he sees no single factor so responsible for the arising of unwholesome states of mind as wrong view, and no factor so helpful for the arising of wholesome states of mind as right view. Again, there is no single factor so responsible for the suffering of living beings as wrong view, and no factor so patent in promoting the good of living beings as right view.[26]

Although Buddhism draws our attention to the importance of right view as a necessary guide to the practice of the moral life, it does not endorse dogmatic adherence to views, even if they are right. Infatuation with one's own view is *sandiṭṭhi-rāga* and

---

[24] Vin. I, 10.
[25] *Ibid.*
[26] A. I, 16.2.

dogmatic adherence to ideologies is *diṭṭhi-paramasa*. Both
manifest themselves as "This alone is true, all else is false."[27] It is
this kind of mentality that provides a fertile ground for bigotry and
dogmatism whose practical manifestations are religious fanaticism
and persecution, not to speak of interpersonal conflicts, sometimes
leading to internecine warfare. When a religion becomes a
dogmatic ideology, it loses its spiritual dimension and paves the
way for ideological conflicts. In fact, it is not incorrect to say that
dogmatic attachment to ideologies is fraught with more danger
than excessive attachment to material things. The religious wars
during the medieval period, referred to by a misnomer as holy wars,
are cases in point. If we do not witness them today, it is perhaps
because the issues have changed and not that we have become
more tolerant. The Buddhist critique of dogmatism shows that a
critical approach, far from being detrimental, is salutary even to
spiritual life. From the Buddhist point of view, a truly religious life
should, therefore, be based on healthy criticism and continual
self-examination.

Another source of ideological dogmatism is the confusion
between the means and the end, the elevation of the means to the
status of the ideal. The Buddhist position on this matter is quite
clear: the *Dhamma* as a means has only relative value, relative to
the realization of the goal. In the "Parable of the Raft" (*kullupama*),
the Buddha tells us that his teaching should be understood not as a
goal in itself, but as a means to the realization of the goal.[28] What
this seems to imply is that even the right view (*sammā diṭṭhi*) is a
conceptual model which serves as an instrument for obtaining a
true vision (*dassana*) to the nature of actuality.[29] Thus, the
emphasis is not on *diṭṭhi* (view) but on *dassana* (vision, insight).
The former is a means paving the way to the latter. Nor does
Buddhism associate itself with any kind of dogmatism and
absolutism as to how the right view should be presented. Hence,
the Buddha says that his doctrine should be understood not as an

---

[27] *Suttanipāta* (= Sn.), PTS. Gatha 895; Dhs 1498.

[28] M. I. 134.

[29] Sn. Gatha 152.

absolutist statement (*nippariyāya*) but as one presented in relative terms (*pariyāya*).[30] What this seems to suggest is that the nature of actuality could be presented in different conceptual models among which one is not held out as superior or interior to another. The validity of each is to be seemed in its ability to realize the ideal, i.e., an insight into the nature of reality.

If right view provides the ideational basis of the moral life, the second path-factor, right intentions (*sammā saṅkappa*), draws our attention to the mind's intentional function, the purposive aspect of mental activity. It is through this factor that values in consonance with the right view and oriented towards the right goal get properly structured. Right intentions are of three kinds: (i) intentions of renunciation, i.e., those free from self-centered desires and ego-centric impulses; (ii) intentions free from aversion; and (iii) harmfulness, i.e., those of benevolence and compassionate love.[31] Such intentions form the psychological foundation for benevolent moral actions. All actions which are socially harmful, all forms of social conflict, violence and oppression can ultimately be traced to our bad intentions. They are the manifestations or the outcroppings of our thoughts motivated by greed, malice and delusion. Thus, our mind's intentional function has a tremendous impact on our social environment. Therefore, the cultivation of right intentions is the surest guarantee for interpersonal concord and peace. Today, when we are living in a global village that cuts across natural barriers and national frontiers, our right or wrong intentions have a wider impact than at any period in the history of the human civilization.

The next three path-factors take into consideration our speech (*vācā*), actions (*kammanta*) and livelihood (*ājīva*). Together they represent the vocal and physical manifestations of our right or wrong intentions, which in turn are guided by our right or wrong views. It is at this level that our thoughts or intentions begin to have a concrete impact on our social environment, for better or worse. In the context of social ethics, therefore, these three factors assume immense significance.

---

[30] S. II, 71.
[31] M. III, 251.

The Buddhist teaching on right speech (*sammā vācā*) takes into consideration four aspects. The first is that it should be dissociated from all forms of falsehood. Positively this means devotion to truth which makes one reliable and worthy of confidence. The second is abstention from calumny or slanderous speech (*pisuṇā vācā*), which is intended to make enmity and dissension among people. Its opposite is the speech that heals divisions and promotes amity, harmony and friendship. The third is abstention from harsh speech (*pharusā vācā*). All forms of abuse, insult, and even sarcastic remarks are its variations. Its opposite is the speech which is "blameless, pleasant to the ear, lovely, reaching to the heart, urbane, pleasing and appealing to the people." Fourthly, right speech consists of abstention from frivolous and vain talk, idle chatter and pointless talk, all lacking in purpose and depth (*saṃphappalāpa*). Its opposite is to be found in one who cultivates meaningful, purposeful, useful and timely speech.[32] The first and the fourth aspects of right speech show that according to Buddhism, even truth must not be stated if it leads to problems. In uttering what is true, one should take into consideration not only its potential effect but also the proper time for its utterance (*kālavādin*).

These four aspects of right speech show how exhaustive and thoroughgoing the Buddhist moral teaching is on how we should exercise our capacity for verbal expression. The effects of speech are as pervasive as those of physical action. Hence, we cannot overlook its potential and consequences for good or harm. A careless word or a sarcastic remark could break lives, make enemies and even start wars. Hence, Buddhism advises us to be ever watchful of our words (*vācānurakkhi*).[33] This advice has more relevance and importance today "when the positive and negative potentials of speech have been vastly multiplied by the tremendous increase in the means, speed and range of communications."[34]

---

[32] D. I, 62.

[33] *Dhammapada* (=Dhp), PTS, gatha 281.

[34] *Ibid.*

If right speech involves the proper cultivation of vocal acts, right action (*sammā kammanta*) requires the cultivation of proper modes of bodily acts. It enjoins first abstention from injury to life and all forms of violence, the laying aside of all cudgels and weapons and, positively the cultivation of love and compassion to all creatures that have life. Secondly, it enjoins one to abstain from "taking what is not given." All kinds of thievery, robbery, fraudulence through false claims, deceiving customers by using false weights and measures, and even literary plagiarism axe some of its many variations. Positively this means cultivation of honesty and purity of heart at all levels of interpersonal relations. Thirdly, right action requires abstention from wrongful gratification of sensual desires through sexual misconduct or illicit sexual relations.

The fifth path-factor is on the necessity of following a morally acceptable means of livelihood (*sammā ājīva*). The Buddha mentions five specific modes of livelihood which are to be avoided: trading in weapons, in human beings (slave trade, for example), in living beings (butchery and meat production), in poison, and in intoxicating drinks. [35] Practicing deceit, treachery, soothsaying, trickery, and usury are among other wrongful means of livelihood. In short, any occupation which entails harmful consequences to others is to be considered as morally reprehensible, although it could be materially rewarding.

The last three factors of the Noble Eightfold Path, namely right effort (*sammā vāyāma*), right mindfulness (*sammā sati*) and right concentration (*sammā samādhi*), form a closely inter-related group involving direct mental training. They have as their basis the purification of conduct brought about by the three prior factors. The first requires putting forth energy to eliminate unwholesome dispositions and to prevent them from arising anew and to cultivate and stabilize wholesome dispositions. This particular path-factor brings into focusing the indispensability of effort, diligence, exertion and unflagging perseverance for the successful practice of the Buddhist moral life. It is the vital factor "necessary for the

---

[35] A. III, 208.

triumph of the moral will over the baser emotions."[36] The second, which is right mindfulness, is presence of mind, attentiveness, alertness, or awareness that plays the role of an inward mentor watching over all mental activity. For purposes of watching the mind, it is necessary that it "should be trained to remain in the present, open, quiet and alert," [37] free from all judgments, evaluations and interpretations. The ultimate aim of right mindfulness is to give proper moral direction to all volitional acts and their mental, vocal and physical manifestations. *Sammā samādhi* or right concentration is the unification of the differentiated mind, the calm, clear, unconfounded state of the mind, "the centering of all mental activity right and evenly."[38] It is this factor that serves as the proper basis for the dawning of wisdom, a true vision to the nature of reality, resulting in the elimination of all unwholesome dispositions and culminating in moral perfection.

This brings us to an end of our general survey of the Noble Eightfold Path, the Buddhist scheme for the practice of the moral life. Here, we would like to make two observations. One is that the eight factors of the path are not like the steps of a ladder, usually followed in sequence and sometimes bypassing some for purposes of expediency. As Bhikkhu Bodhi observes, "they can be more aptly described as components rather than as steps, comparable to the intertwining strands of a single cable that requires the contributions of all for maximal strength." [39] However, at the beginning and until such time when they begin to support each other some degree of sequence is inevitable. The other observation that we would like to make here is that the Noble Eightfold Path should not be understood as a path that we leave behind once we have reached the destination. The path-factors are in fact eight moral qualities to be absorbed and developed internally. Once these eight factors are fully developed, it results in the emergence

---

[36] P. D. Premasiri, *Encyclopedia of Buddhism*, Vol. V (Colombo: Government of Ceylon, 1990), 150.

[37] Bhikkhu Bodhi, *op. cit.*, 84.

[38] *Ibid*, 104.

[39] *Ibid*, 12.

of two other factors, namely right emancipation (*sammā-vimutti*) and right knowledge and vision (*sammā-ñāṇādassana*). These are ten *kusala* qualities which an arahant is said to be endowed with.[40] Thus, the highest level of moral perfection based on the Noble Eightfold Path is *Nibbāna*, to which the other two factors, namely right emancipation and right knowledge and vision, are added. It may not be incorrect to say, therefore, that to follow the Path is to become the Path, for here, to a great extent, the means coincides with the end as well.

One widespread misunderstanding of the Noble Eightfold Path is only for those who have renounced the lay life and not for the laity. This misunderstanding is part of the mistaken view that early Buddhism is an entirely other-worldly religion, an ascetic movement which has nothing to do with worldly life. We would like to submit three specific reasons why this conclusion is not acceptable. The first is that all the Buddhist moral teachings, whether they concern the laity or the monks / nuns, are ultimately traceable to the Noble Eightfold Path. It therefore follows that the Buddhist teachings pertaining to happiness in this world, well-being in the life after and the path leading to the realization of *Nibbāna* are all based on it. It is the repository of Buddhist ethics from which all other ethical teachings emanate. Secondly, the definition given to right livelihood (*sammā ājīva*), for instance, as abstention from five kinds of morally reprehensible trades, shows clearly that the laymen, too, were taken into consideration in defining the Noble Path. The third is the most important since it is based on the words of the Buddha himself. In the *Saṃyutta-nikāya*, the Buddha refers to two kinds of paths. One is the wrong path (*micchā paṭipadā*) and the other is the right path (*sammā paṭipadā*). After defining the wrong path as the direct opposite of the Noble Eightfold Path, the Buddha says, "Monks, I do not uphold the wrong path either for laymen or monks.[41] Thus, the Middle Path which is also the Noble Eightfold Path is the right path not only for monks and nuns but also for laymen and laywomen. The clear

---

[40] M. II, 115.
[41] S. V, 18-9.

implication is that the Path could be followed on different levels or
in varying degrees of intensity. If it cannot be followed fully, it is
better to follow it as far as possible. If the best thing is to realize
the ideal, the next best thing is to be nearer the ideal. This situation
is in fact true of all present-day social, economic and political
ideals. Just because there are varying degrees of differences
between the ideal and the practice, we do not propose to give up
the ideal. The ideal is an invitation to do the right thing and to
resist from doing the wrong thing.

As a religious teacher who upholds the supremacy of the moral
life, the Buddha defines his position as follows: "You yourself
should do what ought to be done; the Tathāgatas are (only)
teachers."[42] Thus, the Buddha is not a savior who could redeem
mankind. On the contrary, he is a spiritual guide who shows the
way, the way to enlightenment and emancipation. Hence, he is also
called "a torch-bearer to mankind."[43] As a moral teacher, he
explains to us what is morally wholesome and unwholesome and
the consequences that follow from our morally wholesome and
unwholesome acts. The Buddhist moral precepts should, therefore,
be understood as descriptive rather than prescriptive. There are no
moral commandments or injunctions as to what ought to be done
and what ought not to be done. This also means that morally good
and bad acts are neither rewarded nor punished, but that they have
their own consequences according to the principles of moral
causation, what the Buddhist commentators call *kammaniyama* or
the moral order.

However, *saddhā* or faith in the Buddha and his Doctrine
(*Dhamma*) is necessary if we are to embark on the course of
spiritual discipline that culminates in moral perfection. Reference
is made in the early Buddhist discourses to two kinds of *saddhā*.
One is called *amūlika saddhā*, i.e., baseless or blind faith. The
other is called *akaravati saddhā* or "rational faith,"[44] i.e., faith or
confidence arrived at by examining reasonable evidence for any

---

[42] *Dhammapada*, gatha 276.
[43] Sn. Gatha 336.
[44] M. I, 320.

claim made. It is this latter kind of faith that Buddhism emphasizes. In fact, excessive faith or devotion to the Buddha could be an obstacle to spiritual progress as is seen from the story of the Buddhist monk called Vakkali.

It, therefore, follows that those who have faith in the efficacy of the *Dhamma* to elevate a person from a morally lower position to a morally higher position come to consider the Buddha as a Moral Authority. Here by authority we do not mean a person who has authoritative power, but one who has authoritative knowledge on the subject. Hence, the followers of the Buddha, both laymen and monks, consider him the highest authority on all problems relating to the moral life. Therefore, they all have faith in the Buddha and the *Dhamma*. There have been some attempts made to minimize the importance of the role of faith in Buddhism. Textual evidence does not support such a conclusion.

However, in presenting the Buddhist moral teachings, the Buddha also took into consideration the necessity of keeping to a minimum what may be called the faith-factor. A moral teaching, if it is to be effective, should be persuasive rather than coercive. In this connection, he also took into consideration that if not all, at least the intelligent members in the society (*viññū parisā*) have the ability to be rationally persuaded as to make a proper distinction between what is morally good and bad. For this purpose, the Buddha has laid down a set of guidelines that each individual could follow in the practice of the moral life.

One such guideline is called *attupama* or self-comparison. This is an invitation to the individual to put himself in another individual's position. If one does not like to be killed, it follows that the other person also does not like to be killed. This is very well illustrated in the well-known *Dhammapada* verse: "All tremble at punishment; and all fear death. Comparing oneself to another, let one refrain from killing another, and let one refrain from killing and tormenting others." [45] The same idea is more poignantly expressed in the *Saṃyutta-nikāya*: "Here, a noble disciple reflects thus: 'I like to live. I do not like to die. I desire

---

[45] Dhp., gatha 129.

happiness and dislike unhappiness. Suppose someone should kill me, since I like to live and do not like to die, it would not be pleasing and delightful to me. Suppose I too should kill another who likes to live and does not like to die, who desires happiness and does not desire unhappiness, it would not be pleasing and delightful to that other person as well. What is not pleasant and delightful to me is not pleasant and delightful to the other person either. How could I inflict upon another that which is not pleasant and delightful to me?' Having reflected in this manner, he (the noble disciple) on his own refrains from killing, and encourages others too to refrain from killing, and speaks in praise of refraining from killing."[46] The basic idea behind this moral guideline is that all living beings, whether they are human or otherwise, are led by the pleasure-principle and therefore recoil from pain.[47] If human beings, as observed in the *Vasettha Sutta*,[48] differ biologically (*jātimaya*) from all other species of living beings, what is common to all is the fact that they like to be happy, they do not like to be unhappy.

A second guideline for moral action is the one based on what the Buddhist commentators call the threefold *ādhipateya* or the three kinds of dominant influence.[49] This requires our examining the moral quality of an act from three different points of view. The first, called *attādhipateya*, invites the individual to examine whether the act he is going to commit results in self-blame or repentance. This is a clear reference to what may be called conscience, although a word corresponding to it does not seem to occur in the early Buddhist discourses. This is a case of allowing oneself to be controlled by oneself. The second, called *lokādhipateya*, requires the individual to examine whether such and such arts will be approved or disapproved by intelligent people. This is a case of allowing oneself to be controlled by public opinion. However, the Buddhist idea of public opinion does not exactly correspond to how we understand it today, i.e., as the

---

[46] S. V, 354.

[47] A. I, 189.

[48] Sn. & M.

[49] *Visuddhimagga*, PTS, 14.

opinion of the majority. According to Buddhism, what matters is neither the opinion of the majority nor that of the minority, but the opinion of those who really know, the intelligent people in society; the term used is *viññū purisā*. This is the yardstick that should be adopted when we are confronted with what others say. Hence, what is morally approvable is referred to as *viññuppasaṭṭha* and conversely what is morally reprehensible as *viñūgarahita*. The third point of view from which our acts are to be examined is called *dhammādhipateya*, i.e., whether they conform to the Moral Norm. This threefold examination is thus intended as a check for refraining from doing what is morally unwholesome and also as an incentive to do what is morally wholesome.

A third guideline is based on a rational appeal to a reasonably intelligent person's moral sense – if this term is permissible. In the *Kālāma Sutta*, it is recorded that the people of Kālāma complained to the Buddha that they were at a loss to discriminate between what is morally good and bad, because they were confronted with a variety of contradictory opinions on this matter. Then, the Buddha put this question to them: "Now what think, you Kālāmas, when greed (for example) arises within a man, does it arise to his profit or to his loss? When the Kālāmas admitted that it conduces to one's own loss, the Buddha continued: "Now, Kālāma, does not this man, thus become greedy, being overcome by greed and losing control of his mind – does he not kill a living creature, take what is not given, go after another's wife, tell lies and induce others, too, to commit deeds that would conduce to disadvantage and unhappiness for a long time?"[50] This same observation was made in respect of malice (*dosa*) and delusion (confusion). A similar argument, with the opposite effect, is repeated in respect of the absence of greed, malice and delusion. It was through this rational appeal to Kālāmas' moral sense that the Buddha was able to convince them of the undesirability of what is morally reprehensible and of the desirability of what is morally rewarding. As P. D. Premasiri observes, the *Kālāma Sutta* is "philosophically

---

[50] A. II, 95.

significant in that it draws attention to the possibility of independent inquiry into moral questions."[51]

The next question that we propose to take up is the relative position which Buddhism assigns to our own good and the good of others. How is the distinction between egoism and altruism maintained?

The Buddhist answer to his question is very well illustrated in a classification of individuals into four groups. The first individual is he who does not strive either for his own well-being (*attahita*) or for the well-being of others (*parahita*).[52] The second individual is he who pursues the well-being of others but fails to pursue his own well-being. The third individual is he who strives for his own well-being and not for the well-being of others. The fourth individual is he who strives for his own well-being as well as for the well-being of others.[53] The most important thing that must not be overlooked here is that in this classification, the words "pursuit of well-being" mean the pursuit of moral well-being, and not any other kind of well-being. We should bear this in mind if we are to draw the correct conclusion as to how Buddhism draws the line between one's own good and the good of others.

This classification of the four kinds of individuals is done in an ascending order of excellence. Therefore, the fourth individual is judged to be the best. An examination of the classification should also show the great importance attached to one's own moral well-being. This is very clear from the fact that the third individual who pursues his own moral well-being is superior to the second person who pursues the moral well-being of others, while neglecting his own moral well-being. This same idea is also applied by the fact that the fourth individual is judged to be the best. If the fourth individual is held out as the best, this means that although he pursues the moral well-being of others, he also pursues his own moral well-being.

---

[51] P. D. Premasiri, *op. cit.*, 155.

[52] A. II, 95.

[53] M. I, 45.

Why does Buddhism attach more importance to one's own moral well-being? Does this mean that the early Buddhist morality is individualistic, that it considers self-interest more important than altruism? An affirmative conclusion is sometimes found in some modern writings on Buddhism. The question we raised need not lead to any kind of unwarranted speculation. For the answer to it is provided in the Buddhist discourses themselves.

The Buddhist answer to this question is that one who is lacking in morality cannot make others morally good. In illustrating this situation, it is observed that a person who is stuck in mud cannot pull out another who is also stuck in mud. The lesson to be drawn is that a person who is stuck in the mud of moral depravity cannot save another who is also in the same predicament. Before one seeks to eliminate another's moral depravity, one must first eliminate it from oneself. This reminds us of the well-known saying: Example is better than precept.

It is also maintained that the benefits of moral cultivation are reciprocal. When a person eliminates from his mind such unwholesome mental disposition as greed, malice and delusion, they will not manifest themselves in practical form in relation to others. Thus, moral cultivation has not only an individual dimension but a social dimension as well. This is the significance of the Buddha's saying: "Monks, one who takes care of oneself, takes care of others. And one who takes care of others takes care of oneself. How, monks, is it that one who takes care of oneself takes care of others. It is by moral training, moral culture and moral development. And how, monks, does one who takes care of others take care of oneself? It is by forbearance, by harmlessness, by goodwill and compassion."[54]

If Buddhism attaches more importance to an individual's own moral well-being, it should not be concluded from this that a person who has attained moral perfection remains indifferent to society. On the contrary, he addresses himself to the pursuit of others' moral well-being. This is clearly shown not only by the life led by the Buddha, but also by the lives led by the arahants, as

---

[54] S. V, 169.

recorded in the Pāli texts. It is best illustrated by the Buddha's admonition to the first sixty arahants to go forth and preach the doctrine of emancipation "for the benefit, well-being and happiness of the man."

Before we conclude this paper, we would like to refer here to another important aspect of the Buddhist teaching on the moral life. It is that according to Buddhism, moral perfection should be accompanied by knowledge and must also be based on knowledge. If they do not go together, moral perfection loses its very foundation. To put it briefly, this means that a person who is morally perfect but is not aware of his moral perfection is not morally perfect. This may appear rather paradoxical, nevertheless from the Buddhist point of view, it is the case.

This situation is very well illustrated in the *Samaṇamaṇḍika Sutta* of the *Majjhima-nikāya* which records the theory of moral perfection as advocated by a religious teacher of the Buddha's day, called Uggahamana. As recorded here, his definition of a morally perfect person is as follows: "A person who does not do an evil act with his body, speaks no evil speech, intends no evil intention, leads no evil livelihood, is to that extent morally perfect." [55] Apparently this seems to be how the Buddha himself teaches moral perfection. However, the fact that it comes to be criticized by the Buddha shows that this definition of moral perfection is not acceptable to Buddhism. In criticizing it, the Buddha makes these observations: "According to this view of moral perfection, even a young baby-boy, lying on its back, would be morally perfect. A young baby-boy, lying on its back, does not think of his own body. How then could he do an evil deed with its body, except for a little kicking about. He does not think of his own voice. How then could he utter an evil speech except for a little crying? He does not think about its own intention. How then could it intend an evil intention, except for a little excitement? He does not think of its own mode of livelihood. How then could he lead an evil mode of livelihood, except for taking its mother's milk?"[56]

---

[55] M. II, 24.
[56] *Middle Length Sayings*, PTS, II, 223-4.

This criticism is based on the observation that the naive innocence of a baby-body, lying on its back, is not based on knowledge and is not accompanied by awareness. It is not something that is deliberately and consciously cultivated. In the same way, moral perfection devoid of the knowledge factor is not moral perfection. This same idea is repeated in a different form elsewhere as follows: "Just as a man whose hands and feet are cut off knows that his hands and feet are cut off, even so one who is morally perfect, whether he is walking or standing still or asleep or awake, in him there is constant and perpetual presence of knowledge to the effect that all mental defilements are destroyed by him."[57]

The Buddhist moral life is not based on a theory which states that either the sense-organs or the corresponding sense-objects are in themselves an obstacle to mental culture. If two oxen, one white and the other black – so runs the argument – are tied by a yoke, it is not correct to say that the black ox is a bond for the white ox or vice versa. For it is the yoke that constitutes the bond, it is that which unites them both. In the same way, what stands as an obstacle to mental culture is neither the sense organs nor the sense objects but craving or attachment. If it were otherwise, then one would have to rule out the very possibility of the practice of the moral life (Brahmacariya). [58] More or less, the same idea is reflected in the Indriyabhāvanā Sutta where the Buddha questions a disciple of Parasariya as to how his Master teaches moral culture. In reply, the latter says that the senses are to be trained to the extent when they fail to fulfill their respective functions: The eye does not see form; the ear does not hear sounds. Then, the Buddha rejoins that this kind of mental culture leads to the conclusion that the blind and the deaf have their senses best cultivated.[59] The clear implication is that mental culture is not to be associated with the suppression of the senses. They should be cultivated to see things as they truly are (yathābhūta).

---

[57] M. I, 523.
[58] S. IV, 163.
[59] M. III, 29ff.

A BUDDHIST ORIENTED RELATIONAL VIEW OF TRANSFORMATION IN MEDIATION

Ran Kuttner[1]

Introduction

In the last few decades, there has been a growing interest in Alternative Dispute Resolution (ADR) as a theoretical and practical academic field that has been presenting new practices for managing interpersonal conflicts. The ADR field is based on a systematic understanding of negotiation and the nature of conflict.

In the burgeoning field of ADR, mediation has had a central place as a process in which a third party helps disputants; there are different views as to the nature of this help: What is the mediator's role? What are the goals of the mediation process? How should the mediator intervene, if at all, throughout the process?

This paper offers an understanding of conflict escalation and of conflict transformation based on Buddhist philosophy, while addressing the abovementioned questions and by showing how the

---

[1] Assistant Professor of Conflict Resolution, Wener Institute for Negotiation and Dispute Resolution, Creighton University School of Law, and Associate Director, Dispute Resolution Program, the Program on Negotiation at Harvard Law School. The following is based on a chapter from a PhD dissertation, titled "Presence of Dialogue in Mediation: Understanding Relational Worldview as Means for Transformation", submitted in Bar-Ilan University, Israel, in The Program on Conflict Management and Negotiation.

Buddhist worldview can shed light on some foundational concepts in the field of conflict management and ADR.

I. Current tendencies in western thought and mediation

In their book *The Promise of Mediation* (1994), Baruch Bush and Joseph Folger claim that in order for mediation to fulfill its promise, its potential to fundamentally transform common adversarial patterns, a different understanding with regard to foundational philosophical questions such as what it means to be a human being, our connection to our surroundings and our freedom, is needed. Transformation is needed, they claim, from an individualistic view of the self to a relational view of the self, where "Individuals are seen as both separate and connected, both individuated and similar. They are being to some degree autonomous, self-aware, and self interested but also to some degree connected, sensitive and responsive to others."[2]

The narrative approach to mediation, as presented by John Winslade and Gerald Monk in their book *Narrative Mediation* (2000), offers a framework that also critically re-examines the common modern western concept of the "self" as having a separate, permanent inner core. The narrative approach emphasizes that a shift is required from the parties' firm, fixed and well-constructed view of the self to a relational realization of its co-construction by the parties. Winslade and Monk elaborate on the quest to re-formulate the idea of the "self," offering a critique of the category of the "self" as a fixed entity, based on postmodern philosophy:

How mediators understand the nature of the self has a bearing on how they manage a dispute between parties... problem-

---

[2] Robert A. Baruch Bush and Joseph P. Folger, *The Promise of Mediation: Responding to Conflict through Empowerment and Recognition* (San Francisco: Jossey-Bass, 1994), 242. (In 2005, a new and revised edition was released). The individualistic worldview, they claim, is rooted in a vision of the individual as a separate being, autonomous and unconnected, who will fulfill his potential and actualize his freedom and independence by personally developing his values and subjective life experiences.

solving and interest-based approaches emphasize the individual as independent, stable, unitary, self-motivating, and self-regulating identity.... Through the postmodern lens, a problem is seen not as a personal deficit of the person but as constructed within a pattern of relationships.... From this perspective, identity is not fixed, nor is it carried around by the individual largely unchanged from one context to another.[3]

The questioning of the "self" as a separate, independent, firm entity is one tendency in current ADR literature, on which these frameworks elaborate. It is a tendency found in late twentieth century thought at large, which involves ontological questioning of Aristotelian metaphysics and Cartesian philosophy with regard to the human agent, the subject or the self.[4] It also involves a call for more focus on relational emphases. Prominent figures in the field of ADR claim that not enough attention is given to relational emphases – another important tendency in late twentieth century thought – attention that if given and emphases that if explored, can improve our understanding of the potential embedded in mediation and even "integrative negotiation", and both our practices and teaching accordingly.[5]

---

[3] John Winslade and Gerald Monk, *Narrative Mediation: A New Approach to Conflict Resolution* (San Francisco: Jossey Bass, 2000), 44-45. While elaborating on the loss of respect under the influence of the dispute, Winslade and Monk refer to the formation of what they call "personality", which can be understood to mean the "self": "A common description of conflict situations is to call them *personality crashes*. Such a description privileges the essential individual qualities that we call personality. The assumption of personality is that individuals carry around with them some kind of stable personhood that is context free. However, people are far more complex than any description.... What is implied in the type of respect we are advocating is a conscious effort not to see people as essentially anything, to refuse to sum people up." (*Ibid*, 132).

[4] Nietzsche, Heidegger, Wittgenstein, Foucault and Derrida are prominent thinkers in creating this intellectual shift, each of them with his unique criticism of the governing western underpinnings.

[5] For example, Tricia Jones writes, "A review of theoretical approaches to conflict and, more specifically, to mediation, reveals that relational context has received little attention.... Although mediation theories may include reference to or discussion of relational context, they rarely highlight its potential for

I suggest that the discourse on the potential embedded in mediation and the understanding the underlying premises of "integrative negotiation" can benefit from analyzing the changes in the view of the "self" as took place in twentieth century thought in various disciplines,[6] as well as from the "relational" philosophy and practices regarding what it is to be human.[7] In addition, further exploration of the philosophical underpinnings of the mediation process at large and of proposed models in particular may contribute to the field of ADR on both the theoretical and practical levels, grounding it in a larger theoretical framework and allowing

---

influence. And, to date, they have failed to seriously unpack how that influence may be exerted" (Tricia S. Jones, "A Dialectical Reframing of the Mediation Process," in *New Directions in Mediation*, eds. Joseph P. Folger and Tricia S. Jones (Thousand Oaks: Sage, 1994), 30). Her utterance, although written in 1994, is still relevant in 2007, and the challenge of shifting from the governing discourse, in which "…disputants are constructed as expressive and utilitarian individuals" (Jonathan Shailor, *Empowerment in Dispute Mediation: A Critical Analysis of Communication* (Westport: Praeger, 1994), 28) is yet to be met. Greenhalgh and Lewicki stress that even when negotiation manuals claim to adopt relational emphases, the teaching of negotiation "was a convenient simplification, because considering 'the party' as a single generic actor allowed scholars to apply all of their individualistically oriented theory to the intra-group, inter-group, intra-organizational, and international levels." (Leonard Greehalgh and Roy Lewicki, "New Directions in Teaching Negotiations From Walton and McKersei to the New Millennium," in *Negotiations and Change: From the Workplace to Society*, eds. Thomas A. Kochan and David B. Lipsky (New York: Cornell University Press, 2003), 27).

[6] See for example Bowling and Hoffman, where the authors describe manners in which new conceptions of the "self" effect various disciplines, and also suggest relevance to the mediation room. (Daniel Bowling and David Hoffman, "Bringing Peace into the Room: The Personal Qualities of the Mediator and their Impact on the Mediation," in *Bringing Peace into the Room: The Personal Qualities of the Mediator and their Impact on the Mediation*, eds. Daniel Bowling and David Hoffman (San Francisco: Jossey Bass, 2003), 13-49).

[7] For example, developments in psychotherapy in the last few decades, as framed under the "Relational Psychotherapy" stream (see Stephen Mitchell and Lewis Aaron, eds., *Relational Psychology: the Emergence of a Tradition* (Hillsdale: The Analytic Press, 1999), or relational postmodern philosophy (see Sheila McNamee and Kenneth J. Gergen, *Relational Responsibility: Resources for Sustainable Dialogue* (Thousand Oaks: Sage, 1999).

new insights to emerge regarding the practice of negotiation and mediation.[8]

While elaborating on the philosophical underpinnings of the relational worldview, the Buddhist philosophy – which in the words of the Japanese Buddhist philosopher Izutsu "...is ontologically a system based upon the category of *relatio*, in contrast to, say, the Platonic-Aristotelian system which is based on the category of *substantia*"[9] – should play an important role. Buddhism offers a 25-centuries long worldview and method of transformation which presents a significant alternative to the view of the "self" as widely accepted in western philosophy. It presents a philosophical, psychological and practical relational framework for transformation, which at its basis includes a radical transformation of the way the "self" is perceived. Prominent ADR scholars have already begun introducing Buddhist concepts and techniques to the discipline of Alternative Dispute Resolution;[10] delving into the philosophical underpinnings of the Buddhist

---

[8] Bush and Folger present the Relational Worldview as a philosophy that sets an alternative to the governing philosophical underpinnings that lay at the basis of the "individualistic worldview." Mediation theory must examine and shape, they claim, the basic philosophical tenets of mediation, as each mediator's philosophical worldview is the foundational layer that needs to be clarified in order to understand his or her orientation to the practice. A clarification of the foundational layers is essential, claim Bush and Folger, in order to allow the mediator to make informed choices ingrained in a "big picture" understanding of and an in-depth orientation to the mediation process. Winslade and Monk go even further to claim that "Those who grasp the philosophical position will relatively easily and quickly master the practices... [while] those who undertake narrative mediation through a simplistic practical orientation of them flounder after a short time and fail to embody the spirit of the approach" (Winslade and Monk, 32).

[9] Tohihiko Izutsu, *Toward a Philosophy of Zen Buddhism* (Tehran: Imperial Iranian Academy of Philosophy, 1977), 23

[10] Riskin 2002/2004/2006, Peppet 2002/2004, Bowling 2003, Rock 2005, Freshman 2006, if to name a few. The 2002 Spring issue (No. 7) of the *Harvard Negotiation Law Review* was dedicated to that subject matter, under the title "Mindfulness in Law and ADR," following a symposium that took place in March that year at Harvard Law School on that matter. For more information see: http://www.pon.harvard.edu/news/2002/ riskin_mindfulness. php3.

framework, I suggest, may help further draw the more practical implications for mediation and negotiation. Buddhist philosophy may also help shed light on the notion of "integration" altogether, and help clarify some central concepts in "integrative negotiation" literature, [11] thus helping to see the path from distributive bargaining and adversity to integrative negotiation and dialogue.

II. Key concepts in Buddhist philosophy

The Relational Worldview as found in various disciplines in current western thought, and the Buddhist Worldview, share similar dissatisfactions and premises. However, there are fundamental differences between the underpinnings of the Buddhist philosophy and the common western philosophical foundations that go back as far as Aristotelian philosophy. According to Aristotelian premises, knowing an object demands knowledge of its 'essence,' its inalterably fixed and determined inner substance. According to the Buddhist worldview, on the other hand, knowledge cannot be attained as long as an object's fixed and determined inner substance is sought. A key term in the understanding of the Buddhist worldview is the term 'dependent co-arising' (*pratītya-samutpāda*): any object – "self" included – is a product of causality, dependently co-arising with other objects that co-arise with it. According to the principle of dependent co-arising, any given situation is a set of connections and relations in which separate entities arise, entities that through a process of abstraction, we grasp as having the characteristics of continuous separate substances. [12] Seeing entities as continuous, separate substances is an abstraction, resulting from observing the situation

---

[11] As presented, for example, by Fisher and Ury, Lewicki and Saunders, Lax and Sebenius, Mnookin, and others.

[12] Izutsu explains, "We may do well to recall at this point that Buddhism in general stands philosophically on the concept of *pratītya-samutpāda*, i.e., the idea that everything comes into being and exists as what it is by virtue of the infinite number of relations it bears to other things, each one of these 'other things' owing again its seemingly self-subsistent existence to other things" (Izutsu, 23).

from outside and while ignoring the process of dependent co-arising as it occurs at the moment. Doing so, we are creating notions of entities that we later perceive to be separate from their arising, having a substantial and permanent inner-nature with which "they" then enter a process of interaction with "another" – similarly substantial and permanent entity. Every "thing," every apparent object we seem to grasp as standing on its own, separate from other objects, is not, according to the Buddhist view, such. The idea that definite objects exist, having their own essence, substance, and unique characteristics that will never change, is perceived by the Buddhist philosophy as an abstraction derived from the human need to arrange the world in such a way and create what Buddhism sees as an illusion.

A key term in the understanding of *dependent co-arising* is the idea of emptiness (*śūnyatā*). The claim that everything is empty means that nothing exists independently, having an internal, substantial, fixed and permanent nature of its own, a core or inner nature (*svabhāva*) which is not a product of causality or dependency in other things with which it stands in relation. The wish to grasp to a separate, fixed and permanent substance – according to the Buddha's teachings – is an illusion that causes human suffering and dissatisfaction or "dis-ease". It involves attachment to psychologically-formed entities, perceived as objects with such characteristics. This constant processes of self-formation (i.e., of forming entities with inner "selves") needs to be transformed, as such a mindset and mental activity, according to the Buddhist worldview, is a partial and insufficient realization of reality, and a form of what is described in the Buddhist framework as ignorance (*avidyā*).

Buddhism aims to release the practitioner from the illusory way in which the "self" is perceived through this constant processes of self-formation in everyday life. Through mental practice, the substantive self is transformed to a realization of the impermanent, empty and dependent co-arising nature of all things, according to which "things" exist only within the given context and web of relations in which they take part. Transformation within the Buddhist framework means letting go of the attachment to the firm, unchanging, independent self, and realizing its "emptiness" of characteristics of substance. [13] A transformation of that attachment (which, as mentioned, is understood in Buddhist philosophy as the cause for suffering and dis-ease) through cultivation of awareness to the process of dependent co-arising – sheds light, I suggest, on the shift sought in negotiation and mediation from adversarial to integrative negotiation. In the latter, viewed from a relational standpoint as understood within the Buddhist framework, the separate, well defined 'self' or 'agent' can be seen in a new way. [14] The either/or polarizing state of mind, as well as the subject/object or mine/yours dichotomy which stems from Aristotelian logic and stressed when in adversity, as will be further discussed in the following section, may be transformed through that process. [15]

Moreover, this illusion – according to the Buddhist worldview – relates not only to the perception of human beings as having a substantial and independent "self", but to the perception of *any* entity seen as a separate, self-substantive entity, i.e., the granting

---

[13] Emptiness is a central term in Buddhism that needs much clarification in order to prevent nihilistic interpretations.

[14] This way of presenting the self helps clarify the philosophical tenets that lay as foundational in some relational theories of human interaction. For example, while quoting Mary Parker Follett and presenting her visionary perception of integrative negotiation, Deborah Kolb and Judith Williams write: "When bargainers put their cards on the table, face the real issue, and bring everything into the open, they relate to each other differently. As Follett wisely points out, 'I never react to you but to you-plus-me; or to be more accurate, it is I-plus-you reacting to you-plus-me…. In the very process of meeting, we both become something different, more receptive to that unknown that the other party knows. When we engage in dialogue instead of talking *at* each other, we learn from the exchange, and the boundaries of set arguments become elastic." (Deborah Kolb and Judith William, *Everyday Negotiation: Navigating the Hidden Agendas in Bargaining* (San Francisco: Jossey Bass, 2003), 235). Cultivating awareness to the I-plus-you and the you-plus-me that is essential for engaging in dialogue, as described by Follett, can be clarified and attained through the process of transformation drawn in Buddhist philosophy.

[15] "Eastern thought," writes Rollo May, "never suffered the radical split between subject and object that has characterized Western thought" (Rollo May, *The Discovery of Being: Writings in Existential Psychology* (New York: Norton, 1983), 59).

of characteristics of permanent, fixed and firm entity to objects, ideas, feelings, etc.

Understanding the Buddhist framework and its governing underpinnings, which include a re-examination and new realizations regarding the self, may assist the practitioner in emphasizing the centrality of the relational aspect and in fact to advance the project that Bush and Folger claim is still in its preliminary stages – to develop relational philosophy, underpinnings for a relationally based approach to mediation. Understanding this framework may also help further integrate systematically the Buddhist philosophy and psychology with ADR literature, and the Buddhist practice with the practice of mediation, developing new techniques to help parties transform their adversary into dialogue.

III. Conflict escalation as a process of self-formation

I suggest that during the escalation of a disagreement into dispute, the disputants minimize the common dialogic space in which dependent co-arising is taking place. The partners withdraw from their common-space to singularity, shutting themselves within their separate, distinct perceptions, which are no longer balanced as dialogue is lost. Such withdrawal creates an illusionary mindset of independent, separate "selfhood." At the same time, it also creates an illusion of "the other": an "other" who is also perceived as independent and separate, and acting outside the common-space. This is where party-ness – the sense of being separate parts that do not dependently co-arise – is created, entrenching within the separate self and creating a private world, a private language and internal grammar. [16] The freedom from the construction of new understandings within the common dialogic space, and moreover – from the relational process that is constantly

---

[16] This illusion involves an instrumental attitude towards others that are perceived in a one-dimensional manner, with no spatial perspective, as being separate from the common-space. It is turning the other into an object, at the same time objectifying their self-consciousness, a one-dimensional and illusive consciousness, lacking space, lacking vividness.

taking place – is part of that illusion. Constructing a common-space with other players (such as one's spouse or one's lawyer), or even dozens of other common spaces that the party moves between, cannot substitute for reconstructing the understandings within the dialogic space in which a dispute has developed.[17]

In the following pages, I wish to present a detailed model of conflict escalation, which was developed by the German scholar Friedrich Glasl, in which the changing mindset of the parties involved throughout the process of escalation was analyzed step-by-step. An understanding of the dynamics of escalation as presented in this model, I suggest, sheds light on the manner the formation of the substantive self plays a central role in the dynamics of conflict escalation. With regard to the process of conflict escalation, my claim is, in general, that when in a conflict, parties withdraw from their 'common dialogic space' as I name it, and fortify or entrench in separate spaces, clinging to – or being attached to, if to use two key concepts in Buddhist psychological analysis – firm, fixed, independent positions.[18]

Friedrich Glasl developed a nine-step model of conflict escalation, each stage accompanied by characteristic patterns of in-group and out-group images, motives, moods, and forms of interaction. [19]

---

[17] This does not come to create dependency in a manner that would lead to blurring the distinctions, but only by emphasizing the relational component as it manifests itself each moment in the common space it would be possible to move to the distinction and give room to the plurality of components that co-arise in the common space. This does not come to suggest that the previous relationship should be restored, but that the illusion and ignorance should be transformed, thus creating a common – non sentimental – dialogic space, in which an agreement to part, for example, may be reached.

[18] "This is what I want" (and I do not intend to move), "I don't care what you think about it" (and I am 'persistent' about it, not open for reconsideration).

[19] Friedrich Glasl, "The Process of Conflict Escalation and Roles of Third Parties," in *Conflict Management and Industrial Relations*, eds. G. B. J. Bomers and R. B. Peterson (The Hague: Kluwer Nijhoff Publishing, 1982), 119-140.

standpoints, i.e., fixed positions on how a certain issue ought to be handled, and tend to defend rigid positions. The transition from the first to the second stage, which Glasl names "polarization and debating style,"[20] is a stage in which "these groups are increasingly consolidated into more well delimited parties."[21] The delimiting process is described by Glasl as the main source of escalation, where separation takes place, as boundaries defining who belongs to the inside and the outside become more and more visible. In order to gain strength, parties become increasingly locked into inflexible standpoints. Glasl describes at that stage the formation not only of firm positions, but the buds of bringing into the process a firm "general position," which is a shift from a discussion over the merits to a more general – even if at this stage only vague – sense of self behind the merits, who needs to be guarded and dealt with.[22] This stage includes growing mistrust among the parties, and a sense of insecurity and loss of control, which the parties try to compensate for with an increased emphasis on a self-image as righteous and strength.[23] Aggressive actions serve at this stage mostly to boost self-esteem.

The main characteristic of stage three is the loss of dependency and the formation of what I see as independent self, independent from the common dialogic space. In this stage, Glasl explains, the antagonists seek to replace the mutual dependencies with unilateral dependency, in order to be able to dominate the counterpart.[24] With that independency arises a wish for unilateral action, where each

---

[20] *Ibid,* 125

[21] Thomas Jordan, "Glasl's Nine Stage Model of Conflict Escalation: A Summary," 2000, p. 1, in http://www.mediate.com/articles/jordan.cfm.

[22] Separating the people from the problems, as advised by Fisher and Ury (Roger Fisher and William Ury, *Getting to Yes: Negotiating Agreement without Giving In* (New York: Penguin, 1981), 17), hence becomes difficult to attain.

[23] In a later stage, the formation will wear a more global picture of "the other," while at this stage it is a patterning process, in which repeated experiences of the counterpart lead to the formation of images of typical behavior patterns, which help dealing with insecurity and loss of control.

[24] *Ibid,* 4. Glasl writes, "The parties stop talking to each other for they become convinced that they will get nowhere. They think positions are fixed and will only be moved by deeds" (Glasl, 126).

party's top priority is to be perceived as not yielding, under any circumstances, to the other's wish to dominate. In order to assure it, the pressure to conform to a common attitude and a common interpretation increases the parties' further entrenchment within the picture of the formed self, which helps guard each of them from the other party.

At stage four, the consolidating process of the self is entering a new phase, as "the 'typicals' that evolved at stages two and three are now consolidating and complemented into full-blown general and consistent images of the counterpart. These images are stereotypical, highly fixed and are very resilient to change through new information." [25] Such images, Glasl explains, serve an important role in providing a sense of orientation: one has the feeling of knowing what to expect from the environment. The sense of insecurity involved is dealt with by also developing that well-structured, known and familiar clear and distinct view of the counterpart and of the situation.[26]

This is true not only for the manner by which "the other" is seen, but also for the manner by which one sees oneself; the power of the stereotypes, he explains, leads to a subtle pressure on each party to conform to roles assigned to her behavioral expectations that are – at this stage of the dynamic – difficult to escape. Stage five is characterized by the parties' sudden insight into the other's "true nature." The formation of the self who is behind the actions is at this stage completed, as one develops conviction as to the other's moral character and identity.

In stage six, a major escalation is taking place, according to Glasl, as the parties make dedicated statements of self-commitment from which they cannot retreat without losing credibility, in order to enhance the seriousness of their threats. The attachment to the

---

[25] Jordan, 4. "The parties' self-image and the image of the enemy," Glasl writes, "become very much polarized" (Glasl, 127).

[26] In a manner that according to the Buddhist worldview only strengthens one's ignorance and creates a barrier from seeing thing as they are, in their suchness. Jordan writes, "The negative images are now screens that occupy the field of vision whenever the parties meet each other. These screens prevent the parties from seeing each other's true complexity and individuality." (Jordan, 5).

self one formed in the dynamics, and the control and firm perception of the situation that one craves for, blinds one from the occurrences in the common space, and from seeing things as they are, each party insisting that its own issues and standpoints must be dealt with in exactly the exact form she has in mind.

At this point, one is most concerned with the protecting and maintaining of one's own formed self,[27] and success is measured in the credibility that this self has as a continuous, firm self-substantive entity, who for that reason clings to his standpoints and threats without any withdrawal whatsoever.

In stage seven, the entrenchment onto the self increases, as there is no longer any real communication. In this stage, each party is only concerned with expressing his own message, and does not care about how it is received, or what the response might be. The further one increases one's entrenchment and attachment to the self, the more one draws away from dialogue. In stage eight, being concerned only with one's own survival, one moves to attacking the "very core" of the other, aiming at destroying his existence as a self and thus to eliminate the adversary. It is a last attempt to preserve the formed self, through annihilating the other's equivalent entity. However, the attempt to preserve the formed self is due to fail, bringing with it additional suffering and destruction. That failure is the threshold to stage nine, when the self-preservation drive is given up and there is no check at all on further destructiveness.

This, according to the Buddhist worldview, is also the case with ignorance, which generates non-dialogic behavior, reinforces negative perceptions, attitudes and behavior, and thus generates further suffering and dis-ease. Glasl's model, I suggest, resonates with the Buddha's description of the cycle of suffering and dis-ease, which presents an analysis of the manner ignorance is generated: The *Twelve Links* model, a detailed 12-stage analysis of the process of "withdrawing" from *wisdom*, its cessation understood in the Buddhist framework as the transformation of

---

[27] "Securing one's own further survival becomes an essential concern." (*Ibid*, 9).

suffering through realization of impermanence, emptiness and dependent co-arising. The twelve-links model can thus be used to understand both the processes of conflict escalation and of conflict transformation, providing a thorough analysis of the described withdrawal from the 'common dialogic space.' Both The twelve-links model and Glasl's model describe a process of escalation in which the process of self-formation is emphasized as playing a central role – in Glasl's model in the context of conflict escalation and in the Buddha's description in the context of the development of suffering and ignorance.

IV. Implications to mediation and negotiation

As mentioned, the process of withdrawing into the 'private space,' or the state of mind as described by Glasl, can be equated with the Buddhist scheme of withdrawal from wisdom and relational awareness to what is viewed as ignorance – self-substantive independent and permanent entities. This has an effect on the well-established view of "Interest Based Negotiation" as laid out by Fisher and Ury in *Getting to Yes* and onwards: Interest Based Negotiation sees the shift from adversarial bargaining to integrative negotiation as a shift away from "positions."[28] In the context of negotiation theory, the characteristics of self-substantive independent and permanent entities can be ascribed to positions, and ignorance can be understood as the inability to be aware of the impermanent nature of every position, and its emptiness as a substantial entity with an inner, independent core, independent from the manner it co-arises in the 'common dialogic space.'

This constant process of producing such entities or positions, according to the Buddhist worldview, is the cause for human suffering or dis-ease: "This is who I am" and "this is what I want," i.e., this is my identity and these are my positions, identical

---

[28] Fisher and Ury define at the opening of *Getting to Yes* the common pattern of bargaining over positions as "The problem," as well as the vast majority of literature, and deal throughout the book with that distinction and with how to turn from "positions" to "interests" (see Fisher and Ury, table of contents and first chapter).

wherever I go, no matter of the "outer variables and changes" (which are also granted similar delusive characteristics, seen as self-substantive, independent and permanent), i.e., no matter what the other's fixed and firm positions are.

This way of looking at the world is challenged by the Buddhist cultivation of wisdom, of developing awareness to the ever-changing, empty nature of all such "things" or "entities," or "selves." Transformation and de-escalation of conflicts, I therefore suggest following the Buddhist worldview, is transformation from this way of looking at "things" and of the process of withdrawing to and entrenching in a separate, fixed and firm well-defined self, to awareness of the ongoing process in which the "things" co-arise, self included. It is a shift from the entrenched self-substantive, self-absorbed and self-sustained self, fortified and captured in fixed, firm independent view of one's "self" and one's perception of the dispute at hand, manifested by fixed, firm and independent positions, to realization of impermanence, emptiness and dependent co-arising.

This, as aforesaid, has an effect on the well established view of Interest Based Negotiation, which sees the shift from adversarial bargaining to integrative negotiation as a shift from "positions" to "interests". Following the view suggested above, positions are diagnosed as a manifestation of the fortified self. The positional self can be viewed in terms of attachment as described above, as clinging to firm, fixed, unchanging positions that are perceived to be secured from the other party's positions. A shift is required, I suggest, not from "positions" to "interests," but from the distinct, bounded and firm self-substantial positions and arguments, to relational awareness in which positions are recognized to be dependently co-arising within each context. [29] Parties' interdependence is thus realized [30] and new information may be

---

[29] Thus meeting challenges as described in footnotes 4 & 14 above.

[30] Lax and Sebenius stress the importance of interdependence, bringing it forth in the opening pages of their book *Managers as Negotiators*, stressing its centrality to integrative negotiation and value creation: "Mutual dependence implies limits to how much one party can do alone, or at what cost, or how desirably joint action may be preferable for everyone. This possibility makes

gathered on their interests, needs, feelings and perspectives, in a manner that I elsewhere define as "dialogic."[31] Through such transformation, one let go of the attachment to a generalized perspective of one's firm and un-effected, determined positions.[32] Seen from a relational standpoint and with the understanding of impermanence – "What was important to the parties last week – or even 20 minutes ago – may not be important now. Interaction between the parties can put some interests to rest, but it may raise others. Thus, the parties must continually be attentive to changes in their own interests and the interests of the other side."[33] Attentiveness, I suggest, should be cultivated also to the manner by which "their own," as well as "the other side's" interests, dependently co-arise in the process. Mindfulness, according to Buddhist philosophy, which one cultivates during the process of transformation through various meditation practices, is the quality of awareness described.

---

interdependence a key element that defines negotiating situations." (See David A. Lax and James K. Sebenius, *The Manager as Negotiator: Bargaining for Cooperation and Competitive Gain* (New York: Free Press, 1986), 7). Although writing within a pragmatic philosophical framework, different from the one suggested in this paper, I suggest that the awareness cultivated to interdependence as described above can support the shift from "claiming value" to "creating value."

[31] Following, I suggest, the foundational premises found in prominent thinkers' view of dialogue, e.g., Martin Buber, David Bohm, Mary Parker Follett and others (see footnote 1 above, chapter 3).

[32] This does not imply accommodating personality, giving up on one's own views (positions, interests, needs or feelings), but on "positionality," i.e., the characterization of each of them in a manner that grants them the characteristics of "self". Sara Cobb sees empowerment in mediation as a process that enhances the destabilization of each party's narrative coherence, reducing the rigidity and the tendency to fixate in it, thus loosening the boundaries that self-perpetuation narratives exhibit. She writes, "[i]n mediation, narrative closure or coherence is problematic because it stabilizes the description of the problem in ways that delimit its transformation." See Sara Cobb, "Empowerment and Mediation: A Narrative Perspective," in *Negotiation Journal* 9.3 (1993): 251.

[33] Lewicki and Saunders, 117.

V. Conclusion

Buddhist psychology offers us a step-by-step micro-focus model of the process in which humans withdraw to what I describe as the illusory "private space."[34] I will not be able in this paper to go into details and present that model, but wish to suggest the idea of "positionality" as a mental attachment, clinging into firm, fixed and independent "things" that serve as a manifestation of the self, i.e., an entity situated behind the asserted positions which produces the separate, independent and well defined or definite "things" – a state of mind that needs to be transformed. We cannot suffice, if to continue with this line of thought, with a shift from positions to interests, but should aim – from a relational point of view – at transforming the mindset to a realization of impermanence, emptiness and dependent co-arising. The aim is to realize that "things" not only "change all the time" but are empty of a core that can be identified as the thing that changes. Put positively, "they" are dependently co-arising in a relational manner in the common dialogic space with whatever takes place and arises in that situation. The challenge is to see that this realization represents neither a state of repression of oneself (or 'accommodation,' as described by Thomas and Kilmann in their Conflict Mode grid),[35] nor a regressive psychological state. The "inner" me and "outer" world cannot be really distinguished, and in order to learn about myself – my needs, my interests, my positions, my fears and my sensations – awareness is needed to the manner in which "my" needs, interests and so on, relationally co-arise – right here, right now.

Walpola Rahula, in his book *What the Buddha Taught*, writes, "Two ideas are psychologically deep-rooted in man: self-protection and self-preservation.... For self-preservation, man has conceived the idea of an immortal Soul or Atman (…) which will live eternally. In his ignorance, weakness, fear, and desire, man

---

[34] Or the illusory of private language, if to draw a parallel to Wittgenstein's later philosophy.

[35] Kenneth W. Thomas and Ralph H. Kilmann, "Thomas-Kilmann Conflict Mode Instrument" (New York: Xicom, 1974), in http://www.kilmann.com/conflict.html.

needs these two things to console himself. Hence, he clings to them deeply and fanatically."[36]

Positions, I suggest, are manifestations of these deep-rooted conceived ideas. In the process of conflict escalation, with all the weaknesses, fears, and desires that it brings, one seeks self-protection and self-preservation, entrenching in firm, fixed and independent self and positions. Buddhism offers a 25 centuries long worldview and method of transformation of suffering and dis-ease embedded in the craving for these mental frames. In order to thoroughly examine its applicability to the mediation process and to further develop the practice of mediation, the added value of the Buddhist analysis to the understanding of conflict escalation and its possible transformation is needed. Analyzed in the manner described above, I suggest, conflict escalation can be seen as a process which the Buddhist methods of transformation – if adapted systematically to conflict settings – can help transform. Cultivating mindfulness and other qualities of mind as emphasized and practiced in the Buddhist tradition can help to develop integrative mindset and dialogic interaction, and to "change the game" of adversarial, competitive bargaining. [37] Stemming from the philosophical underpinnings offered by the Buddhist framework, that shift also incorporates a deep conviction that other models, emphasizing a shift from positional to integrative bargaining, do not necessarily include, as "the claim that opportunities for integrative bargaining make good behavior a simple matter of rational, pecuniary self-interest is not nearly as strong as is sometimes claimed... the case for good behavior cannot rest entirely on pecuniary self-interest".[38] In fact, delving into the

---

[36] Walpola Rahula, *What the Buddha Taught* (England: Oneworld Publication, 1959), 51.

[37] As suggested by Fisher and Ury throughout *Getting to Yes*, or by Ury in his succeeding book *Getting Past No: Negotiating Your Way from Confrontation to Cooperation* (New York: Bantam Books, 1993) where he writes, "Your greatest power is the power to change the game – from face-to-face confrontation to side-by side joint problem-solving" (171).

[38] Gerald Wetlaufer, "The Limits of Integrative Bargaining", in *Georgetown Law Journal* 85 (1996): 372.

philosophical tenets of the Buddhist worldview may add metaphysical rather than moral support: collaborating is not about behaving well, but about being human.

Bibliography

Bowling, Daniel and David Hoffman. "Bringing Peace into the Room: The Personal Qualities of the Mediator and their Impact on the Mediation." Daniel Bowling and David Hoffman, eds. *Bringing Peace into the Room: The Personal Qualities of the Mediator and their Impact on the Mediation.* San Francisco, California: Jossey Bass, 2003. 13-49.

Bowling, Daniel. "Mindfulness Meditation and Mediation: When the Transcendent Meets the Familiar." Daniel Bowling and David Hoffman, eds. *Bringing Peace into the Room: How the Personal Qualities of the Mediator Impact the Process of Conflict Resolution.* San Francisco, California: Jossey-Bass, 2003. 263-278.

Bush, Robert A. Baruch and Joseph P. Folger. *The Promise of Mediation: Responding to Conflict through Empowerment and Recognition.* San Francisco, California: Jossey-Bass, 1994.

Bush, Robert A. Baruch and Joseph P. Folger. *The Promise of Mediation: The Transformative Approach to Conflict.* New and Revised Edition. San Francisco, California: Jossey-Bass, 2005.

Cobb, Sara. "Empowerment and Mediation: A Narrative Perspective." In *Negotiation Journal* 9.3 (1993): 245-255.

Fisher, Roger and William Ury. 1981. *Getting to Yes: Negotiating Agreement without Giving In.* 1981. 2nd edition. New York: Penguin, 1991.

Freshman, Clark. "Identity, Beliefs, Emotion, and Negotiation Success." Michael Moffitt and Robert Bordone, eds. *The Handbook of Dispute Resolution.* San Francisco: Jossey-Bass and The Program on Negotiation at Harvard Law School, 2006. 99-117.

Glasl, Friedrich. "The Process of Conflict Escalation and Roles of Third Parties." G. B. J. Bomers and R. B. Peterson, eds. *Conflict Management and Industrial Relations.* The Hague: Kluwer Nijhoff Publishing, 1982. 119-140.

Greenhalgh, Leonard & Roy Lewicki. "New Directions in Teaching Negotiations from Walton and McKersei to the New Millennium." Thomas A. Kochan and David B. Lipsky, eds. *Negotiations and Change: From the Workplace to Society.* New York: Cornell University Press, 2003. 20-36.

Izutsu, Tohihiko. *Toward a Philosophy of Zen Buddhism.* Tehran: Imperial Iranian Academy of Philosophy, 1977.

Jordan, Thomas. "Glasl's Nine Stage Model of Conflict Escalation: A Summary." 2002. http://www.mediate.com/articles/jordan.cfm.

Jones, Tricia S. "A Dialectical Reframing of the Mediation Process." Folger, Joseph P. and Tricia S. Jones, eds. *New Directions in Mediation.* Thousand Oaks, CA: Sage, 1994. 26-47.

Kolb, Deborah and Judith William. *Everyday Negotiation: Navigating the Hidden Agendas in Bargaining.* San Francisco, California: Jossey Bass, 2003.

Lax, David A. and James K. Sebenius. *The Manager as Negotiator: Bargaining for Cooperation and Competitive Gain.* New York: Free Press, 1986.

Lewicki, Roy and David Saunders. *Negotiation.* Boston: McGraw Hill, 1985.

May, Rollo. *The Discovery of Being: Writings in Existential Psychology.* New York: Norton, 1983.

McNamee, Sheila and Kenneth J. Gergen. *Relational Responsibility: Resources for Sustainable Dialogue.* Thousand Oaks, California: Sage, 1999.

"Mindfulness in the Law and ADR." A symposium held at Harvard University. March 2002. http://www.pon.harvard.edu/news/2002/riskin_mindfulness.php3.

Mitchell, Stephen and Lewis Aaron, eds. *Relational Psychology: the Emergence of a Tradition.* Hillsdale, New Jersey: The Analytic Press, 1999.

Mnookin, Robert, Scott Peppet and Andrew Tulumello. *Beyond Winning: Negotiating to Create Value in Deals and Disputes.* Cambridge, Massachusetts: The Belknap Press of Harvard University Press, 2000.

Peppet, Scott. "Can Saints Negotiate? A Brief Introduction to the Problems of Perfect Ethics in Bargaining." *Harvard Negotiation Law Review* 7.1 (2002): 83-96.

Peppet, Scott. "Mindfulness in the Law and Alternative Dispute Resolution." Carrie Menkel-Meadow and Michael Wheeler, eds. *What's Fair.* San Francisco, California: Jossey-Bass, 2004. 440-453.

Riskin, Leonard L. "The Contemplative Lawyer: On the Potential Contribution of Mindfulness Meditation to Law Students, Lawyers, and their Clients." *Harvard Negotiation Law Review* 7 (2002):1-67.

Riskin, Leonard. "Mindfulness: Foundational Training for Dispute Resolution." *Journal of Legal Education* 54.1 (2004): 79-90.

Riskin, Leonard. "Knowing Yourself: Mindfulness." Andrea Kupfer Schneider and Christopher Honeyman, eds. *The Negotiator's Fieldbook.* ABA Section of Dispute Resolution, 2006. 239-250.

Rock, Evan M. "Mindfulness Meditation, The Cultivation of Awareness, Mediator Neutrality, and the Possibility of Justice." *Cardozo Journal of Conflict Resolution* 6.2 (2005): 347-365.

Shailor, Jonathan. *Empowerment in Dispute Mediation: A Critical Analysis of Communication.* Westport, Connecticut: Praeger, 1994.

Thomas, Kenneth W. and Ralph H. Kilmann. "Thomas-Kilmann Conflict Mode Instrument." Tuexedo, New York: Xicom, 1974. http://www.kilmann.com/conflict.

Ury, William. *Getting Past No: Negotiating Your Way from Confrontation to Cooperation.* New York: Bantam Books, 1993.

Winslade, John and Gerald Monk. *Narrative Mediation: A New Approach to Conflict Resolution.* San Francisco, California: Jossey Bass, 2000.

Wittgenstein, Ludwig. *Philosophical Investigations.* New York: Macmillian, 1945.

PARADIGMS OF BUDDHIST ETHICS: JUDGMENT AND CHARACTER IN THE MODERN WORLD

David Putney

Introduction

This paper will examine the following questions: (1) What should be the role of Buddhist ethics in the modem world? A discussion of this question will necessarily stimulate related questions such as: (2) What is the role of ethics in the larger Buddhist Path?; (3) Is a concern for ethics and karma, necessarily a self-oriented or egoistic enterprise?; (4) Does the attainment of Enlightenment or Realization transcend the concern for ethics?; (5) What is the role of Buddhist ethics for the still unenlightened practitioner?; (6) From the point of view of Western ethical thought, how might we understand Buddhist ethics as a kind of virtue ethics, a kind of utilitarian ethics, a deontological ethics, some combination of these, or is some other framework more appropriate?; (7) Is Buddhist ethics applicable only in regulated Buddhist communities or does it have a role for individual Buddhists in a larger urban society?; and (8) Does Buddhist ethics have anything to say to ethical discussion in general, or is it confined only to practicing Buddhists?

Although I will draw on Buddhist *Nikāya* and Mahāyāna traditional theory and practice, the focus of this paper will be not limited to the historical, but will also address the issue of how

Buddhist ethics might or should be understood and applied in the contemporary world.

The Role of Ethics and Karma in Buddhist Practice

In the most fundamental and traditional formulation of the path of Buddhist is the Eightfold Path, where, traditionally, three major categories are delineated: (1) Wisdom (*paññā; prajñā*), (2) Ethical Practice (*sīla*), and (3) Concentration (*samādhi*).[1] The Eightfold Path is mentioned so frequently in the Pāli *Nikāya* canon and associated with the Four Noble Truths as the foundation of Buddhist practice, and it is impossible to avoid the conclusion that in Early Buddhism,[2] Buddhist Ethics must be understood in the context of the Eightfold Path. In the context of Buddhist causality, or depended arising (*paṭicca-samuppāda*), the three elements of the path, Wisdom, Ethical Practice, and Concentration were inter-dependent. The practitioner could not have one without the others and could not develop one of the paths without developing the others.

Although Buddhism abounds with seemingly legalistic rules such as the extensive vinaya for monks and nuns, the "Five Precepts," the "Eight Precepts" and the "Ten Precepts," etc. for laypersons, the Eightfold Path stands out as fundamentally lacking a legalistic structure. The *sīlas* in the Eightfold Path are spoken of in terms of "Right" *(sammā)*. They are not a list of "shall nots". The traditional "definitions" of Right *sīla* include *examples* of both what should be aspired to and perfected and what should be

---

[1] "*Calavedalla Sutta*," in *Majjhima Nikāya* (1.301; see I. B. Horner, *The Middle Length Savings*, vol. 1 (London and Boston: Routledge & Kegan Paul, 1976), 363. It will be my practice throughout the remainder of this paper to use Pāli spellings for text composed in the Pāli language and representing the oldest texts of Early Buddhism and the Theravādin tradition and the Sanskrit forms for texts in the non-Theravādin and Mahāyāna traditions.

[2] I make no claims in this paper that what I call "Early Buddhism" is identical to "Original Buddhism." This topic is beyond the scope of this paper and, I believe, beyond the ability of scholastic research to decisively demonstrate. Early Buddhism in this paper refers to the Buddhism described in the Pāli *Nikāyas*.

avoided or eliminated, but are by no means exclusive lists of either positive or negative behaviors. The *sīlas,* in the context of the Eightfold Path, defy explicit injunctions or prescriptions about specific activities.

Let us consider first, the traditional Five Precepts for laymen include the vows to abstain from: (1) taking of life, (2) taking what is not given, (3) misconduct in sensual actions, (4) false speech, and (5) intoxication and indolence. [3] The Eight Precepts add abstentions from (6) untimely meals, (7) entertainments, cosmetics and personal ornaments, and (8) the use of high or exalted seats. These three were reserved for special *uposatha* days of intense practice, functioning as a form of short religious retreat. The 10 precepts were meant for especially dedicated laypersons on extended retreats or even for lifelong personal practice. These included an elaboration on the seventh precept, divided into two, a further emphasis on abstaining from "high seats" and finally the vow to abstain from accepting gold and silver. [4] These precepts, however, were never meant to be ends in themselves, but rather as a kind of guideline for self-realization. An analysis of the precepts reveals their justification in terms of the *effects* of the actions described on the practitioner and all other involved persons. [5] It is not the precepts which constitute the core of Buddhist ethics, but rather the *justification* for the precepts in terms of the Four Noble Truths and the Eightfold Path and later in the Bodhisattva Ideal and the *pāramitās* (Perfections) stressed by Mahāyāna Buddhism.

Since all of the items in the Eightfold Path begin with the term "Right" (*sammā*), and since three kinds of interrelated yet distinctive forms of "right" have been identified, it is critical to identify what is meant by "right" in each of the three groups.

Traditionally, the eight items have been arranged as follows: Wisdom includes (1) Right View / Right Understanding (*sammā-diṭṭhi*) and (2) Right Thought (Aims, Intention, Aspiration) (*sammā-saṅkappa*). Ethical Practice has traditionally included (3)

---

[3] H. Saddhatissa, *Buddhist Ethics: Essence of Buddhism* (New York: George Braziller, 1970), 87.

[4] *Ibid,* 87-113.

[5] *Ibid,* 87*ff* and 113*ff.*

Right Speech (*sammā-vācā*), (4) Right Action (*sammā-kammanta*), and (5) Right Livelihood (*sammā-jīva*). Right Concentration has included (6) Right Effort (*sammā-vāyāma*), (7) Right Mindfulness (*sammā-sati*), and (8) Right Concentration / Meditation (*sammā-samādhi*).[6]

I suggest that "Right" for Wisdom should be understood in terms of the Buddhist conception of Truth, "Seeing things as they are or have become" (*yathābhūtam*), without the distortions of prejudice, mental habits, likes and dislikes, etc., and that Right View is a synonym for *Bodhi,* literally meaning Enlightenment or Realization.

I suggest that "Right" in the context of Ethical Practice should be understood in terms of the Buddhist term *kusala,* which has been translated as "good," "skilled," "wholesome," and "healthy."[7] *Kusala* includes all of these English meanings, but is particularly close to the term "healthy" and "wholesome," in the context of the Buddha's common doctor and patient metaphors.

I would also include Right Thought (*sammā-saṅkappa*) in the ethical category, contrary to much Buddhist tradition, because it is described in the context of health rather than truth. The concept includes right aims or intentions, including thoughts of detachment, compassion and non-violence. Since the three traditional ethical categories of speech, action, and livelihood include bodily "action," I argue that *saṅkappa* in this context refers to mental action. As David Kalupahana has pointed out, the *Ambalaṭṭhikā-*

---

[6] M 1.301.

[7] See T. W. Rhys Davids and William Stede, *Pāli-English Dictionary* (PED) (Rpt., New Delhi: Munshirain Manoharlal Publishers, 1975) (It was first published in London by the Pāli Text Society), 223-224, where *kusala* is defined as "skillful", expert", "good", "right", and "meritorious". Kalupahana understands *kusala* as "wholesome" or "healthy". [See David J. Kalupahana, *Buddhist Philosophy* (Honolulu: University of Hawaii Press, 1976), 61*f*]. Taniguchi translates *kusala* as "skillful" in the context of that which leads to a healthy mind. [See Shoyo Taniguchi, "A Study of Biomedical Ethics from a Buddhist Perspective" (Masters Thesis, UC-Berkeley, CA, 1987), 60].

rāhulovāda-sutta of the *Majjhima-nikāya* defines "good" and "bad" in the following fashion, always referring to bodily, mental and verbal actions. He summarizes this *sutta* as follows:

> Whatever action, bodily, verbal, or *mental*, leads to suffering (by *bādha*, literally, illness) [8] for oneself, for others, or for both, that action is bad (*a-kusalam*). Whatever action, bodily, verbal or *mental*, does not lead to suffering for oneself, for others or for both, that action is good (*kusalam*). [9]

"Actions" of the mind may also be thought profitably of as "states of mind." Thus, H. Saddhatissa defines "Right Thought," saying:

> This means that our mind should be pure, free from lust (*rāga*), ill will (*vyāpāda*), cruelty (*vihiṃsā*) and the like. At the same time, we should be willing to relinquish anything that obstructs our onward march and unselfishly transfer merit obtained to all sentient beings. [10]

Thus, Right Thought should not be limited simply to intention, but also the states of the mind as manifested in its activities. Ethical practice would then include the four elements of Right Thought, Right Speech, Right Action, and Right Livelihood. All of these can be thought of in terms of health, and health can best be understood both as things to avoid, and things which need to be actively promoted, learned and developed.

In the Third Category, Concentration, the sixth path, Right Effort, is often described in reference to efforts to control mental action and unwholesome mental states. The traditional "examples" of Right Effort include efforts to (1) prevent evil and unwholesome (unhealthy) (*akusala*) states of mind from arising. (2) Get rid of

---

[8] PED: "evil, wrong, hurt", 492.

[9] M 1.414-418. See Kalupahana, *Buddhist Philosophy*, 62. See I. B. Horner, *Middle Length Savings*, vol. 2, 88-90 for full English translation.

[10] Saddhatissa, *Buddhist Ethics*, 70-71.

such evil and unwholesome states that have already arisen. (3) Produce to cause to arise good and wholesome states of mind not yet arisen. (4) Develop and bring to perfection the good and wholesome (*kusala*) states of mind already present.[11] The first two are negative and the last two are positive. Saddhatissa, however, generalizes these to apply to all of the ethical paths,[12] which could be summarized as: (1) prevent habits of unwholesome thought, speech, actions, and livelihood from arising; (2) get rid of such habits of unwholesome thought speech, actions, and livelihood that have already arisen; (3) produce or cause to arise good and wholesome habits of thought, speech, action and livelihood that have not yet arisen; and (4) develop and bring to perfection the good and wholesome habits of thought, speech and action that are already present.

The Third Category also includes two other important forms of concentration: Right Mindfulness and Right Meditation. These are the particularly Buddhist way in which to develop both Ethical Conduct and Wisdom. Right Mindfulness is the practice of carefully watching and observing (1) the nature and activities of the body (one's own and others'), (2) sensations or feelings, (3) states (or activities) of the mind, and (4) ideas, thoughts, conceptions and phenomena (*dhamma*).[13] Right Concentration or Meditation includes a large variety of ways to focus the mind, including the Four *Jhānas,* the Formless *Jhānas,* various visualizations, and so on.

Buddhism inherits the older Indian word, karma, but understands it in terms of the Buddhist theory of causality or Dependent Arising. Karma is often spoken of in the context of rebirth, but is not limited to rebirth. I argue that the major significance of karma to the practitioner at the present moment of practice is better understood in terms of the Buddhist causal understanding of the psychological processes of delusion and the mutual interrelationships of one person's actions with other

---

[11] See, for example, "Mahā-satipanna Suttanta," *Dīgha-nikāya* 2.312.

[12] Saddhatissa, 72.

[13] See the "Mahā-satipahana-Sutta" of the *Majjhima-nikāya* 1.70 *ff.*

individuals in his or her society and environment, past, present, and future.

It is true that karma can and has often been understood in terms of personal reward, especially in terms of a higher, or even a heavenly rebirth. It has been rightly argued that such a view is essentially egoistic. If one practices "right" ethical practices with a view to ensuring one's own personal reward or salvation, this is, according to the most basic of Buddhist teachings, a form of attachment, a clinging to the "self" and would tend to hinder the way to Realization. Also, understanding karma primarily in terms of rebirth can function as a form of bad faith in that people can tell themselves that such and such need not be done today, it can be done later, or that they do not have the strength to do such and such now, but will later, although this may be in a future life. Also, present and past ills and inequalities can be attributed to the karmic results of previous lives and these are to be patiently born as one's just fate.[14] Such a view can lead to an excuse for non-action, in a situation where action should be taken.

The goal of accumulating personal good karma conveniently ignores the fundamental Buddhist teachings of "No-Self" (Pāli, *anattan*; Skt., *anātman*) and Impermanence (Pāli, *anicca*; Skt., *anatya*), where it is meaningless to say that the person who commits an action is either identical or different to the person who "enjoys" its fruits.[15] An overemphasis on "self" in past or future lives leads to the very substantialization of self opposed by the Buddha.

Winston King has argued that, in the Theravāda tradition, a set of definite goals are "inherently tainted with samsaric impurities" because it is still "ineradicably poisoned with attachment to this

---

[14] Winston L. King, "Is There a Buddhist Ethic for the Modern World," in *Eastern Buddhist* 25.2 (Autumn 1992): 2-3.

[15] See, for example, the "Kassapa Sutta" (S. 2.18-22), where the Buddha tells Kassapa that it is meaningless to say that suffering is wrought by oneself, by others, by both, or neither.

present world, with desire for limited time-space 'goods'."[16] He has also argued that in both the Theravādin and Mahāyāna traditions:

> The portrayal of the individual self and its world as fundamentally transient and unreal has consistently led to a down grading of concrete efforts to "better" the present world order in the daunting knowledge that samsaric entities (self, world) can never be essentially or permanently improved. Thus, Buddhism has on the whole been socially passive.[17]

However, to conclude that there is no point in working for the betterment of self, community and society because any and all results are impermanent is to fall into the trap of using impermanence as an excuse for failing to apply all of the ethical paths, as well as Right Effort. If effort is to be applied only to those results which are necessarily permanent, we need make no effort in any direction. Every concrete situation faced in life is impermanent, and yet in the Buddhist worldview, this is merely an aspect of causality, or Dependent Arising (paṭicca-samuppāda). The whole point of the Buddha's teaching of Dependent Arising, as found in the Four Noble Truths, is to help the individual understand why situations have developed, what results are likely to arise from certain actions, and how to go about correcting problems that have arisen.

The function of Ethical Practice in the Eightfold path was never meant to support such an egocentric viewpoint. Although the ultimate goal of the Buddhist path cannot be formulated specifically in terms of personal and social goals, on the other hand, it cannot be realized without acting on provisional personal and

---

[16] Winston L. King, "Motivated Goodness and Unmotivated Perfection in Buddhist Ethics" (*Anglican Theological Review*, LXXI.2 (1989)) and quoted in his "Is There a Buddhist Ethic," 1.

[17] Winston L. King, "Buddhist Self-World Theory and Buddhist Ethics" (*Eastern Buddhist* 22.2 (Autumn 1989), paraphrased in King, "Is there a Buddhist Ethic," 1.

community goals, depending on the circumstances of place and time. Also, although it is true that realization of the Path of Buddhism cannot be accomplished without Concentration (*samādhi*) and Wisdom, it is also true that Concentration and Wisdom cannot be realized outside of moral action. Indeed, moral action is the manifestation of the realization of Wisdom.

Does Realization transcend the concern for ethics?

Some have argued that Enlightenment or Realization transcends concerns for dualistic thinking: making distinctions such as good or bad. They do not mean, of course, that the enlightened person, whether arahat, bodhisattva or Buddha, is free to commit evil. They mean rather that the enlightened one "naturally" does good, almost by definition. James Whitehill has labeled this the "transcendence trap." In his discussion of Robert Aitken's *The Mind of Clover: Essays in Zen Buddhist Ethics*,[18] he quotes Aitken's conclusion, [incorporating a Mahāyāna view of Emptiness (*śūnyatā*)]: "Thus, in the world, too, there is nothing to be called virtue."[19] According to Whitehill:

> The trap misleads them and us into portraying the perfected moral life as a non-rational expressiveness, something natural, spontaneous, non-linguistic, and uncalculating. This is a 'Taoist-like' view of virtue as 'natural, intuitive, skill / power' (Chn., *te*; Jpn., *toku*) .... This ethical conception results in the kind of ontological dismissal of morality and ethics....[20]

The "Transcendence Trap" ignores the basic reality that the vast majority of sentient beings are *not* enlightened. Buddhist ethics must speak to the practitioner. The Eightfold Path and the

---

[18] Robert Aitken, *The Mind of Clover: Essays in Zen Buddhist Ethics* (San Francisco: North Point Press, 1984).

[19] Aitken, 159.

[20] James Whitehill, "Buddhist Ethics in Western Context: the 'Virtues' Approach," in *Journal of Buddhist Ethics* 1 (1994): 2.

Six *pāramitās,* after all, are not for the Buddha, but for the individual lost in ignorance, selfishness, attachment, and craving.[21] Even in the context of the Buddha Nature and Original Enlightenment doctrines, the vast majority of sentient beings, although essentially Buddhas (depending on how we interpret this doctrine) *perceive themselves* as being unenlightened. It is clear, that in nearly all forms of Buddhism, the remedy to this problem is seen in the reliance of the "unenlightened" person on a good teacher. And yet, no one can make progress on the Buddha path by "leaning" on the teacher. In the terms of Early Buddhism, each person must be their own guide and lamp, looking to the three treasures of the Buddha, Dharma and Saṅgha for assistance. The situation is not fundamentally different in the Mahāyāna where direct assistance from Buddhas and Bodhisattvas is possible. The importance of effort, in some sense, on the part of the practitioner is indispensable, even in the context of "other help" in the Pure Land systems. It is impossible to discuss the full range of Buddhist doctrine on effort and faith in this paper, yet, I believe, the generic conclusion remains true for nearly all, if not all Buddhist schools: the individual practitioner must think, speak, act, and make his or her livelihood in the most wholesome manner possible, given the limits of the individuals personal attainment or understanding.

True enlightenment, King argues, is sometimes thought to bring the realization that, ultimately, the world does not need improvement, or that the real improvement must be wrought instead in one's own view of the world. He quotes the eighteenth-century Zen master Hakuin:

The Buddha Amitāyus is brilliantly manifest here and now.... All kinds of hell-suffering ... are nothing but

---

[21] Whitehill, "The role of Emptiness in Buddhist practice] is true and helpful only within the 'deconstructive' mood and context of '*anyata*' dialectics and metaphysics. When the net of 'no-self' is thrown to catch truth in an ethical context, villains laugh and demons thrive." (p. 6).

Amitāyus Buddha's whole body that shines with the color of burnished gold.[22]

Such an interpretation is a variation on the Buddha Nature Doctrine, which was so pervasive in Japanese Shingon, Tendai and Zen. But even here, the Japanese Zen tradition is not univocal. Dōgen (1200-1253), for example, in his later years, seeing the confusion caused by these doctrines emphasized the traditional understanding of Buddhist ethics in at least four of his last group of writings included in his 12 *Fascicle Shōbōgenzō: "Jinshin Inga"* (Deep Belief in Causality), *"Sanji-ga"* (Karmic Retribution in the Three Stages of Time), *"Ippyaku-hachi Homyo-mon"* (One Hundred and Eight Ways to Enlightenment), and *"Hachi Dainin-gaku"* (The Eight Aspects of Enlightenment).[23]

Furthermore, there is no evidence that Hakuin, or the Zen movement in general in Japan, concluded from the Buddha Nature and Original Enlightenment doctrines that effort in all aspects of the Path was unnecessary, a point which Dōgen stressed relentlessly throughout his career. An examination of the strict regimens in Zen training monasteries in Japan, either Sōtō or Rinzai, makes this point be self-evident.

Western Paradigms for Understanding Buddhist Ethics

In the context of a dialogue with Western ethical thought, how might Buddhist ethics be best explained as a kind of virtue ethics, a kind of utilitarian ethics, and a combination of these, or are none of these appropriate?

---

[22] "Sokkaroku-kaien-fusetsu," Sect. 30, in *Hakuin Osha Zensha*, vol. 2, pp. 403-404, trans. by Tokiwa Gishin. Quoted from King, "Is There a Buddhist Ethics," 5.

[23] For a "preliminary" translation, see Yaha Yokoi and Daizen Victoria, *Zen Master Dōgen: An Introduction with Selected Writings* (New York & Tokyo: Weatherhill, 1976).

Some, such as Whitehill, following Damien Keown, [24] have argued that Buddhist ethics is best understood as an "ethics of Virtue."[25] Whitehill defines this type of virtue ethics as an ethics of "wakened virtue," or more completely as "awakened, compassionate virtue-cultivation."[26] Ken Jones also argues for a form of virtue ethics.[27] According to Whitehill, Jones "affirms ... that Buddhist morality is a matter of character and cultivation, and that it *focuses on cultivating character rather than evaluating particular acts.*"[28] Jones argues that:

> The emphasis in Buddhist morality is therefore on the cultivation of a personality which cannot but be moral *rather than focusing upon the morality of particular choices* and acts. But, to repeat, it is not the will that can create such a personality, no more than I can pick myself up from the ground by my collar. It is to the training the will must be applied, *from which virtue will naturally flow.*[29]

Whitehill constructs his version of a Buddhist ethics of virtue on the Six *pāramitās:* "generosity or gift giving (*dāna*), morality or the five precepts (*śīla*) [30], patience and forgiveness (*kṣānti*), courage and vigor (*vīrya*), concentration [or meditation] (*dhyāna*), and wisdom (*prajñā*).[31] The importance of reason, for Whitehill, was emphasized in the Mahāyāna by the addition of four more

---

[24] Damien Keown, *The Nature of Buddhist Ethics* (New York: St. Martin's Press, 1992).

[25] Whitehill, 4.

[26] Whitehill, 5.

[27] Ken Jones, *The Social Face of Buddhism* (London: Wisdom Publications, 1989).

[28] Whitehill, 7 (my italics).

[29] Jones, 157 (my italics).

[30] H. Wolfgang Schumann translates *sila* as "self discipline". [H. Wolfgang Schumann, *Buddhism: An Outline of its Teachings and Schools*, translated by Georg Feuerstein (London: Rider and Company, 1973), 130.

[31] Whitehill, 9.

pāramitās: resolution, determination, strength, and skillful means.[32]

The notion of the Perfections, of course, is not unique to the Mahāyāna. As Saddhatissa notes, the Ten Perfections in the Theravādin Tradition include: (1) generosity (*dāna*), (2) morality (*sīla*), (3) renunciation (*kekkhamma*), (4) wisdom (*paññā*), (5) energy (*viriya*), (6) patience (*khanti*), (7) honesty and truthfulness (*sacca*), (8) determination (*adiṭṭhāna*), (9) loving kindness (*mettā*), and (10) equanimity (*upekkhā*).[33]

For Whitehill, the fuzziness of the Jones' phrase, "from which virtue will naturally flow," places Jones on the lip of the "transcendence trap" by arguing the Buddhist ethical behavior emerges from the "forms of moral discipline and repetition, *yet* different from them, somehow transcendent, natural and free." For Whitehill, the "schooling in the forms of virtue is a social, emotional, and cognitive process."[34] The role of the *pāramitās* is primarily positive: "to *foster a character* that increasingly encounters each moment, each space, each being, as a 'mother' enjoys and protects her only child."[35]

Whitehill further argues that:

A focus on character tends to obscure or override the role of general principles and rules as guides to decision-making and mutual regulation. ... I acknowledge that *act-evaluations* and rule-adjudications must be *secondary* instruments in Buddhist ethics, necessary as they may be in particular moments of particular communities.[36]

That the Buddhist ethical path includes a form of virtue ethics cannot be discounted. The considerable attention paid to

---

[32] Schumann lists these last four as "right method" (*upāya*), [the Bodhisattva] "vow" (*praṇidhāna*), "strength" (*bāla*), and "knowledge" (*jñāna*). (p. 132).

[33] Saddhatissa, *Buddhist Ethics*, 72. See DhA 1.84.

[34] Whitehill, 7 (my italics).

[35] Whitehill, 9.

[36] Whitehill, 15-16.

psychology in the *Nikāyas, Abhidhamma / Abhidharma* and *Yogācāra* systems attests to this. The Buddhist tradition is certainly in agreement with Aristotle's assertion that:

> Those who have just begun to learn can string together words, but do not yet know; for it *has to become part of themselves,* and that takes time; so that we must suppose that the use of language by men in an unrestrained state [*akṛta*] means no more than its utterance by actors on the stage. [37]

In the Buddhist tradition, a person does evil both out of ignorance and because of deeply ingrained karmic habits (*saṅkhārās / saṃskāras*), defilements (*kleśa / kleta*) and cancer like "outflows" or "cankers" (*āśravas / āsravas).* And through the purification of these character habits, meditative techniques and the realization of Wisdom, the moral becomes possible. [38] Whether or not this realization is attained through "self help" or through the help of Amida Buddha, enlightenment is linked to moral character.

I argue, however, that "act-evaluation" is just as much an integral component of Buddhist ethics as is the development of character. The two go hand in hand, and Buddhist ethics are impoverished when either of them is undervalued. It is clear that Buddhist ethics can also be understood as, at least, including a special form of utilitarian ethics, where the welfare of oneself and others, in terms of health and happiness, forms the basis of *ethical judgments.*

In the *"Ambalaṭṭhikā-Rāhulovāda-sutta"* of the *Majjhima-nikāya,* we read:

---

[37] *Nicomachaen Ethics,* 7.3: 1147a20-24; Translated from Ross and Urmson, *Collected Works of Aristotle,* edited by Jonathan Barnes, vol. 2 (Princeton: Princeton University Press, 1984), 1811.

[38] For a detailed discussion of the psychology of habit in Buddhism, see my dissertation, "The Nature and Practice of Freedom: A Dialogue on Freedom and Determinism in Buddhist and Western Philosophy," Ch. 2, and for a comparative discussion of Plato and Aristotle and Buddhism on the relationship between knowledge or wisdom, habit and freedom, see Ch. 3.

Even so, Rāhula, a deed is to be done with the body (only)
after repeated reflection; a deed is to be done with speech ...
with the mind (only) after repeated reflection. [39]

I have already noted that Kalupahana has formulated such a
general utilitarian principle:

Whatever action, bodily, verbal, or mental, leads to
suffering for oneself, for others, or for both, that action is
bad (*a-kusalam*). Whatever action, bodily, verbal or mental,
does not lead to suffering for oneself, for others or for both,
that action is good (*kusalam*). [40]

Shoyo Taniguchi has stated:

Mental, physical, or verbal actions that are harmful to
oneself, to others, or to both are strongly discouraged in
Buddhism. The Buddha says it is because all beings fear
pain, harm, suffering, and hurt and seek comfort and
fearlessness. [41]

She quotes the *Saṃyutta-nikāya*:

'A state that is not pleasant or delightful to me, it must be
so to him too. Then how could I inflict that upon him?' As
a result of such reflection, he himself abstains from taking
the life of creatures and he encourages others so to abstain,
and speaks in praise of so abstaining. [Repeat for stealing,
adultery, lying, etc.][42]

---

[39] [M 1.415]. I. B. Horner, trans., *Middle Length Sayings*, vol. 2, 88-89.
[40] M 1.414–418. Kalupahana, *Buddhist Philosophy*, 62.
[41] Taniguchi, 52.
[42] [S.5.353-354]. Trans. from F.L. Woodward, vol. 5, *The Book of the
Kindred Sayings* (1930; Rpt., London and Boston: Routledge & Kegan Paul,
1979), 308*f.*

Gunapala Dharmasiri stated:

In Buddhist ethics, the reasoning of morality is deduced to "oneself".... [The Buddha's] appeal to us is to realize that all other beings too think exactly in the way one thinks about oneself.[43]

Dharmasiri goes so far as to identify Buddhist ethics with "act utilitarianism," but is careful to point out that:

It was an ideal utilitarianism rather than a hedonistic because the ultimate end of ethical endeavor went beyond the pleasure-pain principle.[44]

This is because the ultimate goal is *Nibbāna* in Early Buddhism and Buddhahood in the Mahāyāna. In the *Dīgha-nikāya*, we read about *Nibbāna* that:

There will be pleasure (*pāmujjam*), joy (*pati*), composure (*passaddhi*), mindfulness (*sati*), self-possession (*sampajānam*), and happy living (*sukho ca vihāro*).[45]

Although this is an Early Buddhist description of *Nibbāna* as attained in life, this description is also applicable to the Pure Land. And, since the goal of all Buddhas is to free all beings from

---

[43] Gunapala Dharmasiri, *Fundamentals of Buddhist Ethics* (Antioch, Calif.: Golden Leaves Publishing Company, 1989), 27.

[44] Gunapala Dharmasiri, *A Buddhist Critique of the Christian Concept of God* (Colombo: Lake House Investments, 1974). Quoted by Pahalawattage Don Premasiri, "Moral Evaluation in Early Buddhism: From the Perspective of Western Analysis" (Ph.D. Dissertation, University of Hawaii, 1980), 172-173. In his dissertation, Premasiri gives an extended discussion of the relationship between Buddhist Ethics and the utilitarianism of Bentham and Mill. Especially see Chapter 6, "Early Buddhism and Utilitarian Ethics."

[45] D. 1.196, translated by Premasiri, *Ibid,* 179. Also see T. W. Rhys Davids, *Dialogues of the Buddha*, pt. 1 (Pāli Text Society), 261.

suffering, the utilitarian aspect of Buddhist ethics is basic to the Buddhist tradition.

Buddhist ethics is realized through empathy[46] and through judgment. To say, however, that these judgments or incomplete since they are based more or less on ignorance, as opposed to Wisdom, is another aspect of the "transcendence trap," since we cannot avoid making ethical decisions in our daily lives, regardless of our level of attainment. I argue that one of the main functions of the Buddhist teaching of causality is to form a framework for such decisions. What will happen if I think this way, speak this way, act this way, or make my living in this way? Our limited wisdom and perspective will necessarily result in numerous errors. However, it is precisely these errors that lead to an understanding of consequences, the result of experience.

Taniguchi points out:

Since each human nature, character, habit or behaviour is different according to each one's given surroundings, abilities, education and maturity, *sīla* or good conduct differs accordingly to one's development of character and nature.[47]

It is through mindfulness of our experience[48] that we come to see the dependently arisen nature of the fruits of action, leading, as Dharmasiri argues, to judgments based on facts (*yathābhūtam*).[49] This is Right View. It is precisely through a combination of the development of healthy (*kusala*) habits of mind and body (*saṅkhārā*s), along with the Perfections (*pāramitā*s) and the application of the Buddhist utilitarian principle to concrete situations that the true path of ethics is realized.

---

[46] Dharmasiri, 27.

[47] Taniguchi, 53.

[48] See, for example, I. B. Horner, *The Basic Position of Sīla* (Colombo: The Bauddha Sahitya Sabha, 1950), 18.

[49] Dharmasiri, 33.

Buddhist Communities and Mass Society

Is Buddhist ethics applicable only in regulated Buddhist communities, or does it have a role for individual Buddhists in a larger urban society? As a starting point for this discussion, it is important to remember that the Buddha taught "for the good of the many, for the happiness of the many, out of compassion for the world."[50]

Some have advocated that Buddhist ethics is best developed in relatively small Buddhist societies, where a teacher and other members help to reinforce all aspects of Buddhist practice, and that "tend to lack a viable social ethic in modem terms, that is a policy-generating set of principles that can be institutionalized on a mass scale, while protecting individual right-claims with coercive means."[51] This is because "the self is fundamentally incomplete, evolving, and inter-penetratingly co-dependent with others." This training must be carried on in the context of a community of a teacher and practitioners. "The Buddhist believes her moral efforts flow necessarily into the community on many levels, materially, verbally, and mentally, in a subtle, looping reciprocity."[52]

That such communities are vital to Buddhism is clear, but where does this leave such communities in the larger social community of diverse beliefs? What do the Buddhist practitioners or small group of practitioners do?[53] Do initiates or more advanced students live in such communities for a variety of reasons? Does Buddhism have nothing to say to the lone individual or the small group of practitioners, since "ethical strategies focusing on rational rules and *judgments of* particular outward acts are the essential

---

[50] Walpola Rahula, *What the Buddha Taught*, 2nd ed. (New York: Grove Press, 1974), 46.

[51] Whitehill, 12.

[52] Whitehill, 11.

[53] Whitehill argues that communities of four to six "can hardly challenge and support the full range of self-cultivating practices necessary to awakened virtue." He also says that communities of more than 200 active members are too large, since such organizations are "too complex and too absorbed in the entropic tasks of organization maintenance of buildings, mortgages, and so on." [Whitehill, 16].

feature of groups so large that they constitute a society of strangers?"[54] Are act-*evaluations* and rule-adjudications limited only to the status of "secondary instruments in Buddhist ethics, necessary as they may be in particular moments of *particular communities.*"[55] I think not.

It is only a combination of virtue ethics and situational ethical judgments in the context of efforts in all aspects of the Eightfold Path, or the Mahāyāna *Pāramitās* can be practiced, with at least some success, ideally with periodic contact with a teacher and/or Buddhist community. If the lay practitioner is not in the best of possible worlds, the ideal sized and led Buddhist community, this is no excuse for not doing his or her best to cultivate both character and judgment. I am not attempting, in any sense, to devalue the role of the teacher and Buddhist communities, but am stressing that a discussion of Buddhist practice and especially moral practice cannot be *limited* to these communities.

Buddhist Ethics and Societal Ethics

Does Buddhist ethics have anything to say to ethical discussion in general, or need it be confined only to practicing Buddhists?

I argue that Buddhism can engage in a dialogue with Western Ethicists by concentrating on commonalities between Buddhism and the Western tradition in the areas of (1) virtue ethics, (2) situational ethics, and (3) ethical judgments according to the maxim. "Act such that your thoughts, speech, actions and livelihood are of benefit and bring happiness to oneself as well as others and do not act such that your thoughts, speech, actions and livelihood cause harm and suffering to yourself as well as others." A dialogue on virtue ethics is possible because many, though not all, of the Buddhist virtues are held in common with other world religious and ethical traditions. A general interest in developing virtue in the process of educating children, for example, is a good starting point. Buddhism, I believe, has a great deal to say about

---

[54] Whitehill, 16 (my italics).

[55] *Ibid.* (my italics).

ethical judgments and can engage in dialogue with Western ethicists in utilitarian ethical discourse, virtue ethical discourse, and even in a form of Kantian deontological ethics of maxims. Such an engagement can help the Buddhist community to integrate itself into the larger, impersonal society of diversity and help the individual Buddhist develop a working relationship with that society.

THE TEACHINGS OF THE BUDDHA AND JESUS AS RESOURCES FOR A DOCTRINE OF PEACE

J. Bruce Long

Not by hatred is hatred quelled
but only by acts of love.
This is the eternal law.

(Dhp. 5)

But I say to you, Love your enemies and
pray for those who persecute you, so that you
may become children of your Father in heaven....

(Matt. 5.44)

In his introduction to the excellent collection of essays on Comparative Philosophy, *Interpreting Across Boundaries*,[1] Gerald Larson discusses a number of pitfalls in the use of the comparative method, *per se*, each of which, if committed, will ineluctably skew, in some way of another, one's view of the topic under consideration. Two of the four perspectival biases appear more frequently than the other two. First is the temptation to elevate one's own perspective or set of beliefs over that of the 'other,' such that the truth-value of one's own perspective is inflated and

---

[1] See Eliot Deutsche and Gerald Larson, eds., *Interpreting Across Boundaries: New Essays in Comparative Philosophy* (Delhi: Motilal Banarsidass, 1988), 3-18.

that of the 'other' is undervalued. Second is the exact antithesis of
this fault, namely, the tendency to diminish or denigrate one's own
personal or cultural ethos and *idealize* that of the 'other,' as being
more special or superior to one's own cultural system.

In this essay, we will attempt to avoid both of these pitfalls, in
hopes of being in a position to travel, not a *neutral* track (for that is
humanly impossible) but a kind of middle-of-the-road pathway,
cutting between 'pure objectivity' and 'pure subjectivity.' The aim
of this approach is to maximize the chance of giving the ethics of
the Buddha and the ethics of Jesus as fair and balanced a hearing,
as possible, in an attempt to delineate each of them as potential
resources for an Ethics of Peace.

In order to make even this relatively circumscribed subject
manageable, we have chosen to consult two sacred texts, one from
each of the two traditions, as exemplary statements of the central
core of the respective body of teachings on the Ethics of Peace.
The relative brevity and conciseness of each of the two texts,
combined with the wealth of details concerning core ethical
principles contained in each, makes these texts a reasonable basis
for this exploration.

First to be considered is the Buddha's Ethics of Peace as
embodied principally in one of the most eloquent and highly
revered scriptures in the whole of Buddhism, namely, the *Mettā
Sutta*, also, thought to be one of the earliest compendia of the
Buddha's discourses.[2]

Subsequently, we will explore Jesus' Ethics of Peace as
articulated in the earliest known record of what are believed to
have been Jesus' exact words (or as close to those exact words as
we are ever likely to come), a document known simply as "Q" or
more poetically, "The Sayings of Q." For now, it suffices to say

---

[2] *Sutta Nipāta* (I. 8), English translation, K.R. Norman, *Groups of
Discourses*, 2nd ed. (Oxford: Pāli Text Society, 2001). See also, *The Rhinoceros
Horn and Other Early Buddhist Poems*, trans. K.R. Norman (Oxford: Pāli Text
Society, 1996). There is also a large body of material on this *sutta* composed by
various contemporary Pāli scholar-monks, notably, Thanissaro Bhikkhu,
Piyadassi Thera and Ñāṇamoli Thera accessible at the online site,
http://www.accesstoinsight.org.

that "Q" was composed entirely of selected "sayings of Jesus," no stories, no didactic material, no biographical information – just sayings. More will be said about this document, subsequently.[3]

In this comparative exploration of the teachings of the Buddha and Jesus as *models of* and *resources for* the development of an Ethics of Peace, it will be assumed that an Ethics of Peace does not have an existence independently of a general system of ethics in either case but that it is, in every case, inextricably intertwined with the constitutive strands of their more general ethics.

The Buddha's Ethics of Peace

The Buddha's social ethics is based on a set of principles meant to develop and support a society pervaded by peace and amity. In the area of interpersonal relations (or etiquette and ethics), the Buddha promoted a morality of great gentility, gentleness and humaneness, based more on comity and fellowship than on strict moral obligation. The four cardinal virtues – friendliness (*mettā*), compassion (*karuṇā*), joy (*muditā*) and equanimity (*upekkhā*) form the basic quaternity of his comprehensive ethical system. Unlike the ethical systems of all of the other Great Religions (except for the contemporaneous Jainism), the Buddha's concern for the protection of life forms extended well beyond the bounds of the human community, to include "all sentient beings," both great and small, visible and invisible.

The *Jātaka*s, stories concerning the previous lives of the Buddha, urge the adoption of friendly and even compassionate relations between human beings and all the other sentient beings in

---

[3] A very small core body of scholarly literature in English on the subject of "Q" might include the following: Burton Mack, *The Lost Gospel: The Book of Q and Christian Origins* (San Francisco: Harper, 1993); James M. Robinson, Paul Hoffmann, and John S. Kloppenborg, eds., *The Critical Edition of Q: Synopsis including the Gospels of Matthew and Luke, Mark and Thomas with English, German and French Translations of Q and Thomas* (Minneapolis: Fortress, 2000) and of greatest value as a recreation of Jesus' 'theology' from this same text, James M. Robinson's *Jesus: According to the Earliest Witness* (Minneapolis: Fortress Press, 2007).

the universe, based on such cardinal virtues as living for others, devotion to family, brotherhood, honesty, non-injury, and the like. And while the primary focus of the Buddha's ethical instructions was on the monastic community, he provided a broad and varied array of ethics principles, by means of the adherence to which the lay person might hope to achieve a better rebirth in the future, in a celestial realm or Pure Land and ultimately, achieve complete liberation.

Like Jesus (Matt. 6. 19-21), the Buddha counseled his followers to avoid burying a treasure in a deep pit, in hopes that it might come in handy in the eventuality of some personal misfortune. He wisely observes that such a buried treasure may not be of any benefit at all to its owner, "for he may forget where he has hidden it, or goblins may steal it, or his enemies or even his kinsmen may take it when he is careless." (Dhp., 119-120) The Buddha continues that by means of "charity, goodness, restraint, and self-control," a person can store-up a treasure that will be beneficial regardless of the physical circumstance, "a treasure which cannot be given to another person or group and which robbers cannot steal." If such a wise man follows this course, "this treasure will never forsake him."[4]

The key word that synthesizes the diversity of terms used at various points in the *Nikāya*s is the word, "non-attachment." The relevance of this word to the creation of an Ethics of Peace is patently obvious: if a person, a family, a community, or an entire people were to live by this principle of mental, moral and spiritual release, surely it would follow that open warfare would never be a viable option, and every conscientious effort would be made to resort, at most, to a nonviolent form of self-defense or even less than that, a calm and undisturbed silence. For under this ethical rubric, neither the collection, the preservation nor the transmission

---

[4] *Khuddaka Patha* 8. Note that in this passage the statement that "the treasure cannot be given to others" stands in distinction from the belief in later Mahāyāna that merits accruing from good deeds may be transferred to others as a gift, the most exemplary model of which is the compassionate actions of the bodhisattva, whose sole *raison d'etre* is the assistance to all sentient beings in finding their way to emancipation or full Buddhahood.

of any sort of material values or commodities should serve as a motivating force for any kind of bucolic action, of either mind or body. Positively stated, each individual, family, society or nation state would seek under all circumstances to maximize the benefits of 'the other,' regardless of how the 'other' is defined. There would be no self-aggrandizing action in any form; only altruistic and benevolent action on behalf of the welfare of 'the other' and in promotion of the general commonweal.

The *Mettā Sutta* as the Basis for the Buddha's Ethics of Peace

The *Mettā Sutta*, located in the *Sutta Nipāta* (I. 8), is a seminal text in the presentation of the Buddha's Ethics of Peace.

The genius of this text is, in part, its marriage of poetic conciseness and comprehensive inclusion of the prominent ethical principles of the Buddha's teachings. For this reason, this *Sutta* stands as a paradigmatic representation of many of the key principles of the Buddha's ethics.

The first two verses are an extremely concise presentation of the Buddha's concept of the perfected person or a person who is skilled in accomplishing his goals or objectives. In addition, these verses provide a pre-scription for a dedicated Buddhist practitioner to achieve the ultimate goal, namely, "that state of peace" (*taṁ santaṁ padam*) or *Nibbāna*. In a word, they clearly establish the fact that a combination of single-minded dedication and persistent commitment are indispensable to the effective practice of the Dharma.

The first ten lines of the poem enumerate a total of fifteen virtues possessed by the ideal person: skilled in aims, desirous of attaining the state of peace, capable, upright and straightforward, easy to instruct, gentle, of humble nature, contented and easy to support, with few duties, living lightly, with peaceful faculties, modest and not greedy for supporters, not attached to views (of any kind), virtuous and consummate in vision, having subdued the desire for sensual pleasures. All virtues could be viewed as marks of the Way of Peace.

This list is, in effect, a working menu of the virtues that constitute the Buddha's overall ethics (*sīla*), as well as his Ethics of Peace. The first quality in the list is a term meaning, capable or skillful in achieving one's aims (*sakko*). This strong goal orientation should give rise to honesty and forthrightness (*ujū ca sūjū ca*) in one's practice. Then come obedience, gentleness, and humility (*anatimāni*), the last term emphasizing the Buddha's exhortation to pursue a life that is not excessively proud or arrogant.

Following this, there is a list of attributes that seem more intended for monastics than for laity, a fact that would seem to confirm that this *sutta*, as it now stands, is the result of the co-mingling of at least three pieces of material that were once distinct and independence sources. The list includes contentment, easy to support, of few duties and simple lifestyle; restrained senses, masterful, modest and unattached to family. Specifically the text described such people as *subhara* and *sallahuka-vutti*, literally easy to support and simple in livelihood, or characterized by a simplicity of dress, food and shelter, the bulwark of the monk's life and *kulesu ananu-giddha,* meaning separation from lay-life and exercising self-restraint among lay people.

Then follows a succinct summary of the ethical profile of the ideal human being from the Buddhist perspective: "May he not perform the slightest wrong for which the liberated being (*arahant*) might rebuke him." Here the text serves up another succinct summation of the nature of ideal ethical judgment: *pare upavadeyyum* (an action for which a person would rebuke another), indicating that a less than ideal person will be more likely to detect the shortcomings of others than of his own. This point, of course, coincides precisely with the comparable words of Jesus, urging his followers to refrain from judging others, in recognition of the fact that sooner or later, that person will be judged by others by the same ethical criteria by which he has judged others. The

judgmental person is one who sees "the speck in the neighbor's eye," but fails to see "the log in their own eye."[5]

In a most dramatic and highly poetical manner, the *sutta* presents a wish for the well-being of all creatures, great and small: "May all beings be happy and well and may they have joyous minds," a thought that will be foremost in the mind of the ideal person at all times. Thus, without verbal elaboration, the text evokes a person of universal goodwill and loving kindness, whose every thought is pervaded by feelings of friendship, not only for his closest acquaintances but for all creatures in the universe, known and unknown.

The next two stanzas provide a brief inventory of the various genre of creatures to which one should always relate and interact with an attitude of friendliness and loving kindness: (1) feeble or strong, (2) of long, short and medium stature, (3) small and large, (4) visible and invisible, and (5) those who are born and those who are yet to be born. This classification of different types of creatures to whom perpetual good will should be extended, is the most all-encompassing and, indeed, universalistic of any ethical profile known to this writer. Furthermore, the list should be understood to be much more than a frozen taxonomy or a creaturely typology, that is formulated as an intellectual exercise. Rather, it should be seen as a working program in ethical self-development.

The practice of *mettā* must be developed in stages, beginning with the bestowal of *mettā* upon oneself. For the Buddha recognized (as Jesus did in his injunction "you should love your neighbors *as you love yourself*"), that without first loving oneself, a person will be mentally and emotionally incapable of loving others. From the securing of love of oneself, one should, then, practice the bestowal of *mettā* upon people who are closest to the giver and the most well-liked and only then should they extend *mettā* to friendly strangers and finally, to people who have done the person wrong in some way or another and, hence, people that that person may

---

[5] Matthew 7.1-5. In modern psychotherapeutic terminology, the first stance is the product of *maximizing* when judging the faults of others, and *minimizing* when reflecting on one's own faults. This tendency is both an "imbalanced" and an "inaccurate" picture of both one's own and others, virtues and vices.

distrust or dislike. From this sequence of steps, it becomes clear that the practice of *mettā* should be carried out within an enormous geographical stage (i.e., the universe) and with a largesse of emotional empathy for every conscious being.

The next four verses delineate the model for developing and maturing these thoughts of loving kindness. The text is composed of a series of what might be described as "prayerful injunctions": may you avoid deceiving or hating anyone, anywhere, showing neither anger nor ill-will nor wishing harm in any form to anyone. Like a mother who is prepared to risk her own life in order to protect her only child from harm, one should "cultivate boundless love toward all beings."

And then, picking up on the intentionality of the first principle in the Eightfold Path, the text states that one should maintain a state of increasingly purified and alert mindfulness at all times and thereby, develop increasingly pure and clear awareness of one's life-situation, and in the course of things develop Right Views. In addition, one should be always virtuous and possessed of insight into the nature and moral and spiritual directionality of each moment of experience. By this means, "that person will never again be subject to rebirth," declares the *sutta* triumphantly.

To deceive or betray someone else in order to enhance one's own position *vis-à-vis* a desired outcome, is, obviously, to act out of a self-centered attitude of greed and blind self-aggrandizement and to cast an insult on another is to see oneself in a superior light. It is obvious from this context that this injunction covers both external actions of deprecation and debasement of others and internal attitudes of arrogance and superiority toward others. Such attitudes of exaggerated self-regard are likely to give rise to actual desires that other persons against whom one has ill-feelings, actually experience some kind of misfortune.

The final couplet decisively summarizes the viewpoint of the entire *sutta*, as well as, a major portion of the Buddha's teachings contained in the Four Noble Truths and the Eightfold Path. While the Buddha clearly regarded the extension of *mettā* throughout the length and breadth of the universe and to all of its creatures, as crucial to the creation and maintenance of a Culture of Peace, he,

also, made it clear that this practice was not sufficient to gain the ultimate goal, *Nibbāna*. He posits four additional preconditions to the achievement of that goal which, in this context, he states but does not elaborate: namely, (1) to put away all false views and thereby, master the first step in the Eightfold Path, the achievement of "Right Views" (*sammā diṭṭhi*); (2) to become virtuous (*sīlavā*), which includes Right Speech (*sammā vācā*), Right Action (*sammā kammanta*) and Right Livelihood (*sammā ājīva*); (3) to acquire insight (*dassanena sampanna*), Right Knowledge or Right Thought (*sammā saṅkappa*); and (4) to discard all forms of sensual desire (*kāmesu gedham*), which leads to the eradication of suffering by means of the suppression of desire (*taṇhā, tṛṣṇā*).

It is evident from the foregoing that the Buddha's teachings, as well as, his life and actions, are not only instructions *about* an Ethics of Peace, expressive of a mutual loving regard of human beings for each other, but an *existential embodiment of* those ethical principles. At no point does he allow the resorting to aggressive or violent behavior against another human being (or any other creature), either to acquire some desired commodity or value or to protect something already owned. This entire ethics might be epitomized in the paradigmatic declaration: "Not by hatred is hatred quelled but only by acts of love. This is the eternal law."[6]

Jesus' Ethics as Represented in the Pre-biblical "Sayings of Q"

It has long since been proven, by use of the analytical tools of modern biblical criticism, initially developed in Germany in the 1880's, that "the Bible did not fall from heaven like a stone," that is, all at once and in one piece. Both the Old and New Testaments developed over centuries and through the agency of numerous writers and editors /redactors. Like the Pāli Sūttas, the four gospels (Matthew, Mark, Luke and John) were initially transmitted orally and only later committed to writing. It is further known, beyond any reasonable doubt, that the four apostles, to whom each of the four gospels (Matthew, Mark, Luke and John) has been attributed,

---

[6] Dhp. 5.

were not the actual authors of the four texts. It is not known who authored these texts and those facts may never be conclusively determined.

In 1838, a biblical scholar in Leipzig, Germany, Christian Hermann Weisse sensed the presence of a collection of the "sayings of Jesus" embedded, almost incognito, in the gospels of Matthew and Luke, as we now have them. After its discovery and reconstruction as a "ghost text," it came commonly to be referred to simply as "the source," or in German, *Quelle*, abbreviated as "Q."[7]

Since the existence of Q precedes the actual composition of Matthew and Luke, and is the source from which the writers of the two gospels drew the "sayings of Jesus" around which they wove their own narratives of Jesus' life and teachings, this text, in all probability, is our most reliable source for the actual words of Jesus in the entire New Testament canon.

"Q" is not a currently existent text. It is a scholarly reconstruction of a text composed entirely of the "sayings of Jesus," a collection of precious aphorisms that is believed to have been collected around 50 CE, a mere seventeen years after Jesus' death. Two of the four Gospel writers (Matthew and Luke) drew directly from Q in composing their own accounts of the life and teachings of Jesus. Once the gospels came into existence and became authoritatively established within the Christian community, the document "Q" was apparently superseded and ultimately disappeared.

What, then, are the basic principles and requirements of Jesus' Ethics of Peace according to this pre-biblical document, the "Sayings of Q?"

Jesus' first recorded action during his adult years was his leaving his family home in Nazareth to join the apocalyptic movement of John the Baptist, and undergoing John's initiation of the rite of baptism in the Jordan River. This water-rite must have

---

[7] Consult James M. Robinson, *Jesus: According to the Earliest Witness* (Minneapolis: Fortress Press, 2007) for extensive information concerning the personage of Jesus in the "Sayings of Q."

symbolized the discarding one's old worldly identity and the emergence of a new, godly person, prepared to meet the coming of the Kingdom of God within the near future. To interpret, properly, Jesus' ethical teachings, it is necessary to see them within the context of his apocalyptic vision, namely, that the Day of Redemption, the Final Judgment and the End of the World, were all believed to be near-at-hand.

After his baptism by John, Jesus broke away from John's apocalyptic movement and began to preach a message of his own, based on a similar understanding that his mission in the world was to usher in a new era of the Kingdom of Righteousness (*basileia dikaiosuna*) or the Kingdom of God (*basileia tou theou*) to be established, not on power and might but on love and forgiveness. According to a leading biblical scholar, "Jesus did not call for any demonstration of repentance or baptism. For him, God's grace was certain without rites. . . . At the centre of Jesus' message stood the Jewish belief in God: for Jesus, God was a tremendous ethical energy which could soon change the world to bring deliverance to the poor, the weak and the sick."[8]

The core ingredients of Jesus' ethics as found in Q are as follows: (1) A love (Grk., *agape*) not only for one's family, friends and neighbors but for one's enemies as well, contrary to the Old Testament, where "unbelievers" are defined as God's enemies, and hence, to be avoided except, perhaps, to bring them into the company of the faithful, and the corollary to that, (2) the Golden Rule, "do unto others as you would have them do unto you,"[9] (3) a lack of critical judgment towards other people, regardless of who they might be or the circumstances under which one may find oneself dealing with them, (4) a life, devoid of material possessions, and without toil for daily bread, but rather a life dedicated to the service of the Kingdom of God and a looking to God for all of one's daily needs, (5) a life committed to denying self and serving others, regardless of who they might be, and (6) a

---

[8] Gerd Theissen & Annette Merz, *The Historical Jesus: A Comprehensive Guide* (Minneapolis: Fortress Press, 1996), 570.

[9] Cf. Luke 6. 31.

life lived in the awareness that the 'appointed time' (*kairos)*, the day of salvation, the end of the world order and the final judgment is near-at-hand.

Using the metaphor of the tree, Jesus compared good trees that produce healthy fruit and bad trees that produce inedible fruit, with good and evil human beings. His intention in telling this story was to say, "Let me tell you what being a good person really means – I call on you to be just that."[10] As this small story illustrates, Jesus sought to identify the basic *intentions, attitudes* and *motivations* of people, rather than focus on their attention to social proprieties, ritualistic practices or publicly-sanctioned ethical norms. He spoke to people personally to address the kind of person he wanted them to be. He challenged them to adopt a certain way of life as a result of their moment-to-moment decisions and choices. He summoned them to a certain way of life, articulated in his teachings, for he spoke to them as a teacher (Rabbi) or better, a preacher or evangel, rather than a theologian who would, customarily, deal with *ideas* rather than moral and spiritual *injunctions*[11] and life changing commitments.

In Jesus' view, "looking out for number one," or striving for "self-preservation," either for individuals or institutions, is not an acceptable life pathway to follow. Rather, one should not be concerned about one's own life, at all. Just think of the ravens (Q 12. 22-31), he counseled – they do not work in fields or store their harvest in barns, as do human beings. Yet God provides for their nourishment. Like the lilies of the field, they have no need to produce their own clothing and yet the beauty of their adornment is superior even to the royal garments of a king like Solomon. The moral of the story: God always knows what each person needs before they ask for it and he stands ready to provide it, provided they ask for it with uncompromised confidence or faith in His power to provide whatever is needed.

All of these teachings, taken separately and together, present a life-model that cuts across the grain of most natural human

---

[10] Robinson, *op. cit.*, 69.
[11] *Ibid*, 69.

inclinations toward self-preservation, self-aggrandizement, self-advancement, and the acquisition of desired objects or goals (often at the moral and psychological expense of others) or the protection of something already owned but under threat of loss. Jesus counsels a life governed by the ethics of self-abnegation, self-denial, equitable treatment of others regardless of the circumstances and an uncompromised love *of* and compassion *for* others, especially the poor, the socially-despised and the dispossessed. Under such an ethics, there is no accommodation given to self-serving, defensive or offensive moral stances, or any other similar positions that, under extreme circumstances, may serve as a motivation to interpersonal or intra-communal conflict or outright warfare.

One discovers more fully the basic ethics of Jesus and its implications for life, in those passages of Q in which Jesus is either addressing or speaking about his closest disciples, who, in modern parlance, might be referred to as "wandering rebels." They have no money and no need for any. They have no purse or clothes bag, since they take neither money nor supplies with them. (Q 10. 4) They live like the wild birds and animals or like the sparrows that cannot even fall to earth without God knowing it. (Q 12. 7) They must trust implicitly in the power of God to take care of them. They do not even wear sandals on their feet, perhaps a sign of penance (Q 10. 4). Nor do they even carry a stick to protect themselves from wild animals and robbers; rather they go about after the fashion of lambs among ravenous wolves, innocent and vulnerable. (Q 10. 3)[12]

Thus, the archetypal representation of the loyal follower of Jesus is not the powerful potentate or the militaristic defender of the realm, nor the self-serving rich and famous, but rather the lowly, self-sacrificing and self-effacing underlings in society, who live, altruistically, in service *to* and for the benefit *of* other people, the poor, the disenfranchised and the powerless.

---

[12] This passage from Q manifests an ethic that could only be described as *ascetical*, commensurate, in many ways, with the spiritual paths depicted in both the Hindu and Buddhist traditions as the path taken by "wandering homeless yogis," (*sāmañña-s/śramaṇa-s* and *sannyasin-s.*)

Jesus initiates, what has become his most compelling and archetypal body of teachings, his "Sermon on the Mount," with the famous "Beatitudes" (lit., "blessings"), that illuminate vividly the place of love and peace in his overall message. He extends these blessings, not to the rich and powerful, not to kings and wealthy merchants but to the poor in spirit, mourners, the meek and submissive, those who hunger and thirst for righteousness, the merciful, the pure in heart, the peacemakers, etc. He states specifically in the eighth beatitude that those who are persecuted for righteousness' sake will inherit the kingdom of heaven. He promises his followers that many of them will be persecuted on his account but that they can rejoice in the assurance that their reward for their faithfulness on earth will be great in heaven.

But Jesus goes one step further toward the establishment of an Ethics of Peace, by declaring that one should not even offer resistance to anyone who harms one or threatens one's person with harm. (Q 6. 29-30) If someone strikes you on one cheek, offer him the other, as well. If a robber snatches your (outer) coat, you should give him the shirt off your back as a gift. If anyone asks you for something, give it to him willingly and if someone seeks a loan, do not ask him later for repayment (i.e., treat the loan as a gift). And, he concludes, as we ask God to forgive us our sins/moral debts, so should we forgive others their indebtedness to us. These, too, are unquestionably, hallmarks of an Ethics of Peace.

Perhaps, one of the most difficult of all principles in Jesus' Ethics of Peace to embrace is this: love your enemies and pray for those who persecute you. You should do more than love your friends or social equals because even the sinners and tax collectors do as much. Rather, you should follow the lead of God, who sends both rain and sunshine alike, on both the good and the evil. Only by this means can you become a child of God. [13]

A key piece of evidence that points to the very core of Jesus' Ethics of Peace is to be found in a section of "Q" (10. 5-6)

---

[13] As Robinson notes, "Jesus was first called a Son of God, not because he was like a Roman emperor, or like Hercules, or like other sons of God in that society, but because he was like God in loving /and forgiving/ his enemies." *Ibid.* 71.

regarding the customary greeting offered to a fellow member of "the faithful," i.e., the greeting, "Shalom." This was not an empty and casual greeting, as our "good morning, how're you doing?" often is. The greeting was extended with profound sincerity and warmth of spirit, more especially to a fellow members of the "Jesus' people." Whenever a "wandering rebel" knocked at a door and was admitted with a "Shalom," the head of that household came to be known a "son of peace," and the household itself, a "place of peace," when, in point of fact, such a place often existed under great risk of persecution and even, death for its residents, at the hands of the opponents of Jesus, both Jewish and gentile. [14]

The "wandering rebels "who followed Jesus wherever he went on his mission of teaching, healing and exorcisms (the three forms of ministry for which he was largely known) were sent out to go from house to house, seeking minimal hospitality for themselves (simple food – often a small loaf of bread and a single small fish – and a simple homespun robe for clothing) and offering only gestures of "peace" in return. These disciples often healed the sick and extended a reassuring word to the world-weary and the bereaved that "God's power has touched you." (Q 10. 9)

This, then, is the way of life that Jesus and his followers urged people to embrace – unburdened and uncluttered like the life of the ravens and the lilies of the field. For as Jesus promises, one needs only to ask God for something and it will be given: seek and you will find; knock and the door will be opened to you. (Q 11. 9) Hence, the taking of aggressive, self-serving measures to grab something that another person has in their possession or to prevent such a persona from acquiring something one is determined to possess, is never condoned.

In sum, because God's bounty is so abundantly available and only for the asking, no person should be concerned or anxious about their life, what they would eat, what they would put on. Only consider the ravens: they neither sow nor reap nor gather into barns, and yet God feeds them. Are we humans not much better than the birds? For this is what the Gentiles (unbelievers) do; but

---

[14] *Ibid,* 72.

your heavenly Father knows what you need even before you ask
for it. Therefore, seek only the kingdom (Mt 6. 25-34) and all other
things will be granted to you. (Q 12. 22b. 24. 29-31)

A Short Hermeneutical Interlude

There is a paradox at the heart of the teaching, concerning the
superiority of human beings over the birth of the air (and by
extension, all other 'lower animals') a teaching that sets Jesus'
ethics apart from that of the Buddha in a dramatic fashion. On the
one hand, Jesus seems to be expressing unconditional love for the
birds of the air and in a sense, idealizes them as models of the free
and unburdened life. But, then, he quite surprisingly suggests that
the ravens are, by definition, an inferior species of creature, which
is less valuable in God's eyes than are human beings. This
statement re-enforces the long-held belief in the Hebraic tradition
that humans are the crown of God's creation, the most illustrious
of all his creative acts and should, therefore, be held in higher
regard and treated with special concern, over and above the animal
kingdom, over which God gave man dominion at the time of the
creation of the world. (Genesis 1. 26)

This axiological and ethical distinction between human beings
and the, so-called, lower animals, stands in stark contrast to the
Buddha's conviction that the uncompromised avoidance of causing
injury or harm (*ahiṃsā*) to *all sentient beings* is a fundamental
precondition for achieving a purified heart and mind. The
reasoning here seems to be that if one exercises avoids bringing
harm to any sentient being, one will, thereby, be in personal touch
with the deepest of all ethico-spiritual principles, namely, "the
reverence for life," within the life-world (*saṃsāra*).

The doctrine of "*ahiṃsā*" has stood as the hallmark of the
Buddhist tradition for over 2500 years. That same ethics of non-
violence continues to be the elemental guiding principle in
contemporary Buddhism. Two recent examples: first, a huge series
of protests staged by monks in Myanmar (formerly, Burma)
against the repressive policies of the current government, which
the government-controlled military put down with unrestrained

force, causing the disappearance and even the death of numerous monastic demonstrators and second, large groups of Tibetan monks protesting, also through non-violent means, the plethora of violations of common civil rights by the iron rule of the Chinese government in Beijing. The Dalai Lama, the political and spiritual leader of the people of Tibet, made a public declaration that unless his fellow-countrymen halted the violent protests immediately, he would resign as the Dalai Lama. Many other such contemporary public demonstrations on behalf of peace and justice are dramatic exemplifications of the Buddhist-Gandhian conviction that "non-violent resistance" is the most effective and least injurious of all forms of "righteous indignation."

A Brief Counterpoint in Jesus' Ethics of Peace

There is one element in Jesus' ethics that calls for brief but close scrutiny. That is the charge by Jesus (contained in simple form in Q, but provided in a more elaborate and demanding form in the gospel of Matthew) that declares that he came to earth "to bring, not peace but a sword."

The passage in Matthew is as follows: "Don't get the idea that I came to bring peace on earth. I did not come to bring peace but a sword. After all, I have come to pit a son against his father, a daughter against her mother, and a daughter-in-law against her mother-in-law. A person's enemies are members of the same household. Those who love father and mother more than me are not worthy of me, and those who love son or daughter more than me are not worthy of me. And those who do not take their cross and follow after me are not worthy of me. Those who find their life will lose it, and those who lose their life for my sake will find it." (Matthew 10. 34-37) The piece about family conflicts is based on an identical passage from the Old Testament prophet, Micah (7. 5-6). This is another instance in which a gospel "writer/redactor" reaches back to the Hebrew scriptures for a piece of material that he felt would assist him in accomplishing his "theological goal" in recounting the story of Jesus.

The core statement in this passage comes from Q and hence, is in all probability, either the exact words of Jesus or an accurate paraphrase. Like the other three gospel writers, Matthew drew on the simple sayings of Jesus contained in Q and then added his own narrative and theological elaborations to achieve his theological task. It is likely, based on close textual analysis, that only the first sentence of the declaration came from Jesus himself, by way of Q. Thus, Matthew expanded on Jesus' point about peace and the sword, by supplying specifics about family divisions that might occur as a result of following him.

Taking the sentence about bringing not peace but a sword at face value, it seems to be in direct conflict with Jesus' recommendation of unqualified love. (See Matt. 5. 43-48) But, given the love-centered nature of Jesus' overall message and mission, this sentence should be read "metaphorically." The hermeneutical result of such a reading would go something like this: "While I preach peace to everyone, my followers should understand that following me may (and in all likelihood will) put them at odds with certain opponents of the faith. And they should understand that such conflicts may be one of the attendant costs of discipleship."

Another consideration: since, in this saying, Jesus refers to himself in the first person, (it is doubtful that he, customarily, did this) and also, that it harkens back to a verse from Micah, it is, again, likely that much of this passage originated, not with Jesus himself, but with the later Church. In any case, the first sentence in the passage should not be interpreted literally to mean that Jesus' followers should, literally, take up arms to fight for his cause, but only to be prepared to remains faithful to Jesus' teachings and to meet attacks on the community of the faithful with love and forgiveness.

However, one caveat remains: Elsewhere in Q and the gospels, Jesus is teaching in the temple and his parents reportedly think he is mad and urge him to come home with them. Jesus responds with a startling statement: "Who is my family? Only those who do the will of my father in heaven are my family and not necessarily my blood kin, only." This, combined with the passage about hating your family members and cutting family ties, cuts to the very root of the, then current, Mediterranean social and religious practice of supporting one's blood relatives, at all costs, perhaps, even to the point of death. According to some scholars, "The saying probably originated as a retort to people who used family ties as an excuse not to become a follower."[15]

Hence, despite the seemingly contradictory intention of this passage and other gospel passages that will go unmentioned here, Jesus' message remains a message of peace. What needs to be factored into the overall picture is that Jesus obviously realized that his message, though based to some extent on the Hebraic tradition in which he was raised, was at odds with the mainline and conservative branches of that tradition and that, in all likelihood, an adherence to his message would place the believer at odds with the social and religious communities of which they were a part.

The Buddha's and Jesus' Ethics of Peace Compared and Contrasted

The core teaching of both the Buddha and Jesus is this: Before taking action a person should put him/herself in the place of the other person and treat them exactly as they themselves would like to be treated by them – that is with friendship, not animosity; with love, not hatred; with forgiveness, not condemnation; and with compassion and understanding, not abuse.

In hopes of providing the basis for a quick and easy comparison of these two Ethics of Peace, there follows below a listing of some of the most important core commonalities and differences within the respective ethical systems. The Buddha's teaching comes first in each instance, followed by Jesus' teaching regarding the same, or similar topic.

1. <u>B</u>: Extend not only to human beings throughout the world, but to all sentient creatures, the gift of friendliness, loving kindness,

---

[15] Robert W. Funk, *et al.*, *The Five Gospels: What Did Jesus Really Say?* (San Francisco: Harper, 1993), 175.

compassion, joy and equanimity, without any degree of discrimination of any sort, regardless of the nature of the condition or set of conditions in any instance.

J: Love, not only your family, friends and neighbors but also your enemies and those who persecute you, in order, thereby, to become "sons of your Heavenly Father," i.e., to become God-like.

2. B: Like a mother risking everything to protect her only child, one should cultivate boundless love that pervades the whole world, beginning with those one already knows and loves, followed by those one doesn't know, concluding with those one knows but toward whom that one may harbor ill-feelings of dislike or resentment.

J: You should love everyone with equal regard, just as Jesus has loved you for, to lay down your life for your friends, is the greatest love of all.

3. B: To believe one's family and wealth to be enduring personal possessions is self-delusionary, for one does not even own oneself. Even though one may accumulate limitless worldly goods, one succumbs to death in the end. Therefore, cultivate righteousness – a treasure does not pass away and that thieves cannot break in and steal.

J: Do not struggle to acquire wealth and power in this world where time destroys all human accomplishments and where robbers break in and steal; rather build up treasures in heaven which can neither be destroyed nor stolen.

4. B: One should abstain from killing, from stealing, from lying and from illicit sexual acts, in order to maintain a life of moral purity.

J: In keeping with the ancient commandment, one should not murder, steal, lie, commit murder, commit adultery or dishonor one's parents.

5. B: The Buddha began his search for Truth by becoming a "homeless wanderer" (*śramaṇa*), traveling about with no place to lay his head; even after Enlightenment, he continued to wander from place to place, intent on instructing all those who were willing to listen and believe.

J: Jesus was a Palestinian peasant and a homeless itinerant preacher and a charismatic healer and declared that he "has nowhere to lay his head."

6. B: The Buddha renounced the world of power and wealth and abandoned his family (parents, wife and newborn son) to go out, he knew not where, to search for, he knew not what – perhaps the answer to his many questions and liberation from the angst that overwhelmed him after witnessing the "Four Signs."

J: You should "hate father and mother .... son and daughter," in order to become his disciple – meaning, love Jesus more than your family and realize that, following Jesus often entails abandoning family and your domestic responsibilities.

Despite the existence of a remarkable number of correspondent ethical principles in these two Ethics of Peace, there remain, perhaps, an equal number of dissimilarities. This is not an occasion for puzzlement or amazement, for given the dramatic points of disparity between the ancient Indian and the Palestinian religious and cultural historical contexts, the wonder is not the plethora of cultural contrasts, but the remarkable number of correspondences. Here, then, are a few of the defining differences between the Buddha's and Jesus' ethics:

1. B: A knowledge of the Truth about the nature of the world does not come through divine revelation from God but through the

practice of the principles of the Dharma, which the Buddha himself discovered under the Bo tree and has delivered to mankind through his ministry.

J: A knowledge of the Truth comes through divine revelation from the Heavenly Father, that brings with it a requirement of a life of obedience to the divine will as communicated through the ministry of Jesus.

2. B: Salvation or liberation is acquired not through the grace of a divine being but by each individual working out their own salvation with diligence, in recognition that everything, including the universe as a whole, is subject to change and decay.

J: Salvation comes through faith in Jesus' message of love and hope. Hence, no need to be anxious about daily needs; rather invest complete trust in the reign of God's power throughout the universe, His readiness to provide all basic needs and, ultimately, his power to grant deliverance from a self-centered, strife-ridden and self-defeating life, to all those who believe.

3. B: No apocalyptic vision of the coming "end of the world," nor an appeal to any sort of kingdom, whether worldly or celestial but rather complete renunciation of any notion of a "kingdom," in order to escape from all forms of suffering and the realization of a life of peace and joy.

J.: An "apocalyptic" vision of his mission to usher in a new historical era, characterized by the advent of the "Kingdom of God" which is, paradoxically, both "at hand" and also "not of this world."

4. B: No invocation of a divine or celestial "deliverer" and no human teacher; only an unswerving conviction in the power of the Dharma to provide the way to enlightenment and deliverance from suffering to all those who embrace it and practice its principles.

J: Teachings established on a single-minded faith in Yahweh, the solitary God of the Jews and in his power to provide, not only ordinary needs but, ultimately, salvation and, thereby, deliverance to a state of righteousness, love and peace.

4. B: Belief, not in a divinely created and sanctioned Universal Law but a cosmological law (*Dhamma/Dharma*) operative on the basis of the principle of Dependent Co-arising and the impermanence of all entities in the phenomenal world.

J: Belief in a divinely established and sanctioned universal Law, revealed, initially, in and through the Law of Moses (notably, the Ten Commandments) and all of the attendant ritual practices, to his Chosen People (the Children of Israel), but consummated and fulfilled in Jesus' life and teachings (and according to the later Church in Jesus' death and resurrection on behalf of a sinful humanity).

Conclusion

In summation, it is abundantly clear that the central doctrine of both the Buddha's and Jesus' ethics is in the case of the Buddha the injunction to practice universal loving kindness and equanimity toward all creatures and in the case of Jesus, the love of all human beings. Viewed historically, the Buddhist tradition has created a far better record in living up to this universal love-ethics, than has the Christian Church.[16]

Second, it is both self-destructive and self-delusionary, according to both traditions, to invest one's full attention and energies to the amassing of wealth, power and prestige during a given lifetime, to the exclusion of other, more personally and socially beneficial values (such as the cultivation of moral and spiritual principles, the amelioration of social ills arising from social inequality, and the development of one's own human

---

[16] In a future project, I will explore, comparatively, the histories of these two traditions under the rubric of "Religion and War."

potential for "the good"). The ultimate self-delusion is the ignorance of the inevitability of death that will, in a moment's time, wipe away all that has been garnered during a lifetime.

Third, both Founders agree that all human beings should subscribe to such basic and irreplaceable human values as not killing, not stealing, not lying, and not honoring the fundamental worth of each individual human being, simply, by virtue of their birth in the world as a human being.

Fourth, and finally, one should anchor one's life in commitment to *know* and *do* the Good, understood minimally, as "doing no harm to others," and more than that, living to the best of one's ability, given one's intellectual, moral, spiritual and material resources, for the good of others.

This essay will close with a few brief remarks on a few of the major differences between the ethics of the Buddha and Jesus and the social and political manifestations of those differences in historical perspective.

First, it can be said that Buddhism has managed, to a large extent, to honor and live by its ethics of non-violence and peaceful coexistence with a wide variety of other religions and cultures. The historical facts confirm, with little or no room for doubt or qualification on this point, that, unlike the history of Christianity, the history of Buddhism, by and large, has spread through many different cultures throughout the world, unscarred by outbreaks of religious warfare, i.e., wars launched by or joined in defense of the faith. Christianity, on the other hand, has been marked by attacks on Christianity itself by members of others faiths (principally, Islam), the Church's launching of eight Crusades against the Muslim world, the Spanish Inquisition of the 14th - 15th centuries contain the outbreak of heresies against orthodox belief and, in the case of the Thirty Year's War in the 17th century, the warfare between European Catholics and Protestants.

Second, the lack of a belief in a creator / ruler God in Buddhism, in addition, to a shift by the Buddha of the focus of his teachings away from himself and toward the teachings themselves away, juxtaposed with the uncompromised Christian belief in a single God, believed to be the lord of the entire universe (and consequently, of all peoples inhabiting that universe), and in his Son, Jesus Christ (according to the later Church), believed to be the only "Way, the Truth and the Life," for all peoples, has given rise to very different histories: (1) In the case of Buddhism, more openness *to* and tolerance *of* other faiths, less doctrinal and ritualistic exclusivism, and less compelled to defend, forcefully and militaristically, its own understanding of the Truth, (2) in the case of Christianity, ostensibly committed to the ethics of "turn the other cheek," love both neighbor and enemy and forgive wrongs committed by others, but in reality, compromising or outright transgressing that ethics repeatedly, throughout its two-thousand plus year history of "wars and rumors of wars."

And, finally, the Buddhist ethics is, theoretically, more comprehensively environmentally friendly, by virtue of its commitment to the ethics of non-injury and non-violence and its adherence to a "reverence for life," in all of its myriad forms, than is the Judeo-Christian ethics, which is committed to the love of human beings, only. For its parts, the Judeo-Christian ethics, as articulated in the biblical account of the creation of the world, included Gods investiture in human beings of the dominion over all the lower, non-human creatures. It has been argued that one of the fundamental reasons that modern science and technology developed in the western world rather than in Asia is the twin Judeo-Christian notions that the world is *real* and therefore, worthy of concerted attention and physical development, and the superiority of mankind over the whole of nature. It goes without saying, the outcome of this "naturalistic drama" remains to be seen in future times.

And, as the French saying goes, *"plus ca change, plus c'est la meme chose"* ("the more things change, the more they remain the same").

APPENDIX

CHRISTIANITY AND WAR

Kenneth A. Locke

At first glance, it may seem odd to find a paper on Christianity and war in a volume dedicated to exploring religions' contributions to peace. Why speak of war when the goal should always by peace and loving-kindness? Is not war something that should be eradicated? The answer to both these questions is, of course, "yes," but we must be careful not to fall into a simplistic naiveté. To say that war is bad is not the same as saying that war is always the worst possible course of action. At times, war may be the lesser of two evils. While it would be nice if all peoples and nations could resolve their differences through non-military means, reality presents us with a far more complicated, ambiguous and disturbing picture. Imperialist policies, violent ideologies, selfish desires and megalomania continue to shape human interaction, giving rise to violence, oppression, invasion and occupation. To insist on the complete rejection of military action in the face of such destructive forces is not only naive, it is foolhardy. It can lead to torture, enslavement and extermination. Indeed, few today would argue that it would have been better if the world had dealt with Adolf Hitler through non-military means. In our ambiguous and deeply flawed world, wars are sometimes necessary.[1] The problem is not

---

[1] Peter Mayhew, *A Theology of Force and Violence* (London & Philadelphia: SCM Press, Trinity Press International, 1989), 93, 97.

war, but unnecessary war. How are we to distinguish between the
two? This paper explores a Christian response to this question.

Christians must explore and talk about this question because
politicians rarely hesitate to invoke religion to justify military
action. In the run-up to the Iraq War, George W. Bush repeatedly
insisted that "our cause is just" and that President Saddam Hussein
was an "evil" dictator who had to be removed from power, thereby
combining the concept of justice with metaphysical / religious
ideas of good and evil. More blatantly, on March 17, 2003, when
President Bush announced military action against Iraq, he ended
his address with the words "may God continue to bless America,"
implying that God, at least up until then, was on America's side.
However, probably most astounding was Bush's statement at a
ceremony honoring soldiers killed in the Iraqi conflict: He
announced that these soldiers were now closer to God. Christians
cannot sit idly by while politicians use such religious language to
further their geo-political and military goals. They must speak out
and show what it truly means to be a Christian in our, at times,
violent world.

An almost immediate, but unfortunately not very helpful,
response to Bush's language is to argue that Christianity rejects
completely all acts of violence. A number of scriptural passages
seem to support this view. Probably the most famous is Matthew
5:38-41:

> You have heard that it was said, 'An eye for an eye and
> a tooth for a tooth.' But I say to you, 'Do not resist an
> evil doer.' But if anyone strikes you on the right cheek,
> turn the other also; and if anyone wants to sue you and
> take your coat, give your cloak as well; and if anyone
> forces you to go one mile, go also the second mile.[2]

In the Beatitudes, Jesus states, "Blessed are the peacemakers
for they will be called children of God" (Matthew 5:9), and on the

---

[2] All biblical quotations are from the *New Revised Standard Version*.

night of his arrest, he appears to condemn using violence for self-defense:

> Then they came and laid hands on Jesus and arrested him.
> Suddenly, one of those with Jesus put his hand on his
> sword, drew it, and struck the slave of the high priest,
> cutting off his ear. Then Jesus said to him, "Put your sword
> back into its place; for all who takes the sword will perish
> by the sword." (Matt. 26:50-52)

These scriptural passages illustrate Christianity commitment to non-violence, even in the face of violent aggression.

Nevertheless, one must be careful not to overstate the case. In spite of this non-violent message and preference for peace, from the beginning, Christianity did allow for the possibility that violence may sometimes be necessary. Jesus himself appears to have engaged in violent action when he cleansed the Jerusalem Temple:

> In the temple he found people selling cattle, sheep, and
> doves, and the money changers seated at their tables.
> Making a whip of cords, he drove all of them out of the
> temple, both the sheep and the cattle. He also poured out
> the coins of the money changers and overturned their
> tables. (John 2:14-15)

What is significant, however, is the reason Jesus engaged in such action: In Luke 19:46, Jesus' outburst at the Temple is followed by the proclamation, "It is written, 'My house shall be a house of prayer, but you have made it a den of robbers.'" Jesus was upset because money, rather than prayer and focus on God, had become the center of Temple life. At issue, here was the problem of idolatry, the worship of something other than God as though it were God. The sellers and money changers in the Temple were more interested in profit than in a relationship with God; they had chosen to worship money rather than the true God. As a result, they had lost their connection with God and had degenerated into "robbers." In order to put an end to this idolatry in the House of God, Jesus drove them from the temple. It would seem that violence is justified when it is in service to the true God.

Connected to preventing idolatry is the fight for justice. Repeatedly in the biblical literature, the idea of justified violence is closely connected to the prevention of innocent suffering: "Wash yourselves; make yourselves clean; remove the evil of your doings from before my eyes; cease to do evil, learn to do good; seek justice, rescue the oppressed, defend the orphan, plead for the widow." (Isaiah 1:16-17) God demands justice from his people and holds them accountable for their actions. Those who fail to do good will face violent consequences: "But if you refuse and rebel, you shall be devoured by the sword...." (Isaiah 1:20) Simply worshipping God is not enough: "What to me is the multitude of your sacrifices? Says the LORD; I have had enough of burnt offerings of rams and the fat of fed beasts; I do not delight in the blood of bulls, or of lambs, or of goats." (Isaiah 1:11) What is noticeable is that idolatry and injustice often overlap. Worship of the one true God and the ability to maintain and defend justice are two sides of the same coin:

> "Teacher, which commandment in the law is the greatest?" [Jesus] said to him, "'You shall love the Lord your God with all your heart, and will all your soul, and with all your mind.' This is the greatest and first commandment. And a second is like it: 'You shall love your neighbour as yourself.' On these two commandments hang all the laws and the prophets." (Matt. 22: 36-40)

There is a never-ending dialectic between loving God and loving one's neighbor. Failure to love God is to fall into idolatry, it is to consider something else (e.g., money, power, ego) as more important than God, and it invariably leads to injustice and the mistreatment of others. At the same time, failure to love others, and the invariable suffering it causes, leads to idolatry, the worship of a false God.

This uncompromising call to be both loving and just, however, is at the same time a reminder of human weakness and failing: How are imperfect humans to perfectly combine love and justice? The two often appear incompatible. The acceptance, flexibility, empathy and forgiveness cultivated by love seem at odds with the rigidity, sternness, exactness and judgment demanded by justice. Humans find it difficult to reconcile the two, and often end up choosing between emphasizing love at the cost of justice, or celebrating justice to the detriment of compassion. For Christians, this human shortcoming is summed up in the word "sin." Few words are more misunderstood. In the Bible, a sin is not so much the violation of a taboo or the transgression of an external ordinance, as it is an action and/or thought which touches upon and distorts a human's personal standing with God. To commit a sin is to alienate oneself from the divine.[3] It is the failure to love God, and thus it is the failure to love one's neighbor and to maintain justice.[4] This is the profound negative implication the term "sin" is meant to convey: a sin damages and distorts a person's loving relationship with God. Since it is God who perfectly combines the practice of love with the practice of justice, sin separates humans from the divine source which would enable them to do the same.

Nor can this separation be completely overcome. For Christians, the problem is not just sin, but "original sin." The modern world tends to dismiss the idea of original sin too quickly. Although in its classic formulation by Augustine (354-430) it is no longer acceptable today, the fundamental message it was meant to express remains relevant. Augustine formulated his description of original sin in response to Pelagius (late 4th to early 5th century), who taught that every human being could learn to avoid sin. Augustine rejected Pelagius' teaching because he believed it failed to appreciate the tragic element in human life. Augustine argued

---

[3] S. J. de Vries, "Sins, Sinners," in *The Interpreter's Dictionary of the Bible,* vol. 4 (Nashville: Abingdon, 1962), 362-363.

[4] Catholic Church, *Catechism of the Catholic Church* (New Hope, Kentucky: Urbi et Orbi Communications, 1994), 453, para. 1849.

instead that when Adam sinned against God, he ruined the entire race.

Since then, Adam's sin has been passed down from generation to generation through the act of procreation. Every child is, from moment of birth, infected with this sin.[5] While it is probably best to discard Augustine's negative attitude toward sex and unfair portrait of the newborn child, one must be careful not to lose sight of the deeper truth he was trying to convey. Human behavior is almost always morally and psychologically ambivalent. Humans' best intentions go wrong and their hidden motivations remain unclear even to themselves. The doctrine of original sin expresses the deep tragedy that affects all human action. It reveals human flaws and reminds people that their best efforts are often not good enough. From the moment of birth, people are divided against themselves, others and God. Humans are self-destructive, even when they do not want to be.[6] Nowhere is this better expressed than in the words of Paul: "I do not understand my own actions. For I do not do what I want, but I do the very thing I hate.... For I do not do the good I want, but the evil I do not want is what I do." (Romans 7:15, 19)

War is inevitable because sin (failure to love God and neighbor) is inevitable. Thus, from a Christian perspective, it is the reality of idolatry and injustice that fuels war. Consequently, Christians are faced with an insoluble dilemma: as sinful humans, they contribute to the cause of war, yet at the same time they are called by God to struggle against those who cause war. Furthermore, this struggle may itself involve military action. From its inception, Christianity has acknowledged that the practice of war is not necessarily incompatible with the Christian message. In the Gospel of Luke, a soldier is praised for his deep faith:

---

[5] J. N. D. Kelly, *Early Christian Doctrines* (London: A&C Black, 1977), 362-366.

[6] Gabriel Daly, *Creation and Redemption* (Dublin: Gill and Macmillan, 1988), 126-128.

As Jesus had finished all his sayings in the hearing of the people, he entered Capernaum. A centurion there had a slave whom he valued highly, and who was ill and close to death. When he heard about Jesus, he sent some Jewish elders to him, asking him to come and heal his slave. When they came to Jesus, they appealed to him earnestly.... And Jesus went with them, but when he was not far from the house, the centurion sent friends to say to him, "Lord, do not trouble yourself, for I am not worthy to have you come under my roof; therefore I did not presume to come to you. But only speak the word, and let me servant healed. For I also am a man set under authority, with soldiers under me; and I say to one, 'Go,' and he goes, and to another, 'Come,' and he comes, and to my slave, 'Do this,' and the slave does it." When Jesus heard this, he was amazed at him, and turning to the crowd that followed him, he said, "I tell you, not even in Israel have I found such faith." When those who had been sent returned to the house, they found the slave in good health. (Luke 7:1-10)

And no time in this exchange is the centurion's military profession held against him, nor is he required to abandon it for his slave to be healed. The Book of Acts contains a long passage on the centurion Cornelius, who finds favor with God and is baptized into the Christian faith. Described as a devout man who gave alms and prayed constantly, he experiences a vision of God which leads him to contact the apostle Peter. Peter comes to his household and tells him the story of Jesus Christ. The story culminates with the Holy Spirit descending upon all who are listening, upon which they are baptized in the name of Jesus Christ (Acts 10:1-48). As in Luke, Cornelius' military service is neither held against him nor considered a stumbling block to becoming a Christian.

In the post-New Testament period, as Christians began to contemplate military service at a deeper level, there arose the recognition that being both a soldier and a Christian could be problematic. A number of Christian writers began to urge their fellows to avoid military service. What is noteworthy, however, is that they did so not so much out of a desire to practice non-violence, but to avoid the danger of idolatry, the worshipping of false gods. Tertullian (*c.* 160 – *c.* 225), for instance, while decrying the pain and destruction caused by war, argued that the Roman emperor, state and army were part of God's plan on earth:

> They know from whom they have obtained their power; they know, as they are men, from whom they have received life itself.... Without ceasing, for all our emperors we offer prayers. We pray for life prolonged; for security to the empire; for protection to the imperial house; for brave armies, a faithful senate, a virtuous people, the world at rest, whatever, as man or Caesar, an emperor would wish.[7]

The military might of the Roman empire was necessary to assure stability, security and peace. Nevertheless, Tertullian's support for the army did not extend to an endorsement of Christian military service. For him Christian life and military life stood in total opposition:

> But now inquiry is made ... whether a believer may turn himself unto military service, and whether the military way be admitted unto the faith, even the rank and file, or each inferior grade, to whom there is no necessity for taking part in sacrifices or capital punishments. There is no agreement between the divine and the human sacrament [the Latin word *sacramentum* could also mean "a military oath"], the standard of Christ and the standard of the devil, the camp of light and the camp of darkness. One cannot be due to two masters – God and Caesar.[8]

---

[7] Tertullian, *Apology*, 30, in *The Ante-Nicene Fathers: Translations of the Writings of the Fathers down to A.D. 325*, eds. Alexander Roberts and James Donaldson, vol. 3 (Grand Rapids, Michigan: Eerdmans, 1973).

[8] Tertullian, *On Idolatry*, 19, in *ibid.*

Tertullian's reference to "sacrifices" is important, for it highlights what disturbed him most about the Roman army: It was first and foremost a religious system with rituals that honored not only Roman gods, but pledged obedience to the emperor, who was considered a god. This was the key issue for Tertullian: Christian participation in such a system was tantamount to worshipping something other than God.[9] This is why he chose to discuss the problem of military service in his *Treatise on Idolatry*. Tertullian even felt that wearing military dress was incompatible with Christianity,[10] and lauded a Christian soldier for refusing to wear a laurel crown because it conflicted with his faith.[11] Hippolytus (*c.*170 – 236), a contemporary of Tertullian's, took a similar view. In his Apostolic Tradition, he placed the occupation of the army under the same footing as idolatry.[12] While he argued that soldiers who converted to Christianity "must be taught not to kill men," he particularly considered the soldier's swearing of oaths and wearing of "the purple" inconsistent with Christian practice. Indeed, he insisted that "If a catechumen or a believer seeks to become a soldier, they must be rejected, for they have despised God."[13] Hippolytus was aware of the religious nature of military service: the very practices of swearing oaths and wearing military garments expressed a commitment to Roman religious beliefs. Like Tertullian, he feared that the religious rituals and symbols that permeated the Roman army would lead Christians away from the worship of the one true God of Jesus Christ.

Origin (*c.* 184 – 254) represents a slightly different perspective. He clearly linked being Christian with an inability to serve in the military, but, unlike Tertullian and Hippolytus, he did not focus on

---

[9] John Helgeland, Robert J. Daly and J. Patout Burns, *Christians and the Military: The Early Experience* (London: SCM Press, 1987), 23.

[10] Tertullian, *On Idolatry*, 19, in *The Ante-Nicene Fathers*, vol. 3.

[11] Tertullian, *De Corona*, 1, in *ibid.*

[12] Helgeland, Daly and Burns, 36.

[13] Hippolytus, *Apostolic Tradition*, 16, in *The Apostolic Tradition of Hippolytus*, trans. Burton Scott Easton (1934; reprint, Cambridge: Cambridge University Press, 1962).

idolatry. Instead, he insisted that living the Christian life was completely incompatible with the practice of any form of violence:

> And yet, if a revolt had led to the formation of the Christian commonwealth, so that it derived its existence in this way from that of the Jews, who were permitted to take up arms in defence of the members of their families, and to slay their enemies, the Christian Lawgiver would not have altogether forbidden the putting of men to death; and yet He nowhere teaches that it is right for His own disciples to offer violence to any one, however wicked. [14]

Origin agreed that the ancient Israelites were justified in resorting to war to ensure their survival, but he argued that such an approach had never been meant to last in perpetuity. The Jewish law, which permitted the making of war and the putting to death of criminals, had been replaced by the Gospel of Jesus Christ, which did not. [15] Nevertheless, Origin's position did not lead to a total blanket condemnation of war. While he rejected Christians serving in the army, he did allow them to pray for the success of those engaged in military action. For him all Christians were "priests," and, like their pagan counterparts serving in the Roman temples, could not be required to enlist in the army, even in times of war. [16] However, since Christians were "priests" in service of the one true God, their prayers could help guarantee military success:

> And to those enemies of our faith who require us to bear arms for the commonwealth, and to slay men, we can reply: "Do not those who are priests at certain shrines, and those who attend on certain gods, as you account them, keep their

---

[14] Origin, *Against Celsus*, III, 7, in *The Ante-Nicene Fathers: Translations of the Writings of the Fathers down to A.D. 325*, vol. 4 (Grand Rapids, Michigan: Eerdmans, 1972).

[15] *Ibid*, VII, 26.

[16] *Ibid*, VIII, 73.

hands free from blood, that they may with hands unstained and free from human blood offer the appointed sacrifices to your gods; and even when war is upon you, you never enlist the priests in the army. If that then is a laudable custom, how much more so, that while others are engaged in battle, these too should engage as the priests and ministers of God, keeping their hands pure, and wrestling in prayers to God on behalf of those who are fighting in a righteous cause, and for the king who reigns righteously, that whatever is opposed to those who act righteously may be destroyed." And as we by our prayers vanquish all demons who stir up war, and lead to the violation of oaths, and disturb the peace, we in this way are much more helpful to the kings than those who go into the field to fight for them. [17]

Origin thought that war was caused by sin, and that sin was caused by demons. It was these demonic forces that threatened civil order and sometimes made war necessary. For him, a righteous war was one undertaken to uphold social peace and stability, and Christians had a God-given duty to support such wars. Through their prayers, they could weaken the demons and ensure victory. Ironically, although Origin forbade Christians to fight, his concession that war could be righteous laid the groundwork for what would later become the Christian theory of just war. [18]

Origin's trust in the power of Christian prayer led him to argue that the spread of Christianity throughout the Roman empire would lead to the decline and eventual end of war:

But if all Romans ... embrace the Christian faith, they will, when they pray, overcome their enemies; or rather, they will not war at all, being guarded by that divine power

---

[17] *Ibid,* VII, 73.
[18] Helgeland, Daly, and Burns, 40-42.

which promised to save five entire cities for the sake of
fifty just persons. [19]

Needless to say, this hope proved naive, and as Christianity
spread, no such decline took place. Furthermore, as the Roman
world became more Christian, it became more difficult to justify
Christian avoidance of military service. This proved especially the
case once the emperor himself converted to Christianity. In 312,
during a civil war over the imperial succession, Constantine I (*c.*
280 – 337) openly declared his commitment to Christianity before
battling his opponent Maxentius (*c.* 278 – 312) at the Milvian
Bridge near Rome. Constantine's victory in the battle not only
made him emperor of the Roman west, but also guaranteed
Christianity state support. Twelve years later, he defeated the
emperor of the Roman east, Licinius (*c.* 250 – 325), and become
the undisputed ruler of the entire empire. With the head of the
Roman military state now a Christian, it was no longer politically
correct to insist that commitment to Christianity required the
unconditional avoidance of war and army service.

Consequently, Christians began to explore in more detail the
extent to which military service and the waging of war could be
compatible with service to God. For Eusebius (*c.* 260 – *c.* 340) the
answer was straightforward: Constantine's military battles for the
imperial throne had actually been battles between the Christian
God and the pagan gods of Rome. Good had fought evil, and good
had triumphed. Commenting on Constantine's final military
confrontation with Licinius, Eusebius argued that war was justified
when it was the only way to overcome evil:

[Constantine], perceiving the evils of which he had heard
[i.e., the persecution of the Christian Church] to be no
longer tolerable, took wise counsel, and tempering the
natural clemency of his character with a certain measure of
severity, hastened to succour those who were thus
grievously oppressed. For he judged that it would rightly be

---

[19] Origin, *Against Celsus*, VIII, 70, in *The Ante-Nicene Father*, vol. 4.

deemed a pious and holy task to secure, by the removal of an individual [i.e., Licinius], the safety of the greater part of the human race. He judged too, that if he listened to the dictates of clemency only, and bestowed his pity on one utterly unworthy of it, this would, on the one hand, confer no real benefit on a man whom nothing would induce to abandoñ his evil practices, and whose fury against his subjects would only be likely to increase; while, on the other hand, those who suffered from his oppression would thus be forever deprived of all hope of deliverance.[20]

Eusebius appears to have had two criteria for justifying Christian engagement in military conflict: (1) It had to be the only remaining viable option for overcoming evil and oppression, and (2) not going to war would cause greater suffering than going to war. Since Constantine and his Christian soldiers had fulfilled these criteria, their military actions were justified and righteous in the eyes of God.[21] Christian reflection on war had shifted from debating whether Christians could fight, to when they should fight. It was Augustine (354 – 430) who probably made the most significant and lasting contribution to this debate, laying the foundations for what eventually became Christian just war theory.

Augustine's ruminations on war were deeply affected by his thoughts on good and evil. He concluded that supreme good was achieved when "the flesh should cease to lust against the spirit, and that there be no vice in us against which the spirit may lust."[22] Since all humans were tainted by sin, it was not possible in this life to attain this supreme good; the best humans could hope for was, through God's help, "to preserve the soul from succumbing and yielding to the flesh that lusts against it, and to refuse our consent

---

[20] Eusebius, *Life of Constantine*, II, 3, in *A Select Library of Nicene and Post-Nicene Fathers of the Christian Church*, eds. Philip Schaff and Henry Wace, second series, vol. 1 (Grand Rapids, Michigan: Eerdmans, 1952).

[21] Helgeland, Daly and Burns, 67-71.

[22] Augustine, *City of God*, XIX, 4, in *A Select Library of the Nicene and Post-Nicene Fathers of the Christian Church*, ed. Philip Schaff, vol. 2 (Grand Rapids, Michigan: Eerdmans, 1973).

to the perpetuation of sin."[23] By "lust" Augustine did not only mean sex, but such desires as ambition and greed that led people to pursue their own selfish goals for power, recognition and wealth. These selfish desires were evil, for they left humans feeling dissatisfied, disappointed and distraught, and eventually turned them against their fellows. This understanding of good and evil deeply shaped Augustine's thoughts on war, for it led him to judge the rightness of military action not so much by its outer manifestations, than by the inner disposition of its combatants.

Augustine believed that serving in the army and serving God were perfectly compatible. Writing to the Christian military officer Boniface in 421, Augustine advised him not to think "that it is impossible for any one to please God while engaged in active military service."[24] The Bible itself contained numerous examples of warriors and soldiers who found favor with God. What was vital for Augustine was that soldiers engage in combat with the proper goals and inner disposition:

> Think, then, of this first of all, when you are arming for the battle, that even your bodily strength is a gift of God; for, considering this, you will not employ the gift of God against God. For, when faith is pledged, it is to be kept even with the enemy against whom the war is waged, how much more with the friend for whom the battle is fought! Peace should be the object of your desire; war should be waged only as a necessity, and waged only that God may by it deliver men from the necessity and preserve them in peace. For peace is not sought in order to the kindling of war, but war is waged in order that peace may be obtained. Therefore, even in waging war, cherish the spirit of a peacemaker.... Let necessity, therefore, and not your will, slay the enemy who fights against you. As violence is used

---

[23] *Ibid.*

[24] Augustine, *Letters*, CLXXXIX, 4, in *A Select Library of the Nicene and Post-Nicene Fathers of the Christian Church*, ed. Philip Schaff, vol. 1 (Grand Rapids, Michigan: Eerdmans, 1974).

towards him who rebels and resists, so mercy is due to the vanquished or the captive....[25]

For Augustine, the key to a just war was service to the causes of peace and mercy and the avoidance of one's own selfish desires. Quoting Matthew 22: 37-40, he insisted that the Christian soldier's guiding principle must be the selfless love of God and neighbor.[26] War itself was not evil, its evil lay in negative passions it could invoke: lust for domination, ferocity of rebellion, and savagery and cruelty. As long as soldiers served God and avoided these evil passions, their engagement in combat was just, even if their rulers instigated the war for unjust reasons.[27]

Augustine's ideas proved paradigmatic, and laid the foundation for what would eventually become a Christian systematic theory for just war. This theory received one of its first distinct formulations in the work of Thomas Aquinas (1224/5 – 1274), who drew heavily on Augustine. Like Augustine, he did not consider war in itself sinful; as long as three specific criteria were fulfilled, Christians could engage in warfare:

First, the authority of the sovereign by whose command the war is to be waged. For it is not the business of a private individual to declare war, because he can seek redress of his rights from the tribunal of his superior. Moreover, it is not the business of a private individual to summon together the people, which have to be done in wartime. And as the care of the common weal is committed to those who are in authority, it is their business to watch over the common weal of the city, kingdom or province subject to them. And just as it is lawful for them to have recourse to the sword in defending that common weal

---

[25] *Ibid,* 6.

[26] *Ibid,* 2.

[27] Augustine, *Reply to Faustus,* XXII, 74-75, in *A Select Library of the Nicene and Post-Nicene Fathers of the Christian Church,* ed. Philip Schaff, vol. 4 (Grand Rapids, Michigan: Eerdmans, 1974).

against internal disturbances, when they punish evil-doers
...; so too, it is their business to have recourse to the sword
of war in defending the common weal against external
enemies....

Secondly, a just cause is required, namely that those
who are attacked, should be attacked because they deserve
it on account of some fault....

Thirdly, it is necessary that the belligerents should have
a rightful intention, so that they intend the advancement of
good, or the avoidance of evil.... For it may happen that
war is declared by the legitimate authority, and for a just
cause, and yet be rendered unlawful through a wicked
intention.[28]

Like a number of his predecessors, Aquinas considered war
just if it was undertaken with the intention to safeguard social
peace and stability. Rulers not only had the right, but the duty, to
engage in warfare if evil forces of invasion and chaos threatened
society. In short, war was allowed if no other recourse was
possible, a legitimate authority declared war, those being attacked
deserved it because of their evil actions, and the guiding intent was
the quest for peace and order, not the fulfillment of selfish desires.
Although Aquinas' thoughts on war have undergone
considerable elaboration and modification over the centuries, they
remain influential today. In a recent contribution to the topic, the
Roman Catholic Church's Magisterium urged "everyone to prayer
and to action so that the divine Goodness may free us from the
ancient bondage of war," but also acknowledged the right to self-
defense once all peace efforts had failed.[29] The use of military
force was allowed only under the following conditions:

---

[28] Thomas Aquinas, *Summa Theologica*, II-II, Q. 40, Article 1, in *St.*
Thomas Aquinas Summa Theologica: Complete English Edition in Five
Volumes, vol. 2 (Westminster, Maryland: Christian Classics, 1981).
[29] *Catechism of the Catholic Church*, 555, paras. 2307-2308.

- the damage inflicted by the aggressor on the nation or community of nations must be lasting, grave, and certain;
- all other means of putting an end to it must have been shown to be impractical or ineffective;
- there must be serious prospect of success;
- the use of arms must not produce evils and disorders graver than the evil to be eliminated. The power of modern means of destruction weighs very heavily in evaluating this condition.[30]

The Magisterium emphasized that the ruling authorities had a grave moral responsibility to ensure that these conditions were fulfilled. Furthermore, once hostilities began, just war theory demanded that equitable provision was made "for those who for reasons of conscience refuse to bear arms," that "non-combatants, wounded soldiers, and prisoners ... be respected and treated humanely," that "the extermination of a people, nation, or ethnic minority" was a mortal sin, that people "were morally bound to resist orders that command genocide," and that "the indiscriminate destruction of whole cities or vast areas with their inhabitants" was "a crime against God and man...."[31]

The debates over Christian just war theory are far from resolved, but the above outlined developments over the last two millennia have, at least, brought into focus the main issues of concern: (1) The cause must be just: military force should only be used to correct evils that threaten the massive violation of a population's basic human rights. (2) There must be right intention: the just cause must be the actual reason for going to war, not a pretext to hide less acceptable and selfish motivations.[32] (3) There must be comparative justice: the injustice suffered by the one side must significantly outweigh that suffered by the other. (4) Only a

---

[30] *Ibid*, para. 2309.

[31] *Ibid*, 556, paras. 2311-2314

[32] Joseph Boyle, "Just War Thinking in Catholic Natural Law," in *The Ethics of War and Peace: Religious and Secular Perspectives*, ed. Terry Nardin (Princeton: Princeton University Press, 1996), 45-46.

legitimate authority may declare war. (5) There must be a probability of success: arms, soldier and civilian lives must not be wasted on lost causes, nor may disproportionate measures by used to achieve minimal successes. (6) War must always be a last resort: all peaceful and viable alternatives must have been seriously tried and exhausted. (7) The benefits must outweigh the costs: not going to war must result in greater evil than going to war. Only when these criteria are fulfilled may a war be considered just. Furthermore, once combat is initiated, there is the constant danger that a just war may deteriorate into an unjust one. In order to prevent this, combatants must abide by the following rules: (1) War must only be directed at enemy combatants, never non-combatants; deliberate destruction of civilian residential areas that lack military targets and acts of terrorism or reprisals against ordinary civilians are prohibited. (2) The amount of force used must be proportional to the evil suffered: the more disproportional collateral civilian injuries and deaths, the more likely the war is unjust. (3) The principle of minimum force must apply: only the strength necessary to defeat the enemy should be employed.[33]

As helpful as these guidelines may be, they also highlight the very painful reality of human weakness, frailty and failure. These criteria for just war are open to massive interpretation, and it is unlikely that any person or nation could satisfy them completely. The difficulties are manifold. Determining just cause and right intentions requires a level of self-honesty and self-reflection by rulers and nations that is seldom achieved. Humans have great difficulties being honest to themselves and others, and are masters of self-deception. Truth is also often the first casualty of war, greatly increasing the possibility that what was initially just becomes unjust. How does one weigh the levels of suffering of one side over against the other? Suffering is to some extent a subjective experience, and one person's great pain and sense of injustice may be another's minor irritation. What is a legitimate authority? Must

---

[33] James F. Childress, "Just-War Theories: The Bases, Interrelations, Priorities, and Functions of Their Criteria," in *Theological Studies* 39 (1978): 427-445.

it be a democracy and, if so, what kind of democracy? What qualifies as a military success, how may innocent casualties be acceptable? Other issues are also difficult to resolve. How does one determine whether all peaceful alternatives have been exhausted? Since the believed benefits of going to war lie in future expectations, how reliable are they for judging whether not going to war would be the greater evil? The future rarely turns out as expected.

These difficulties illustrate the great tragedy of human existence. It is simply impossible for human to be certain that they have fulfilled and maintained all the criteria for a just war. Anyone who claims such certainty is either lying in a dangerous state of denial, or in the grip of demonic forces. In the end, human sin permeates all, a fact Christians must keep in mind when they contemplate military action. In our sinful world, driven by self-serving passions, war may at times be necessary to prevent even greater evil. But even when war is justified, Christians must constantly ask themselves how they failed: How did their own sin contribute to the disaster, and how could their sin make the disaster worse. We fear and rebel against such brutal self-honesty, yet it is commanded by Jesus:

> Why do you see the speck in your neighbour's eye, but do not notice the log in your own eye? Or how can you say to your neighbour, 'Friend, let me take out the speck in your eye,' when you yourself do not see the log in your own eye? You hypocrite, first take the log out of your own eye, and then you will see clearly to take the speck out of your neighbour's eye. (Luke 6:42).

Under no circumstances should Christians engage in ware out of a sense of self-righteousness, for this will invariably lead to a dehumanizing of the enemy and greater tragedy. [34] Finally,

---

[34] Roland H. Bainton, *Christian Attitudes toward War and Peace: A Historical Survey and Critical Re-evaluation* (New York, Nashville: Abingdon Press, 1960), 243.

Christians would do well to remember that victory could never be an automatic retroactive justification for war.

INDEX

EDITORS

Ven. **Chanju Mun** (Ordination Name: Seongwon) is the founder and chief editor of Blue Pine Books. He taught East Asian Buddhist Studies at the University of the West in Los Angeles between Summer 2004 and Spring 2007 and is currently teaching Buddhist philosophy at the University of Hawaii – Manoa beginning Fall 2007.

He is also assigned to lead the International Seminar on Buddhism and Leadership for Peace, initiated in 1983 by Ven. Daewon Ki, founder of Dae Won Sa Buddhist Temple of Hawaii, the largest Korean temple in North America and Dr. Glenn D. Paige, professor emeritus of political science at the University of Hawaii – Manoa.

The editor received a Ph.D. in Buddhist Studies from the University of Wisconsin – Madison in 2002 and a Master's Degree in Philosophy from Seoul National University in 1991. He has been a researcher at exiled Tibetan Drepung Monastic University in South India and at the University of Tokyo.

His recent publications include *Mediators and Meditators: Buddhism and Peacemaking, The World is One Flower: Buddhist Leadership for Peace, Buddhism and Peace: Theory and Practice, Buddhist Exploration of Peace and Justice, The History of Doctrinal Classification in Chinese Buddhism: A Study of the* Panjiao *Systems*, and others.

Ronald S. Green is editor for Blue Pine Books. He received a Ph.D. in Buddhist Studies from the University of Wisconsin-Madison in 2003. He also holds a Master of Arts Degree in Japanese Literature from the University of Oregon and a Master of Science Degree in Sociology from Virginia Tech. In addition to his interest in engaged Buddhism, his research focuses on meditation, non-monastic Buddhist practices, and Buddhism in literature and film. He currently teaches Buddhism and World Religions at Coastal Carolina University.